TRANSFORMING
A RAPE CULTURE

TRANSFORMING
A RAPE CULTURE

· ·

REVISED EDITION

· ·

EDITED BY

EMILIE BUCHWALD
PAMELA R. FLETCHER
MARTHA ROTH

MILKWEED ◐ EDITIONS

Published 2005 by Milkweed Editions
Printed in the United States of America
The text of this book is set in Adobe Garamond.
05 06 07 08 09   5 4 3 2 1
Revised Edition

Special underwriting for this book was provided by the Women's Foundation of Minnesota

Milkweed Editions, a nonprofit publisher, gratefully acknowledges support from Emilie and Henry Buchwald; Bush Foundation; Cargill Value Investment; Timothy and Tara Clark Family Charitable Fund; DeL Corazón Family Fund; Dougherty Family Foundation; Ecolab Foundation; Joe B. Foster Family Foundation; General Mills Foundation; Jerome Foundation; Kathleen Jones; Constance B. Kunin; D. K. Light; Chris and Ann Malecek; McKnight Foundation; a grant from the Minnesota State Arts Board, through an appropriation by the Minnesota State Legislature, a grant from the National Endowment for the Arts, and private funders; Sheila C. Morgan; Laura Jane Musser Fund; an award from the National Endowment for the Arts, which believes that a great nation deserves great art; Navarre Corporation; Kate and Stuart Nielsen; Outagamie Charitable Foundation; Qwest Foundation; Debbie Reynolds; St. Paul Travelers Foundation; Ellen and Sheldon Sturgis; Surdna Foundation; Target, Marshall Field's, and Mervyn's with support from the Target Foundation; Gertrude Sexton Thompson Charitable Trust (George R.A. Johnson, Trustee); James R. Thorpe Foundation; Toro Foundation; Weyerhaeuser Family Foundation; and Xcel Energy Foundation.

Library of Congress Cataloging-in-Publication Data

Transforming a rape culture / edited by Emilie Buchwald, Pamela R.
Fletcher, and Martha Roth.— Rev. ed.
    p.   cm.
Includes bibliographical references (p.) and indexes.
ISBN 1-57131-269-2 (pbk.)
    1. Sexual harassment of women.   2. Rape.   3. Women—Crimes against.
I. Buchwald, Emilie.   II. Fletcher, Pamela R.   III. Roth, Martha.
HV6556.T73 2004
306.7—dc22   2004000560

MINNESOTA
STATE ARTS BOARD

TO THOSE WHO HAVE SUFFERED
SEXUAL VIOLENCE, AND TO THE
NOT-YET-BORN, WHO ARE ENTITLED
TO LIVE IN A VIOLENCE-FREE SOCIETY

TRANSFORMING A RAPE CULTURE

STRATEGIES AND ACTIVISM

VISIONS AND POSSIBILITIES

PREAMBLE

· · · · · · · · · ·

WHAT IS A RAPE CULTURE? It is a complex of beliefs that encourages male sexual aggression and supports violence against women. It is a society where violence is seen as sexy and sexuality as violent. In a rape culture, women perceive a continuum of threatened violence that ranges from sexual remarks to sexual touching to rape itself. A rape culture condones physical and emotional terrorism against women and presents it as the norm.

In a rape culture, both men and women assume that sexual violence is a fact of life, as inevitable as death or taxes. This violence, however, is neither biologically nor divinely ordained. Much of what we accept as inevitable is in fact the expression of values and attitudes that can change.

More than half of all reported rapes are committed by someone the survivor knows. Once we as a society take in the meaning of that fact, we will begin to understand the deeper issues of power, sexuality, and gender relationships surrounding sexual violence.

Most of these essays were written at the editors' invitation to provide models or processes for change. Transforming a rape culture involves imaginative leaps from our present state of institutionalized violence to a future that is safer and more just. We must summon our imaginations for this task, because history and society have so few precedents for us.

When the editors held focus groups among women and men, white and of color, to help us think our way into this book, we found great depth of concern and a commonality of experience that statistics cannot begin to reflect. Almost everyone has been touched by rape culture.

The result is a sourcebook of visions for a future without rape, strategies to achieve it, and current programs of action that are having some success in changing the climate that encourages sexual violence. A few previously published pieces add perspective. This book is intended to spark private reflection, spur public discussion, and lead to action.

ACKNOWLEDGMENTS

THE EDITORS WISH TO THANK the following people for their significant contributions to the revised edition of *Transforming a Rape Culture:* Milkweed editor Ben Barnhart for his resourcefulness and unflagging diligence, as well as the necessary oversight to bring our long process to fulfillment; managing editor Laurie Buss for overseeing all aspects of the revision; intern Kirsten Bohl for her highly organized assistance with the early stages of this project; writer and editor Mai Neng Moua for helping to find writers and activists in the Hmong community; contributor Inés Hernández for her generous suggestions of Hispanic and Native writers; Professor Carol Hogard of Minneapolis Community and Technical College for sharing with us her ten years of experience teaching the first edition; Professor Elzbieta Matynia of New School University; University of Minnesota Press editor Carrie Mullen for suggesting Michael Messner's work; and Professors Carole Sheffield and Susanne Scholz for thoughtful evaluations. Special thanks to Milkweed interns Brandi Brown and Clara Berridge for excellent record keeping and fastidious research. Their assistance and insights strengthen this collection in immeasurable ways.

INTRODUCTION

· · · · · · · · · · · · ·

T HE ORIGINAL EDITION of *Transforming a Rape Culture,* published in 1993, was about changing fundamental attitudes and values.
This revised edition is equally concerned—of necessity—with those same
fundamental attitudes and values, including rethinking the nurture and education of children, sharing power between genders, and revising the abject,
monotonous stereotypes of women presented in the popular media.

Although the media—especially newspapers and TV—give headline attention to particularly brutal sex crimes and dwell on their lurid details, they
play down or ignore the reality of relentless, everyday sexual violence. In
some cases, rapists are receiving severe punishments, but escalation of punishment in and of itself will not lead to significant change. Incarceration and
treatment programs for offenders, as many cases make clear, are merely holding actions to deal with today's violent men. The rate of recidivism indicates
that these measures are not successful deterrents or solutions. Allegations of
rape at our military service academies remind us that even young men who
are considered an elite group regard their women classmates as potential
sexual prey.

Until we identify and confront the issues that lead to sexual violence, we
will need more prisons and we will mete out stricter punishment—after the
fact. The reality that must be reckoned with is that the real causes are found
in the underlying attitudes toward women expressed in our culture—a fact
that many of the essays in this book discuss. We believe that these attitudes
can be changed.

In the year before the first edition of this book came into being, we
studied the large and growing body of factual literature on sexual violence,
beginning with Susan Brownmiller's landmark 1975 work *Against Our Will:
Men, Women and Rape.* Brownmiller's book established decisively that rape

is a crime of violence rather than passion. From Brownmiller's book we went on to the stacks of books we found in library searches and bookstore expeditions: theories of causality; studies of rapists and of survivors; books on the relationship between pornography and sexual violence (ranging from those that deny any causal connection to those that consider pornographic materials as practice manuals for rape); works on the intersection of racism and sexual violence; studies of gang rape; books about incest and the sexual abuse of children; articles about sexual harassment; books about how women can avoid rape and books about self-defense; as well as statistical data that showed continuing yearly increases in reports of sexual violence.

We realized that throughout history rapes have been treated as pardonable, sometimes even welcome, spasms of uncontrollable lust—a view that utterly ignores the woman who has been raped and silences her response. In the twentieth century, women's voices at last were heard on this subject. In this new century, we believe that their work has given us a foundation on which to build.

Our reading led us to understand that we need to change our way of thinking, from reaction to a proactive search for possible solutions, and this understanding shaped our concept of the book. At one of several focus groups held in our community before the creation of the original edition, women responded enthusiastically to our emphasis on transformation. More than one person told us, "We don't want to live in this culture as it is anymore. We've got to *change* it."

In our first edition, we shifted our focus from the violent present—which could have filled many volumes—to visions of possibility. What would it take, we asked, to build a future without rape? We saw with increasing clarity the extent of the problem: On TV programs and ads, in newspapers, novels, poetry, songs, opera, rock, and rap, on every billboard, in every shop window, on every museum wall we found evidence of rape culture. We began to understand the ways girls and boys are programmed to be victims and rapists, and we saw how training for this behavior begins early—before nursery school, even before birth, in most cases, with our own parental notions of the (highly artificial) distinctions between male and female.

As a society, we claim to deplore the sexual violence that characterizes our culture, yet we rear our sons and daughters in such ignorance of their sexuality that many confuse pleasure with pain and domination. We omit the word *pleasure* from sex education altogether. Interestingly, sexual arousal is the most undertheorized topic in human psychology. Women who have been attacked feel shame at their victimization, and other women collude by blaming them. Male and female are presented as polar opposites instead of close variations of one human model. We could hardly do worse if we set out deliberately to promote rape.

Since publication of the original hardcover edition, we have spoken and read to many audiences in the United States and beyond, and their responses have shown us how urgently needed are the cultural transformations called for in this book. Many readers have written to tell us that the book has increased their understanding that the causes of sexual violence are cultural, that they are interrelated, and that, once acknowledged and understood, they can indeed be changed.

For this revised edition, our course was set in part by the realization that the first edition has been widely used as a text for undergraduate and graduate classes in women's studies, family sociology, criminal justice studies, and other disciplines. To make room for new voices that would increase the book's value in the classroom, we made the difficult decision to cut essays that seemed to us to repeat material, or that were no longer as relevant as they had been in 1993. Essays that have become classics have been retained intact, without being updated. These include Andrea Dworkin's "I Want a Twenty-Four-Hour Truce during Which There Is No Rape," Carolyn Levy's "The Date Rape Play," Ntozake Shange's "comin to terms," and Inéz Hernández-Avila's "In Praise of Insubordination, or, What Makes a Good Woman Go Bad." Both Michael Kimmel and Richard Orton have recast their essays for the twenty-first century. Other authors whose essays were retained have updated their references and, in some cases, cut or added to the original piece.

One of the most satisfying aspects of putting together this new edition was the opportunity to commission and find new essays that would enter into dialogue with our original material. When we talked about what we needed to include in the revised edition, one of the first topics that came to mind was wartime rape, the mass rapes of women in genocidal struggles in Europe and Africa. In "Establishing Rape as a War Crime" Vesna Kesić, a journalist and women's activist from the former Yugoslavia, offers a measured, scholarly look at how international tribunals have finally—after how many thousand years?—judged the rape of civilian women by soldiers to be a war crime. Sociologist Cynthia Enloe allowed us to include an excerpt from a chapter in her book *Maneuvers: The Militarization of Women's Lives*, which places Kesić's work in a historical military context. Kesić's account of rape as a war crime struck sparks from both Haki Madhubuti's essay, "On Becoming Antirapist," and John Stoltenberg's "Making Rape an Election Issue."

Michael Messner's "The Triad of Violence in Men's Sports" describes the ways in which participation in sports trains young men to become sexual aggressors, amplifying and extending the insights in Myriam Miedzian's "How Rape Is Encouraged in American Boys and What We Can Do to Stop It." What Messner calls the "triad of violence" consists of violence towards other men (willingness to crush opponents in team play); violence toward the self (a numbing of normal feeling that allows team athletes to play when hurt); and violence toward women (sexual aggression and an unwillingness or inability to hear no).

For the first edition, we were not successful in finding an essay from an Asian American writer that spoke to our question: What needs to be changed in order to end sexual violence? In this edition we are lucky enough to have two such essays. "Hmong Women's Peace" is written by MayKao Yangblongsua Hang and Tru Hang Thao, two activists who started a women's center in the Hmong community of St. Paul, Minnesota—one of the largest in the United States. Traditional Hmong practices like multiple marriage, arranged marriages, and family guardianship of women's sexuality may have had positive cultural value in earlier phases of Hmong life, but in twenty-first century America they incite violence against women and are crimes.

Korean American poet Sun Yung Shin, who was adopted as an infant into a white Midwestern family, brings her experience to bear on a critique of rape culture. Working as a rape crisis counselor, Shin made personal discoveries that illuminated her work with clients and her political commitment, as she describes in "Rape, Color, and Global Feminism: A Converging Consciousness."

With recent scandals uncovered among the clergy, we wanted to include a piece that would speak to the problem directly. Rev. Marie Fortune, founder of Seattle's Center for the Prevention of Sexual and Domestic Violence, now called FaithTrust Institute, wrote an overview of the subject, with recommendations for reforming church practice that chimed with Carol J. Adams's "'I Just Raped My Wife! What Are You Going to Do about It, Pastor?': The

Church and Sexual Violence" and looked ahead to Yvette G. Flores's "'Why Did He Want to Hurt Me? All I Ever Did Was Love Him': Understanding Sexual Violence in Latino Marriages."

Flores, a family therapist, wrote about the specific ways in which Hispanic American culture renders women vulnerable to domestic and sexual assault, including the complicity of some clergy. *Familismo,* the ties that bind Latinas to their loved ones, has been a source of strength but also—as is true for women in the Hmong culture—a precondition for abuse. The dynamics of domestic and sexual violence point clearly to economic injustice as a form of violence against all.

We knew the e-world held a rich vein of pertinent material, ranging from consensual cybersex through Internet harassment to transformative potential, and we're fortunate to have two eloquent essays on the subject. In "Unmasking the Pornography Industry: From Fantasy to Reality," radical feminist Gail Dines describes the growth of cyberporn. To an astonishing degree, the pornography industry has developed along with electronic communications; some innovations in cyberscience seem to have appeared specifically to ease the production and consumption of pornography.

In "More Gender, Less Presumption: Cybersex as an Alternative to a Culture of Violent Sexuality," genderqueer activist Kim Surkan describes the vision of a pleasure-positive sexuality that can carry individuals beyond the narrow definitions of gender on which pornography depends. Many young people define themselves as Q, for *questioning* or *questing,* and search for alternatives, interstitial sexual identities that will permit a free play of erotic energy. This essay is annotated with other exploratory Web sites.

Our contributors describe both institutional change and simple individual behaviors—things we all can do to begin to change ourselves and our society—and readers have enthusiastically joined in this ambitious project. As editors, we acknowledge our debt to the writing and activism of the past several decades, which opened the eyes of many to the misogyny and gender terrorism that create a rape culture. No book can touch upon every arena, nor does this one claim to. To bring about positive change, the public conversation must become general and ongoing, and open to new ideas.

Every man, woman, and child is negatively affected by living in a rape culture, in which children, females, and some males are perceived as sexual prey. No one is safe as long as anyone is physically and spiritually violated. We are all responsible for doing what we can to change the status quo. Finally we must imagine a different world. If we can dream of a safe place, surely we can build one. As editors of *Transforming a Rape Culture,* we challenge our readers to help us make these changes. Please join us in envisioning and building a humane future.

EMILIE BUCHWALD
PAMELA R. FLETCHER
MARTHA ROTH

TRANSFORMING
A RAPE CULTURE

LIVING IN A RAPE CULTURE

In addition to the numbers and facts given here, stories of sexual violence, of tragedy and survival, could have filled these pages. Instead, we have chosen voices of resistance. In 1983, Andrea Dworkin called for a day without rape; such a day has not yet dawned. Nor will it ever come to be without ongoing efforts to spur change.

ARE WE REALLY LIVING IN A RAPE CULTURE?

THE MEDIA ARE QUICK to report on sensational cases of sexual violence and domestic abuse. Beyond these instances, however, here are the facts about sexual and domestic violence in the United States. Current information is derived primarily from two programs administered by the U.S. Department of Justice—the Uniform Crime Report and the National Crime Victimization Survey—and from other studies focused on rape and child sexual abuse.

· · · · ·

THE UNIFORM CRIME REPORT: The FBI's Uniform Crime Report (UCR)[1] data is compiled from monthly reports from over 17,000 law enforcement agencies covering 96 percent of the nation's population. Complaints found to be baseless or unfounded are excluded from the counts. A frequent, recurring criticism of the UCR figures has been that rape is notoriously underreported to the police; thus, the UCR figures represent only a portion of the actual number of rape victimizations.

- In 2002, marking the third consecutive year of increase, the UCR program's estimate of female forcible rape was 95,136 offenses. That's 264 rapes each day of the year, or 11 rapes every hour.
- The UCR reported 1.8 million female survivors of forcible rape or forcible rape attempts in the United States during the twenty year period from 1983 to 2002 alone. *These are the most conservative numbers available and should be considered the baseline or minimum rape figure.*[2]
- The UCR program has traditionally collected rape data only for female victims. Although the rate dropped from 1993 to 1998, it has once again been rising. During 2002, the estimated rate of female forcible rapes increased for all community types. The greatest increase was seen in

cities outside metropolitan areas, where forcible rapes occurred at the estimated rate of 75.9 per 100,000 females, an increase of 12.1 percent over 2001. Metropolitan areas had an estimated rate of 66.5 forcible rapes for each 100,000 females, a 3.3 percent increase over 2001. In rural counties, female rapes occurred at an estimated rate of 46.8 per 100,000 females, up 6.8 percent from 2001.

* * * * *

THE NATIONAL CRIME VICTIMIZATION SURVEY: Re-designed in 1992, the National Crime Victimization Survey (NCVS)[3] is the largest nationally representative, household-interview crime survey in the United States; it is administered by the Bureau of the Census for the Bureau of Justice Statistics. Each year, data are obtained from a nationally representative sample of 42,000 households comprising nearly 76,000 persons, enabling the Bureau of Justice to estimate the likelihood of victimization for the population as a whole. The NCVS provides the largest national forum for victims to describe the impact of crime and the characteristics of violent offenders. The NCVS reported 247,730 rapes and/or sexual assaults for 2002. That's 678 rapes each day of the year, or 28 each hour.

* * * * *

IN AUGUST 2002, the Bureau of Justice Statistics issued a white paper called *Selected Findings on Rape and Sexual Assault: Reporting to Police and Medical Attention, 1992–2000*.[4] According to this study, persons age twelve or older experienced an annual 249,000 rapes or attempted rapes and 152,680 sexual assaults between 1992 and 2000.

All completed rapes, 39 percent of attempted rapes, and 17 percent of sexual assaults against females resulted in injured victims. Of these, 59 percent of victims whose victimizations were reported were treated for their injuries, compared to 17 percent of rape victims with unreported victimizations.

It is telling that even at the end of the twentieth century most rapes and sexual assaults against females were not reported to the police; only 36 percent of rapes, 34 percent of attempted rapes, and 26 percent of sexual assaults were reported to the police. Thus, even as recently as 2002, a majority of women were choosing not to report these crimes and were not treated for their injuries. The reasons they cited for not reporting included keeping the assault as a personal matter, fear of reprisal, and protecting the offender. The closer the relationship between the female victim and the offender, the greater the likelihood that the police would not be told about a rape or sexual assault. When the offender was a current or former husband or boyfriend, about 75 percent of all victimizations were not reported to police, and when the offender was a friend or acquaintance, about 71 percent were not reported. When the offender was a stranger, only 44 percent of the assaults were not reported to the police. Most of those uninjured (77 percent) did not report to the police. Thus, even in the early years of the twenty-first century, a majority of women who suffer sexual assaults are not willing to come forward to report a crime that they view as stigmatizing them.

· · · · ·

CONSIDER THE IMPLICATIONS of the findings of the National Violence against Women Survey, published in November 2000.[5] To further understanding of violence against women, the National Institute of Justice and the Centers for Disease Control and Prevention jointly sponsored a national survey. The findings include these:

- Physical assault is widespread among adults in the United States: 52 percent of women surveyed said that they had been physically assaulted as children by an adult caretaker and/or as adults by any type of attacker. An estimated 1.9 million women are physically assaulted annually in the United States.
- Many American women are raped at an early age: Of the 17.6 percent of all women surveyed who said they had been the victims of a completed or attempted rape, 21.6 percent were younger than age twelve when they were first raped, and 32.4 percent were between the ages of twelve and seventeen.
- Women who reported that they were raped before age eighteen were twice as likely to report being raped as adults. Women who reported they were physically abused by an adult caretaker were twice as likely to report being physically assaulted as adults.
- Stalking is more prevalent than previously thought: 8.1 percent of the women surveyed reported being stalked at some time in their lives.

Approximately one million women are stalked annually in the United States.

- Violence against women is primarily intimate partner violence: 64 percent of the women who reported being raped, physically assaulted, or stalked since age eighteen were victimized by a current or former husband, cohabiting partner, boyfriend, or date.
- Women are significantly more likely than men to be injured during an assault: 31.5 percent of female rape victims, compared with 16.1 percent of male rape victims, reported being injured. The risk of injury increases among female rape victims when their assailant is a current or former intimate.

The report concludes with the statement that violence against women, particularly intimate partner violence, should be classified as a major public health and criminal justice concern in the United States, and that violence prevention strategies should be considered in future policy applications.

· · · · ·

IN LIGHT OF THOSE STATISTICS, the answer to the question "Are we living in a rape culture?" is yes. Rape continues to be a pervasive fact of American life. In addition to the unreported and underreported family and close-relative violence against children, many unreported assaults are categorized by the victims simply as bad dates and domestic disputes. In immigrant populations with differing social mores, including those from East Africa and Southeast Asia, cultural misogyny puts women at risk in arranged marriages and from customs that treat rape as acceptable behavior.

Both the victims and their attackers carry the fact of rape and sexual violence through their lives and, one can argue, through their families' lives as well. We will continue to live in a rape culture until our society understands these facts and chooses to eradicate the beliefs and practices that beget sexual violence in this country.

NOTES

1. Federal Bureau of Investigation, U.S. Department of Justice, Crime in the United States, 2002, "Forcible Rape Statistics," http://www.fbi.gov.
2. Federal Bureau of Investigation, "Table 1, Index of Crimes, United States, 1972–1991."

3. Bureau of Justice Statistics, The National Crime Victimization Survey Report, "Criminal Victimization in the United States," table 26, http://www.icpsr.umich.edu/NACJD/NCVS.

4. Bureau of Justice, *Selected Findings on Rape and Sexual Assault: Reporting to Police and Medical Attention, 1992–2000* (Washington, DC, 2002, publication NCJ 194530). (Available by e-mail from ASKBJS@ojp.usdoj.gov, or go to www.ojp.usdoj.gov/bjs/publications).

5. "Full Report of the Prevalence, Incidence, and Consequence of Violence against Women," by Patricia Tjaden and Nancy Thoennes. The National Violence against Women Survey, NIJ, November 2000 (NCJ 183781).

I WANT A TWENTY-FOUR-HOUR TRUCE DURING WHICH THERE IS NO RAPE

ANDREA DWORKIN

It is astonishing that in all our worlds of feminism and anti-sexism we never talk seriously about ending rape. Ending it. Stopping it. No more. No more rape.

This was a speech given at the Midwest regional conference of the National Organization for Changing Men in the fall of 1983 in St. Paul, Minnesota. One of the organizers kindly sent me a tape and a transcript of my speech. The magazine of the men's movement, M., published it. I was teaching in Minneapolis. This was before Catharine MacKinnon and I had proposed or developed the civil rights approach to pornography as a legislative strategy. Lots of people were in the audience who later became key players in the fight for the civil rights bill. I didn't know them then. It was an audience of about 500 men, with scattered women. I spoke from notes and was actually on my way to Idaho—an eight-hour trip each way (because of bad air connections) to give a one-hour speech on Art—fly out Saturday, come back Sunday, can't talk more than one hour or you'll miss the only plane leaving that day, you have to run from the podium to the car for the two-hour drive to the plane. Why would a militant feminist under this kind of pressure stop off on her way to the airport to say hi to 500 men? In a sense, this was a feminist dream come true. What would you say to 500 men if you could? This is what I said, how I used my chance. The men reacted with considerable love and support and also with considerable anger. Both. I hurried out to get my plane, the first hurdle for getting to Idaho. Only one man in the 500 threatened me physically. He was stopped by a woman bodyguard (and friend) who had accompanied me.

· · · · ·

I HAVE THOUGHT A GREAT DEAL about how a feminist, like myself, addresses an audience primarily of political men who say that they are antisexist. And I thought a lot about whether there should be a qualitative difference in the kind of speech I address to you. And then I found myself incapable of pretending that I really believe that that qualitative difference exists. I have watched the men's movement for many years. I am close with some of the people who participate in it. I can't come here as a friend even though I might very much want to. What I would like to do is to scream: and in that scream I would have the screams of the raped, and the sobs of the battered; and even worse, in the center of that scream I would have the deafening sound of women's silence, that silence into which we are born because we are women and in which most of us die.

And if there would be a plea or a question or a human address in that scream, it would be this: why are you so slow? Why are you so slow to understand the simplest things; not the complicated ideological things. You understand those. The simple things. The clichés. Simply that women are human to precisely the degree and quality that you are.

And also: that we do not have time. We women. We don't have forever. Some of us don't have another week or another day to take time for you to discuss whatever it is that will enable you to go out into those streets and do something. We are very close to death. All women are. And we are very close to rape and we are very close to beating. And we are inside a system of humiliation from which there is no escape for us. We use statistics not to try to quantify the injuries, but to convince the world that those injuries even exist. Those statistics are not abstractions. It is easy to say, "Ah, the statistics, somebody writes them up one way and somebody writes them up another way." That's true. But I hear about the rapes one by one by one by one by one, which is also how they happen. Those statistics are not abstract to me. Every three minutes a woman is being raped. Every eighteen seconds a woman is being beaten. There is nothing abstract about it. It is happening right now as I am speaking.

And it is happening for a simple reason. There is nothing complex and difficult about the reason. Men are doing it, because of the kind of power that men have over women. That power is real, concrete, exercised from one body to another body, exercised by someone who feels he has a right to exercise it, exercised in public and exercised in private. It is the sum and substance of women's oppression.

It is not done five thousand miles away or three thousand miles away. It is done here and it is done now and it is done by the people in this room as well as by other contemporaries: our friends, our neighbors, people that we know. Women don't have to go to school to learn about power. We just have to be women, walking down the street or trying to get the housework done after having given one's body in marriage and then having no rights over it.

The power exercised by men day to day in life is power that is institutionalized. It is protected by law. It is protected by religion and religious practice. It is protected by universities, which are strongholds of male supremacy. It is protected by a police force. It is protected by those whom Shelley called "the unacknowledged legislators of the world": the poets, the artists. Against that power, we have silence.

It is an extraordinary thing to try to understand and confront why it is that men believe—and men do believe—that they have the right to rape. Men may not believe it when asked. Everybody raise your hand who believes you have the right to rape. Not too many hands will go up. It's in life that men believe they have the right to force sex, which they don't call rape. And it is an extraordinary thing to try to understand that men really believe that they have the right to hit and to hurt. And it is an equally extraordinary thing to try to understand that men really believe that they have the right to buy a woman's body for the purpose of having sex: that that is a right. And it is very amazing to try to understand that men believe that the $7-billion-a-year industry that provides men with cunts is something that men have a right to.

That is the way the power of men is manifest in real life. That is what theory about male supremacy means. It means you can rape. It means you can hit. It means you can hurt. It means you can buy and sell women. It means that there is a class of people there to provide you with what you need. You stay richer than they are, so that they have to sell you sex. Not just on street corners, but in the workplace. That's another right that you can presume to have: sexual access to any woman in your environment, when you want.

Now, the men's movement suggests that men don't want the kind of power I have just described. I've actually heard explicit whole sentences to that effect. And yet, everything is a reason not to do something about changing the fact that you do have that power.

Hiding behind guilt, that's my favorite. I love that one. Oh, it's horrible, yes, and I'm so sorry. You have the time to feel guilty. We don't have the time for you to feel guilty. Your guilt is a form of acquiescence in what continues to occur. Your guilt helps keep things the way they are.

I have heard in the last several years a great deal about the suffering of men over sexism. Of course, I have heard a great deal about the suffering of men all my life. Needless to say, I have read *Hamlet*. I have read *King Lear*. I am an educated woman. I know that men suffer. This is a new wrinkle. Implicit in the idea that this is a different kind of suffering is the claim, I think, that in part you are actually suffering because of something that you know happens to someone else. That would indeed be new.

But mostly your guilt, your suffering, reduces to: gee, we really feel so bad. Everything makes men feel so bad: what you do, what you don't do, what you want to do, what you don't want to want to do but are going to do anyway. I think most of your distress is: gee, we really feel so bad. And I'm sorry that you feel so bad—so uselessly and stupidly bad—because there is a way in which this really is your tragedy. And I don't mean because you can't cry. And I don't mean because there is no real intimacy in your lives. And I don't mean because the armor that you have to live with as men is stultifying: and I don't doubt that it is. But I don't mean any of that.

I mean that there is a relationship between the way that women are raped and your socialization to rape and the war machine that grinds you up and spits you out: the war machine that you go through just like that woman went through Larry Flynt's meat grinder on the cover of *Hustler*. You damn well better believe that you're involved in this tragedy and that it's your tragedy too. Because you're turned into little soldier boys from the day that you are born and everything that you learn about how to avoid the humanity of women becomes part of the militarism of the country in which you live and the world in which you live. It is also part of the economy that you frequently claim to protest.

And the problem is that you think it's out there: and it's not out there. It's in you. The pimps and the warmongers speak for you. Rape and war are not so different. And what the pimps and the warmongers do is that they make you so proud of being men who can get it up and give it hard. And they take that acculturated sexuality and they put you in little uniforms and they send you out to kill and to die. Now, I am not going to suggest to you that I think that's more important than what you do to women, because I don't.

But I think that if you want to look at what this system does to you, then that is where you should start looking: the sexual politics of aggression; the sexual politics of militarism. I think that men are very afraid of other men. That is something that you sometimes try to address in your small groups, as if if you changed your attitudes toward each other, you wouldn't be afraid of each other.

But as long as your sexuality has to do with aggression and your sense of entitlement to humanity has to do with being superior to other people, and there is so much contempt and hostility in your attitudes toward women and children, how could you not be afraid of each other? I think that you rightly perceive—without being willing to face it politically—that men are very dangerous: because you are.

The solution of the men's movement to make men less dangerous to each other by changing the way you touch and feel each other is not a solution. It's a recreational break.

These conferences are also concerned with homophobia. Homophobia is very important: it is very important to the way male supremacy works. In my opinion, the prohibitions against male homosexuality exist in order to protect male power. *Do it to her.* That is to say: as long as men rape, it is very important that men be directed to rape women. As long as sex is full of hostility and expresses both power over and contempt for the other person, it is very important that men not be declassed, stigmatized as female, used similarly. The power of men as a class depends on keeping men sexually inviolate and women sexually used by men. Homophobia helps maintain that class power: it also helps keep you as individuals safe from each other, safe from rape. If you want to do something about homophobia, you are going to have to do something about the fact that men rape, and that forced sex is not incidental to male sexuality but is in practice paradigmatic.

Some of you are very concerned about the rise of the right in this country, as if that is something separate from the issues of feminism or the men's movement. There is a cartoon I saw that brought it all together nicely. It was a big picture of Ronald Reagan as a cowboy with a big hat and a gun. And it said: "A gun in every holster; a pregnant woman in every home. Make America a man again." Those are the politics of the right.

If you are afraid of the ascendancy of fascism in this country—and you would be very foolish not to be right now—then you had better understand that the root issue here has to do with male supremacy and the control of women: sexual access to women; women as reproductive slaves; private ownership of women. That is the program of the right. That is the morality they talk about. That is what they mean. That is what they want. And the only opposition to them that matters is an opposition to men owning women.

What's involved in doing something about all of this? The men's movement seems to stay stuck on two points. The first is that men don't really feel very good about themselves. How could you? The second is that men come to me or to other feminists and say: "What you're saying about men isn't true. It isn't true of me. I don't feel that way. I'm opposed to all of this."

And I say: don't tell me. Tell the pornographers. Tell the pimps. Tell the warmakers. Tell the rape apologists and the rape celebrationists and the prorape ideologues. Tell the novelists who think that rape is wonderful. Tell Larry Flynt. Tell Hugh Hefner. There's no point in telling me. I'm only a woman. There's nothing I can do about it. These men presume to speak for you. They are in the public arena saying that they represent you. If they don't, then you had better let them know.

Then there is the private world of misogyny: what you know about each other; what you say in private life; the exploitation that you see in the private sphere; the relationships called love, based on exploitation. It's not enough to find some traveling feminist on the road and go up to her and say: "Gee, I hate it."

Say it to your friends who are doing it. And there are streets out there on which you can say these things loud and clear, so as to affect the actual institutions that maintain these abuses. You don't like pornography? I wish I could believe it's true. I will believe it when I see you on the streets. I will believe it when I see an organized political opposition. I will believe it when pimps go out of business because there are no more male consumers.

You want to organize men. You don't have to search for issues. The issues are part of the fabric of your everyday lives.

I want to talk to you about equality, what equality is and what it means. It isn't just an idea. It's not some insipid word that ends up being bullshit. It doesn't have anything at all to do with all those statements like: "Oh, that happens to men too." I name an abuse and I hear: "Oh, it happens to men too." That is not the equality we are struggling for. We could change our strategy and say: well, okay, we want equality; we'll stick something up the ass of a man every three minutes.

You've never heard that from the feminist movement, because for us equality has real dignity and importance—it's not some dumb word that can be twisted and made to look stupid as if it had no real meaning.

As a way of practicing equality, some vague idea about giving up power is useless. Some men have vague thoughts about a future in which men are going to give up power or an individual man is going to give up some kind of privilege that he has. That is not what equality means either.

Equality is a practice. It is an action. It is a way of life. It is a social practice. It is an economic practice. It is a sexual practice. It can't exist in a vacuum. You can't have it in your home if, when the people leave the home, he is in a world of his supremacy based on the existence of his cock and she is in a world of humiliation and degradation because she is perceived to be inferior and because her sexuality is a curse.

This is not to say that the attempt to practice equality in the home doesn't matter. It matters, but it is not enough. If you love equality, if you believe in it, if it is the way you want to live—not just men and women together in a home, but men and men together in a home and women and women together in a home—if equality is what you want and what you care about, then you have to fight for the institutions that will make it socially real.

It is not just a matter of your attitude. You can't think it and make it exist. You can't try sometimes, when it works to your advantage, and throw it out the rest of the time. Equality is a discipline. It is a way of life. It is a political necessity to create equality in institutions. And another thing about equality is that it cannot coexist with rape. It cannot. And it cannot coexist with pornography or with prostitution or with the economic degradation of women on any level, in any way. It cannot coexist, because implicit in all those things is the inferiority of women.

I want to see this men's movement make a commitment to ending rape because that is the only meaningful commitment to equality. It is astonishing that in all our worlds of feminism and antisexism we never talk seriously about ending rape. Ending it. Stopping it. No more. No more rape. In the back of our minds, are we holding on to its inevitability as the last preserve of the biological? Do we think that it is always going to exist no matter what we do? All of our political actions are lies if we don't make a commitment to ending the practice of rape. This commitment has to be political. It has to be serious. It has to be systematic. It has to be public. It can't be self-indulgent.

The things the men's movement has wanted are things worth having. Intimacy is worth having. Tenderness is worth having. Cooperation is worth having. A real emotional life is worth having. But you can't have them in a world with rape. Ending homophobia is worth doing. But you can't do it in a world with rape. Rape stands in the way of each and every one of those things you say you want. And by rape you know what I mean. A judge does not have to walk into this room and say that according to statute such and such these are the elements of proof. We're talking about any kind of coerced sex, including sex coerced by poverty.

You can't have equality or tenderness or intimacy as long as there is rape, because rape means terror. It means that part of the population lives in a state of terror and pretends—to please and pacify you—that it doesn't. So there is no honesty. How can there be? Can you imagine what it is like to live as a woman day in and day out with the threat of rape? Or what it is like to live with the reality? I want to see you use those legendary bodies and that legendary strength and that legendary courage and the tenderness that you say you have on behalf of women; and that means against the rapists, against the pimps, and against the pornographers. It means something more than a personal renunciation. It means a systematic, political, active, public attack. And there has been very little of that.

I came here today because I don't believe that rape is inevitable or natural. If I did, I would have no reason to be here. If I did, my political practice would be different than it is. Have you ever wondered why we are not just in armed combat against you? It's not because there's a shortage of kitchen knives in this country. It is because we believe in your humanity, against all the evidence.

We do not want to do the work of helping you to believe in your humanity. We cannot do it anymore. We have always tried. We have been repaid with systematic exploitation and systematic abuse. You are going to have to do this yourselves from now on and you know it.

The shame of men in front of women is, I think, an appropriate response both to what men do do and to what men do not do. I think you should be ashamed. But what you do with that shame is to use it as an excuse to keep doing what you want and to keep not doing anything else: and you've got to stop. You've got to stop. Your psychology doesn't matter. How much you hurt doesn't matter in the end any more than how much we hurt matters. If we sat around and only talked about how much rape hurt us, do you think there would have been one of the changes that you have seen in this country in the last fifteen years? There wouldn't have been.

It is true that we had to talk to each other. How else, after all, were we supposed to find out that each of us was not the only woman in the world not asking for it to whom rape or battery had ever happened? We couldn't read it in the newspapers, not then. We couldn't find a book about it. But you do know and now the question is what you are going to do; and so your shame and your guilt are very much beside the point. They don't matter to us at all, in any way. They're not good enough. They don't do anything.

As a feminist, I carry the rape of all the women I've talked to over the past ten years personally with me. As a woman, I carry my own rape with me. Do you remember pictures that you've seen of European cities during the plague, when there were wheelbarrows that would go along and people would just pick up corpses and throw them in? Well, that is what it is like knowing about rape. Piles and piles and piles of bodies that have whole lives and human names and human faces.

I speak for many feminists, not only myself, when I tell you that I am tired of what I know and sad beyond any words I have about what has already been done to women up to this point, now, up to 2:24 P.M. on this day, here in this place.

And I want one day of respite, one day off, one day in which no new bodies are piled up, one day in which no new agony is added to the old, and I am asking you to give it to me. And how could I ask you for less—it is so little. And how could you offer me less: it is so little. Even in wars, there are days of truce. Go and organize a truce. Stop your side for one day. I want a twenty-four-hour truce during which there is no rape.

I dare you to try it. I demand that you try it. I don't mind begging you to try it. What else could you possibly be here to do? What else could this movement possibly mean? What else could matter so much?

And on that day, that day of truce, that day when not one woman is raped, we will begin the real practice of equality, because we can't begin it before that day. Before that day it means nothing because it is nothing: it is not real; it is not true. But on that day it becomes real. And then, instead of rape we will for the first time in our lives—both men and women—begin to experience freedom.

If you have a conception of freedom that includes the existence of rape, you are wrong. You cannot change what you say you want to change. For myself, I want to experience just one day of real freedom before I die. I leave you here to do that for me and for the women whom you say you love.

. . . .

ANDREA DWORKIN is the author of thirteen books, including *Pornography: Men Possessing Women* (Perigree Books, 1981), *Intercourse* (Simon and Schuster, 1987), and *Letters from a War Zone* (Penguin USA, 1981). Her most recent book is *Heartbreak: The Political Memoir of a Feminist Militant* (Basic Books, 2002). She is the coauthor of a law that would recognize pornography as a form of sex discrimination.

THE TRIAD OF VIOLENCE IN MEN'S SPORTS

. . . .

MICHAEL A. MESSNER

Boys and men learn to bond with each other through sexually aggressive, erotically exciting talk that forges an aggressive, even violent, hierarchical ordering of bodies, both within the male peer group and between groups.

T HESE DAYS, we seem to hear story after story describing male athletes' violent acts: ritualized hazing on athletic teams, acquaintance rapes
and gang rapes of women, and verbal and physical abuse of girlfriends
and spouses.[1] Statements of shock and surprise always follow these stories;
school officials and coaches, backed up by psychologists and other professionals, vow to develop better means of weeding out the problem players in
the future.

A common working assumption is that these violent acts are deviations
from the norms of behavior in school and on athletic teams. On the contrary, I believe that far from being an aberration, male athletes' off-the-field
violence stems from the normal dynamics at the center of male athletic culture. Studies of men's college athletics have shown significant relationships
between athletic participation and sexual aggression,[2] and the athletes most
likely to engage in sexual and other violent assault off the field play on teams
I define as being at the institutional center of sport: basketball, football, and
ice hockey.[3]

This issue often raises concerns about race and ethnicity. Indeed, American
culture seems obsessed with what Stuart Alan Clarke has called images of
"black men misbehaving," especially if the alleged misbehaviors involve a
combination of sex and violence.[4] Because racist stereotypes of black men as
violent sexual predators have historically justified the profiling and persecution of African Americans, I'm wary of the ways in which these images continue to surface.[5] When data reveal that college athletes in revenue-producing
sports have higher rates of sexual assault against women, the term *athletes in
revenue-producing sports* threatens to smuggle in racist stereotypes as a thinly
veiled code for *black male athletes.*[6]

Maybe more black men are charged with sexual assault in college because
more black men play the central team sports of football and basketball. In
high schools, where white males are more evenly represented in the student
athlete population, white male athletes perpetrate many of the most egregious
examples of sexual assault. In Canada, where the central sport, ice hockey, is
dominated by white men, the vast majority of sexual assaults by athletes are
committed by white males.[7] So I assume that it is not their race or ethnicity but their central position that makes certain male athletes more likely to
engage in sexual assault than others.

Most male athletes do *not* commit off-the-field violence against women or other men. Those who do, though in the numerical minority, tend to come from the center of their athletic peer group, and I believe they are expressing the most honored form of masculinity. The complicity of other men helps to sustain this form of masculinity and to give it power, even though some (or many) men may be uncomfortable with its beliefs and practices. To change this behavior, it will be necessary to confront the root causes of men's violence against women, and to help the silent majority of men move away from quiet complicity with the culture of misogyny, homophobia, and violence at the center of men's sports culture.

MALE ATHLETES' VIOLENCE AGAINST WOMEN

In a riveting account of the infamous 1989 Glen Ridge, New Jersey, gang rape case, journalist Bernard Lefkowitz describes how thirteen high-status white male high school athletes lured a seventeen-year-old "slightly retarded" girl into a basement.[8] They set up chairs, theater style, in front of a couch. While some boys sat in the chairs to watch, others led the girl to the couch and induced her to begin giving one of the highest-status boys oral sex. As the assault escalated, one sophomore boy noticed "puzzlement and confusion" in the girl's eyes, turned to a friend, and said, "Let's get out of here." Another senior baseball player felt queasy, thought "I don't belong here," and left with another baseball player. On the way out, he told another guy, "It's wrong. C'mon with me," but the other guy stayed.[9] In all, six young men left the scene, while seven—six seniors and one junior—remained in the basement.

While the girl was forced to continue giving oral sex to the boy, other boys laughed, yelled encouragement to their friends, and shouted, "You whore!" at the girl. One boy decided it would be amusing to force a baseball bat up her vagina. When he did this (and followed it with a broomstick), the girl heard one boy say, "Stop. You're hurting her," but another said, "Do it more." Later, the girl remembered that the boys were all laughing while she was crying. When they were done, they warned her not to tell anyone and concluded with an athletic ritual of togetherness by standing in a circle and clasping "one hand on top of the other, all their hands together, like a basketball team on the sidelines at the end of a timeout."[10]

The factors that led up to the gang rape in Glen Ridge are the same factors that studies of men, sexual violence, and sport have pointed to in recent years:

1. Competitive, homophobic, and misogynistic talk and joking
2. A group practice of voyeuring, where boys can watch their friends have sex with girls and sometimes join in
3. Suppression of empathy toward others, especially toward the girls
4. A culture of silence among peers, in families, and in the community

Four football players and wrestlers physically perpetrated the Glen Ridge assault. Three others sat and watched, sometimes laughing or cheering but not joining in.[11] Six boys left the scene.

Although those six boys felt uncomfortable enough to leave, they did nothing at the time to stop their friends, nor did they report the assault to parents, teachers, or the police. And they all refused, during the subsequent long and painful years of litigation, to turn on their male friends and provide incriminating evidence. Their complicity is central.

SEXUAL TALK AND DOMINANCE BONDING

Reading and thinking about these issues brought back memories of cut fights, or competitive insults, from my own childhood. I learned in grade school that boys achieve and maintain high status not only through athletic prowess but also through homophobic and misogynistic banter on the playgrounds, streets, and playing fields. The most ruthless cut fighters seemed always able to one-up another boy's insults. Following another boy's cutting insult with silence or with a lame comment like "you, too" left one open to derision.

I learned this firsthand one day while walking home from fifth grade. Chris, a boy well known for his verbal prowess, and I were in a cut fight. I thought I was doing pretty well until Chris hit me with one for which I had no answer: "Messner," he said, "blow me!" I didn't know what to say back, and so of course I lost. But behind my lack of response was confusion. At eleven, I knew a few things about sex but was unclear about others. I had recently learned that some men had sex with other men. They were called homosexuals, and I was told they were sick and sinful individuals. So, my confused mind told me, if Chris was saying "blow me," he was in effect asking me to be involved in some homosexual act with him. If homosexuality is such a bad and shameful thing, why did *he* win the cut fight?

It took me years to figure that one out. Meanwhile, I simply added "blow me" to my own cut-fight repertoire. Now I can see that insults like "you suck," "blow me," or "fuck you" smuggle into childhood and early adolescence a powerful pedagogy about sexuality, power, and domination.[12] Although children may not fully understand or intend it, through this sort of sexual banter they teach each other that sex, homosexual or heterosexual, is an act of domination and subordination. The men are the ones who are on top, in control, doing the penetrating and fucking. Women or penetrated men are subordinate, degraded, and ultimately dehumanized objects of sexual aggression.

Rarely will two boys alone engage in a cut fight. But put the same two boys in a group and they often feel compelled to insult each other or another boy in the group. A cut fight requires an audience. At center stage are the higher-status boys; around the periphery are the lower-status boys, an admiring audience who, by their presence, attention, and laughter, validate the higher status of the boys at the center. This dynamic starts as early as first grade and is well established by high school.

Trash talking on high school basketball courts and insult talk among teammates off the field have common traits: They establish hierarchies, they involve personal insults or put-downs, often as calls to defend masculinity and honor, and they often degrade objects defined as feminine.[13] In men's locker rooms, there is a conversational style of loud, competitive banter and sexual boasting that is clearly intended as a performance for the group audience and that takes center stage. Other, more personal conversations remain marginal, quiet and private, partly because boys and young men have had the experience of being (or seeing other boys) humiliated in male groups for expressing vulnerability or care for a particular girl.[14]

Boys and men who reveal themselves as vulnerable are subsequently targeted as the symbolic women—the "pussies" and "faggots"—on athletic teams and in other male groups. Most boys learn early to avoid offering themselves as targets for this kind of abuse.[15] The power of this group dynamic was illustrated in an interview I conducted with a former world-class athlete who, during his athletic career, had been a closeted gay man. He found that one of the best ways to keep his sexual identity secret within this aggressively homophobic world was to participate in what he called "locker room garbage" talk about heterosexual conquests.[16]

But it's not simply fear that keeps marginal boys in silent complicity with the group's practices; it's also pleasure. The bonds of the male peer group often have a decidedly erotic base.[17] To say that male groups' dominance bonding is erotic does not necessarily mean that men's bonds in sports are a way of sublimating sexual desire for each other. Undoubtedly, that is true with some boys and men, for whom sports are a heterosexualization process; they learn to repress same-sex desire, which is perhaps sublimated into aggression and eventually converted to sexual desire for women.[18] This same-sex desire may remain submerged in the unconscious of young men who define themselves as 100 percent heterosexual, but whether it does or not, the erotic bond among male athletes tends to be overtly coded as fiercely heterosexual. Boys and men learn to bond with each other through sexually aggressive, erotically exciting talk that forges an aggressive, even violent, hierarchical ordering of bodies, both within the male peer group and between groups. To thwart the dominant modes of the peer group is not simply to risk ridicule and ostracism, it also threatens to undermine the major way that young men learn to experience erotic excitement and pleasure with their peers.

VOYEURING: WOMEN AS OBJECTS OF CONQUEST

By the time they were teens, the jocks of Glen Ridge used more than talk for their erotic dominance bonding. They sometimes gathered in a home when parents were away to watch pornographic films and masturbate together. Next they developed a group entertainment called *voyeuring,* in which one guy at a party would try to convince a girl to go upstairs to a bedroom to have sex. But first his buddies would go up and hide in a closet, under the bed, or behind the door, where they could watch. Sex with a girl, for these guys, was less an intimate encounter with a valued human being than it was the use of a woman's body as a sexual performance for male buddies, a way to create their own porn movie.[19]

Similarly, the white California high school footballers known in the early

1990s as Spur Posse had multiple sexual encounters with girls and young women as a competition among the boys to see who could score the most times. Significantly, it was the competitive talk among the boys, not sex with the girls, that seemed to be the major driving force in their pursuit of this scoring.[20] In 2001, a case of voyeuring by male athletes came to light in a Maryland high school when a sixteen-year-old lacrosse player secretly filmed himself having sex with a fifteen-year-old girl and later showed the film to his teammates.[21]

In gang rape, men use female bodies to bond with each other. Anthropologist Peggy Sanday and others who have studied gang rape are careful to argue that, from the point of view of the woman, the rape is not a sexual experience but a violent, degrading, and painful assault. For the perpetrators, however, gang rape certainly is a sexual experience—but it is not about sex with a woman; rather, the males in the group use the violated woman's body as an object through which to have vicarious sex with each other.[22] Underlying gang rape is male anxiety about status in a hierarchy of power, expressed through denigration of women and erotic bonding among men, and rooted in the misogynist joking culture of athletic teams.

Most heterosexual boys and young men go through a period of insecurity and even discomfort in learning to establish sexual relations with girls and women. Men who were former athletes told me that in high school, and even in college, talking with girls and women made them feel anxious and inadequate.[23] These young men dealt with their feelings of lameness with young women primarily by listening to and watching their male peers deliver a rap to women. This peer pedagogy of heterosexual relations taught them to put on a performance for girls that seemed to work. The success of this learned heterosexual come-on allowed a young man to mask, even overcome, his sense of insecurity and lameness in his own eyes and, just as important, in the eyes of his male teammates. It also deepened his erotic bond with other members of his male peer group by collectively constructing women as objects of conquest.

As a freshman in college, I was a marginal member of my community college basketball team.[24] After having been a reasonably good high school player, I found myself thirteenth on a thirteen-player team. Moreover, off the court I could not hold my own in the competitive sexual banter. Early in the season, on a road trip, the guys lounged around in a motel room, talking and joking about sex. Drew, our starting center and one of the highest-status guys on the team, noticed that Rob (another marginal player) and I had not been contributing anything to the raucous chronicling of sexual exploits. "Hey, Robby T., hey Mess," Drew asked, "you guys ever had a piece of ass?"

A virgin with little to brag about, I tensed up. Kess, another reserve player, had recently been labeled the team fag after he refused to jump into the middle of a brawl with another team. I wanted to avoid becoming such a target of joking put-downs, so I employed what I thought was a subtle strategy. "Naw," I replied, but with diverted eyes and a knowing smile I hoped would suggest I was simply too cool to brag about sex with my girl-friend, a high school girl. Rob followed the same strategy. Drew, missing the subtleties, clobbered us: "Wow! We got two virgins on this team! We can't have that! Mess, Robby T., we gotta get you laid, and soon! We can't go having any virgins on the team. Havin' Kess is bad enough!"

A couple of weeks later, Drew invited us to a party. Robby T. and I showed up together, with our six-packs of beer. Soon Drew announced to Rob and me, loudly, "Hey, you two virgins ain't gonna be virgins after to-night, eh?" Not knowing what he was talking about, we just agreed and laughed, "Sure, Drew. We're trying to figure out who we're going to lay to-night." Drew replied, "Man, you don't have to worry about that, because me and the guys have taken care of it. We got a lady comin' over here in a couple of hours. She's real special, and since you guys are the only two virgins on the team, you get to go first." As I felt my palms get sweaty, I knew I was supposed to act grateful. "Wow, Drew. Like, is she some kind of prostitute or something?"

Drew smiled. "You could say that. She's kind of a friend of mine, you know?" He laughed loud and hard, and so did we. I took some long pulls on my beer, drained it, and opened another one. I whispered to Robby T., "Let's get the hell out of here," and we escaped out the back door.

Rob and I never did find out whether Drew was serious about his plan to get us laid, or if the guys were just pulling a joke on the two lower-status guys on the team. We felt a bit ashamed, and we knew that leaving the party did nothing to enhance our status, so we decided that the way to handle the guys when we next saw them was to lie: We were now laying our girlfriends and just couldn't do it with someone else because we were faithful. That's how we escaped being put in the fag bag with Kess. We were accepted now; we had learned how to bullshit with the best of them.

After this embarrassing incident, I began to step up the pressure on my girlfriend to put out. Like many young men, I wanted to have sex. But the urgency of my desire was not driven simply by my attraction to my girlfriend. I desperately wanted access to the sexual experience that would put me on a par with the guys on the team. Fortunately, my girlfriend had a mind of her own and asserted her own timetable for what we would do and when we would do it. However, I can see in retrospect how my experiences with my teammates evoked fear, embarrassment, and frustration over my virgin status, and this in turn encouraged a tendency to treat my girlfriend more as an object of conquest than as a person with feelings of her own. This experience eventually helped me to understand how athletic male peer groups' voyeuring—forming bonds by watching each other have sex or listening to each other talk about sex—works. It doesn't always lead to gang rape; it can also feed a more private dynamic of date and acquaintance rape, even among young men who are marginal in their athletic peer group.[25]

WOMEN'S SEXUAL AGENCY

As my story suggests, the idea that young male athletes view women as objects of sexual conquest oversimplifies relations between women and men. After all, although I had begun to pressure my girlfriend in order to gain status with my male peers, she did not become a passive object of my actions and desires; she expressed and asserted her own will. When I talk with college male athletes these days, they describe women as anything but passive objects. High-status male college and professional athletes learn to take for granted that some women will seek out sex with them. What Jeffrey Benedict calls the "jock–groupie tango" tends to socialize many male athletes to "an image of women as sexually compliant. The sex-for-fame commerce that exists between athletes and groupies undermines autonomy and trivializes the fundamental component of consent."[26]

Sports has a subculture of sexually assertive and active women and men, and some antirape activists may blanch at the ways that women's "complicity reinforces the athletes' attitude of sexual license,"[27] fearing that this will fuel the tendency to blame the victim that surfaces when women are raped by male athletes. A fine line has to be navigated here: On the one hand, acknowledging women's agency risks letting men off the hook and, once again, blaming women for men's acts of sexual violence. On the other hand, ignoring women's agency risks academic complicity in seeing women as passive sexual objects. A key, I think, to understanding the complexity of this situation lies in viewing both women's and men's sexual agencies as embedded in unequal power relations.

Gail McKabe studied male Canadian hockey players (elite athletes, aged fifteen to twenty) and the women who call themselves puck bunnies and aggressively seek out sex with the jocks.[28] McKabe says the puck bunnies are "relentless in their pursuit . . . and 'proud as punch' to have sex with the jock," because this will "entitle the puck bunny to 'bragging rights.'" The male jocks are often happy to have sex with the puck bunnies and even see it as "tangible evidence of their celebrity status." However, in a crude variant of the madonna/whore dichotomy, the jocks tend to define the puck bunnies as "the dirties," in opposition to girlfriends, with whom they expect to have broader and longer-term relationships.

These activities take place in a decidedly asymmetrical context with respect to gender and social status. The puck bunnies' attempts to gain status through sex with the high-status males may be a way of resisting the gender and age constraints they face in their communities. But the jocks have high social status as respected male ice hockey players, and this asymmetry serves ultimately to advantage them and to disadvantage the "dirties," whose bragging rights are short lived. Relations of the two groups ultimately reproduce the social asymmetry.

SUPPRESSION OF EMPATHY

To treat a person as an object of conquest means to suppress empathy for such a person. But boys and men have mothers, sisters, female cousins, and friends whom they know as people and whom they are taught to protect and care for. How can they conjure up the emotional distance to sexually assault women?

Homosocial bonding among men, especially the sort of sexualized dominance bonding I discussed above, is a poor environment for the development of empathy (or respect) for women. The Glen Ridge boys who were most central in the actual assault grew up without sisters, in families headed by domineering male figures. Moreover, their peer group, family, and community experiences taught them to value boys' and men's activities over girls' and women's. Most of the boys who left the scene and felt uncomfortable with the assault grew up in homes with sisters. They seemed more open to seeing the pain in the victim's eyes and were less able to suppress their empathy for her.[29]

MALE ATHLETES' CULTURE OF SILENCE

Why did the six Glen Ridge boys who left the scene remain silent, both on the day of the rape and during the subsequent years of litigation? At least some of these young men were uncomfortable with what happened, even thought it was wrong, but nobody in the group raised a hand or voice to stop it. Two other young men did, however. The case broke when another male athlete, who had not been at the scene of the assault, reported to teachers that he had overheard other guys laughing and bragging about the rape. Significantly, this African American young man who blew the whistle had always felt excluded from the tightly knit, high-status clique of white athletes. A second boy, who became an activist in the school and community in his quest to see that the jocks did not get away with their crime, was a long-haired "gigger" (a name for the small minority of radical, arty, antijock students at the school). Both of these boys—one an athlete, one not—were outside the dominant athletic male peer group. Those inside, even those who were marginal within the group, maintained a complicit silence.

This culture of silence is built into the group's spoken and unspoken codes. The eroticized dominance bond has already established that "the guys" are part of a high-status, privileged in-group (and very little during adolescence can solidify this sort of feeling as much as being part of an athletic team). Others—nonathlete boys, racial and ethnic minority boys, girls, parents, teachers, police, and so on—are outsiders. Years of experience within the group taught these boys that they would be rewarded for remaining silent and punished for speaking out. A whistle-blower might be banished from the group and possibly also beaten up, or he might remain in the group, but as a degraded, feminized "faggot" who betrayed the "men."

MEN'S VIOLENCE AGAINST OTHER MEN

In February 2000, a professional basketball player with the San Antonio Spurs, Sean Elliot, announced that he was returning to play after a life-threatening illness that had resulted in a kidney transplant. Considerable media discussion ensued about whether it was appropriate for Elliot to return to play at all, given the risk of further damage to his kidney. Lakers star Kobe Bryant, when asked how he would respond to playing against Elliot, said, "As soon as he steps on the court, that means he's healthy. I'll have no problem putting an elbow in his gut."[30]

Players and coaches know that in order to be competitive, they will need to put their bodies on opposing players in ways that could cause harm. In football and ice hockey, overt aggression against other players is even more intense. One former National Football League player told me that before a playoff game his coach implored his defensive players to hurt the opposing star running back if they could. This is apparently not unusual. A 1998 *Sports Illustrated* cover story on "the NFL's dirtiest players" admiringly described San Fransisco 49ers guard Kevin Gogan's tendencies, sometimes even after a play had been whistled dead, to "punch, kick, trip, cut-block, sit on or attempt to neuter the man lined up across from him." Gogan's coach, Steve Mariucci, approved: "Coaches want tough guys, players who love to hit and fly around and do things that are mean and nasty. Not everyone can be like that, but if . . . one or two players . . . are a little overaggressive, that's great."[31]

Bodily aggression toward opponents on the field or court, whether of the routine kind that takes place within the rules or the dirty, illegal kind that aims to injure an opponent, is supposed to end when players cross back into the real world. The gentle giant football player who growls, curses, and tears opponents limb from limb on the field but is a kind and caring teddy bear off the field is part of our national lore. But is he real? Or is aggression on the field related to aggression off the field? Former Dallas Cowboys football star John Niland now says that he and many of his former teammates were involved in drugs, alcohol, and spouse abuse:

> I'm not going to name names, but my wife at the time knew
> of other wives who were abused. . . . We're paid to be violent.
> We're paid to beat up on the guy across from you. When you're
> in the game and your emotions are so high and the aura of
> the whole environment is so unbelievable. When the game's
> over, technically, it's to be turned off. But you can't. . . . Quite
> frankly, if you got every player who did drugs or alcohol or
> played stoned or who was a spousal abuser, you couldn't field
> an NFL team. It's still going on.[32]

And consider a comment by NBA coach Pat Riley, of the Miami Heat. Bemoaning an unusually long break between his team's playoff games, Riley said, "Several days between games allows a player to become a person. During the playoffs, you don't want players to be people."[33] If it is acknowledged that the supposedly civilizing influences of a player's life outside sports can (negatively!) humanize him, then doesn't it follow that it might also work the other way—that dehumanizing attitudes and experiences within sports might spill over into life outside sports?

BOYS' EMBODIMENTS OF TOUGHNESS

Most children are taught that it is unacceptable to hurt other people. In order to get athletes (or soldiers) to inflict harm on others, the opponent must be made into an enemy, and the situation must be defined in such a way that it's either the enemy or the athlete himself. As one athlete put it, "Somebody's gonna get hurt. It could be you, it could be him—most of the time, it's better if it's him." The most obvious motive for suppressing empathy is the reward one gets for the successful use of violence: "The coach loved it," the same man said. "Everybody loved it."[34] And he received more than just immediate positive reinforcement; he also received a college scholarship, all-American honors, and eventually all-pro status in the NFL.

But rewards do not tell the whole story behind athletes' suppression of empathy for their opponents. In fact, when I probed athletes' early experiences in sports, I found stories not of victories, trophies, and public adulation. Instead, these men were more likely to talk about connection with others, especially fathers, older brothers, uncles, and eventually same-age male peers. For some, sports were the primary or the only site where they connected with their otherwise emotionally or physically absent fathers. Many also said they felt alone, unsure of themselves, and cut off from others, and they found acceptance through sports participation, especially those who had some early successes.

Why sports? An important part of the answer is that boys' early experiences teach them not to show fear or weakness, to appear invulnerable. Little boys begin to learn this at a very young age. Learning to embody and display toughness, even if it is a veneer that covers quivering insecurity, can help boys stay safe in a hostile environment. In his eloquent description of street life for African American boys in poor communities, Geoffrey Canada describes how learning to fight, or at least displaying an attitude that one was ready and willing to fight, was necessary. Losing a fight, and "taking it like a man," was far better (and ultimately *safer*) than being labeled a coward.[35] Learning early to mask one's vulnerability with a display of toughness may help boys survive on the street, but it can also hinder their emotional development. Even in an emotional straitjacket, boys and men retain a human need to connect with others, and for those who have some early athletic successes, sports can become the context for closeness with others.[36]

But as they move further into competitive athletic careers, men learn that they must be winners in order to continue to receive approval and respect. And to be a winner, you must be willing to suppress your empathy for other athletes. In the context of sports careers, you do not experience your body as a means of connecting intimately with others; rather, your body becomes a weapon, which you train to defeat a dehumanized opponent.[37] It's a dog-eat-dog world out there; you gotta have that killer instinct.

Homophobic bullying of nonathlete boys is a common occurrence on high school and college campuses. A window was opened on this in 1999, when Eric Harris and Dylan Klebold, armed to the teeth, entered Columbine High School, in Littleton, Colorado, and proceeded to kill thirteen and wound twenty-one of their schoolmates and teachers. "All jocks stand up," the killers yelled when they began their slaughter. "Anybody with a white hat or a shirt with a sports emblem on it is dead."[38] In the aftermath of this tragedy, public discussions sought the origins of the anger expressed by the two boys and asked how in the future to prevent others from violently going off. Very little discussion dealt with the ways such outsider boys are commonly targeted as nerds and symbolic pussies who serve as foils for athletes' own in-group status. Indeed, Columbine High School was like many other high schools in this regard. There was a tough little group of about seven guys, mostly football players and wrestlers, who were known for painful, degrading hazing of younger male athletes, for harassing and physically abusing girls, for destroying property, and basically for getting away with it all. They also abused the outsider boys, one of whom was shoved into a locker by three football players who taunted, "Fag, what are you looking at?"

Homophobic taunting and bullying does not always result in such serious physical violence,[39] but it is common. Homophobia plays a role within male peer groups that I compare to Elmer's glue bonding two pieces of wood. Once the white glue is dried, it becomes clear, nearly invisible, and it acts simultaneously (and paradoxically) as a bond that holds the two pieces of wood together and as an invisible barrier, or shield, that keeps the pieces of wood from actually touching each other. Homophobia works the same way. While it bonds boys as part of the in-group (we are men, they are faggots), it also places clear limits on intimacy.

This is where alcohol often comes in. Although it is part of the system of competitive status enhancement to drink a lot of alcohol, young men also find that one of the short-term benefits of drinking with the guys is that it loosens constraints on verbal and emotional expression.[40] The key desires underlying boys' and men's affiliations with each other—for acceptance, emotional connection, respect—seem more accessible after a few drinks. The constraints normally placed on expressions of physical closeness among men relax after a few drinks; the arms draped around a teammate's shoulders and the words "I love you, man" can be forgotten in the fog of tomorrow's hangover.

MALE ATHLETES' VIOLENCE AGAINST THEMSELVES

In June 2000, future Hall of Fame quarterback Steve Young ended several months of speculation by announcing his retirement after fifteen years of professional football. He actually had played his last down ten months earlier, when a knockout hit by an opposing player caused his fourth concussion in three years. "I'll miss so many things," said Young. "What I won't miss are the hits that made my body tingle."[41] Young's announcement was not surprising. In fact, many had wondered why it took him so long to retire, given mounting evidence about the dangerous cumulative effects of head injuries. But Young's desire to continue playing must be seen in the context of an entire career in which he was rewarded for taking tremendous risks on the football field, playing hurt and with reckless abandon.

Steve Young is not unusual in this respect. In November 2000, Denver Broncos quarterback Brian Griese suffered a shoulder separation in the first half of the game. Told by team doctors that he had a third-degree separation, the most severe type, he took a painkilling injection and returned to the game to lead his team to victory.

Football players live with the knowledge that minor and moderate injuries are an expected outcome of the game and that a serious career-ending or even life-threatening injury is always a possibility. Indeed, during the 1999 NFL season, 364 injuries were serious enough to cause a player to miss at least one game. Knee (122) and ankle injuries (52) were the most common, but 11 were concussions. In U.S. high schools, football players suffer by far the greatest number of fatal, disabling, and serious sports injuries (although the injury rates per 100,000 participants are higher in ice hockey and gymnastics).[42] Among children, falls and sports-related injuries are the leading causes of hospital stays and emergency room visits.[43] A survey of hospital emergency rooms and medical clinics in 1997 found a staggering number of sports injuries among U.S. children aged fourteen and under, led by bicycling (901,716), basketball (574,434), football (448,244), baseball (252,665), and soccer (227,157).[44] In Canada, injuries—many of them head, neck, and cervical-spine injuries—among children ice hockey players are also escalating.[45]

THE BODY AS MACHINE

Several years ago, I was watching a football game on television with a friend. A big fan, he knew his team had to win this game to secure home-field advantage for the playoffs. Suddenly the announcer observed that a key player on my friend's team was hurt. The camera focused on the player, slowly walking off the field and looking at his hand in a puzzled way. His index finger, it turned out, was dislocated and sticking out sideways, at a ninety-degree angle. "Oh, good," my friend sighed in relief. "It's only his finger—he can still play." Indeed, a few plays later, the man was back on the field with his hand taped up (presumably popped back into place by the trainer and perhaps injected with painkiller).

What struck me about this moment was how normal it seemed. Announcers, coaches, other players, and fans like my friend all fully expected this man to suck it up and keep on playing. We all have high expectations of football players' (and other professional, college, and even high school athletes') willingness and ability to play hurt, often risking their long-term health. Injuries and pain that in other contexts would result in emergency room visits, bed rest, and time off work or school are considered a normal part of the workday for many athletes.

A former major league baseball player described a series of injuries and rehabilitations that spanned not only the everyday aches and bruises one would expect a catcher to endure but also year after year of ankle, knee, shoulder, neck, and spinal injuries requiring several operations. Players routinely decide to play hurt, to "give their bodies up for the team" in this way, even with full knowledge that they are risking long-term disability. But when, in his early thirties, this man's eleven-year pro baseball career finally came to an end, he described it as a "shock. . . . I had felt that, the way I had conditioned myself and taken care of myself, that I would play until I was thirty-seven, thirty-eight."[46] To describe the way he had lived his life as taking care of himself seemed to me to express a particularly alienated relationship to his own body. Like many athletes, he had a wide range of knowledge about his body, but this self-knowledge was shallow; it was not an expansive sense of his body as a living organism, a self that connects in healthy ways with others and with the environment.[47] Rather, it was an instrumental view of his body as a machine or tool to be built, disciplined, used (if necessary, used up) to get a job done.

This kind of self-knowledge—what psychologist William Pollack calls the "hardening of boys"—starts early in life, especially for athletes.[48] Boys learn that to show pain and vulnerability risks their being seen as soft, and they know from the media, from coaches, and from their peers that this is a very bad thing. Instead, they learn that they can hope for high status, privilege, respect, and connection with others if they suppress their feelings and show they can take pain and risk injury.[49] In the context of the athletic team, risking one's health by playing hurt is more than a way to avoid misogynist or homophobic ridicule; it is also a way of performing a highly honored form of masculinity.

There are concrete rewards—status, prestige, public adulation, scholarships, and even money—for men who are willing to pay the price. But we must also remember that underlying men's performances for each other is a powerful need to belong, to connect, to be respected. A player who refuses to play hurt, especially in a team sport, risks losing his tenuous but powerful connection with the male group. Given both the negative enforcement mechanisms and the positive rewards a player can expect from choosing to play hurt, it should surprise us more when a player decides *not* to risk his long-term health, refuses the needle, sits down and says "no más."[50]

PERFORMING THE TRIAD OF MEN'S VIOLENCE

The triad of men's violence in sports—violence against women, against other men, and against their own bodies—is an explicable outcome of behavior and performance in male athletic groups. A small group of high-status males at the center of these groups sets the tone with misogynist and homophobic banter, teasing, and actions. Less central boys and men within the group, some of whom may feel uncomfortable with the group's dominant values and actions, still tend to actively support or passively go along.

But how are these three kinds of violence connected? I've found two intertwined clusters of behavior that connect these three seemingly separate phenomena. The first is *misogynist and homophobic talk and actions,* through which boys and men learn two contradictory lessons about the group's sexual aggression: It forms an exciting and pleasurable erotic bond that holds the group together (and places it above other groups), and it constantly threatens humiliation, ostracism, and even violence against a boy or man who fails to conform with the group values and practices.

The second is *suppression of empathy.* Through athletic peer groups, boys and men learn to suppress their empathy toward women and to make them objects of the group's jokes and assaults. One's own body becomes a sexual machine or a weapon for the conquest of a woman and for displaying heterosexual masculinity to male peers. Men also learn to suppress their empathy toward other men, both on and off the field, turning them into outsiders and enemies to be defeated by violence, if necessary. Again, one's own body is experienced as a weapon to be used against an objectified opponent. Ultimately, the body-as-weapon turns back on the male athlete as an alien force: As he has learned to suppress his own self-empathy, to endure pain and injury to get the job done, his body is experienced not as a human self to be nurtured and cared for but as a machine or a tool to be used to get the job done.

This essay is an adaptation of "Playing Center: The Triad of Violence in Men's Sports" in Taking the Field: Women, Men, and Sports *(Minneapolis: University of Minnesota Press, 2002). Copyright © 2002 by the Regents of the University of Minnesota. Reprinted with permission from the University of Minnesota Press.*

NOTES

1. See Jeffrey R. Benedict, *Athletes and Acquaintance Rape* (Thousand Oaks, Calif.: Sage, 1998) and Mark D. Totten, *Guys, Gangs, and Girlfriend Abuse* (Peterborough, Canada: Broadview, 2000). Journalist Laura Robinson offers an especially chilling description of violence and sexual assaults by Canadian hockey players. See Laura Robinson, *Crossing the Line: Violence and Sexual Assault in Canada's National Sport* (Toronto: McClelland and Stewart, 1998).

2. S. D. Boeringer, "Influences of Fraternity Membership, Athletics, and Male Living Arrangements on Sexual Aggression," *Violence against Women* 2 (1996): 134–147; M. P. Fritner and L. Robinson, "Acquaintance Rape: The Influence of Alcohol, Fraternity Membership, and Sports Team Membership," *Journal of Sex Education and Therapy* 19 (1993): 272–284; Mary Koss and J. Gaines, "The Prediction of Sexual Aggression by Alcohol Use, Athletic Participation, and Fraternity Affiliation," *Journal of Interpersonal Violence* 8 (1993): 94–108.

3. Todd Crosset, "Athletic Affiliation and Violence against Women: Toward a Structural Prevention Project," in *Masculinities, Gender Relations, and Sport,* edited by Jim McKay, Michael A. Messner, and Donald F. Sabo (Thousand Oaks, Calif.: Sage, 2000), 147–161; Todd Crosset, et al., "Male Student Athletes and Violence Against Women: A Survey of Campus Judicial Affairs Offices," *Violence against Women* 2 (1996): 163–179.

4. Stuart Allan Clarke, "Fear of a Black Planet," *Socialist Review* 21 (1991): 37–59.

5. Angela Davis, *Woman, Race, and Class* (New York: Vintage, 1981); Robert Staples, *Black Masculinity: The Black Male's Role in American Society* (San Francisco: Black Scholar, 1982).

6. For a thoughtful discussion of this dilemma, see Bonnie Berry and Earl Smith, "Race, Sport, and Crime: The Misrepresentation of African Americans in Team Sports and Crime," *Sociology of Sport Journal* 17 (2000): 171–197.

7. Robinson, *Crossing the Line.*

8. This section of the essay is a substantially revised version of Michael A. Messner and Mark Stevens, "Scoring without Consent: Confronting Male Athletes' Sexual Violence against Women," in *Paradoxes of Youth and Sport,* edited by Margaret Gatz, Sandra Ball Rokeach, and Michael A. Messner (Albany: State University of New York Press, 2002), 225–240.

9. Bernard Lefkowitz, *Our Guys* (New York: Vintage, 1997), 23–24.

10. Lefkowitz, *Our Guys,* 25.

11. Lefkowitz's descriptions of the assault are retrospective constructions, based in part on the victim's descriptions and on subsequent bits of information that came out in the trials. Precise numbers of just how many boys in the basement participated physically in the assault and how many acted as a supportive audience are thus somewhat speculative.

12. Julian Wood argues that this sort of competitive sexual talk among boys is a sort of group pedagogy through which boys are "groping toward sexism" in their attitudes and practices toward girls and women. Julian Wood, "Groping toward Sexism: Boys' Sex Talk," in *Gender and Generation,* edited by Angela McRobbie and Mica Nava (London: Macmillan, 1984), 54–84.

13. Scott Eveslage and Kevin Delaney, "Trash Talkin' at Hardwick High: A Case Study of Insult Talk on a Boys' Basketball Team," *International Review for the Sociology of Sport* 33 (1998): 239–253.

14. Donald F. Sabo, "The Myth of the Sexual Athlete," in *Sex, Violence and Power in Sport: Rethinking Masculinity,* edited by Michael A. Messner and Donald F. Sabo (Freedom, Calif.: Crossing, 1994), 83–88.

15. Cynthia A. Hasbrook and Othello Harris, "Wrestling with Gender: Physicality and Masculinities among Inner-City First and Second Graders," in *Masculinities, Gender Relations, and Sport,* edited by Jim McKay, Michael A. Messner, and Donald F. Sabo, (Thousand Oaks, Calif.: Sage, 2000), 13–30. Hasbrook and Harris report this sort of verbal and physical aggression by higher-status boys toward lower-status boys taking place in their study of first graders.

16. Michael A. Messner, *Power at Play: Sports and the Problem of Masculinity* (Boston: Beacon, 1992).

17. Peter Lyman, "The Fraternal Bond as a Joking Relationship: A Case Study of Sexist Jokes in Male Group Bonding," in *Changing Men: New Directions in Research on Men and Masculinity,* edited by Michael S. Kimmel (Newbury Park, Calif.: Sage, 1987), 148–163.

18. I develop this argument in Michael A. Messner, "Studying Up on Sex," *Sociology of Sport Journal* 13 (1996): 221–237.

19. Lefkowitz, *Our Guys,* 183–184.

20. Michael A. Messner, "Riding with the Spur Posse," *Sex, Violence and Power in Sports,* 16–27.

21. As a result, the high school removed eight players from the nationally ranked lacrosse team and cancelled the rest of the season. See Lynn Anderson and Lem Satterfield, "St. Paul's School Cancels Varsity Lacrosse Season," *Baltimore Sun,* April 4, 2001.

22. Peggy Sanday, *Fraternity Gang Rape: Sex, Brotherhood, and Privilege on Campus* (New York: New York University Press, 1990).

23. Messner, *Power at Play*, 94–95.

24. I originally wrote about this incident as part of an autobiographical short story, "Indignities: A Short Story," in Messner and Sabo, *Sex, Violence and Power*.

25. James Messerschmidt argues that when a boy is teased or ridiculed in school for not being enough of a man, he experiences this as a "masculinity challenge." Some boys respond to this subordination among other boys by using sexual violence against women as a "hegemonic masculine project." James W. Messerschmidt, "Becoming 'Real Men': Adolescent Masculinity Challenges and Sexual Violence," *Men and Masculinities* 2 (2000): 286–307; James W. Messerschmidt, *Nine Lives: Adolescent Masculinities, the Body, and Violence* (Boulder, Colo.: Westview, 2000).

26. Benedict, *Athletes and Acquaintance Rape*, 2.

27. Benedict, *Athletes and Acquaintance Rape*, 1–2.

28. Gail McKabe, "Jocks and Puck Bunnies: Intimate Relations, Cultural Negotiations, and Sport Subjectivities" (paper, American Sociological Association meeting, San Francisco, August 1998).

29. Lefkowitz, *Our Guys*, 280.

30. "They Said It: Kobe Bryant."

31. Michael Silver, "Dirty Dogs," *Sports Illustrated*, October 26, 1998.

32. Bob Glauber, "We're Paid to Be Violent: Cost Was High for Ex-Dallas Star John Niland," *Newsday*, January 12, 1997.

33. "Quotebook," *Los Angeles Times*, May 11, 2000.

34. Messner, *Power at Play*, 65–66.

35. Geoffrey Canada, *Fist Stick Knife Gun* (Boston: Beacon, 1995).

36. I develop this line of argument in much more depth in *Power at Play*, where I argue that the specific kind of connection that boys and men experience in sports is a distant and thus emotionally safe form of connection. This has (mostly negative) ramifications for the development of friendships, for intimate relations with women, and for athletes' retirement and disengagement from sports. Psychologist William Pollack reaches a similar conclusion, arguing that boys often find sports to be one place where they find emotional connection. Pollack concedes that "the positive benefits to boys dim when sports cease to be played"; still, he tends to overstate the benefits of sports and ignores the range of social-scientific studies of sport that point to negative outcomes. William Pollack, *Real Boys: Rescuing Our Sons from the Myths of Boyhood* (New York: Henry Holt, 1998), 273.

37. Philosopher Brian Pronger has argued that an oppressive territorialization of the male body, which closes off intimate and erotic connection with other bodies and channels desire into violent directions, is the key outcome of modern sport, which he sees as a major expression of fascism. Brian Pronger, "Outta My Endzone: Sport and the Territorial Anus," *Journal of Sport and Social Issues* 23 (1999): 373–389; and Brian Pronger, "Homosexuality and Sport: Who's Winning?" *Masculinities, Gender Relations, and Sport*, 222–244.

38. Lorraine Adams and Dale Russakoff, "At Columbine High, a Darker Picture Emerges: Were Athletes Given Preferential Treatment and Allowed to Misbehave with Impunity?" *Washington Post National Weekly Edition*, June 21, 1999.

39. Indeed, Messerschmidt points out that although many boys are challenged by bullying, not

all respond with violence. Boys' responses to bullying vary, and this variance can be explained by boys' being differently situated in family, school, and peer contexts. Messerschmidt, *Nine Lives*.

40. As Rocco L. Capraro puts it, "College men's drinking appears to be profoundly paradoxical. . . . [They drink] not only to enact male privilege but also to help them negotiate the emotional hazards of being a man in the contemporary American college." Rocco L. Capraro, "Why College Men Drink: Alcohol, Adventure, and the Paradox of Masculinity," *Journal of American College Health* 48, no. 6 (May 2000): 307–315.

41. Steve Young, "Young at Heart," *Sports Illustrated*, June 19, 2000, 55–61.

42. Kevin Young and Philip White, "Researching Sports Injury," in McKay, Messner, and Sabo, *Masculinities, Gender Relations, and Sport*.

43. Janny Dwyer Brust, William O. Roberts, and Barbara J. Leonard, "Gladiators on Ice: An Overview of Ice Hockey Injuries in Youth," *Medical Journal of Allina* 5 (1996): 26–30.

44. Scott Gold and Tracy Weber, "Youth Sports Grind Is Tough on Body, Spirit," *Los Angeles Times*, February 28, 2000.

45. Dwyer Brust, Roberts, and Leonard, "Gladiators on Ice."

46. Messner, *Power at Play*, 122–123.

47. Brian Pronger has written about sport as a disciplinary practice particular to modernity, through which men learn to close off their bodies to connection with others. Instead, the body is experienced as a means of overcoming others. Pronger, "Outta My Endzone."

48. Pollack, *Real Boys*.

49. Don Sabo, "Pigskin, Patriarchy and Pain," in Messner and Sabo, *Sex, Violence and Power in Sport*, 82–88. The pain principle in sport can also be seen as paradigmatic of (and indeed, a pedagogy for) a more general cultural view of men's instrumental orientation to their own bodies. A few scholars have recently pointed to gender-related health patterns among men that help explain why, on average, men die seven years earlier than women do and have higher death rates from suicide, heart disease, accidents, and other major killers. Research points to the conclusion that these health risks among men are closely correlated with boys' and men's conformity to narrow conceptions of masculinity, including risk-taking, violence, and instrumental orientations to the body. For excellent general overviews, see *Men's Health and Illness: Gender, Power, and the Body*, edited by Donald Sabo and David E. Gordon, (Thousand Oaks, Calif.: Sage, 1995), 121–139; and Will H. Courtenay, "Constructions of Masculinity and Their Influence on Men's Well-Being: A Theory of Gender and Health," *Social Science and Medicine* 50 (2000): 1385–1401. Taking this observation to a different level, scholars have pointed out how different groups of men—broken down by social class, race/ethnicity, sexual orientation, age, and so forth—have very different levels of vulnerability to certain diseases and dangers. See, for instance, Robert Staples, "Health Among African American Males," in Sabo and Gordon, *Men's Health and Illness*.

50. The "no más" reference is to the famous 1980 welterweight championship fight between Roberto Duran and Sugar Ray Leonard. Feeling that he was losing the fight, Duran refused to return to the ring for a new round, saying, "No más (no more)." He was roundly criticized for quitting instead of continuing the fight until he was knocked out. I examined this idea that boxers must

fight until the very end in Michael A. Messner, "Why Rocky III?" in Messner and Sabo, *Sex, Violence and Power in Sports*.

. . . .

MICHAEL A. MESSNER is a professor of sociology and gender studies at the University of Southern California, where he currently chairs the sociology department. His books include *Taking the Field: Women, Men, and* Sports (University of Minnesota Press, 2002), *Paradoxes of Youth and Sport* (State University of New York Press, 2002), and *Power at Play: Sports and the Problem of Masculinity* (Beacon Press, 1992). He has conducted several commissioned studies on gender and sports media, and he speaks frequently on sex equity and violence in sports to students, academics, educators, and coaches' associations.

RAPE, COLOR, AND GLOBAL FEMINISM
A CONVERGING CONSCIOUSNESS

· ·

SUN YUNG SHIN

The subject of rape was not polite dinner conversation. It made people uncomfortable, and yet I wanted to understand how it operated in our society to keep all women hostage.

In my own life, borders have come in many guises,
and I live with them inside as well as across racialized
women's communities.

— CHANDRA TALPADE MOHANTY

I HAD NEVER HEARD THE TERM *vulnerable adult* before answering my first rape crisis call. The apartment was bare, and a woman sat on the couch holding her stomach and telling the female police officer, "He was my friend at the group home. After he did it, he jumped on my stomach. His father had a video camera and taped the whole thing. My stomach hurts." She was whimpering softly, like a wounded domestic animal, while I—a new on-call counselor from Sexual Offense Services—retrieved some clean clothes and a stuffed animal from her bureau.

I don't remember if she used the word rape. I believe she just described the actions without labeling them. At the hospital, we waited as different officers and nurses wandered in and out, usually without telling us what they were doing or why, or when they or someone else would be back. It was the middle of the night. I asked the woman if she wanted me to hold her hand and I was surprised when she said yes. She said little as she was being poked, prodded, and ignored. Was her silence because she was "vulnerable" or because she was in shock? She was a large person (as was her rapist, who she said weighed almost three hundred pounds) and her face had a childlike openness, now clearly registering pain. I sat with her until early morning and then went to work.

I couldn't stop thinking about the woman and what had been done to her, and how this happened over and over, with barely a murmur from any official voice. A seam of disbelief, sadness, and rage had opened for me, and I was drawn in completely. She was called a vulnerable adult because of mental and emotional difficulties that made her dependent on social services, but the crime that had been committed against her had nothing to do with that level of vulnerability.

A month before, I had gone to Ramsey County's Sexual Offense Services volunteer information table, where I signed on to become a counselor. My reasons for doing this weren't clear to me at the time, but it changed my life. What I experienced as a sexual assault crisis counselor—in forty-five hours of training, in the field, and on the phone—continues to fuel my inquiries into the intersections of sexual assault, race, class, and activism.

I was the only woman of color in our volunteer training sessions, and the two main leaders were white women. I had just transferred from a university in Boston, where for the first time in my life as an American I had been surrounded by Asians and made friends with other Koreans. Now I was in St. Paul, Minnesota, an English major at Macalester College.

A Korean adoptee, I was raised near Chicago. Being a transracially adopted person and an immigrant has always complicated my sense of ethnicity, nationality, race, and female sexuality. As I learned more about rape—the theory and the practices—I saw America as a rape culture, a culture of misogyny, and I also saw that as part of the Korean diaspora I lived with a hidden legacy of rape culture, both real (Korean "comfort women," who were the sexual slaves of the Japanese military) and speculative (rape or sexual exploitation of birth mothers of Korean orphans).

When a white woman came to speak to us about white privilege, to prepare us for working with a population that might include women of color and women who spoke languages other than English, I was strongly moved. We had already learned that rape affected women from all cultures and communities, but I had never heard the term *white privilege* before—never had that language to name it—and it validated my sense of racialized reality. I had not thought it possible for a white person to truly be my ally (and teacher) in this way.

Other women were moved as well. One red-haired white woman said that she often told people she was Irish but she really wasn't, she didn't know what she was and felt she had no ethnic identity. Other white women nodded. This is how whiteness operates as a human standard: A white person is only "raced" if there are people of color in the room. I realized that it wasn't just women of color who struggled with feelings of authenticity, belonging, and invisibility, and I wondered how we would bring our knowledge of ourselves as "raced" to our work with sexual assault victims.

STEREOTYPE OF THE COMPLIANT WOMAN

Asian Pacific American women are at particular risk of being
racially and sexually harassed because of the synergism that
results when sexualized racial stereotypes combine with

racialized gender stereotypes. The "model minority myth," a much criticized racial stereotype of Asian Pacific Americans, has been shown to paint a misleading portrait of groupwide economic, educational, and professional super-success. In addition, the mythical model minority is further overdetermined by associated images of political passivity and submissiveness to authority. . . . Model minority traits of passivity and submissiveness are intensified and gendered through the stock portrayal of obedient and servile Asian Pacific women in popular culture.[1]

The stereotypical images of Madame Butterfly and Suzie Wong reflected completely irrelevant qualities for me and the other young women I knew. Of course I had been subject to street harassment and endured my share of stereotyping and prejudicial encounters, but what the model minority quote illustrates most for me is the need to rehabilitate Asian American identity, to move it from passive to active, politically engaged, and noncompliant (sometimes in complex, subversive ways) with authoritarian culture. As a college student, I began to question what my role was, globally, as a transplanted Korean—a "lucky" American—and an evolving feminist.

Like many adoptive parents, mine had always told me how lucky I was to be an American, how I would be starving, or a prostitute, or dead had I stayed in Korea. They told me that North Korea was an evil Communist country and that my South Korean mother was too poor to keep me. This master narrative is worn to the point of grim hilarity among the cynical adoptees I know. How little we were taught about our places of birth is almost laughable, but the power of our adoptive families' belief in their love and assimilationist efforts shaped our lives and our sense of malleability and anonymity. No one had ever told me that I belonged to 10 percent of all Korean Americans. I had virtually no past, thus I had no context in the present—and as Buddhists say, the only power we have is in the present. My adoptedness was largely invisible, yet on some level it informed everything I did. I wanted it to be a strength, not a weakness, in my work as a feminist. Because I'd been given a so-called second chance, I strongly wanted to contribute to my community, to make a mark but also to be marked—to transform and be transformed.

But were my people the women still living on the Korean peninsula, or (and?) were they so-called Asian Americans? Could I expand my consciousness to include all women, especially women of color? How could I make the most difference when rape seemed to be both everywhere and grievously invisible? The subject of rape was not polite dinner conversation. It made people uncomfortable, and yet I wanted to understand how it operated in our society to keep all women hostage.

WOMEN IN CRISIS

One of the hardest calls I ever took was from a woman whose daughter was being molested by her ex-husband, with whom she shared custody. The mother felt outrage but also guilt at not knowing sooner, at not being able to prevent the abuse, at having chosen to mate with a man who would later sexually assault his own offspring. After hearing her panic, I gave her the phone numbers of potentially helpful agencies and affirmed that she was doing the right thing in taking action. I walked through some options she had for speaking with her daughter herself or going to a professional counselor. I told her it wasn't her fault, but that she could and must take action now. She agreed. She was angry and ready to assert her rights.

Her anguish was hard to witness, but her fierce decisiveness in the light of her daughter's victimization made me think that we all need to take responsibility for each other with the same ferocity and to understand that one mother's daughter is all of our daughters. It led me to do some research on incest, divorce, and blended families, and in several studies on girls who are victims of incest I saw statistics showing that girls are more at risk when a man who is not biologically related to them lives in the household. Other correlating factors include the presence of a passive mother. Passive women make passive mothers who put their daughters at risk for abuse and who, if the logic follows, are more likely to pair with dominating males, which sent me back to the stereotype of the compliant Asian woman.

I wondered why there wasn't more investigation into the converging issues of working women's economic status, marriage and divorce, the American-style nuclear family, and girls' (and boys') basic human rights to be safe from sexual abuse by their own household or family members. As an adoptee, I've always had a heightened consciousness of the construction of the family and the mysteries and conflicts of nature and nurture. As a person of color raised by white people, my reality was unknown, unnamed, and discounted, and as a girl/woman I felt I was under the thumb of my depressed, raging white father. Once I became a rape crisis counselor, it was never difficult for me to understand rape victims' psychological responses of dissociation, shame, silence, fear, and fear of secondary victimization. My Asian body-self had long been a source of feelings of unreality, which easily translated into a deep well of empathy for women (of any color) who had been raped or assaulted. Though I don't consider myself a victim of physical abuse (and I would never diminish or obscure the nature of rape by equating it with the complex and variable nature of international transracial adoption) I did and can relate to an enduring sense of loss of control and even of damage.

Another caller was a young woman who was being stalked and sexually threatened by a male coworker. She kept saying, "All I want to know is why. Why would someone do such a thing? I don't understand! Why do you think he would do that to me? I don't get it. I just want to know why."

I stumbled through different responses, from the standard "It's not your fault" to referral to a litany of practical services. None of these responses answered her anguished need to know why, on a psychological level, a man she hardly knew would terrorize her in this manner. She seemed genuinely interested in the causes, not simply in whether she had done anything wrong. She said she believed it wasn't her fault, but it seemed as though all her life she'd believed in rationality, cause and effect, logical behavior, and this man defied all of it and broke open her sense of reality. I (re)realized that even the threat of sexual assault is a profound violation of the victim's sense of reality, of her most basic right to control what happens to her body—the materiality of her essence as a human being.

Another incident that stands out in my mind was another middle-of-the-night call to the Ramsey County hospital. A white teenager who lived in a kind of juvenile halfway house said she had been raped at gunpoint around 4 A.M. while she was walking on a main street. The police officer asked her to describe the gun, and the girl faltered, changing the details. I sensed that the police officer might not believe her story. As the morning wore on, the girl pleaded with her caseworker to let her stay in the psychiatric ward of the hospital, and I wondered what had really happened, and what we as part of the social services systems could do to help her.

The girl had been cutting herself in the past weeks and said she wanted to kill herself. There was some issue over how many hours she had already spent in the hospital recently, and the officials had to be sure that she really was in danger of committing suicide. I sat silently and observed. It seemed surreal that this young woman, clearly troubled and vulnerable in many ways, had to beg and plead within a bureaucracy to get the help she needed. She made me think of my friends in high school who lived at a teen orphanage because their adoptive parents had abused them.

Coming into contact with these at-risk women and girls who lived within a few miles of my college made me sharply aware of the paradox of my class privilege as a student and my shared vulnerability as a female. Because my status as a missing daughter of Korea converges with my adopted family's traditional white patriarchal patterns, I've come to see the convergence of all my personal and political understandings—my sense of the broad effects of imperialism on the Korean peninsula; U.S. foreign and domestic policy as it relates to women's rights; and the need for a more historical and political analysis of transracial adoption—dovetail into a critique of sexism and state-sanctioned silence, silence that women cannot afford to continue.

Sexual aggression is an integral aspect of the othering that we recognize more readily as racial hatred. As I have learned, and continue to learn, women of color can make common cause with white women against sexism and violence while creating our own spaces and leaders. We can recognize and understand difference without making a fetish of it. We can place rape in a framework of global justice work. And it's our mission to end rape's power as a tool of domination against women of all cultures, nations, and neighborhoods. I embrace my generation (X) and the work we have to do. Thus it is abundantly clear to me that as an Asian (naturalized) American adopted Korean woman/mother/worker, I (we) have no more time to waste in obscurity.

Smoking, breast cancer, depression, and alcoholism and other addictions have now become well-known public health issues due to the passionate and dedicated work of activists and the institutions they have created and funded. Other activists have called for the same unrelenting public focus on rape [see Dworkin, p. 12ff, and Stoltenberg, p. 259ff]. We must support and fund centers that specialize in preventing sexual assault and assisting its victims, but we cannot allow the issue of rape and its broad causes and consequences to be relegated in the public's mind to a problem only for liberal social services, hormone-fueled college campuses, and underfunded urban criminal courts.

I was a counselor for three years and was sad when, pregnant with my first child and exhausted, I decided to take a break from counseling. I began my journey as a rape crisis counselor by externalizing vulnerability, thinking of the women who survived attack as somehow different from me. I soon came to recognize that we are all vulnerable, and because of this we are all responsible for transforming our rape culture.

NOTES

1. Sumi K. Cho. "Asian Pacific American Women and Racialized Sexual Harassment," in *Making More Waves: New Writing by Asian American Women,* edited by Elaine H. Kim, Lilia V. Villanueva, and Asian Women United of California (Boston: Beacon, 1997), 164–73.

SUN YUNG SHIN is from South Korea, then Chicago, then Boston. Her poems have been published in journals such as *Indiana Review, Mid-American Review, Xcp,* and the anthology *Echoes upon Echoes: New Korean American Writings* (Asian American Writers' Workshop). She is the author of the illustrated children's book *Cooper's Lesson* (Children's Book Press, 2004). Shin now lives in Minneapolis with her husband and their two children.

STILL NO LAUGHING MATTER
SEXUAL HARASSMENT IN K-12 SCHOOLS

. . . .

NAN STEIN

Listening to the stories of young women's experiences of sexual harassment in schools has led me to see that schools may in fact be training grounds for domestic violence: Girls learn that they are on their own, that the adults and others around them will not believe or help them when they report sexual harassment or assault.

T HE PRESENCE OF SEXUAL HARASSMENT in schools is no longer a contested phenomenon. Its existence has been acknowledged by federal courts, including in two cases heard by the U.S. Supreme Court; by a plethora of surveys; and by countless personal testimonials from children and adolescents, both boys and girls, who have been targets of harassment or witnesses and bystanders. The families of children whose lives were affected by sexual harassment have taken great personal risks to pursue complaints and lawsuits against their school districts for failure to maintain a learning environment that was free from sex discrimination and sexual harassment.

However, bringing sexual harassment to national consciousness also took years of unrelenting effort from feminist lawyers, activists, and researchers, and from equity-focused education employees at the local, state, and national levels. No one whose life is lived in and around schools can doubt that sexual harassment in schools exists and that it exerts a powerful influence on the quality of school life.

The educational establishment paid little attention to the subject of sexual harassment in K–12 schools until it was propelled into the national discourse in February 1992 and again in May 1999. In the 1992 case, *Franklin v. Gwinnett County (Georgia) Public Schools,* an increasingly rare unanimous ruling of the United States Supreme Court found that schools could be held financially liable for sexual harassment.[1]

Although sexual harassment in K–12 schools had not been widely acknowledged before this 1992 Supreme Court decision, some state-level education agencies and individuals were paying attention to the problem.[2] A few academic and popular articles have also been published on the subject.[3] Although the larger educational community sometimes acknowledged the problem of sexual harassment anecdotally, it was usually treated like a secret that just happened to occur in public.

In addition, the school reform movement of the 1980s generally ignored both the issue of gender and the phenomenon of sexual harassment. In the landmark 1992 study "How Schools Shortchange Girls," written at the Wellesley College Center for Research on Women and coincidentally released two weeks prior to the *Franklin* decision, discussion of gender was found to be missing from thirty-one of the thirty-five school reform reports that the researchers reviewed. Only four of the commissions that issued reports about the condition of America's schools included gender or sex discrimination issues (the rubric under which sexual harassment is legally located) in their analyses. Girls' problems were limited to pregnancy at an early age and dropping out of school. The Wellesley report concluded that "the concentration on these [two] issues to the exclusion of others leads to strategies directed toward individual rather than systemic change and programs focused on girls' personal decisions rather than policy initiatives to improve the educational system."[4]

Seven years later, in May 1999, the Supreme Court ruled again on sexual harassment in school. In a five to four decision in *Davis v. Monroe County (Georgia) Board of Education,* the court ruled that schools are indeed liable for student-to-student sexual harassment when they know about the harassment and fail to stop it. However, the standard for school liability was set very high. To quote from the majority opinion written by Justice Sandra Day O'Connor, "Damages are not available for simple acts of teasing and name-calling among schoolchildren" but rather for behavior "so severe, pervasive and objectively offensive that it denies its victims the equal access to education" guaranteed under Title IX of the Education Amendments of 1972.[5]

Even though a lawsuit is a sample size of one, lawsuits can be prototypical and serve as guideposts for future directions. If social scientists and educators who are interested in documenting the problem of sexual harassment in schools would use lawsuits as a new source of evidence, valuable lessons might emerge. A summary of the major federal lawsuits and the complaints filed through the Office for Civil Rights of the U.S. Department of Education documents the impact of sexual harassment on the lives of the targets.

Among the consequences of sexual harassment that have been stipulated through lawsuits are:

- absenteeism
- dropping out of a particular class or school
- lower grades
- sleeplessness and physical symptoms or complaints
- fear of separation from adults, either parents or school personnel (for example, refusing to take the school bus, refusing to participate in recess, asking to stay in the classroom or be sent to the principal's or nurse's

office during recess, refusing to eat lunch in the cafeteria, and choosing
to stay in the classroom or library during lunch)

- depression
- weight loss or gain
- threats to commit suicide.[6]

Students also have expressed a lessening of trust toward adults and in their
beliefs that school is a safe and fair environment. They have felt betrayed, trivialized, and dismissed if and when they told school personnel about incidents
of sexual harassment they had experienced. These lessons can linger far beyond the actual episodes of the sexual harassment: Trust in adults is eroded,
school becomes a place to be avoided, and justice is not delivered.

Granted, some of the evidence gleaned from lawsuits is biased in that it is
provided by the plaintiff or the experts who have been hired by the plaintiff's
attorney. On the other hand, the opposing counsel's grueling interrogation
of the plaintiff (especially in the discovery or deposition phase of the case,
when no judge or jury is present) makes the process of proceeding with a
lawsuit very difficult and leaves the pursuit of lawsuits to those plaintiffs and
their parents who are particularly zealous and motivated. Thus, it is unclear
whether lawsuits are typical. Even so, many lessons can be drawn that could
spare others from heading in the same direction in the future. To that extent,
the lessons that can be derived from the lawsuits should not be dismissed,
whether these cases are won, lost, or settled out of court. Beyond the power
and precedent that lawsuits can establish, narratives and anecdotal information from girls and young women parallel the experiences of sexual harassment in schools that are documented in the lawsuits and complaints. In
other words, there is nothing atypical about the lawsuits.[7]

Listening to the stories of young women's experiences of sexual harassment in schools has led me to see that schools may in fact be training grounds
for domestic violence: Girls learn that they are on their own, that the adults
and others around them will not believe or help them when they report
sexual harassment or assault. The harassers find that their conduct is treated
with impunity, sometimes even glorified. And other students, who may be
witnesses of and bystanders to the harassing behaviors, absorb the lesson that
sexual harassment is a public performance which is normalized, expected,
and tolerated. What follow are excerpts from young women's experiences

with sexual harassment as they appeared in responses to a survey published in *Seventeen* magazine.[8]

> It came to the point where I was skipping almost all of my
> classes, therefore getting kicked out of the honors program.
> It was *very* painful for me. I dreaded school each morning,
> I started to wear clothes that wouldn't flatter my figure, and
> I kept to myself. I never had a boyfriend that year. I'd cry
> every night I got home, and I thought I was a total loser. . . .
> Sometimes the teachers were right there when it was going on.
> They did nothing. . . . I felt very angry that these arrogant,
> narrow-minded people never took the time to see who really
> was inside. . . . I'm also very angry that they took away my
> self-esteem, my social life, and kept me from getting a good
> education. (Sixteen-year-old from a midsized city in Illinois)

> Being sexually harassed at school made me feel upset, angry,
> and violated. I mean, I shouldn't have to take this crap at
> school, should I? It's my right to go to school and not be
> harassed, isn't it? I feel confused because I wonder if *all guys*
> think those things about me! I feel insecure after this hap-
> pens. I hate it. I shouldn't have to feel sexually intimidated
> by people who barely know me. (Sixteen-year-old from a
> midsized city in northern New England)

> The problem is, this is middle school, and they think it doesn't
> happen, but it does! He only gets a warning or, if I'm lucky,
> detention. It's so unfair! It's all over our school. (Twelve-year-
> old, Atlanta area)

> He had a habit of trying to sneak up on girls and try(ing)
> to pull their shorts down. All the girls complained to the
> teacher—who yelled at him but did nothing. What made
> things harder was that some girls kidded with him, which
> may have encouraged him further. For about three months he
> continued. Some days were better than others; most people
> tried to avoid him. What angers me is that even though I filed

a formal complaint, the gym teacher didn't get in trouble.
The boy was watched for a while until the principal had more
evidence—then suspended for six days. The "big picture" is
scarier than isolated incidents. (Seventeen-year-old from New
Jersey)

It was like fighting an invisible, invincible enemy alone.
I didn't have a clue as to what to do to stop it, so I experi-
mented [with] different approaches. Ignoring it only made
it worse. It made it easier for them to do it, so they did it
more. Laughing at the perpetrators during the assaults didn't
dent the problem at all, and soon my friends became tired of
doing this. They thought it was a game. Finally I wrote them
threatening letters. This got me in trouble. But perhaps it did
work. I told the school administrators what had been happening to me. They didn't seem to think it a big deal, but they did
talk to the three biggest perpetrators. The boys ignored the
administrators and it continued. And they were even worse.
(Fifteen-year-old from a midsized city in Massachusetts)

Of the times I was sexually harassed at school, one of them
made me feel really bad. I was in class and the teacher was
looking right at me when this guy grabbed my butt. The
teacher saw it happen. I slapped the guy and told him not to
do that. My teacher didn't say anything and looked away and
went on with the lesson like nothing out of the ordinary had
happened. It really confused me because I knew guys weren't
supposed to do that, but the teacher didn't do anything. I felt
like the teacher (who was a man) betrayed me and thought I
was making a big deal out of nothing. But most of all, I felt
really bad about myself because it made me feel slutty and
cheap. It made me feel mad too because we shouldn't have to
put up with that stuff, but no one will do anything to stop it.
Now sexual harassment doesn't bother me as much because
it happens so much it almost seems normal. I know that
sounds awful, but the longer it goes on without anyone doing

anything, the more I think of it as just one of those things that
I have to put up with. (Fourteen-year-old from a midsized city
in the Pacific Northwest)

The silence of adults in the school community represents negligence, allowing and encouraging the sexual harassment to continue. The cynical, bitter lessons of silence and neglect affect not only the subjects of sexual harassment but also the witnesses. Boys as well as girls become mistrustful of adults who fail to intervene, provide equal protection, and safeguard the educational environment. Too many of our schools have become unsafe, uncaring and unjust.

Peer-to-peer sexual harassment is rampant in elementary and secondary schools. While it is sometimes identified and curtailed, more often than not it is tolerated, characterized as a normal stage in healthy American adolescent development. Frequently it is identified as flirting or dismissed as part of acceptable initiation rites. "No harm done," the adults often say, or "no big deal." Regardless of the ways school authorities rationalize its existence, sexual harassment interferes with a student's right to receive equal educational opportunities and is a violation of Title IX, the federal law passed in 1972 that outlaws sex discrimination in educational institutions receiving federal financial assistance.[9]

Sexual harassment in schools happens in full view of others. Boys harass girls with impunity while people watch. Examples of sexual harassment that happen in public include attempts to snap bras, grope at girls' bodies, pull down gym shorts, or flip up skirts; circulating "summa cum slutty" or "piece of ass of the week" lists; designating special weeks for grabbing the private parts of girls; nasty, personalized graffiti written on bathroom walls; sexualized jokes, taunts, and skits that mock girls' bodies, performed at school-sponsored pep rallies, assemblies, or halftime performances during sporting events; and outright physical assault and even rape in schools.[10]

Sexual harassment is a form of sex discrimination and is illegal as defined by Title IX of the Educational Amendments of 1972, Title VII of the Civil Rights Act (1964, amended 1972), the equal protection clause of the Fourteenth Amendment of the U.S. Constitution, and numerous state criminal and civil statues.[11] The presence or absence of sexual harassment depends on the victim's perception of "unwelcome" sexual behavior. Sexual harassment can range from touching, tickling, pinching, patting, or grabbing to comments about one's body, sexual remarks, innuendos, jokes that cause discomfort, obscene gestures, staring, leering, assault, or rape.

Both students and employees are legally protected against sexual harassment, regardless of whether the perpetrator is an employee, a student, or an individual who is connected to the school district only by being part of an organization with which the school has a contractual agreement. Some forms of sexual harassment may also be actionable as child abuse, sexual assault, rape, criminal or civil libel, slander, or defamation of character. Victims, as well as educators or community members acting on the victim's behalf, may file sexual harassment complaints. Sexual harassment contaminates the whole school environment, and its reach may embrace more than the immediate and intended target(s). Indeed, the school environment becomes poisoned for everyone—innocent witnesses and bystanders alike—in addition to the intended subject/victim of the sexual harassment.

The examples of peer-to-peer sexual harassment cited above are commonplace occurrences in elementary and secondary schools across the country, in small towns with homogeneous populations as well as in large cities with more culturally diverse populations. The desperate dilemma facing victims of sexual harassment is how to avoid the upsetting and degrading incidents when they have become so acceptable, ordinary, and public. What happens in public, if not interrupted, becomes normalized and acceptable over time. Moreover, students have expectations that if something scary, unpleasant, or illegal is happening in school, especially if it occurs in public, someone with authority will intervene to stop it, help out, or at least believe the victim afterwards. Yet sexual harassment seems to proceed mostly without adult intervention, thereby exacerbating and broadening its reach and reign of terror. In schools, sexual harassment is tenacious, pervasive, and operates as a kind of gendered violence.

CONFIRMATION FROM RESEARCH STUDIES

Sexual harassment in schools has been studied since the early 1980s, generally one school or one state at a time.[12] It wasn't until 1993 that a scientific national sample was gathered by the American Association of University Women (AAUW) Educational Foundation for its Hostile Hallways study, which was repeated in 2001. The 1993 AAUW/Harris poll established a surprisingly high prevalence of sexual harassment in public schools, and the 2001 survey affirmed that the school environment had not changed much in the interim. Additionally, the 2001 study covered a much larger sample in order to obtain greater reliability.[13]

The 2001 survey sampled 2,064 students (1,094 girls and 970 boys), attending randomly selected public schools in grades eight through eleven. It found that 83 percent of girls and 79 percent of boys have experienced sexual harassment at some point during their lives. Although the percentage of girls experiencing sexual harassment has remained fairly steady, the percentage of boys who are harassed "often or occasionally" has risen since 1993 (from 49 percent to 56 percent). The majority of students who experience sexual harassment are harassed by their peers (85 percent), which is similar to the 1993 figure (86 percent).

HARASSMENT OF GAY, LESBIAN, AND BISEXUAL STUDENTS

Very few data have been collected on the sexual harassment of gay, lesbian, and bisexual students. According to a 2001 Hatred in the Hallways survey by Human Rights Watch, the United States had more than 2 million sexual minority students.[14] In fact, until the Washington State Safe Schools Coalition Five-Year Project began in 1994, no one had even studied antigay harassment, either "qualitative[ly] or [with] a population based quantitative sample."[15]

In 1999, Massachusetts and Washington collected some data on the subject. In addition, quite a number of incidents have been reported to advocacy organizations such as the Gay, Lesbian, and Straight Education Network (GLSEN) and Human Rights Watch. The Massachusetts data belong to a national and statewide survey, the Youth Risk Behavior Survey (YRBS), which was expanded to include harassment of gay, lesbian, and bisexual students. Additionally, only five states, Massachusetts, Vermont, Wisconsin, California, and Connecticut, have passed laws to protect the civil rights of gay and lesbian students. The advocacy work of organizations such as GLSEN and other legal actions in federal courts undertaken by students against their school systems for failure to protect them from harassment have brought attention to the discrimination, harassment, and violence suffered by gay and lesbian students.[16]

MASSACHUSETTS YOUTH RISK BEHAVIOR SURVEY

The Massachusetts Youth Risk Behavior Survey (MYRBS) has been conducted every two years since 1990 by the Massachusetts Department of Education. Massachusetts was among thirty-four states that administered their own YRBS in order to keep an eye on the prevalence of risky behaviors that adolescents engage in, such as using tobacco, not using seat belts, and high-risk sex acts.

The MYRBS was completed by students in several randomly selected public high schools throughout Massachusetts in 1999. In each selected school, three to five classes were randomly selected to complete the MYRBS questionnaire. The overall response rate was 79 percent (4,415 completed surveys out of 5,589 selected students). Of these 4,415 students, 5.5 percent described themselves as "gay, lesbian, bisexual and/or students with any same-sex sexual experience." Of the students who have a "sexual history," 9.4 percent were sexual minority students.[17]

Sexual minority students were engaged in significantly higher rates of school violence than non–sexual minority students. Sexual minority students reported being in twice as many physical fights at school and were three times as likely to carry a weapon to school, to be threatened or injured with a weapon at school, and to miss school because they felt unsafe.

CONCLUSION FROM THE RESEARCH

Students, whether they are the targets, witnesses or perpetrators of harassment, overwhelmingly acknowledge the existence of sexual harassment in their schools. There is no shortage of evidence pointing to a firm and well-substantiated conclusion that sexual harassment in schools exists and is rampant and that the targets (predominantly girls) are not passive in the face of this harassment. Yet despite the cumulative evidence from these studies, both those with well-substantiated results and those that provide only a basis for informed speculation, researchers and public policy advocates continue to study the phenomenon of sexual harassment. It is safe to assume at this point that educators can believe the results, which amounts to believing the students. It is time to expand research to include longitudinal studies that examine the effects of sexual harassment on perpetrators and victims over time. In addition, studies should be undertaken to test the effectiveness of a variety of interventions designed to reduce and prevent sexual harassment.

The findings that have emerged from the research conducted to date could have been easily ignored were it not for the complaints and lawsuits that girls, young women, and in rare instances boys have been filing and winning in state and federal courts in the past decade. Perhaps these lawsuits have made the survey results all the more powerful and credible.

BULLYING AS AN ANTECEDENT TO SEXUAL HARASSMENT

The antecedents to peer-to-peer sexual harassment in schools may be found in bullying—behaviors children learn, practice, and experience beginning at a very young age. All boys know what a bully is, and many boys, as well as girls, have been victims of bullying. Teachers and parents know about bullying, and many accept it as an unfortunate stage that some children go through on their way to adolescence and adulthood. Left unchecked and unchallenged, bullying may in fact serve as a practice ground for sexual harassment.

Like its older cousin, sexual harassment, bullying deprives children of their entitlement to be educated and secure in the knowledge that they will be safe and free from harm. While laws in many states outlaw the practice in educational institutions of hazing (defined as the organized practice of induction, usually into a fraternity or sports team, through degrading behaviors or physical assault), antibullying laws have been passed in slightly more than a dozen states since the year 2000. Discussion of bullying should be a deliberate part of the school curriculum but frequently is not.

One promising violence prevention study began in 1997 with fifth-grade students and their teachers in Austin, Texas, with multiyear funding from the Division of Violence Prevention at the Centers for Disease Control and Prevention (CDC). This scientific study, with control and experimental groups, and with pre- and post-tests of both students and their teachers, has shown that long-term curricular interventions, along with training for faculty, staff, and parents, and along with school-based and districtwide policy implementation, can have a great impact on reducing gender-based bullying and sexual harassment. This project was conducted by SafePlace, a combined sexual assault and domestic violence center in Austin, along with its partners in the Austin Independent School District and at the School of Social Work at the University of Texas, with scientific oversight from the research scientists at the CDC.

The project, called Expect Respect, was based on the curriculum *Bullyproof: A Teacher's Guide on Teasing and Bullying for Use with Fourth and Fifth Grade Students.*[18] Results from the project showed a significant increase in awareness of bullying followed the educational intervention.[19]

ELIMINATING SEXUAL HARASSMENT IN SCHOOLS

Schools need to resist the temptation to treat sexual harassment symptomatically—a videotape here, a workshop there. Sexual harassment is a systemic problem; solutions must be systemic as well. To accomplish this, a multipronged effort must be undertaken. What follow are several components of such an effort:

Training programs for staff and students. Everyone in the school community, from custodians to bus drivers, classroom teachers to coaches, extracurricular advisors to superintendents and school board members, needs mandated professional development workshops and seminars on sexual harassment. Everyone must be trained to recognize sexual harassment, to know their responsibilities to report it to the proper individuals and agencies, and to create strategies to prevent and eliminate it. A cadre of both male and female staff members should receive intensive training and be designated to serve as ombuds available to the students.

Ongoing professional development must be required for those who work or plan to work in the schools *in any capacity,* in order to prevent and eliminate sexual harassment. Teacher preparation programs need to offer courses to preservice teachers, explaining their responsibilities to intervene in order to discourage discrimination and harassment. Beyond this, such programs need to develop strategies for intervention and models to resolve the problem.

The students must also be included in ongoing conversations about sexual harassment and child sexual abuse in schools. Through orientation, assemblies, student handbooks, support/rap groups, peer advising, and activities and lessons infused into the classroom curriculum, the subject of sexual harassment must become a deliberate and frequent part of formal and informal curricula.

Policies and procedures. An effective sexual harassment policy should begin with a clear statement that expresses disapproval of sexual harassment and a strong commitment to eliminating it. Victims should be encouraged to come forward, and all community members should be reminded of their responsibilities, as bystanders and potential witnesses, to report incidents of sexual harassment. Anything the school system writes should be in language accessible to all the students and community members. The policy should include definitions of sexual harassment that embrace peer-to-peer, adult-to-student, student-to-adult, and same-sex harassment.[20] It is helpful to include examples of sexual harassment and child sexual abuse, indicating that these incidents and behaviors can happen both in public and in private.

Policy development. Concerned educators, parents, students, community members, and feminists must press policymakers to extend the new national awareness about sexual harassment in schools into the domain of legislation, regulation, and school board policy. First, policymakers must disentangle the jurisdictional confusion about which state agencies have authority to investigate complaints of sexual harassment and child sexual abuse in schools, and then they must publicize those lines of authority to the public and to students.

In addition, they must design models for public policy, procedures, regulations, and delivery of services to ensure that children who experience sexual abuse and sexual harassment in school settings are heard and protected. Antihazing laws must be passed or strengthened to include those institutional and group acts of sexual harassment that sometimes pass for initiation rites.

Moreover, every state needs to pass laws that offer protections to teens who are involved in violent dating relationships. These laws, known often as civil restraining orders or stay-away orders, typically are available for adults who are in abusive relationships. As awareness of the violence in teen dating relationships becomes more widespread, state legislators are making such protections available for teenagers.[21]

CONCLUSION

Ultimately, a strategy to attack sexual harassment in schools needs to aim at transformation of the broader school culture. Dealing effectively with sexual harassment is much easier if a school has committed itself to infusing a spirit of equity and a critique of injustice into its curriculum and pedagogy. On the other hand, harassment flourishes where children are practiced in the art of doing nothing in the face of unjust treatment by others. When teachers subject children to a sit-down-shut-up-and-do-your-work pedagogy, they don't learn to think of themselves as moral subjects, capable of speaking out when they witness bullying or other forms of harassment. If youngsters haven't been encouraged to critique the sexism of the curriculum, hidden and overt, then they are less likely to recognize it when they confront it in their midst. Too often, the entire school structure offers children no meaningful involvement in decision-making about school policy, climate, or curriculum. Life in school rehearses children to be social spectators.[22] Particularly in an era of zero tolerance, with its mandatory sentencing policies of one strike and you're out, school administrators and teachers need to balance the needs of creating and maintaining a safe (as in gender-safe) school along with humane, just discipline policies.[23]

Sexual harassment in schools, a well-known social secret and a national disgrace, must become a public concern in order for it to be obliterated from educational settings. With sustained and multipronged educational efforts, we can crack the denial and casualness surrounding the problem. Only in conjunction with efforts to reduce other practices that promote and institutionalize inequalities in schools—such as tracking and ability grouping; standardized testing; biased curricula; and biased classroom practices and pedagogies—will our schools become safe and welcoming learning environments for all students, with equal educational opportunities and justice available for both females and males. In order to live out the democracy, we need to practice it in our schools.

The author thanks Bill Bigelow—teacher and author from Portland, Oregon— for his help with the original version of this essay, which appeared in the 1993 edition of this book, and for his overall editorial suggestions, provocative and incisive comments about educational transformation, resistance, and activism.

NOTES

1. *Franklin v. Gwinnett County (Georgia) Public Schools,* 112 S. Ct. 1028 (1992), *Davis v. Monroe County (Georgia) Board of Education,* 119 S. Ct. (1999).

2. These pioneering efforts include the curriculum materials developed and surveys administered by the Massachusetts Department of Education (1979, 1982, 1983, and 1986) and the Programs in Equal Educational Opportunity at the University of Michigan (one of the federally funded Desegregation Assistance Centers, now called Equity Assistance Centers). In addition, training efforts were established through the sex-equity offices in departments of education in several states, including California, Florida, Hawaii, Maryland, Massachusetts, Minnesota, Montana, Nebraska, New Jersey, Pennsylvania, South Dakota, Washington, and Wisconsin. Nan Stein, "Sexual Harassment of High School Students: Preliminary Research Results" (unpublished report, 1981); Nan Stein, ed. *Who's Hurt and Who's Liable: Sexual Harassment in Massachusetts Schools* (Malden: Massachusetts Department of Education, 1986; originally published in 1979).

3. Karen Bogart and Nan Stein, "Breaking the Silence: Sexual Harassment in Education," *Peabody Journal of Education* 64, no. 4 (1987): 146–163; Nan Stein, "It Happens Here Too: Sexual Harassment in the Schools," *Education Week* 11, no. 13 (1991): 32; Susan Strauss, "Sexual Harassment in the School: Legal Implications for Principals," *NASSP Bulletin* 72, no. 506 (March 1988): 93–97 (available from National Association of Secondary School Principals, Reston, VA).

4. American Association of University Women, *How Schools Shortchange Girls: A Study of Major Findings on Girls and Education* (Washington, DC, 1992).

5. *Davis v. Monroe County (Georgia) Board of Education,* 526 U.S. 629 (1999); Linda Greenhouse, "Sex Harassment in Class Is Ruled Schools' Liability," *New York Times,* May 25, 1999.

6. Nan Stein, *Classrooms and Courtrooms: Facing Sexual Harassment in K–12 Schools,* (New York: Teachers College Press, 1999).

7. Millicent Lawton, "Sexual Harassment of Students Target of District Policies," *Education Week* 12, no. 20 (1993): 1, 15–16; Millicent Lawton, "District May Be Held Liable for Harassment, Court Rules." *Education Week* 15, no. 22 (1996): 5, Tamar Lewin, "Students Seeking Damages for Sex Bias," *New York Times,* July 15, 1994; Tamar Lewin, "Students Use Law on Discrimination in Sex-Abuse Suits," *New York Times,* June 26, 1995; Nan Stein, "School Harassment: An Update," *Education Week* 12, no. 9 (1992): 37. Nan Stein, "Secrets in Public: Sexual Harassment in Public (and Private) Schools" (working paper #256, Wellesley College Center for Research on Women,

Wellesley, Mass., 1992); Nan Stein, "Sexual Harassment in K–12 Schools: The Public Performance of Gendered Violence," *Harvard Educational Review* 65, no. 2 (1995): 145–162.

8. Adrian LeBlanc, "Harassment in the Halls," *Seventeen,* September 1992, 162–165, 170.

9. U.S. Department of Health, Education, and Welfare, "Title IX of Education Amendment of 1972," 20 U.S.C. sec. 1681 (P.L. 92–318), *Federal Register* 40, no. 108 (June 4, 1975): 24,128: "No person in the United States shall, on the basis of sex, be excluded from participation in, be denied the benefits of, or be subjected to discrimination under any education program or activity receiving Federal financial assistance."

10. Stein, *Classrooms and Courtrooms,* 1999; Stein, "School Harassment"; Stein, "Secrets in Public."

11. U.S. Department of Health, Education, and Welfare, Title VII, Equal Employment Opportunity Commission, "Guidelines on Discrimination Because of Sex," 29 C.F.R Section 1604.11, Part 1604, *Federal Register,* (November 10, 1980): 746,676: "Harassment on the basis of sex is a violation of Sec. 703 of Title VII. Unwelcome sexual advances, requests for sexual favors, and other verbal or physical conduct of a sexual nature constitute sexual harassment when (1) submission to or rejection of such conduct is made either explicitly or implicitly a term or condition of an individual's employment, (2) submission to or rejection of such conduct by an individual is used as the basis of an employment decision affecting such individual, or (3) such conduct has the purpose or effect of unreasonably interfering with an individual's work performance or creating an intimidating, hostile, or offensive working environment."

    Civil Rights Act of 1871, 42 U.S.C. sec. 1983: "Every person who, under color of any statute, ordinance, regulation, custom, usage, or any state or territory, subjects or causes to be subjected, any citizen of the United States or any person within the jurisdiction thereof to the deprivation of any rights, privileges, or immunities secured by the Constitution and laws, shall be liable to the party injured in an action at law, suit in equity, or other proper proceeding for redress."

    Section 1983, which is a federal statute, provides an avenue of redress for individuals who have been deprived of their federal constitutional or statutory rights at the behest of state authority. Section 1983 provides redress for violation of explicit constitutional rights (e.g., the right to due process) and also of federal statutory rights passed pursuant to constitutional authority.

12. Stein, *Classrooms and Courtrooms.*

13. American Association of University Women, "Hostile Hallways: The AAUW Survey on Sexual Harassment in America's Schools" (Washington, DC, 1993); "Hostile Hallways" (2001).

14. Human Rights Watch, "Hatred in the Hallways: Violence and Discrimination against Lesbian, Gay, Bisexual, and Transgender Students in U.S. Schools" (New York, 2001).

15. B. Reis and E. Saewyc, "Safe Schools Coalition of Washington State: Selected Findings of Eight Population-Based Studies" (Seattle, WA: Safe Schools Coalition, 1999).

16. *Nabozny v. Podlesny,* 92 F. 3d 446 (7th Cir. 1996).

17. Massachusetts Department of Education, *1999 Massachusetts Youth Risk Behavior Survey Results* (Malden, 2000) 25, 30.

18. Lisa Sjostrom and Nan Stein, *Bullyproof: A Teacher's Guide on Teasing and Bullying for Fourth and Fifth Grade Students* (Wellesley, Mass.: Wellesley College Center for Research on Women, 1996).

19. Martha G. Meraviglia et al., "The Expect Respect Project: Creating a Positive Elementary School Climate" *Journal of Interpersonal Violence* (November 2003): 1347–60.

20. Deborah Brake and Verna Williams, *Do the Right Thing: Understanding, Addressing, and Preventing Sexual Harassment in School* (Washington DC: National Women's Law Center, 1998).

21. Roger Levesque, "Dating Violence, Adolescents, and the Law," *Virginia Journal of Social Policy and the Law* 4, no. 2 (1997): 339–379; Jay Silverman et al., "Dating Violence against Adolescent Girls and Associated Substance Use, Unhealthy Weight Control, Sexual Risk Behavior, Pregnancy, and Suicidality," *Journal of the American Medical Association* 286, no. 5 (August 1, 2001): 575–579. Stein, *Classrooms and Courtrooms*.

22. William Bigelow, personal communication, October 1993.

23. Nan Stein, "Sexual Harassment Meets Zero Tolerance: Life in K–12 Schools," in *Zero Tolerance: Resisting the Drive for Punishment: A Handbook for Parents, Students, Educators, and Citizens*, edited by William Ayers, Bernardine Dohrn, and Richard Ayers (New York: New Press, 2001) 143–154; Nan Stein et al., "Gender Safety: A New Concept for Safer and More Equitable Schools," *Journal of School Violence* 1, no. 2 (2002): 35–50.

. . . .

NAN STEIN is a senior research scientist at the Center for Research on Women at Wellesley College, where she directs research projects on sexual harassment, bullying, and gender violence in the schools. She served for five years as codirector of a national center for the prevention of violence against women, funded by the Centers for Disease Control and Prevention. She is the author of *Classrooms and Courtrooms: Facing Sexual Harassment in K–12 Schools* (Teachers College Press, 1999). Stein frequently provides training to school personnel and students around the country on the problem of sexual harassment in schools and has served as an expert witness in lawsuits on sexual harassment in schools. She is a former middle-school social studies teacher.

"I JUST RAPED MY WIFE! WHAT ARE YOU GOING TO DO ABOUT IT, PASTOR?"
THE CHURCH AND SEXUAL VIOLENCE

. . . .

CAROL J. ADAMS

An understanding of battering and marital rape could transform the clergy from being unhelpful or harmful to being catalysts for safety and change. Ministers have an opportunity that few other service providers have of interacting with congregants who are being battered and raped or who are doing the battering and raping.

Where language and naming are power,
silence is oppression, is violence.

—ADRIENNE RICH, 1976

PROLOGUE: THE RAPE OF SHIRLEY

L ET ME INTRODUCE YOU TO SHIRLEY, a woman who was
despised and rejected by men, a woman of sorrows, a woman acquainted
with grief. Shirley was battered and raped, and she tried to stop the terror. Her husband at times seemed like a perfect gentleman—caring, playful,
kind. But—there were other times. Once, he rammed her head into a cabinet
when she was pregnant; she sustained a concussion and had a miscarriage.
Another time, he spilled milk on the floor, then knocked her onto the floor
and mopped the milk up with her hair and clothes. Once, when she sought
refuge in her mother's house, he showed up with a knife and said, "If I can't
have her, no one can." Sometimes he raped her during or after beatings.
Shirley told her fundamentalist pastor about the violence; he counseled her
to forgive her husband. During a particularly savage assault

> they had had an argument and she had gone into the shower
> to try to put some distance between them. He came into the
> bathroom and kept ripping back the curtain. She slapped him,
> something she had never done before (and never did again:
> "That taught me"). He started socking her in the stomach,
> until she vomited. Then he forced her to have sex. Distraught,
> she thought she might finally get some assistance from her
> pastor and quickly dialed his number. Before she could tell
> him what had happened, however, her husband picked up the
> phone on another extension and shouted, "I just raped my
> wife! What are you going to do about it, pastor?"[1]

The rapist's taunt is also our question: What should the church do about
sexual violence, especially marital rape? In the responses of both Shirley and
her rapist to the pastor—one faithfully seeking help, one expressing extreme
contempt—we find a clue to the problem the church faces. When it fails to
help the victim, it simultaneously colludes with the rapist while demonstrat-
ing its powerlessness to him. The rapist is thus enabled to view the church

and its representatives with the same scorn he holds for his victim. And the victim faces further violence, deserted by her faith community and, from her perspective, by her God as well.

Even without Shirley's story, we know that ministers are doing harm when women abused by their male partners seek their counseling. We know that battered women who escape their abusers rank the assistance they receive from clergy at the bottom of their list.[2] We also know that women who turn to their clergy for guidance stay longer with the men who hurt them. We know that battered women's shelters often shy away from working with clergy because of their poor track record.

An understanding of battering and marital rape, however, could transform the clergy from being unhelpful or harmful to being catalysts for safety and change. Dedicated clergy can make a difference. Ministers have an opportunity that few other service providers have of interacting with congregants who are being battered and raped or who are doing the battering and raping. Women who distrust secular authorities, who might never consider going to a shelter for battered women or calling a rape hotline, often do talk to their ministers. Moreover, unlike social workers and other service providers, pastors enter freely into the domain where most injury to women occurs—the home.

There are some specific reasons for the inadequacy of the church in responding to sexual victimization; this essay will examine the barriers to effective response and conclude by providing some suggestions for removing them.[3]

THE WIDESPREAD PROBLEM OF SILENCE AND NAMING

The church, like society at large, has had difficulty naming sexual violence and believing the victims who break the silence. The failure to name accurately plagues our culture, as the following anecdote exemplifies:

An anthropologist went to South America to live with the Yanomami—a people whose culture had been identified as intensely violent. In a book he later wrote about that experience, he concluded that this label was wrong. Ugly incidents may occur in this culture, he argued, but to focus on them distorts the Yanomami way of life. When his book was reviewed in the *New York Times Book Review*, the reviewer praised the book and its approach because it refused to allow reported incidents of violence to dominate any definitive interpretation of this culture.

This book, the review, and the reaction to them help identify some of the issues that will concern us as we discuss the church and sexual violence. It turns out that a great deal of the violence in the Yanomami culture is violence against women by men. Single women beyond the age of puberty are routinely raped. Witnessing the gang rape of a woman from another village who had run away from her husband, the anthropologist was shaken with anger. Though he pondered the question of whether he should stop this violence, he finally allowed another man to pull him away.

The anthropologist left the community for a while, leaving his young Yanomami wife as well. She was put in an extremely perilous situation. When word came back that the anthropologist had died, tribesmen repeatedly raped the woman, and one of her ears was badly ripped.

In response to the book review recounting these incidents, as well as to the conclusion that violence is not the central theme of Yanomami life, a letter was sent to the *Times*. In part it read:

> Here is a society in which the lives of half the population
> (women) are overtly controlled by the other half (men) through
> the threat and actuality of rape as an institutionalized, cultur-
> ally sanctioned norm; in which any woman of childbearing
> age not married and subservient to a man from her own
> village is "routinely raped" by the men of her own or another
> village. If this is not violence as a central theme of societal life,
> what would be?[4]

It could be argued that this disparity in interpretation—in which some people minimize the significance of violence while others see sanctioned cultural violence—is true for our culture as well. This becomes clear when researchers use open-ended questions in surveys and approach women about their experiences. Although the questions may not focus specifically on violence, by their open-ended nature they allow for the disclosure of information on violence. In fact, women disclose violent acts against them to such a degree that researchers must redesign their studies. For example, in their project to identify ways in which women's self-concepts and ways of knowing are intertwined, the authors of *Women's Ways of Knowing* report:

> Although we did not initially intend to collect information on sexual abuse, it became clear to us, after we started interviewing, that women spontaneously mention childhood and adolescent sexual trauma as an important factor affecting their learning and relationships to male authority. Midway into the study we began to survey the women systematically on their history of sexual and physical abuse. . . .
>
> Based on our data, sexual abuse appears to be a shockingly common experience for women. . . .
>
> . . . We believe that sexual trauma among women is a far more serious problem than is acknowledged by the medical and psychiatric establishment and the public at large.[5]

Once named and no longer invisible, sexual violence moves from the margin to the center of a discussion of women's lives. For the church to be effective, this movement of sexual violence from margin to center must occur within its own structures. Church leaders must acknowledge that they know sexual violence exists in society and, therefore, in their congregations. Are they prepared to offer helpful responses? When clergy do name violence from the pulpit or in their other capacities as church leaders, they report surprise at the number of people who come forward who have been personally affected by sexual violence. Just as clergy must begin by naming violence to announce their concern, just as victims begin to regain control in their world by naming their experiences, questions of naming and interpretation must concern us first.

FROM DENIAL TO NAMING

The question of naming and perceiving violence is an urgent one for the church. The church has had difficulty naming violence. Biblical stories about violence against women are not a part of the lectionary (the assigned readings from the Bible for weekly church services). In the absence of naming violence and understanding the dynamics of sexual victimization, it is difficult to believe victims, even though they usually understate the abuse. There is also an expectation that victims will self-disclose the information about their abuse.

As silence is the opposite of speaking, denial is the opposite of naming. In other words, the absence of any discussion within the theological community at whatever level—in seminary or church, in counseling or sermons—might be considered silence, but it is actually denial. In this response, the Christian community resembles the abuser, who actively denies the violence or his responsibility for the violence. Silence "not only immobilizes victims but encourages the behavior of perpetrators."[6] As long as violence is both invisible and unnamed, it is tacitly, although perhaps unintentionally, condoned.

Paulo Freire writes: "Dialogue cannot occur between those who want to name the world and those who do not wish this naming."[7] Victims need to name their world so that the terror and violence will stop and so that they will no longer be victimized but will become survivors. Perpetrators do not want their acts to be acknowledged through naming. How has the church faced this problem of dialogue? Some within the church have been afraid to learn about private terrors because of antiquated notions about family or marital bliss, fears of inadequacy in terms of counseling abilities, close friendships with abusers, or an unwillingness to hear of the immense suffering, or because clergy are at times abusers themselves. A problem inadequately named cannot be adequately addressed.

Freire writes further that "to speak a true word is to transform the world." What are the true words that must be spoken about sexual violence? Before anything else can happen, we must admit that next to the police and the military, the home is the most violent institution in the United States. Women and children are considerably less safe in the home than are men. Rape, child sexual victimization, and physical abuse all occur behind the closed doors of parishioners' homes. We must create a climate of safety in which acts of naming can overthrow acts of violation and denial.

WHY HASN'T NAMING OCCURRED?

Our language has a tendency to mask violence. It may highlight someone's victimization while simultaneously cloaking the agency and actions of the perpetrator of that violence. Sarah Lucia Hoagland demonstrates how this works: "John beat Shirley" becomes "Shirley was beaten by John," then "Shirley was beaten," then "a woman beaten," and thus "a battered woman."

Hoagland observes that "now something *men do to women* has become instead something that is a part of *women's nature.* And we lose consideration of John entirely."[8] Pushing Hoagland's insights, we see that when Shirley says, "I was raped, abused, battered," she is not only saying something about herself, she is saying something about another: the rapist, abuser, batterer. The difficulty of doing this is that you are announcing that someone has inflicted evil, someone has been evil. In her moving autobiography *My Father's House,* Sylvia Fraser depicts the process of coming to the point where she can actually say "my father raped me." She is naming something about herself and her father simultaneously. This dialectic of naming—that one is saying something about oneself and another—results in a complex process of denial and resistance to naming. The maxim "do not speak ill of another" carries terrifying weight for victims of battering, rape, and child sexual abuse.

Language that excludes women will exclude their experiences. The continual use of *man* and *mankind* as generic terms implies that the male human being is the norm. It also denies women's experiences and women themselves, presupposing that they can be included within the term *man.* When women are rendered invisible through androcentric language, it is "difficult for women to recognize their own needs for health and safety as legitimate, [and] also makes recognition difficult for the entire community."[9]

Naming may not occur for many because they have no name to give to their experience. But when, through representation and identification, an image is offered by the media, naming pours forth. For instance, after the first showing of *The Burning Bed,* a film that portrays a wife who kills her husband after enduring years of beatings, women responded by an inundation of calls to shelters and hotlines for battered women.[10] Suddenly, naming became possible because what happened to these women had been represented by the media. Similarly, after a clergyperson mentions battering from the pulpit, women abused by their partners will be more likely to approach her or him and discuss their own beatings. When one minister announced that he was attending a seminar on family violence, four families in which violence was ongoing contacted him. "He was horrified at first; he thought there was an epidemic in his congregation. Then he realized that these things had always existed, but no one had ever spoken to him of them, because he had never given them a signal that he knew about them, cared about them, and thought they were appropriate subjects to deal with in the church."[11]

Women are more likely to speak about the experiences of rape that conform to society's notion of rape—that is to say, violently coerced sexual acts by strangers. This, as Susan Estrich has shown, is what people think of as *real* rape. The further one's own experience strays from this cultural notion of being "really raped, the less likely is one to speak about one's experience as rape,"[12] or even to think of it as rape. Many women do not call nonconsensual sex rape, or they classify it as the lesser crime of assault or battery. It is especially difficult for a wife to admit that her husband raped her. "She doesn't want to face the fact that she is living with a rapist, that she is making herself vulnerable to rape."[13] This is denial. Yet Diana Russell's monumental study indicates that marital rape is the most common kind of rape.

In her landmark survey on marital rape, Russell discovered that women who did not see themselves as having been raped confirmed that they had been forced to have intercourse or that intercourse had been obtained by threat. In one study, more than twice as many women were raped by their husbands as by strangers. Anywhere from one-third to one-half of battered women are victims of marital sexual assault.[14] In *License to Rape*, David Finkelhor and Kersti Yllo identified three categories of marital rape. The first is battering rape, in which violent sex is another aspect of controlling behavior and physical abuse by the male partner. Of the women they interviewed who were battered by their husbands, 50 percent had been sexually assaulted twenty times or more. Women are often raped as a continuation of a beating, threatened with more violence if they fail to comply with their husbands' sexual requests, or forced to have sex to oblige the abuser's need to "make up" after a beating. Women who survived battering rapes often felt that the sexual abuse was the most devastating element. The second category is force-only rape, or nonbattering rape, in which forced sex was related to specifically sexual contexts. And the third category is obsessive rape, in which the husbands had bizarre sexual obsessions and were heavily involved with pornography. A third of the women in Finkelhor and Yllo's study reported anal rape.

Once sexual violence has been named, additional forces may make it difficult for an individual to speak about her experience of violation. Elsewhere, Finkelhor and Yllo tell us, "No doubt raped wives, like battered wives, use many self-deceptions to avoid facing the realities of an intolerable marriage because the alternatives—loneliness, loss of financial security, admission of failure—are so frightening."[15]

Lack of comfort in discussing a woman's body compounds the problem of naming. We must be able to name female body parts—breast, clitoris, vagina—and to hear them named without feeling squeamish if we are to name what has happened or hear it named. In the absence of comfort about the words themselves, a woman will feel awkward describing what was done to those body parts. Moreover, in a culture in which images of these body parts are so heavily eroticized, the victim who speaks of violation may be experienced as speaking pornographically.[16] The overcoming of denial by naming is complicated by this patriarchal contamination of the space into which women must speak about their experience of sexual violation.

NAMING, DENIAL, AND THE CHURCH'S RESPONSE TO SEXUAL VIOLENCE

In addition to these forces that impede naming, the commitment of the church to educating its leaders on the subject of sexual violence faces several structural impediments.[17]

First, pastoral care has no category for the crises of battering, date rape, and marital rape. The classic book on pastoral counseling, Howard Clinebell's *Basic Types of Pastoral Care and Counseling*, proposes that the vast majority of pastoral care in the church occurs around life crises and identifies two kinds of crises: developmental crises "that occur around the normal stressful transitions in the life journey" and accidental crises.[18] What Clinebell reveals is something many survivors have experienced: Pastoral care has no category for ongoing, nondevelopmental crises perpetuated by someone with whom the victim is in a caring relationship, such as childhood sexual victimization, marital rape, and wife battering. Without such a category, pastoral care has attempted to fit the crises of sexual and domestic violence into preexisting categories. As a result, what is actually a chronic problem (the abuser's behavior) is treated within an inadequate crisis framework.

Second, ministers have a tendency to minimize the lethality of sexual and domestic violence by focusing instead on relationship issues. This distorts the responsibility of the abuser. Because of this focus on the relationship rather than on the violence, reconciliation may be encouraged before the abuse has been stopped. Or, as happened in Shirley's case, forgiveness may be encouraged even though the abuser has not repented of his behavior.

Third, inadequate counseling techniques are taken as adequate. For instance, domestic violence protocol holds that couples counseling that takes place when battering is ongoing may contribute to increasing, rather than decreasing, the violence. Yet pastoral care courses often encourage couples counseling without noting when it is inadvisable. When ministers are not trained to identify and act on the evidence of sexual and domestic violence, they will put women at risk if they follow traditional counseling techniques.

Fourth, criminal behavior has been defined as a psychological problem for the victim. Questions about her behavior enter into the counseling, again minimizing the abuser's accountability by implying the victim's provocation. The psychological focus also means that the victim must go through "recovery" rather than achieve justice. Moreover, the church, often uncomfortable with the use of secular resources, has difficulty seeing the role of criminal justice in Christian justice.

Fifth, there is a lack of clarity on the issue of confidentiality. While reporting requirements for child sexual abuse may or may not be seen to apply to clergy—and many clergy do not want to be held to this reporting requirement—it is sadly the case that clergy often call the perpetrators after learning from their victims about abuse. Without the permission or knowledge of the victims, this violation of confidentiality can seriously endanger them.

Sixth, clergy have little comprehension that abuse provides rewards for the abuser, and that he is thus unlikely to stop without intervention. Several issues are apparent here:

1. Sometimes clergy identify with the abuser, especially if he is a church member. Thus the tendency is to see the violence as an aberration rather than as a chronic problem. This protects the offender.
2. Often the church believes in the abuser's contriteness and thus emphasizes forgiveness, especially when there is any sign of remorse. Abusers can manipulate religious language in their own interest. Remorse is confused with repentance. But forgiveness without any guarantee that the abuser has changed, has truly repented, will not stop the abuse. It also short-circuits the legitimate anger of the victim while endangering her.
3. All involved—the church, the batterer, and his victim—may misinterpret the meaning of the marriage covenant, and when the covenant is broken:

A woman victimized in an abusive domestic relationship feels serious ethical/spiritual dilemmas about the marriage covenant. She has made promises that are still important and meaningful to her. One of those is that the relationship will be a lasting one. To stay in the relationship means to suffer further abuse, but to leave (temporarily or permanently) makes her feel as if she is breaking her promise. Many women thus stay and suffer the abuse, precisely because they take their commitment seriously. Seldom does it occur to the victim of the abuse (at least in the beginning)—or to friends, family, or the church—that the covenant has already been broken by the behavior of her partner. . . .

. . . The victim who seeks safety, or eventually decides to seek separation or divorce, *is* acknowledging that the covenant which she had established with another no longer exists, *but she is not the one breaking the covenant.*[19]

In other words, rather than asserting that the family must stay together, the church could acknowledge that violence has already sundered the family, and that it is the abuser who has broken the covenant.

NAMING, GOD-TALK, AND SEXUAL VIOLENCE

Men who abuse and rape their partners are men who seek to control others. In being abusive, they are not out of control; rather, they establish control.[20] Images of control, authority, and maleness combine in traditional representations of God as Father, which upholds the petit-godhead established within each family by the abusive husband. In this, God the Father sacralizes domination by a father/husband who in turn usurps the role of this patriarchal God: assigning guilt, punishing, and controlling. Sallie McFague argues that we need language appropriate for our time, not language that supports hierarchical, dualistic, external, unchanging, atomistic, and deterministic ways of understanding the relationship between God and the world, but language that understands the God–world relationship as open, caring, inclusive, interdependent, changing, mutual, and creative.[21] Were we to replace the harmful monarchical language about God—king, ruler, lord, sovereign—with language that embedded God within the world, the abuser would lose the sacralized reinforcement of authoritarianism.

It is not surprising that an abuser might gravitate to any hints of misogyny in the Christian tradition. This tradition provides excellent raw material for his authoritarianism. What Rosemary Radford Ruether terms patriarchal anthropology has proclaimed women as sinful, women as the cause of sin, and subjugation to men as the punishment for women's sinful behavior.[22] This positioning of women provides legitimations for rapist behavior: seeing woman as temptress and each woman's duty as submission to her husband. From Eve, who was sinful, who tempted Adam, who deserved God's punishment, through to the New Testament and the apparent absence of female disciples, the Biblical tradition appears to be on the side of the abuser. This tradition gets incorporated into justifications for the abuser's behavior. Just as an abuser twists everything—claiming as reasons for his actions such things as adding mushrooms to a pizza, vacuuming a room at the wrong time of day, taking a job, or refusing to have sex—how much more salient are selected texts from the Bible about women being obedient or sinful.

Of course, twisted Biblical interpretations seem to confirm women's subjugation to abuse as well. In a search for the meaning of her abuse, the victim may see Jesus's suffering as a model for her own and think that she must accept her cross (especially if this is what her clergyperson exhorts). She may think sinfulness lies in her assertion of self and believe that she must become more self-denying. She may conclude that she must forgive all who have hurt her. It is understandable that battered and raped women might gravitate to this idea of Jesus's suffering and his forgiveness of his abusers in order to cope with the abusive behavior of their partners. Our culture encourages the sacrifices of wives and mothers. Women are said to be the caretakers and nurturers of the family. Women's self-development is sacrificed to the family and this sacrifice is considered redemptive for all involved, including the women.[23] The perceived Christian emphasis on sacrifice as something good matches the way girls are taught to consider others rather than themselves, to be self-sacrificing in a social situation. The religious meaning of sacrifice is thus layered on top of the social view of women as sacrificial. The idea that bodily suffering is spiritually redemptive also intersects with the traditional Christian notion of denial of the body. Thus women's bodies are separated from the idea of being redeemed in and of themselves, of having bodily worth or bodily integrity.

By failing to provide a prophetic word against interpretations that on one hand justify domination and on the other reinforce subordination, the church becomes complicit in perpetuating these images and ideas so ripe for misapplication. The church becomes a party to dominant–subordinate relationships.

In the face of this appeal to authority by the abuser and the gravitation to Biblical messages that entrap the victim, the church must side clearly with the abused. It must challenge interpretations that accept abuse as appropriate, offering instead a liberating, prophetic word about setting captives and rape victims free. It must declare to the assaultive man and his victim that the person who has been violent is the person who has endangered this marriage. It must remind victims of marital rape and battering that when Jesus had the opportunity to stop or prevent suffering, he did. Often, the suffering individuals were women: the woman whose bleeding would not stop, the woman taken in adultery, the Samaritan woman. If Jesus were ministering today, would he say, "Yes, continue suffering as I did"? Or would he say, "Stop suffering! Whenever I could, I stopped suffering, and your suffering can be stopped."

Furthermore, the church must proclaim that God is not male, and that the male—especially in his own home—is not God. It must challenge the domination–subordination model of the God–human relationship and proclaim that for victims of rape and battering, sin is not self-assertion, love is not self-sacrifice, forgiveness does not involve condoning or excusing abusive behavior. The church has been unable to do this, in part, because marital rape and battering have been seen as interpersonal problems rather than as widespread institutional violence against which the church must take a firm stance.

SEXUAL VIOLENCE IS INSTITUTIONAL VIOLENCE

PROLOGUE: THE RAPE OF MARIA GORETTI

In July 1902, Maria Goretti, a 12-year old Italian girl, was stabbed in a sexual assault and died. Although details of the story have been influenced over the years by constant retelling

and adaptation, the basic facts are as follows: Maria Goretti
was from a poor rural family. Home alone one day, Maria was
attacked by a young man, Alessandro Serenelli. He threatened
to kill her if she did not have sex with him. Maria refused,
and he stabbed her repeatedly with a knife. She died 24 hours
after the attack. Serenelli was caught and tried for murder. He
was sentenced to 30 years in prison. When he was released,
Serenelli went to live with an order of monks. Reportedly,
Maria appeared to him in a vision during his imprisonment.
She forgave him, and he repented of his sin. When she was
canonized by the Roman Catholic Church in 1950, Serenelli
was present, along with Maria's mother and her family.[24]

What for Maria was a murderous rape was described as an attractive
pleasure in Pope Pius XII's homily at her canonization.[25] Here Pius XII, like
the dominant culture, resists seeing the violence in sexual assault. Rape is
not "an attractive pleasure" for the victim, nor is the victim of rape sinful.
As Marie M. Fortune points out, the major problem with religious attention
to the murder of Maria Goretti is that the wrong lessons are drawn. "Unfortunately, this story does not teach women to resist male sexual aggression
for the right reasons, i.e., because it is violent and aggressive and women have
a right to maintain their bodily integrity."[26]

The minister's response to Shirley was that she should pray for her assailant and forgive him; this is the message derived from the story of the suffering of Maria Goretti as well, that the sexually victimized should forgive their
abusers. To be adequately understood, the rape of Shirley and the attempted
rape of Maria Goretti—and these embarrassingly inadequate responses—must
be set within a context that recognizes sexual violence as institutional violence and proclaims that sexual violence will no longer be minimized, mis-
named, and misunderstood.

Elsewhere I have identified what I consider to be the major components
of institutional violence.[27] For something to be institutional violence, it must
be a widespread, unethical practice in a society. As this anthology demonstrates, a large number of children and women are at risk of being battered,
raped, or sexually victimized. In addition, institutional violence consists of
six interrelated factors:

1. *Institutional violence is an infringement on or a failure to acknowledge another's inviolability.* Sovereignty over our own bodies is a basic right, and this sovereignty is undermined by sexual violence. Abuse is aggressive, destructive behavior that violates and often annihilates another human being. Sexual violence is a violation of right relationships; it is evidence of the abuser's alienation, brokenness, estrangement. It also causes alienation, brokenness, and estrangement in the victims. Abuse involves destruction of the ego. For women who are battered and raped by their partners, the assault on their self-esteem accompanies assaults on their bodies. Children who are sexually victimized live in a climate of constant danger. Dissociation "becomes not merely a defensive adaptation but the fundamental principle of personality organization."[28]

Victims of rape and sexual abuse often feel dirty, embarrassed, and guilty. In the face of the violation of their bodies, they also carry the stigma in our culture that it was their fault.

David Finkelhor and Kersti Yllo's *License to Rape: Sexual Abuse of Wives* argues that "rape by intimates in general is more, not less, traumatic than rape by strangers" because the rapist continues to live with his victim. Moreover, women victimized by battering rapes said that rapes were especially traumatizing because of "the more personal, intimate nature of the sexual abuse," as opposed to the sense that the "beatings seem[ed] more external."[29]

If we listen to the victims, we can learn precisely how they feel about losing their sense of inviolability. They feel devastated, demeaned, humiliated, degraded, despondent, depressed, shocked, defiled, betrayed, powerless, isolated, entrapped. Moreover, because they were raped by their husbands, some felt like prostitutes, and many worried about whether they would be able to trust intimates again.

2. *Institutional violence is any treatment or physical force that injures or abuses.* By *treatment,* I mean *ongoing* conditions that are abusive or injurious. By *physical force,* I mean *specific* actions that cause injuries. Incest, rape, and battering are violent and coercive acts that provide to the husband, father, or partner the ability to control, intimidate, and subordinate his wife, his daughter or son, or his partner.

Child sexual abuse often begins when a child is between the ages of four and eight and continues until the child reaches adolescence and is able to escape from the abuse. The average age of a child who is being sexually victimized is between eight and eleven. The average length of time of an incestuous relationship is three years. Child sexual abuse "may include fondling, masturbation, genital penetration, or exhibitionism. It is a crime in every state."[30]

Battering is "assaultive behavior occurring in an intimate, sexual, theoretically peer, usually cohabitating relationship. . . . [It is] a *pattern* of behavior, not isolated individual events. One form of battering builds on another and sets the stage for the next battering episode."[31]

Sexual violence "includes any physical, visual, verbal or sexual act that is experienced by the woman or girl, at the time or later, as a threat, invasion or assault, that has the effect of hurting her or degrading her and/or takes away her ability to control intimate contact."[32]

These are all physical violations that produce trauma and somatic responses. The trauma of marital rape can cause nausea and vomiting, soreness, bruising, muscle tension, headaches, fatigue, and injuries to the genital area. The marital rape victim may feel strain and stress because she is constantly reminded by the presence of her rapist-husband of the incident and the possibility of another attack. Women can experience flashbacks as well as haunting nightmares for years after an assault.

3. *Institutional violence involves a series of denial mechanisms that deflect attention from the violence.* Denial of the extent and nature of violence is an important protective device for maintaining institutional violence. It communicates that the violence that is an integral part of our culture is neither troublesome nor severe. The pastor who told Shirley to forgive her husband was denying the criminal actions of her husband. Pope Pius XII, in misnaming the act of rape, was denying it.

To accomplish denial, *false naming* is a major component of institutional violence. False naming means that we can avoid responsibility. False naming creates false consciousness. As the church struggles with the issue of violence, it often relies on terms such as *marital aggression* or *husband-wife violence, the incestuous family,* or *the battering system.* These terms avoid assigning responsibility, thus cloaking who the incest offender is, who the batterer is, who the rapist is, and who the victim is. This false naming inadvertently sends a message to the perpetrator that he has still not been found out, that the church is not concerned specifically with what he is doing. These efforts minimize the violence and deny responsibility. Contrary to these terms, the facts are that husbands and fathers perpetrate the majority of sexually and physically abusive acts; women and children are the victims and suffer emotional, medical, and spiritual consequences.

Perpetrators deny, evade, or minimize their actions. Denial occurs through the perpetrators' excuses: Victims are portrayed as having enjoyed the experience. (Even rapists who use weapons think their victims enjoy the violence.) The child sexual abuser often sees himself as providing a positive experience for the victim. Other denials by perpetrators include refrains such as "She asked for it," "She enjoyed it," "She deserved it," or "I did it for her."

Where there is denial, *there is no call to accountability* for the perpetrators of sexual violence. Rape, child sexual victimization, and battering are all against the law. Marital rape, too, is criminalized in every state.[33] Ministers, police, doctors, and other authorities have often discouraged rather than encouraged the reporting of sexual violence. Studies, statistics, and individual testimony demonstrate clearly that the most effective way to stop violence against women and children is to hold the abuser accountable. As long as individual women and children who are sexually and physically abused seek help from the church and do not receive any direct cultural message that names the abuse as illegal and the abuser as a sinner and a perpetrator, the violence will most likely not stop. Indeed, it may escalate. When Shirley finally escaped to a shelter, her furious husband sought her out there. "She was frightened to death, she remembers, so immobilized that it was all she could do to crawl upstairs to safety on her hands and knees."[34] Even after Shirley's divorce, her husband hid in her bedroom closet and then forced her to do something he knew she hated—oral sex.

In the absence of accountability, abuse continues. The problem is that crimes of sexual violence are the least likely to be reported and have the lowest conviction rate: "On a national average, one rapist in twenty is arrested, one out of thirty [is] prosecuted, and one in sixty is convicted."[35] Despite this, criminal prosecution should be encouraged for several reasons. First, it is the only way to establish that sexual violence is criminal activity rather than interpersonal problems gone awry. Second, continued appeal to the criminal justice system eventually brings about some reforms, as has been seen in some cities where successful prosecution of batterers resulted in a decrease in incidents of violence.[36] And third, there is even less accountability when legal sanctions are not invoked.

What should Shirley's minister have done? He should have said to her rapist, "You have just told me that you broke a law. You have also violated the church's most basic ethical position on covenantal relationships. Will you call the police or shall I?" This offers the opportunity to say to the assailant, "What you did was wrong. You need to get counseling to learn more appropriate ways of responding. I know that court-ordered counseling is often the only way that perpetrators actually participate fully in the counseling program. Through the prosecution for your offense, you are being offered the chance to change, to learn more effective ways of interacting, and to respect your partner. I will support you in this."

4. *Institutional violence targets "appropriate" victims.* Ideology makes the existence of appropriate victims appear to be natural and inevitable. If one raped or sexually assaulted one's boss, professor, clergyperson, or doctor, the assault would clearly be seen and responded to as the criminal act that it is. Women and children are seen as appropriate victims in our culture, which sees the adult (white) male as the normative person. We can find cultural definitions of women and children as male property; for that reason, fathers and husbands may believe they have the right to control and punish.

The misapplication of certain Biblical passages is evident in the making of appropriate victims. Fathers and husbands come to believe that their authority is divinely mandated, that God ordains men's authority in marriage and women's and children's subordination. Problematic passages such as Genesis 2, 1 Timothy 2:12–14, 1 Corinthians 11:8, and Ephesians 5:22–24 are taken as affirming theological justification for women's subordination. In fact, it has been found that egalitarian, democratic families are less likely to have an abusive husband or incest offender than families in which fundamentalist religious beliefs are held and sex role stereotypes are rigidly adhered to.

A logic of domination accompanies the making of appropriate victims. Differences of age and differences between the sexes have been deemed to carry meanings of superiority and inferiority. According to a logic of domination, that which is morally superior—maleness and adulthood—is morally justified in subordinating that which is not—femaleness and childhood.[37] Associated with this, we find the equation of masculinity with dominance and power in sexual relationships, the view that male aggression is a natural and normal part of sexual intercourse, and the eroticization of male domination. Many see rape as related to our culture's contempt for female qualities. They also argue that rape is an act of social control that keeps women in their place.[38] The fact that marital rape was not outlawed for many years indicated precisely who were—and are—the appropriate victims.

The church, in its emphasis on certain virtues, reinforces marital rape and married women as the appropriate victims. Social conventions about women's duty in marriage are often parroted within religious communities. Thus women who believe it is their duty to have sex with their husbands whenever their husbands desire may tragically find this belief confirmed by church authorities to whom they turn for assistance. When this occurs, the church provides a mirror for the abuser's reality. Moreover, married women may come to believe that God has made them the appropriate victim—that is, that God is punishing them.

The difference between the ways women resist stranger rape as opposed to marital rape illustrates the making of appropriate victims. While gouging the rapist's eyes, kicking him in the groin, running out of the house, calling the police, and brandishing or using a weapon are all possible responses to stranger rape, they are seldom enacted against husbands. Finkelhor and Yllo report that they "heard remarkably few stories of successful resistance to marital rape."[39] Instead, they more frequently found tactics of appeasement: keeping the peace, giving in, preventing anal rape or forced fellatio by substituting vaginal rape. Women found that trying to talk their husbands out of it was ineffective, and running away and hiding brought about broken doors. Some threatened to leave, some left temporarily, some left and divorced, and some used violence, but overall the decision to choose appeasement over outright resistance revolved on several perceptions: that the husband was stronger, that if the wife resisted she would be hurt even worse (especially if there was a history of battering), that resistance prolonged the assault, that appeasement protected the children, that unless she was ready to leave she would have to face the man again, that it was good to keep the peace, and that she was at fault. Catharine MacKinnon has pointed out that the strategies needed to survive day-to-day violence are the exact opposite of those needed to end violence. Appropriate victims are those for whom the need to survive day-to-day violence overwhelms the ability to end the violence; thus they must find ways to accommodate the rapist rather than resist him, they find themselves feeling guilty rather than angry, and they keep the peace rather than holding the husband accountable. "An inability to respond with anger is one way in which multiple experiences of sexual abuse destroy women."[40]

A rapist's sinful acts should be understood as a consequence of his own brokenness and alienation, not as in any way caused by the woman. There are no appropriate victims.

Misunderstanding of theological issues such as suffering, forgiveness, and redemption contributes to maintaining women and children as appropriate victims. They may begin to interpret their suffering as ordained by God, as acceptable because it recalls Jesus's suffering, as having a purpose in redeeming another. In place of the legitimate anger and rage they should feel for the violation of their bodies, they are encouraged to forgive their abusers. Instead of the abusers being encouraged to repent, their victims are encouraged to be forgiving, like Christ from the cross. The victim should not be asked to forgive her abuser, as Maria Goretti was in her enormous pain. In the absence of the abuser's repentance—which would include both accepting responsibility for having been abusive and stopping the abuse—women and children will continue to be abused. Forgiveness in the absence of repentance by the abuser is a salve for the conscience of society, but it is not a healing experience for the victim.

In the absence of a liberation theology that clearly sides with the violated, traditional theological formulations encourage the victims to find meaning in their abuse, rather than in resisting that abuse. Sermons that speak generally on topics such as the necessity for forgiveness or the inappropriateness of anger, without recognizing how they are heard specifically by survivors, can perpetuate victimization.

5. *Institutional violence has identifiable detrimental effects on society as a whole.* Besides the obvious unethical behavior manifested in sexual violence, there are other costs to the human community. More than one-third to one-half of all homeless women are fleeing domestic violence. Runaway children are often running away from sexual abuse. "It is estimated that over seventy-five percent of all adolescents involved in prostitution—female and

male—were victims of prior sexual violence: rape, incestuous abuse, or molestation."[41] We have no adequate way to measure the effect on society as a whole of the fact that for numerous women and children basic trust relationships have been violated, and the result of this is that they rightly have difficulty trusting others.

6. *Institutional violence manipulates others into passivity regarding its practices.* Like the anthropologist mentioned at the beginning of this article, we are pulled away from considering just how we might stop the violence. The result is that the violence continues. We are not empowered to believe we can stop it. We have difficulty recognizing that violence is a choice, one of several options. Rather than asking judgmental questions such as "Why doesn't she leave?" about a battered woman, "What was she wearing or doing?" about a rape victim, and "Can we believe her?" about a child abuse victim, we need to ask, "Why does he choose to batter, rape, and abuse?"

The seminary community has most likely not equipped ministers to respond to the issue of violence in their own congregations. Though often shocked by information about violence and feeling the urgency for action, ministers do not know what to do. Or they may be afraid to act. Or, if they do respond, they often rely on general counseling techniques that they may later learn were totally inadequate.

MARITAL RAPE: A PASTORAL RESPONSE

Calling upon Paulo Freire's insights again, we must acknowledge that "no one can say a true word alone—nor can she say it *for* another, in a prescriptive act which robs others of their words."[42] I envision a community that invites the saying of a true word, not alone, but in a supportive presence. Such a community does not describe and delimit by asking the question, "Have you been abused?" Instead, it invites someone to expand her relationship with the outer world, to transform herself by stating what is happening now, to begin to change the now into the reconstructed and liberating future. Sexual violence requires that we respond appropriately and directly. It requires that we name the violence, that we offer protection and advocacy for the victims, that we hold the perpetrator accountable, and that we work as a society to prevent further abuse.

Freire observes that "to exist, humanly, is to *name* the world, to change it." The power of naming is the power of self-authorization. This is what the church must offer survivors of sexual violence.

Abused women and children see their victimization as a spiritual issue and seek out religiously affiliated people, such as pastors, to help them interpret their experience. Some religious women may not trust secular resources that do not acknowledge the religious crisis they may be undergoing. A secular program that offers safety without addressing deeply important issues such as spirituality and a religious institution that addresses spiritual issues divested from safety issues are fragmented responses.

Three qualities of the pastoral counselor are essential when survivors disclose their experiences: the ability to process information about the dehumanizing violence enacted by one person against another; the ability to provide practical assistance; and the ability to reflect theologically. Most importantly, these three abilities must be constantly balanced, and the boundaries between them must be understood and maintained. So many of the don'ts of pastoral care in this area involve respecting the difference between process, practical advice, and theology, and not substituting a response from one area when a response from another area is called for. If clergypersons act shocked or horrified, they have failed to process the information adequately. If they offer a general prayer for someone's suffering or discuss forgiveness, they have relied on the theological dimension in an unrealistic way that ignores the victim's safety. The primary goal that must be pursued is the victim's safety; this requires practical advice. Diana Russell observes:

> It seems to me that if wives were in a position to threaten to
> leave the marriages in which husbands were violent toward
> them, and if they really meant it and were able to convey this
> to their husbands, we would be at least half way toward a solu-
> tion to the problem of violence against wives.[43]

In order for a woman to speak the truth about her situation, to be able to say, "John has been battering me" or "John anally raped me last night," she must feel safe and be assured that the information she provides will be kept confidential. Insuring sufficient time and safe space for a discussion is essential. Questions that allow for disclosure should be asked, rather than questions that sound like accusations, including questions that focus on her own background ("What was your family life like?") or that focus on her action ("What did you do?"). Instead, beginning with the obvious can be helpful:

> "You seem so unhappy. Do you want to talk about it? I'd like to listen, and I'll keep it between us." Even if she rejects the offer, your observation about her unhappiness supports her by affirming some of her feelings. And you've left the door open for a confidential conversation in the future.[44]

Once naming has occurred, the church must ensure that the pastoral response does not do damage, does not revictimize, but instead empowers the victims and holds the abusers accountable. The counselor must offer to be with a woman in her suffering and her healing. The solidarity model of counseling that I envision has at the minimum these components:[45]

1. *Caring.* First, the counselor can say, "I am sorry this happened to you." She has been courageous in breaking the silence; this should be acknowledged. She should be assisted in grieving the loss of safety and security. She can mourn what she has lost. She should be told no one ever deserves to be hit or hurt. Then the counselor can affirm that her reactions are normal; she is not going crazy even though she has never experienced such a range of emotions before. The counselor can validate her feelings: "It's all right to feel betrayed, hurt, angry, etc." Questions might include, "How are you doing?" and "How are you sleeping?" Solidarity begins with caring.

2. *Concern for safety.* Immediately, however, counseling must acknowledge the trauma of marital rape and the life-threatening nature of battering. The violence must be unequivocally challenged. Women must be encouraged to take their husbands' violence seriously and to find support for challenging it. They have no duty to submit to their husbands' violence. The marital rape victim's first moral responsibility is to herself. Questions to be asked focus on safety, such as "Are you safe?" and "What would it take for you to be safe?"[46] Referral is essential. Information should be repeated; she should know the name of a hotline and be aware of resources for battered women. Referral ensures that neither the clergyperson nor the victim interprets the violence as an interpersonal problem and that the response is placed where it appropriately lies—with the community. The clergyperson could offer to accompany her to meet with a hotline representative if she shows some hesitancy about relying on secular services.

3. *Empowerment.* She should be reassured that it is possible to reestablish control over her life. She has choices. Resources are available. Prosecution of her assailant is an important resource. She could benefit from the creation of new support groups, help in increasing her problem-solving skills, and help in increasing her sense of responsibility toward herself. By asking questions such as "What can I do?" the pastoral counselor empowers her to make decisions. We can help her understand her alternatives while increasing her sense of control. We can ask her, "What decisions have you made so far? What are your concerns?"

Affirmations are extremely valuable. Her courageous act of speaking about the violence should be affirmed. She should be told:

> I believe you.
> I care about you.
> I'm glad you told me.
> You are not alone.
> Violent behavior toward you is never appropriate or deserved.
> It's okay to be afraid.
> I'm glad you survived.
> It's okay to be angry with your husband.
> It's okay to be angry with God.
> You deserve a nonviolent life.
> You can change your life.
> You are not responsible for your husband's behavior.
> You have the right to make choices. You are not to blame.
> You have a right to privacy.
> I do not believe that God is punishing you for a sin.
> I believe that God does not want you to suffer.
> Whatever you did, you did not deserve to be raped.

Once safety issues have been addressed, many religious issues may come up. Most importantly, if the woman feels abandoned by God, the counselor needs to ask, "What kind of God do you feel has abandoned you?" Before her images of God are refuted, she must have the space to describe just how she has experienced her God during her victimization. Feelings such as betrayal and anger at this God are legitimate and should not be short-circuited by attempting to substitute a benign and loving God for the punishing or absent God she has experienced. As Annie Imbens and Ineke Jonker observe about incest survivors:

> We found that it is vital for these women to have the room to express their rage and sorrow about God. Even more crucial is the response. One reaction given to her oppressive image of God and the problems she still has with it is: "Well, God isn't like that, you're looking at this all wrong. That's a false image of God you're describing." This response does not take her seriously and it gives her no room to liberate herself from her oppressive image of God. "This God" should not be the subject of these discussions. It is more pleasant for the priest or minister, because it takes a great deal of resilience and restraint to talk about God in the way that incest survivors need to talk about their oppressive image of God. When the minister or priest starts talking about "this God" during such a conversation, he or she creates a safe distance from his or her own experience of God, and then he or she cannot feel how threatening it is for a woman like Nell to express her rage and sorrow about God in her experience. For *her*, God is not "this God," which people are not supposed to struggle with. For her, it is her only image of God. And that's why she still has so many problems with it.[47]

Women must be provided with the space to discuss their experience of the images of God that have been imposed on them by others. Then they can begin to seek their own image of God. "This makes them more resistant in their lives. The space that is created when they liberate themselves from their oppressive images of God should be left open."[48] Only then can a God who abandoned them be abandoned by them. Only then can a God who would ordain a woman's suffering as punishment for some sinful act on her part, a God who would require submission to rape as marital duty, a God who would not want the abuser called to accountability, a God who would be content with injustice, be told, "You are not my God."

We all must say, to anyone we know, "If you've been given advice to stay or submit because that is your duty, or because God ordains it, if you are told to forgive the rapist, you have talked to the wrong person. If you are given this advice, no matter who the counselor is, no matter how inspiring or spiritually attuned he or she is, you have the wrong advisor. It is not you who are mistaken for resisting this advice, it is the counselor who is mistaken for suggesting it. You have the right to be safe."

What, finally, should the minister have told Shirley when informed of her sexual and physical victimization at the hands of her husband? These are the words I believe Shirley should have heard when she bravely overcame the silence about her victimization:

> Shirley, being long-suffering should not be confused with being actively engaged in change. Whatever you have suffered, you know somehow, by talking to me and by exploring this issue, that that suffering is enough. No more suffering is necessary. The question now is how do we create the reality by which those beatings and rapes can be stopped? To continue to suffer is, in part, to deny the validity of your past suffering. You can say, "It is enough. The suffering is finished. I deserve a life free of violence. My moral responsibility must be, at this moment, to myself. It is time to move on to new life."

I would like to thank Pat Davis, Marjorie Procter-Smith, Nancy Tuana, Mary E. Hunt, and Meredith Pond for their suggestions, and Marie M. Fortune for her encouragement. This article incorporates material from "Naming, Denial, and Sexual Violence," in Miriam's Song V *(Priests for Equality, 1992).*

NOTES

1. Shirley's story is told in David Finkelhor and Kersti Yllo, *License to Rape: Sexual Abuse of Wives* (New York: Holt, Rinehart, and Winston, 1985) 19–21.

2. See Lee H. Bowker, *Beating Wife-Beating* (Lexington, Mass.: Lexington Books, 1983).

3. The FaithTrust Institute (2400 North 45th Street, Suite 10, Seattle, WA 98103) has been a pioneer in developing training material for churches and clergy, trying to reverse the churches' track record. They have published information on how individual congregations can become responsive to sexual and domestic violence: Thelma Burgonio-Watson, "One Congregation at a Time," *Working Together: A News Journal* 22, no. 3 (Fall/Winter 2002): 1. See also http://www.faithtrustinstitute.org.

4. Lynn Hecht Shafron, letter, *New York Times Book Review,* January 20, 1991. The writer was

responding to Tim Cahill's review of Kenneth Good, with David Chanoff, *Into the Heart: One Man's Pursuit of Love and Knowledge among the Yanomama* (New York: Simon and Schuster, 1991).

5. Mary Field Belenky, et al., *Women's Way of Knowing: The Development of Self, Voice, and Mind* (New York: Basic Books, 1986), 58, 89.

6. Anne L. Horton and Judith A. Williamson, *Abuse and Religion: When Praying Isn't Enough* (Lexington, Mass.: Lexington Books, 1989), 9.

7. Paulo Freire, *Pedagogy of the Oppressed: New Revised 20th Anniversary Edition* (New York: Continuum, 1990, 1993), 69.

8. Sarah Lucia Hoagland, *Lesbian Ethics: Toward New Values* (Palo Alto: Institute for Lesbian Studies, 1988), 17–18.

9. Marjorie Procter-Smith, "Reorganizing Victimization: The Intersection between Liturgy and Domestic Violence," in *Violence Against Women and Children: A Christian Theological Sourcebook*, edited by Carol J. Adams and Marie M. Fortune (New York: Continuum International, 1995), 433.

10. *Albany Times Union*, October 11, 1984.

11. Peggy Halsey, "Will the Silence Be Unbroken," *South of the Garden* 9, no. 3: 3.

12. See Susan Estrich, *Real Rape: How the Legal System Victimizes Women Who Say No* (Cambridge: Harvard University Press, 1987).

13. Finkelhor and Yllo, *License to Rape*, 115.

14. Finkelhor and Yllo, *License to Rape*, 22.

15. David Finkelhor and Kersti Yllo, "Rape in Marriage: A Sociological View," in *The Darker Side of Families: Current Family Violence Research*, edited by David Finkelhor, et al. (Beverly Hills, Calif.: Sage, 1983), 121.

16. "Perhaps men respond sexually when women give an account of sexual violation because sexual words are a sexual reality, in the same way that men respond to pornography, which is (among other things) an account of the sexual violation of a woman. Seen in this way, much therapy as well as court testimony in sexual abuse cases is live oral pornography." Catharine MacKinnon, *Toward a Feminist Theory of the State* (Cambridge: Harvard University Press, 1989), 152.

17. The following section draws upon my book *Woman-Battering* (Minneapolis: Augsburg Fortress, 1994).

18. Howard Clinebell, *Basic Types of Pastoral Care and Counseling: Resources for the Ministry of Healing and Growth* (Nashville, TN: Abingdon, 1966, 1984), 35.

19. Mitzi N. Eilts, "Saving the Family: When Is Covenant Broken?" in Adams and Fortune, *Violence Against Women and Children*, 448–9. Emphasis is in the original.

20. See Ann Jones and Susan Schecter, *When Love Goes Wrong: What to Do When You Can't Do Anything Right* (New York: HarperCollins, 1992).

21. Sallie McFague, *Models of God: Theology for an Ecological, Nuclear Age* (Minneapolis: Augsburg Fortress, 1987), 13.

22. See Rosemary Radford Ruether, *Sexism and God-Talk: Toward a Feminist Theology* (Boston: Beacon, 1983), 94–99.

23. See Carol S. Pearson, *The Hero Within: Six Archetypes We Live By* (San Francisco: HarperSanFrancisco, 1986), 99.

24. Kathleen Z. Young, "The Imperishable Virginity of Saint Maria Goretti," in Adams and Fortune, *Violence Against Women and Children,* 279–280. Young notes numerous discrepancies in the story depending on the source.

25. Young, "Imperishable Virginity," 282.

26. Marie M. Fortune, *Sexual Violence, the Unmentionable Sin: An Ethical and Pastoral Perspective* (New York: Pilgrim, 1983), 65–66.

27. See "Feeding on Grace: Institutional Violence, Feminist Ethics, and Vegetarianism," in Carol J. Adams, *Neither Man nor Beast: Feminism and the Defense of Animals* (New York: Continuum International, 1994), 162–178.

28. Judith Herman, *Trauma and Recovery* (New York: Basic Books, 1992), 102.

29. Finkelhor and Yllo, *License to Rape,* 127, 135.

30. Lee W. Carlson, *Child Sexual Abuse: A Handbook for Clergy and Church Members* (Valley Forge, PA: Judson, 1988), 11.

31. Anne L. Ganley, "Integrating Feminist and Social Learning Analyses of Aggression: Creating Multiple Models for Intervention with Men Who Batter," in *Treating Men Who Batter: Theory, Practice, and Programs,* edited by P. Lynn Caesar and L. Kevin Hamberger (New York: Springer, 1989), 202.

32. Liz Kelly, *Surviving Sexual Violence* (Minneapolis: University of Minnesota Press, 1989), 41.

33. While marital rape is criminalized, the majority of states contain some spousal exemptions. Rape in marriage is thus treated differently than other rapes, conveying the message that the wife is still the property of her husband.

34. Finkelhor and Yllo, *License to Rape,* 21.

35. Carole J. Sheffield, "Sexual Terrorism," in *Women: A Feminist Perspective,* third edition, edited by Jo Freeman (Palo Alto, Calif.: Mayfield, 1984), 11.

36. The most successful model for creating accountability for the abuser is the Domestic Abuse Intervention Project (DAIP), developed in Duluth, Minnesota. See www.duluth-model.org.

37. For an analysis of the logic of domination, see Karen Warren, "A Feminist Philosophic Perspective on Ecofeminist Spiritualities," in *Ecofeminism and the Sacred,* edited by Carol J. Adams (New York: Continuum International, 1993), 119–132.

38. See Susan Brownmiller, *Against Our Will: Men, Women and Rape* (New York: Simon and Schuster, 1975).

39. Finkelhor and Yllo, *License to Rape,* 100.

40. Diana E. H. Russell, *Rape in Marriage: Expanded and Revised Edition* (Bloomington: Indiana University Press, 1982), 318.

41. Marie M. Fortune, *Sexual Abuse Prevention: A Study for Teenagers* (New York: United Church Press, 1986), 9.

42. Freire, *Pedagogy of the Oppressed,* 61.

43. Russell, *Rape in Marriage,* 321.

44. Jones and Schecter, *When Love Goes Wrong,* 307.

45. I am not delineating here long-term counseling such as described in Herman's *Trauma and Recovery.* I am sketching the counseling needs of women still trapped within victimizing relationships, those issues that Herman addresses in part in her chapter on safety.

46. Space does not allow me to discuss in detail the safety issues that a pastoral counselor can raise with a victim of marital rape or battering. For a more in-depth description, see my book, *Woman-Battering.*

47. Annie Imbens and Ineke Jonker, *Christianity and Incest* (Minneapolis: Fortress, 1992), 209–210.

48. Imbens and Jonker, *Christianity and Incest,* 210.

. . . .

CAROL J. ADAMS is the author of *Woman-Battering* (Augsburg Fortress, 1994), which is part of the Creative Pastoral Care and Counseling series. She created and has taught the course on sexual and domestic violence at Perkins School of Theology and has been involved in the violence against women movement since the mid-1970s. She is also the author of *The Sexual Politics of Meat: A Feminist-Vegetarian Critical Theory* (Continuum, 1990) and *The Pornography of Meat* (Continuum, 2003), and the editor, with Marie Fortune, of *Violence Against Women and Children: A Christian Theological Sourcebook* (Continuum, 1995).

UNMASKING THE PORNOGRAPHY INDUSTRY
FROM FANTASY TO REALITY
. . . .
GAIL DINES

The new image of the porn user is a computer-savvy male who knows his way around cutting-edge technology. It is the technology that thus glorifies pornography for the consumer, while for the new media industries it is the pornography that has glorified the technology.

T HE RADICAL FEMINIST CRITIQUE of pornography grew out
of the larger struggle to stop male violence against women. Rape, battery, child sexual assault, and sexual harassment were conceptualized as
forms of sexual terrorism that maintained men's power in patriarchy. Rather
than being defined as deviant, men's violence against women was seen as
predictable behavior in a woman-hating culture.

Refusing to accept male violence as natural, many radical feminists turned
their attention to exploring how the culture teaches men to become violent.
Writers such as Andrea Dworkin, Alice Walker, and Diana Russell argued
that one of the major teaching tools was pornography.[1] Using images and
words, these how-to manuals legitimized and objectified women as fuck objects, where violence against women was sexualized and thus rendered invisible. These feminist critics argued that discussions of pornography needed
to go beyond issues of morality (the religious right's approach), or free speech
(the liberal perspective), in order to focus on real women's lives. For the first
time, questions were asked about the nature of the harm done to women by
and through pornography production and consumption.

Because radical feminism has always linked theory with action, we have
been organizing against this female-flesh-eating business for more than three
decades. We have picketed, given thousands of presentations, attempted to get
the Dworkin/MacKinnon proposed legislation passed, lobbied international
bodies, and developed global networks of activism.[2] We have also documented the connections between this industry, the prostitution industry, and
the global trafficking in women, which supplies a steady stream of bodies to
the pimps.[3] This work has led us to the conclusion that pornography is not
an industry that can be saved by unionizing or legitimizing. It is an industry
that has to be abolished if we are to take women's lives seriously. Hence, no
meeting ground exists between the pro- and antipornography camps, as we
are hell-bent on getting rid of pornography and no amount of postmodern
discourse will change our minds.

Many liberal feminists argue that we have always had pornography (cave
images are usually the examples given), and that antipornography feminists
are fighting a losing battle. What is missing from this is an examination
of how pornography actually became the industry it is today. It did not
simply fall from the cave walls into the magazines and videos but rather is

the product of a carefully crafted marketing strategy that could be used in any business school as a case study. By exploring the history and economics of this industry, we can take away its magical quality as a "natural" part of male sexuality and unmask it for what it is: a global industry founded on capitalism, racism, and patriarchy.

In order to examine the socioeconomic framework that informs the production of pornography, it makes sense to begin with the magazine industry, since it was this genre, not cave drawings, that brought pornography out of the back streets and into the mainstream. Specifically, it was the success of *Playboy,* followed by *Penthouse* and *Hustler,* that laid the groundwork for the present-day multibillion-dollar industry. The videos, DVDs, and computer Web sites that make up this industry are a direct outcome of the legal, economic, and cultural spaces that the pornography magazines of the 1950s, '60s, and '70s created through the marketing techniques they developed.

DEVELOPING THE PORNOGRAPHIC MAGAZINE INDUSTRY: FROM *PLAYBOY* TO *HUSTLER*

While *Playboy* (circulation 3.4 million a month) and *Hustler* (circulation 1.4 million a month) are often lumped together under the heading of pornography, they played very different but connected roles in the development of the industry. In terms of the continuum from soft core to hard core—hard core being distinguished by the presence of spread female genitalia (called *pink* in the magazines), erect penises, and sexually explicit activity—*Playboy* was the premier publication of the soft-core end of the market and *Hustler* of the hard-core end. *Hustler*'s aim to be the "first nationally distributed magazine to show pink"[4] could never have been realized without Hugh Hefner's uncanny ability to develop *Playboy* into a mass-circulation soft-core pornography magazine. He did this by cloaking it in an aura of upper-middle-class respectability which would, according to John Mastro, former product manager of *Playboy,* "take some of the shock off nudity."[5] This quality magazine would have at its center airbrushed, soft-focus, pinup-style photographs of women. As a way to encourage men to see themselves as playboys and not porn users, Hefner wrote in the April 1956 issue,

What is a playboy? He can be a sharp-minded young business executive, a worker in the arts, a university professor, an
architect or an engineer. . . . He must be an alert man, a man
of taste, a man sensitive to pleasure, a man who—can live life
to the hilt.

Larry Flynt was equally clear about the *Hustler* reader. He wrote in the
first issue, "Anyone can be a playboy and have a penthouse, but it takes a
man to be a Hustler." Flynt repeatedly writes in *Hustler* that his target audience is "the average American" whose income makes it impossible to identify with the high-level consumption and lifestyle associated with *Playboy*
and *Penthouse*. Mocking *Playboy* and *Penthouse* for taking themselves too
seriously, and for masquerading the "pornography as art by wrapping it in
articles purporting to have socially redeeming values," *Hustler* carved out a
niche for itself in a glutted market as a no-holds-barred magazine.[6]

In 1974, twenty-one years after *Playboy* first appeared, Flynt could indeed
be more explicit in his images. *Playboy* had seasoned men to accept, and indeed
want, more hard-core pornography and thus provided the cultural space for
the mass distribution of a more hard-core magazine targeted at the working-
class guy who liked no-frills pornography. By positioning itself as a magazine
unashamedly for the lower-working-class white male, *Hustler* continues to
promote an image of itself as targeting a specific audience that few readers
see themselves as belonging to. This is because most whites see themselves
as middle class, since, in a racist society, "class differences become racial differences."[7] Herein lies the brilliant marketing strategy of *Hustler*: No one is
meant to see himself as the implied reader. This allows the white male reader
of any class to buy the magazine while keeping a safe distance from images
of semen, feces, child molesters, and women with leaking vaginas. For the
duration of the reading and masturbation, he is slumming in the world of
white trash, an observer of a social class that is clearly not his.

This strategy helped open up the way for men to buy more hard-core
porn by allowing them to separate themselves from the supposed audience.
Thus, the Armani-clad businessman, the athletic frat boy, or the suburban
father can buy or download pornography, believing that he is not a porn user
but a man visiting the world that the other half inhabits. When he is finished
with a particular video, he can zip up his pants and go back to his real world.

Unfortunately for women, the two worlds collapse into each other, and we have to deal with men whose notions of sexuality, femininity, and masculinity are constructed through the cultural images they see. The vast majority of these cultural images are found in mainstream media as pornographic codes, and their conventions filter down to everyday images, albeit in a subtler form. Thus the billboards, the ads on buses, the images in *Cosmopolitan, Vogue,* and *Maxim,* and the videos on MTV all combine to construct a visual landscape that is increasingly pornographic. This not only normalizes violence against women, it also opens up a cultural space for actual pornography to become even more explicit and violent.

FROM THE GIRLS NEXT DOOR TO BACKDOOR GIRLS

The soft-focus pictures of naked women provocatively staring at the camera (mouth slightly open, neck exposed, inviting eyes), popularized by *Playboy,* have been replaced by videos that compete to see which can use and abuse the female body in new and more creative ways. Hefner's marketing strategy, which sexualized commodities while commodifying sexuality, promised the consumer that by buying the right products he would get the real prize: women who looked like the women in the magazine. For this to work, each woman had to be sold as the girl next door, rather than an out-of-reach model or actress. Today, mainstream pornography is not made up of the wholesome girls next door but rather insatiable fuck objects who appear to crave bondage, anal sex (referred to as backdoor penetration in pornospeak), multiple penetration, and outright abuse. In a recent content analysis of popular pornographic videos, Robert Jensen and I found that in our fourteen examples the presence of violent sex was almost routine. The most common forms were "slapping a woman's buttocks during intercourse; slapping the woman's face or vagina with the penis; pulling on hair before and during sex; and deep thrusting in a woman's throat, even if it provoked a gag reflex."[8] In the best-selling video *Latex,* by Michael Ninn (a film that is not advertised as S/M), a woman is gagged with a man's tie and then blindfolded as he slaps her.

Many of the videos document gang rape, although it is presented as consensual sex. It needs to be stressed that the images are not classified as violent; however, this definition is from a male perspective. The big lie of pornography is that women want such treatment and that men are just doing us a favor by meeting our insatiable needs.

Violent videos have now overtaken the magazine industry, and *Playboy*, *Penthouse*, and *Hustler* magazines are difficult to find in porn shops. They have migrated to local newsstands, chain bookstores, neighborhood grocery stores, and the Internet. The porn shop is itself becoming a thing of the past, since the Internet has brought the porn shop into the home. While this may not be new information, what is less well known is the role that pornography played in developing the Internet. Pornography has now become the leading driver of innovation in Internet technology, pioneering streaming audio and visual, flash and chat, the click-through ad banner, the pop-up window, high-speed Internet connections, security improvements, and a new form of à la carte pay services.[9] Thus, while the pornography business can thank the Internet for its massive growth over the last few years, the Internet industry owes an even bigger debt to the pornographers.

NEW TECHNOLOGIES AND THE PORNOGRAPHY INDUSTRY: WHAT NEXT?

At a recent panel on the Internet, entertainment executives in television, film, and digital communications focused on the perplexing question of why most dot-coms fail. Larry Kasanoff, chairman and CEO of the Los Angeles–based Threshold Entertainment asked why no one was talking about the adult entertainment business. "[Porn was first] in cable TV, it was first in home video and [it's first] on the Internet. . . . So you know what? Porn is great for all of us. We should all study it."[10]

This is not the first time porn has been a leading innovator in developing new technologies. It has been credited with helping to drive the evolution of the camera at the turn of the twentieth century, the home video business, cable TV, and DVDs.[11] It is no surprise that *Playboy* was a major player in the development of Internet pornography. Its Web site has been around since 1994, making it one of the first national magazines to go digital. In August 1999, the site partnered with TheKnot.com, a New York–based online wedding resource, to create Playboy BachelorParty.com, a complete online guide for future grooms (lucky brides!). The pornographers are well aware of their power. As the operator of Bondagemistress.com succinctly puts it, "Technology is driven by adult entertainment because sex then sells the technology."[12] Businesses that fail to follow this strategy pay a heavy price. For example, many entertainment analysts maintain that Sony, by refusing to license its Betamax technology to pornographers, allowed VHS to monopolize the market by the early 1980s.

Studies of online pornography demonstrate that the money to be made is staggering. Datamonitor, a New York– and London–based research company, found that in 1998 nearly $1 billion was spent by users accessing pornography through an estimated 50,000 porn-specific sites worldwide, an amount that was expected to triple by 2003.[13] Offline, porn accounts for 69 percent of the current $1.4 billion domestic cable TV pay-per-view market, compared to 4 percent for video games and 2 percent for sports, according to a study conducted in March 2000 for *U.S. News & World Report.* According to *Forbes* magazine, "today's legal porn business is a $56 billion global industry." Andrew Edmond, President and CEO of Flying Crocodile, a $20 million Internet pornography business, stated that "a lot of people [outside adult entertainment] get distracted from the business model by [the sex]. . . . [It] is just as sophisticated and multilayered as any other marketplace. We operate just like any Fortune 500 company."[14]

Indeed, many Fortune 500 companies have links to the pornography industry. General Motors, the world's largest company, now sells more pornographic films than Larry Flynt. According to the New York *Times,* "The 8.7 million Americans who subscribe to DirecTV, a General Motors subsidiary, buy nearly $200 million a year in pay-per-view sex films from satellite." The *Times* also reports that AT&T, the nation's biggest communication company, offers subscribers to its broadband cable service a hard-core porn channel called Hot Network and owns a company that sells porn videos to nearly a million hotel rooms.[15]

The second largest satellite provider, EchoStar Communications Corporation, makes more money selling hard-core pornography films through its satellite subsidiary than all of *Playboy* holdings combined.[16] EchoStar's chief financial backer is Rupert Murdoch, CEO of News Corporation. Murdoch also owns the Fox Television Network, Twentieth Century Fox, the New York *Post,* and the Los Angeles Dodgers, to name just a few of his holdings.

Frontier Media, one of the most popular Web properties, features links to sites such as Virgin Sluts and See Teens Have Sex and does business with In Demand, the nation's largest pay-per-view distributor, which is owned in part by AT&T, TimeWarner, Advance-Newhouse, Cox Communications, and Comcast. The financial connections between mainstream companies and pornography highlight the degree to which pornography is not a marginalized industry but rather a major player in the development of sophisticated, multibillion-dollar new media technologies.

Today, porn users can think of themselves as sophisticated Internet users. Whereas *Playboy* once used its content to provide the reader with an idealized image of himself as a sophisticated male, today technology has taken over this role. The new image of the porn user is a the computer-savvy male who knows his way around cutting-edge technology. It is the technology that thus glorifies pornography for the consumer, while for the new media industries it is the pornography that has glorified the technology. Where all this will end is unclear because we have newer and newer technologies that no doubt will use pornography to make them user friendly. Virtual reality is just around the corner, and already the pornographers are investing in its development.

STOPPING PORNOGRAPHY: TURNING OUR FANTASY INTO REALITY

The mainstreaming of pornography in our culture normalizes violence against women. This is the reason feminists have a vested interest in fighting the pornographers. We must continue our efforts against the pornographers, and one potentially creative form of activism would be to target the big corporations that make money from pornography. General Motors, AT&T, TimeWarner and News Corporation (to name just a few) are vulnerable to consumer pressure. Boycotts, letter writing, and organized protests are the last things these corporations want, thus making them the first things we should do. We can refuse to stay in hotels that carry cable pornography; we can refuse to rent videos or buy books from stores that carry pornography; we can change our phone companies; we can put pressure on the stockholders of corporations that are linked to pornography. Corporations as a collective body have one major interest, to make money, and we can hit them where it really hurts.

The fight against pornography is part of the larger battle against violence against women. Stopping pornography will not end all the violence done to us, but it will deny the patriarchy a major propaganda system that legitimizes men's power over women. Pornography is a powerful delivery service that sends messages to the brain via the genitals. As feminists, we must also fight against the abuse of the women who are used in pornography. No woman was put on this earth to serve as men's fuck object, to be abused for the sake of facilitating male masturbation. Radical feminism is about sisterhood, not partial sisterhood for a few, but full sisterhood, which means that we cannot fall into the patriarchal trap of believing that some women are to serve as men's whores in order to save other women from this fate. Our collective well-being is our agenda, and liberation is our goal. Pornography stands in the way of our liberation, so it has to go. This might seem like a fantasy on my part, but as we know, fantasy doesn't just reside in the head, it has real implications in the social world.

Adapted from an essay in Sisterhood Is Forever: The Women's Anthology for the New Millennium, *edited by Robin Morgan (Simon and Schuster, 2003).*

NOTES

1. Andrea Dworkin, *Pornography: Men Possessing Women* (New York: Dutton, 1981); Alice Walker, "Coming Apart," in *Take Back the Night: Women on Pornography,* edited by Laura Lederer (New York: Morrow, 1980) 218–238; Diana Russell, ed., *Making Violence Sexy: Feminist Views on Pornography* (New York: Teacher's College Press, 1993).

2. The Dworkin/MacKinnon proposed legislation defines pornography as the graphic, sexually explicit subordination of women through pictures/and or words that also includes one or more of the following: (a) Women are presented as dehumanized sexual objects, things or commodities; or (b) women are presented as sexual objects who enjoy humiliation or pain; or (c) women are presented as sexual objects experiencing sexual pleasure in rape, incest, or other sexual assaults; or (d) women are presented as sexual objects tied up or cut up or mutilated or bruised or physically hurt; or (e) women are presented in postures or positions of sexual submission or servility; or (f) women's body parts—including but not limited to vaginas, breasts, or buttocks—are exhibited such that women are reduced to these parts; or (g) women are presented being penetrated by objects or animals; or (h) women are presented in scenarios of degradation, humiliation, injury,

or torture, or shown as filthy or inferior, bleeding, bruised, or hurt in a context that makes these conditions sexual. Andrea Dworkin and Katharine MacKinnon, *Pornography and Civil Rights: A New Day for Women's Equality* (Minneapolis: Organizing against Pornography, 1988).

3. K. Barry, *The Prostitution of Sexuality* (New York: New York University Press, 1995).

4. Larry Flynt, "Ten Great Years," *Hustler,* July 1984, 7.

5. John Mastro, quoted in Thomas Weyr, *Reaching for Paradise: The Playboy Vision of America* (New York: Times Books, 1978), 33.

6. Larry Flynt, *Hustler,* 1974, 4; November 1983, 5; and July 1984, 7.

7. Sut Jhally and Justin Lewis, *Enlightened Racism: The Cosby Show, Audiences, and the Myth of the American Dream* (Boulder: Westview, 1992), 83.

8. Robert Jensen and Gail Dines, "The Content of Mass-Marketed Pornography," in *Pornography: The Production and Consumption of Inequality,* edited by G. Dines, R. Jensen, and Ann Russo (New York: Routledge, 1998), 82.

9. *New York Times,* October 23, 2000; *American Heritage* 51, September 2000: 19; *National Journal,* January 2, 2000, 38.

10. *Brandweek* 41, October 2000, 1Q48.

11. *Video Age International,* 20 (November 2000): 3.

12. *PC/Computing,* January 24, 2000, 64.

13. *Brandweek* 41, 1Q48.

14. *Brandweek* 41; *Forbes,* June 14, 1999.

15. *New York Times,* October 23, 2000.

16. *New York Times,* October 23, 2000.

. . . .

GAIL DINES is professor of sociology at Wheelock College in Boston and a longtime antipornography activist. She is coauthor (with Robert Jensen and Ann Russo) of *Pornography: The Production and Consumption of Inequality* (Routledge, 1997). She is also coeditor with Jean M. Humez of the best-selling textbook *Gender, Race, and Class in Media* (Sage, 1994, 2003). She has written numerous articles on pornography, the media, and violence against women, and she lectures across the country on the effects of pornographic images on women and men.

MANEUVERS
WHEN SOLDIERS RAPE
. . . .

CYNTHIA ENLOE

The male militarized rapist in some way imposes his understanding of enemy, soldiering, victory, and defeat on both the woman to be raped and on the act of sexual assault.

MILITARIZED RAPE HAS GAINED VISIBILITY on the stage of international politics in recent years because of the incidence of mass rape that occurred in Bosnia during its 1992–1995 war and in Rwanda during its 1994 attempted genocide. Yet militarized rapes are far more diverse. Often, as in Haiti and Indonesia, action has been required through the organizing by women for women to uncover soldiers' systematic political uses of rape. Rape perpetrated by men as soldiers has been experienced by women in a variety of forms:

- Rape by a male soldier of a woman he thinks of as a "foreigner"
- Rape by an individual male soldier of a civilian woman of the same nationality while that soldier is "off duty"
- Rape by a male soldier of a woman soldier in the same army, perhaps because he resents her presence in a previously all-male unit or because he is angry at her for her unwillingness to date him or flirt with him
- Rapes of women held in military prisons by male soldiers serving as guards; rapes perpetrated by a soldier acting as an interrogator with the apparent purpose of forcing the woman victim to give information
- Rapes by a group of invading soldiers to force women of a different ethnicity or race to flee their home regions
- Rapes of captured women by soldiers of one communal or national group aimed principally at humiliating the men of the opposing group
- Rapes by men of one ethnicity, race, or nationality of men from the "enemy" group to make the latter feel humiliated because they have been, via rape, reduced to "mere women"
- Rapes of women by men in accordance to male officers' system of morale-boosting rewards to their men after battle
- Rapes of women taking refuge in wartime refugee camps by men also taking refuge in those camps or by men who are assigned to protect women in those camps
- Rapes of women by those men who are prostitution procurers, to "prepare" them for later service in a brothel organized for soldier-clients
- Rapes of women in wartime by civilian men of their same ethnic or national community who are acting out a misogyny nurtured by and licensed by the militarized climate

- Rapes of women who publicly oppose militarization by men of their own supposed community who support militarization

This list may be exhausting, but it is not exhaustive.

There are as many different forms of militarized rape as there are subtle nuances in the relationships between militarized women and militarized men. Nonetheless, they share some important common features—features that will affect not only the rapist's sense of what he is doing and of what gives him license to do it but also the raped woman's responses to that assault. First, the male militarized rapist in some way imposes his understanding of "enemy," "soldiering," "victory," and "defeat" on both the woman to be raped and on the act of sexual assault. Second, consequently, the militarized rape is harder to privatize than the nonmilitarized rape is, since it draws so much of its rationale from an imagining of societal conflict and/or the functions of a formal institution such as the state's national security or defense apparatus or an insurgency's military arm. Third, the woman who has endured militarized rape must devise her responses in the minutes, weeks, and years after that assault not only by weighing her relationships to the rapist and to her personal friends and relatives, to the prevailing norms of feminine respectability, and perhaps to the criminal justice system, but *in addition,* she must weigh her relationships to collective memory, collective notions of national destiny, and the very institutions of the organized violence.

This essay is an excerpt from "When Soldiers Rape" in Maneuvers: The International Politics of Militarizing Women's Lives *(Berkeley: University of California Press, 2000). Copyright © 2000 by the Regents of the University of California. Reprinted with permission from the University of California Press.*

. . . .

CYNTHIA ENLOE is a research professor at Clark University and a well-known feminist writer-theorist. Her books include *Maneuvers: The International Politics of Militarizing Women's Lives* (University of California Press, 2000), *The Morning After: Sexual Politics at the End of the Cold War* (University of California Press, 1993), and *Bananas, Beaches and Bases: Making Feminist Sense of International Politics* (University of California Press, 1991, 2001).

STRATEGIES AND ACTIVISM

According to the late Audre Lorde, "The master's tools will never dismantle the master's house." The writers in this section describe the new tools they have forged for transforming the world, from changing how we raise our sons and daughters to learning to speak a language that will not lie. Putting theory into practice, a college teacher uses the collaborative writing of plays to help her students come to consciousness; women reach through the cultural barriers surrounding their immigrant communities; and men and women learn and teach one another to care for survivors of assault in the rape culture. They share the goal of changing consciousness, of creating new commitments to the long human journey away from violence and toward abundant life.

THE LANGUAGE OF RAPE

· · · · · · · · · · · · · · · · · ·

HELEN BENEDICT

Some might argue that changes in our language can only follow changes in legislation and the social balance of genders, but I believe changes in language can also lead the way.

F EMINIST LINGUISTS HAVE POINTED OUT for some years now the sexist bias in the English language. Dale Spender, for example, told us in her seminal book *Man Made Language* that there are 220 words for a sexually promiscuous woman and only 20 for an equally promiscuous man. This antiwoman bias in our language not only reflects the culture of rape but encourages it, because it portrays women as sexual objects, fair prey for the hunter-man. In short, English is a language of rape.

By "a language of rape," I mean vocabulary that portrays women as sexual, as subhuman, or as childlike temptresses, and that perpetuates the idea of women as legitimate sexual prey. I also mean the vocabulary used to describe rape itself as an act of pleasure, or of comedy, rather than of violence.

Take as illustration the tradition of treating rape as a joke. I watched the 1967 British comedy *Bedazzled,* starring Peter Cook as the devil and Dudley Moore as a pathetic short-order-cook version of Faust. I had loved that movie as a teenager, but as an adult feminist I had quite a different reaction. The film was still amusing, but its misogyny was relentless, culminating in two full scenes making fun of rape. In the first, Eleanor Bron, the object of Moore's desires (and I use the word *object* deliberately), cries rape when Moore leaps on her, and keeps on crying it after the devil has caused him to vanish into thin air. The scene leaves her lying on her back, screaming "Rape!" and kicking with no one else in the room—enacting the traditional view of rape as a figment of a frigid woman's imagination, or, more accurately, as something that doesn't exist.

In the second scene, a police inspector is showing Bron bodies in the morgue. He mentions that he has dealt with a lot of rape cases recently and immediately follows with the sentence, "And that's a nice dress you're wearing, as well," or some such non sequitur. He then goes on to say, "Mind you, the girls always bring it on themselves, you know."

I may not have the exact words, but I have the gist: Rape is sex, rape is attraction, rape is the woman's fault—that is to say, rape doesn't exist.

That film was made in the swinging sixties, but its attitude, and the language in which the attitude is expressed, has barely changed. I spent five years looking at newspaper coverage of rape in the late twentieth century, and I found that same language everywhere, in ordinary people's comments ("He had plenty of girls, he didn't need to rape her"), in lawyers' arguments ("It was Jennifer [Levin] who was pursuing Robert [Chambers] for sex . . . that's why we wound up with this terrible tragedy"), in the jokes of friends I told about my work ("A book about rape? Are you for it or against it?"), and, most of all, in the language of the reporters and headline writers themselves.

Here are some examples of the words I found used by newspapers for female victims of sex crimes: "pretty," "hysterical," "attractive," "flirtatious," "bright," "bubbly," "petite," "pert," "vivacious," "girl" (for a grown woman). These words, never used for men, either infantilize women (the woman is bright, the man intelligent; the woman is bubbly, the man energetic; the woman is hysterical, the man terrified; the woman is a girl, the man is a man), or, in the context of a sex crime, make them sound like sexual tempt-resses (a male crime victim is *never* described as attractive, pretty, or the sug-gestive equivalent). To see the bias, simply change the subject's gender: "Petite, bubbly John Harris took the witness stand today," or, "Friends described Robert Smith as a pert, vivacious boy who liked to flirt in the bars," or, "Alan Peterson ran from the scene half naked, crying hysterically."

Examples of the vocabulary I found used to describe rape and sexual assault are "fondled," "caressed," and "had sex with," all words written by so-called objective journalists who were unconsciously reflecting the rapist's point of view. These words were used to describe not an ambiguous case of date rape but the brutal and bloody attack in 1989 on the woman who came to be known as the Central Park jogger.

True, the language of rape is insidious and it is used unconsciously, quickly, carelessly; yet I maintain that we need not listen passively in the face of its bias. Language can be and has been reformed in the media and, symbiotically, in everyday life. The media, for instance, long ago learned not to use the word *Negro* and is switching from *black* to *African American* as I write; it has also dropped the routine use of *Miss* and *buxom blonde* in its references to women. The media, therefore, can learn to reform its language about rape. Reporters and editors can be taught to apply a simple test to the words they use about women and crime victims: "Would I use this word for a man? What does this word imply in context?"

Some might argue that changes in our language can only *follow* changes in legislation and the social balance of genders, but I believe changes in lan-guage can also lead the way. Again, take the media. If we grew used to seeing women treated as equal to men in the news, if we read and heard descriptions of sex crimes as only horrible and not titillating, of female victims as ordinary people and not whores or martyrs, it would be harder to accept the status quo of women as objects of prey. The media reflects public opinion, to be sure, but it also shapes it, for it is through the media that the public receives all its news and most of its information. The media, therefore, can lead the reform of the language of rape.

Journalists can begin this reform by fighting for a fairer and less sexist use of vocabulary, and consumers can do their part by writing in to object to biased language. Everyone concerned—reporters, columnists, consumers, feminists, writers, and upcoming editors—must argue until the established media is ready to accept a feminist view of rape: that rape is an act of torture in which sex is used as the weapon; that desire and lust have nothing to do with rape except in the sickest of ways (the assailant is aroused by his own acts of sadism, anger, and violence); and that women are not objects of prey but human beings who must be treated with the same respect and consideration a civilized society would like to accord its male citizens.

Once the media accepts the feminist view of rape as neither extreme nor radical but merely realistic, then perhaps women will no longer have to cry "Rape!" to an empty room.

. . . .

HELEN BENEDICT is the author of *Virgin or Vamp: How the Press Covers Sex Crimes* (Oxford University Press, 1993), upon which this article is based. She has written extensively about rape for magazines and newspapers and is the author of six other books, two of which concern rape and sexual assault: *Recovery: How to Survive Sexual Assault* (revised edition, Columbia University Press, 1994) and *Safe, Strong, and Streetwise* (Little, Brown, 1987). Her other books are the novels *A World Like This* (Dutton, 1990), *Bad Angel* (Dutton, 1997) and *The Sailor's Wife* (Zoland, 2000), and *Portraits in Print* (Columbia University Press, 1992). *The Opposite of Love,* a novel, is forthcoming from Viking. Benedict is a professor at the Graduate School of Journalism at Columbia University and lives in New York.

"WHY DID HE WANT TO HURT ME? ALL I EVER DID WAS LOVE HIM"
UNDERSTANDING SEXUAL VIOLENCE IN LATINO MARRIAGES

. . . .

YVETTE G. FLORES

We talked about loyalty to family, attempting to deconstruct rigid patriarchal notions and the history of colonization that has framed *familismo* for generations. She came to see the connections between the exploitation of indigenous men and women in Latin America and the legacy of miscegenation that affects all women of the continent.

MAGDA'S STORY[1]

THE RAPES DID NOT HAPPEN RIGHT AWAY, she said. The violence did not either; it began gradually, first with words that wounded, then with bitter arguments, a shove there, a pull here, and objects that flew across the room. The few bruises they left were the only trace of the disrespect and despair that began to invade the marriage. At first she did not think it was abuse, because there were no injuries. She never understood why she became his punching bag. She felt she was a good wife; she tried to anticipate his every need. His meals were always on time. She ironed his underwear, just like her mother had taught her. She placed him above all else. He was her life.

After each outburst, she talked herself into forgiving him; after all, he worked so hard. She knew how badly he was treated at work. She knew that the American dream that had brought them here had become a nightmare. She had followed him, leaving her family behind; here she had no one.

Who could she confide in? She needed guidance. She went to church. Slowly she approached the old priest because he spoke Spanish. She thought he was a *gachupin*.[2] She thought that he looked at her with condescending eyes: another Mexican seeking refuge in his holy place. She lowered her eyes and never looked at him directly again. He sounded impatient when she confessed her husband's sins. He seemed more interested in whether or not she was a good wife, a good cook, whether she was willing to please him. She left feeling more disheartened than when she arrived. "Be patient," he said, urging her to have faith and pray to God to be a better wife. She never went to church again. But she continued to pray.

With the passage of time, the beatings increased, as did her desolation. Her love for him was quietly transformed into fear. She no longer desired his touch or his sporadic words of affection. She was revolted at his beer breath, his brusque approach. She dreaded his arrival home; she dreaded nighttime. She developed chest pains, migraines, backaches. She spoke less and less. And then it happened. He came home early from work bringing her flowers. He seemed to be in a good mood. He wanted to take her to the movies. She smiled without enthusiasm but acquiesced. They sat in silence; he reached for her hand; she felt a knot grow in her stomach. He touched her thigh and caressed her breast. She tensed, unaccustomed to being fondled in public. She tried to move his hand. She felt tension enter his body.

When they got home, he screamed and accused her of cheating. Why else would she reject his "loving advances"? She denied the accusation. With each denial, he became more outraged. She pleaded; he hit. Suddenly he threw her on the bed and raped her. All the while he called her a whore; he told her she would now know what a real man was like. He had made love to her before, he told her. Now *se la iba a chingar,* he would fuck her, like the whore she was.

She remembers little else. Her spirit left her body. She woke up in a pool of blood. She bathed herself and made him breakfast. From then on, he forced himself upon her at will. She felt nothing. She had two children during this time; she loves them, she says, although she knows they were conceived in hate and disrespect.

But she cannot leave him; she has nowhere to go. She should not leave him and break up the family. Her sons need a father, a role model, she says. She is twenty-seven years old; she looks much older. "*Me siento muerta en vida,*" I feel dead, she says. How could this happen, she asks without expecting an answer.

We are taught as children that our culture values women, that a woman should not be hit even with the petal of a rose, "*a la mujer no se le pega ni con el pétalo de una rosa,*" she says. What went wrong? How could men who grow up in a culture that claims to love and respect women behave in such a way? As she told her story for the first time, she quietly asked, "Why did he want to hurt me? All I ever did was love him."

TRANSFORMING A RAPE CULTURE: DECONSTRUCTING *FAMILISMO*

Latino social scientists, among others, have described *familismo* as a value central to most Latino groups.[3] Familism involves identification with and attachment to nuclear and extended family relationships and strong feelings of loyalty, reciprocity, and solidarity among members of the same family.[4] In a number of studies, familism has been shown to include three types of value orientations: First, the perceived obligation to provide material and emotional support to the members of the extended family; second, reliance on relatives for help and support; and third, the perception of relatives as behavioral and attitudinal referents.[5] These values appear to change very little with acculturation or long residence in the United States.

Moreover, Latina feminists have argued that women and men are socialized differently within the parameters of familism.[6] Men are expected to provide materially and women emotionally. Thus, men are not generally taught to safeguard the psychological and emotional well-being of the women in their lives. The male code of honor emphasizes patriarchal notions of being a provider for and proprietor of the family. Women are expected to anticipate and meet a man's every need, particularly his emotional ones, so he will not even know he has such needs. In this way, he can save face; he will not have to acknowledge having an emotional need.

I argue that such socialization impedes the development of empathy in men. If a man is unable to recognize his own emotional needs, he will be incapable of recognizing such needs in others. Women will then be viewed as having irrational needs or desires if they expect, ask, or dare to demand emotional presence or availability from their male partners. Moreover, within patriarchal cultures men are socialized to expect (if not demand) absolute loyalty from their partners and children.

The reliance on family for support often isolates women in abusive relationships. Moreover, marital rape engenders feelings of shame and dissociation. A woman's mind, body, and spirit disconnect. In order to withstand the violence, the body feels nothing, the spirit leaves the body, and the heart is silenced.[7]

Since the family and loved ones provide the mirroring for what is culturally appropriate and acceptable, dysfunctional families where unfairness is normalized, where the abuse of women is not contested but encouraged, silence women and make them feel responsible for the horrors they experience. As Inés Hernández-Avila has noted [see p. 323], the sexual victimization of Latinas must be understood in terms of the history of sexual violence against indigenous women in the Americas and their subsequent vilification by native and Latino men. The disempowerment of Latino men as a result of their conquest and colonization, and the continuing racism they experience, results in rage and violence which is often turned against women. Women within the culture are socialized to understand the men's victimization and through cultural narratives, *dichos* (sayings), and by example, are taught to absolve the men of responsibility. I call this process the *pobrecito* syndrome.[8] When the man is viewed as not responsible for his violence because of his own victimization, he is not held accountable and is therefore not forced to change. In this way, cultural values and practices help maintain the cycle of violence.

As a clinical psychologist, I have heard women's testimonies of violence and despair for more than twenty years. Few women initially feel entitled to leave abusive relationships. Few find support in their own families. Sometimes with good intentions, sometimes with cruelty, mothers, siblings, and others encourage women to stay in unhappy marriages for the good of the family. Using powerful religious imagery, Latinas often are told that a bad marriage is a cross that they must bear. Appeals to a woman's sense of loyalty and obligation to family are often successful in curbing her agency.

It can be dangerous to challenge fundamental notions of familism within the context of psychotherapy. Women in therapy can experience the questioning of cultural expectations or practices as disrespectful and insensitive. Furthermore, the economic realities of life for immigrant Latinas indeed make it difficult for many to leave abusive relationships. Likewise, few culturally competent treatment programs address intimate partner violence. Few women seek services on their own when they are battered or raped. Referrals then come from physicians who examine the women after injuries, occasionally from clergy, or from law enforcement officers who have been called to the home.

Few women disclose physical marital violence. Fewer still report marital rape. "I was told that as a wife it was my responsibility to have sex with him when he wanted it, even if I didn't," Magda told me. "I didn't know I had the right to say no. Besides, when I did, he got mad and hit me." It took Magda many years to see the sexual violence she experienced as abuse, as rape. It never occurred to her to report the incidents; she believed that as a wife it was her duty to take it.

THE ROAD TO HEALING: RECONSTRUCTING FAMILISM

Magda came to see me after her primary care physician could not find a medical cause for her physical distress. She never told him about the violence, as she put it, because he never asked. Carefully, tentatively her story unfolded after we had established some trust. As a Latina socialized within the context of traditional family beliefs and values, I understood Magda's sense of obligation. I too had stayed in a marriage decades longer than I needed to. While I never suffered the degree of violence she endured, I understood the binding chains of loyalty and obligation, the guilt induced by breaking up a family. I recalled the way in which a dear aunt fell to her knees in prayer when I announced my divorce. Unlike Magda, however, I had a large group of cousins, *comadres* (literally, godmothers, a term describing close, supportive friends) and sisters who supported my choice and reminded me that I had the right to be treated with respect.

Magda and I then began a series of conversations about the culture we shared. We spoke of growing up in a Latin country; she told me stories of her childhood, of happier times, of how her mother taught her to be a woman. Slowly, respectfully, I posed questions regarding her sense of justice. What did she consider fair treatment? We explored issues of entitlement; using humor, we examined how men and women are socialized differently in Latin America; how class status often plays a role. She agreed that affluent Latinas often receive a smaller dosage of *familismo* and a larger dosage of entitlement. We spoke about the process of migration and how her life had changed, and about her losses and the resources she had acquired. We explored her dreams. I shared with her my writings on intimate partner violence, the *testimonios* (testimony) of Latina feminists, college students, and community residents I have collected over the years. I introduced her to the writings of Chicana feminists and Gloria Anzaldúa's ideas of *la nueva mestiza* (the new mestiza).[9]

We talked about loyalty to family, attempting to deconstruct rigid patriarchal notions and the history of colonization that has framed *familismo* for generations. She came to see the connections between the exploitation of indigenous men and women in Latin America and the legacy of miscegenation that affects all women in the continent. She came to see the relationship between her husband's oppression and his rage. She also realized that she was not responsible for healing his rage or tolerating his violence.

We examined the indigenous roots of our culture and traditional ways of healing from shame, grief, and despair. She began to form a more balanced view of family loyalty and obligation, one where her own needs and rights would be considered. Magda read all the writings I recommended and was inspired to begin her own process of transformation. How would healing from the violence she had endured affect her sons, I asked? What could her sisters and *comadres* learn from her courage to hold her husband accountable?

Magda never lost compassion for her husband. She began to gain it towards herself. In the new balance that developed between obligation to others and to her own self, Magda found her voice again. As she healed her wounded spirit and reconnected to her body, she found the courage to leave her husband.

She did not want to leave him, but he refused to change. She would have stayed with him, she said, if only he would have sought treatment. But she no longer felt obligated to sacrifice herself in the service of others.

Few women who are abused have the privilege or resources to seek counseling or psychotherapy. However, if mental health providers understand the complex roots of violence among Latinos and the burden of obligation Latinas are taught to carry, perhaps they can respectfully engage with their clients to preserve the positive aspects of familism while challenging rigid notions that bind women.

As educators, we can engage with our students in a critical analysis of culture and seek ways to transform unfair expectations and behaviors into liberatory discourses and new ways of relating. This may be one small step in the transformation of a rape culture.

I want to thank Inés Hernández-Avila for her continued inspiration and Roney Miranda for showing me that love can exist without violence. To "Magda" and the hundreds of women clients, students, and friends who have given me the gift of their testimonios, *my profound appreciation.*

NOTES

1. *Magda* is a pseudonym used to protect the identity of the courageous woman whose testimony informed this essay.
2. Term used to refer to Spaniards.
3. Gerardo Marin and Barbara VanOss Marin, *Research with Hispanic Populations* (Newbury Park, Calif.: Sage, 1991).
4. Harry C. Triandis, et al., *Dimensions of Familism among Hispanics and Mainstream Navy Recruits* (Chicago: University of Illinois, 1982).

5. F. Sabogal, et al., "Hispanic Familism and Acculturation: What Changes and What Doesn't," *Hispanic Journal of Behavioral Sciences* 9 (1987): 397–412.

6. See Oliva Espin, *Latina Realities: Essays on Healing, Migration, and Sexuality* (Boulder: Westview, 1997); and Yvette Flores-Ortiz, "Voices from the Couch: The Co-Construction of a Chicana Psychology," in *Living Chicana Theory*, edited by Carla Trujillo (Berkeley: Third Woman, 1997), 102–122.

7. See Yvette Flores-Ortiz, "Broken Covenant: Incest in Latino Families," *Voces: A Journal of Chicana/Latina Studies* 1, no. 1 (1997): 48–70.

8. Yvette Flores-Ortiz, "La Mujer y la violencia," in *Chicana Critical Theory* edited by Norma Alarcon et al. (Third Woman, 1989). I argue that considering men as *pobrecitos,* poor little ones, who are not capable of handling their own feelings is a direct legacy of colonization, which positioned indigenous and mestizo men as castrated and disempowered beings. The view that women should be responsible for protecting men from their emotions and healing them from their pain is perpetuated by the notions of loyalty and abnegation, which are part of the values of familism.

9. Latina Feminist Group, *Telling to Live: Latina Feminist Testimonios* (Durham, N.C.: Duke University Press, 2001); Gloria Anzaldúa, *Borderlands/La Frontera: The New Mestiza* (San Francisco: Aunt Lute, 1999).

. . . .

YVETTE G. FLORES is a Panamanian–Costa Rican clinical psychologist. An associate professor of psychology in Chicana/o Studies at University of California–Davis, she has researched intimate partner violence among Mexicans on both sides of the border and has written extensively on Latina mental health. She is coeditor of *Telling to Live: Latina Feminist Testimonios* (Duke University Press, 2001). She lives in Berkeley, California.

MEN, MASCULINITY, AND THE RAPE CULTURE

MICHAEL KIMMEL

What is it about groups that seems to bring out the worst in men? I think it is because the animating condition for most American men is a deeply rooted fear of other men—a fear that other men will see us as weak, feminine, not manly.

NOT A WEEK GOES BY without another entry in the seemingly endless parade of men behaving badly, men who embody the seamier side of male sexuality—entitlement, predation, and violence: athletes, politicians, TV and movie stars, rappers, ordained clergy. When confronted by this parade, many men react defensively. "Men on Trial" could be the common headline linking all these disparate cases.

But it's not men on trial here; it's masculinity, or rather the traditional definition of masculinity, a definition that leads to certain behaviors that we now see as politically problematic and often physically threatening. Under prevailing definitions, men have and are the politically incorrect sex. Perhaps we should slap a warning label on penises across the land: Warning: Operating this instrument can be dangerous to your and others' health.

Why have these issues emerged now? Why are sexual harassment and date rape the particular issues we're facing? Most importantly, how can we change the meanings of masculinity so that sexual harassment and date rape will disappear from our workplaces and our relationships?

CONSTRUCTING MALE SEXUALITY

To speak of transforming masculinity is to begin with the way men are sexual in our culture. As social scientists see it, sexuality is less about biological urges and more about the meanings we attach to those urges, meanings that vary dramatically across cultures, over time, and among social groups within any particular culture. Sexual beings are made, not born. John Gagnon, a well-known theoretician of this approach, argues that people learn when they are quite young a few of the things that they are expected to be, and they continue slowly to accumulate a belief in who they are and ought to be through the rest of childhood, adolescence, and adulthood. Sexual conduct is learned in the same ways and through the same processes; it is acquired and assembled in human interaction, judged and performed in specific cultural and historical worlds.[1]

The major item in that assemblage, chief building block in the social construction of sexuality, is gender. We experience our sexual selves through a gendered prism, and the rules of masculinity and femininity are strictly enforced. Difference equals power. The difference between male and female sexuality reproduces men's power over women, and simultaneously the power of some men over other men, especially of the dominant, hegemonic form of manhood—white, straight, middle class—over marginal masculinities. Those who dare to cross over—women who are sexually adventurous and men who are sexually passive—risk being seen as gender (not sexual) nonconformists. And we all know how homophobia links gender nonconformity to homo-sexuality. The stakes are high if you don't play along.

Sexual behavior confirms manhood. It makes men feel manly. A quarter-century ago, psychologist Robert Brannon identified the four traditional rules of American manhood: (1) No sissy stuff. Men can never do anything that even remotely suggests femininity. Manhood is a relentless repudiation and devaluation of the feminine. (2) Be a big wheel. Manhood is measured by power, wealth, and success. Whoever has the most toys when he dies, wins. (3) Be a sturdy oak. Manhood depends on emotional reserve. Dependability in a crisis requires that men not reveal their feelings. And (4) Give 'em hell. Exude an aura of manly daring and aggression. Go for it. Take risks.[2]

These four rules lead to a sexuality built around accumulating partners (scoring), emotional distance, and risk-taking. The emotional distancing of the sturdy oak is considered necessary for adequate male sexual functioning, but it leads to some strange behaviors. For example, to keep from ejaculating too soon, men devise a fascinating array of distractions, such as counting, doing multiplication tables in their heads, or thinking about sports. Risk-taking is a centerpiece of male sexuality. Sex is about adventure, excitement, danger. Taking chances. *Responsibility* is a word that seldom turns up in male sexual discourse. And this, of course, has serious medical side effects: sexually transmitted diseases, the possibility of impregnation, and AIDS—currently the most gendered disease in American history. To reign in this constructed male appetite, women have been assigned the role of asexual gatekeepers; women decide, metaphorically and literally, who enters the desired garden of earthly delights and who doesn't. Women's sexual agency, women's sense of entitlement to desire, is drowned out by the incessant humming of male desire. A man's job is to wear down her resistance. Sometimes that hum can be so loud that it drowns out the actual voice of the real live woman that he's with. Men suffer from socialized deafness, a hearing impairment that strikes only when women say no.

Some campus fraternities have adapted the business text *Getting to Yes* and applied it to scoring. Some campus men's groups offer seminars to other men about how to spike women's drinks with roofies—basically using the drug Rohypnol to render women unconscious, and consequently more compliant. I'm sure I'm not the first person to point out that having sex with someone who is unconscious is closer to necrophilia than it is to sex. I wouldn't imagine you could count it on your scorecard.

WHO ARE THE REAL SEXUAL REVOLUTIONARIES?

Of course, a lot has changed along the frontiers of the sexual landscape since the 1960s. We've had a sexual revolution, after all. But as the dust settles, what emerges in fine detail is that it's been women, not men, who are our era's real sexual pioneers. We men like to think that the sexual revolution, with its promises of more access to more partners with less emotional commitment, was tailor-made for male sexuality's fullest flowering. But, in fact, it's been women's sexuality that's changed, not men's. Women now feel capable of and entitled to sexual pleasure. They have learned to say yes to their own desires, claiming, in the process, sexual agency.

And men? We're still dancing the same tired dance of the sexual conquistadors. Look, for a minute, at those late-night and cable TV shows like *The Man Show* or those men's magazines like *Maxim* or *Stuff*. Men seem to need to feel reassured that although women are working right alongside men in every conceivable field of endeavor, women are still, at heart, jiggly sexpots who fetishize consumer goods and jump on trampolines in bikinis, with oversized mammary glands not quite completely stuffed into too-tight tops. Or what about those so-called reality shows like *The Bachelor* in which women literally and symbolically prostrate themselves on the altar of masculinity to get some media-defined version of Mr. Right—handsome, rich, and vacuous—to marry them. (Even *The Bachelorette,* which pretends to reverse roles, makes women into the object of men's attraction, for which men are supposed to compete—which is hardly a role reversal. What it shows is that women are equally capable of objectifying men—not quite the revolution one might have hoped for.)

Some might argue that this simply confirms that women can have male sex, that male sexuality was victorious because we've convinced women to be more like us. But then why are so many men wilting in the face of women's desire? Why are sex therapists' offices crammed with men who complain not of premature ejaculation (the most common sexual problem in the 1970s) but of what therapists euphemistically call inhibited desire—that is, men who don't want to have sex now that all these women are able to claim their sexual rights.

And how about the legions of men now clamoring for Viagra, choosing to medicate a problem whose origins lie in their other sexual organ, their brains? (At least two-thirds of all men with erectile dysfunction experience morning erections, indicating that the problem is not with the physiological apparatus but in the message they send to that apparatus in the presence of a corporeal, desiring being.) But men look to Viagra not to help pump their erections but to revive their libidos. Many men believe that Viagra is a foolproof aphrodisiac, guaranteed to enable them to achieve functioning erections even in the absence of sexual desire. (And it is among the most successful new drugs ever to hit the global market.) It does no such thing; it enables an erection to be achieved and sustained only in the presence of desire. This dubious pharmaceutical solution may make desire actionable but it does not replace it. That would require some rethinking about what sex is and could be. Only in the most hydraulic model of male sexuality—ten inches, hard as steel, goes all night—could Viagra be seen as priming the pump.

DATE RAPE AND SEXUAL PREDATION, AGGRESSION, AND ENTITLEMENT

As women have claimed the right to say yes, they've also begun to assert their right to say no. Women are now demanding that men be more sexually responsible and they are holding men accountable for their sexual behaviors. And, yes, it is women who have changed the rules of sexual conduct. What used to be (and in many places still is) called male sexual etiquette—forcing a woman to have sex when she says no; conniving, coercing, pushing, ignoring her efforts to get him to stop; getting her so drunk that she loses the ability (or consciousness) that one needs for consent—is now defined as date rape. Charges of date rape are brought every year on campuses all over the

United States against all sorts of men, but most frequently against fraternity men (some with an enlarged sense of entitlement, like that of JFK's nephew William Kennedy Smith) and athletes. In American life, it sometimes seems as though we expect sexual aggression from athletes [see Messner, p. 23]. Barely a week goes by in which the sports pages do not tell of yet another professional athlete like Christian Peters, the former Nebraska lineman, or Randy Moss, the star receiver for the Minnesota Vikings (who was tossed off the Notre Dame team before he ever played for them because he had been accused of sexual assault in high school; he then went on to star at Marshall, where he was also accused of rape). The Center for the Study of Sport and Society at Northeastern University posts the names of all athletes accused of sexual assault, and they have to update the list weekly. And what about Latrell Sprewell, who when upset that his coach worked the team too hard in practice decided to try and strangle him? In high schools, in colleges, and on professional teams, we're getting the message that our young male athletes, trained for fearless aggression on the field, are translating that into predatory sexual aggression in relationships with women. Our task is to make it clear that what we want from our athletes when they are on the playing field is not the same as what we want from them when they are playing the field.

MEN IN GROUPS AND MASCULINE FRAGILITY

Focusing on athletes only illustrates the problem of male entitlement, which seems to flow unquestioningly to men in groups. Most athletes, after all, play on teams; much of their social life and much of their public personas are constructed through association with their teammates. At scores of campus and corporate workshops over the past fifteen years, women have shared the complaint that, while individual men may appear sympathetic when they are alone with women, they suddenly turn out to be macho louts, capable of the vilest misogynist statements, when they are in groups of other men.

What is it about groups that seem to bring out the worst in men? I think it is because the animating condition for most American men is a deeply rooted fear of other men—a fear that other men will see us as weak, feminine, not manly. The fear of humiliation, of losing in the competitive ranking among men, of being dominated by other men—these are the fears that keep men in line and that reinforce traditional notions of masculinity as a false sense of safety.

Homophobia—which appears to be the fear of homosexual men but is really the fear of other men—keeps men acting like men, keeps us exaggerating our adherence to traditional norms so that no other men will get the wrong idea that we might really be that most dreaded person of all: a sissy. Don't believe me, though. Listen to the words of my favorite contemporary gender theorist, Eminem. When asked in an interview why he uses homophobic epithets in his raps, Eminem poignantly illustrated the role of gay baiting in peer interactions. In his view, calling someone a faggot is not a slur on his sexuality but on his gender. "The lowest degrading thing that you can say to a man when you're battling him is to call him a faggot and try to take away his manhood," said America's premier rap artist. "Call him a sissy, call him a punk. 'Faggot' to me doesn't necessarily mean gay people. 'Faggot' to me just means taking away your manhood."[3]

That fear of being seen as a sissy, of being gay-baited, taunted, and bullied because one is not a real man is certainly what lies behind so much adolescent masculine risk-taking and violence. A recent survey asked high school students what they were most afraid of. The girls answered that they were most afraid of being assaulted, raped, killed. The boys? They said they were most afraid of "being laughed at." Boys laugh at each other, tease each other, make fun of each other, bully each other constantly. When we consider the myriad school shootings that have occurred between 1992 and 2002 (there have been twenty-eight cases), several constants stand out. All twenty-eight cases were committed by boys. All but one was committed by a white boy in a suburban or rural school. We speak of teen violence, youth violence, violence in the schools, but no one in the media ever seems to call it suburban white boy violence, although that is exactly what it is. Try a little thought experiment: Imagine that all the killers in the more famous school shootings in the 1990s—Littleton, Colorado; Pearl, Mississippi; Paducah, Kentucky; Springfield, Oregon; and Jonesboro, Arkansas—were black girls from poor families who lived instead in New Haven, Boston, Chicago, or Newark. Wouldn't we now be having a national debate about inner-city poor black girls? Would not the media focus entirely on race, class, and gender?

Of course it would: We'd hear about the culture of poverty; about how life in the city breeds crime and violence; about some putative natural tendency among blacks towards violence. Someone would probably even blame feminism for causing girls to become violent in vain imitation of boys. Yet the obvious fact that these school killers were all middle-class white boys seems to have escaped the media's notice, in part because race, class, or gender are only visible when speaking of those who are not privileged by race, class, and gender but invisible when speaking of those who are privileged by them—which might account for some of that media myopia. But it's not just middle-class white boys. It's something else—it's the interactions among middle-class white boys. All the boys who committed these terrible acts had stories of being bullied, beaten up, and, most significantly for this analysis, gay-baited. All seem to have stories of being mercilessly and constantly teased, picked on, and threatened. And, most strikingly, it was not because they were gay (none of them was, as far as I can tell), but because they were different from the other boys—shy, bookish, honor students, geeks, or nerds.

The prevalence of this homophobic bullying, teasing, and violence is staggering. Probably the most common put-down in America's high schools and middle schools today is "that's so gay." And as we've seen, it has less to do with sexual orientation than it does with gender. Boys act as the gender police, making sure that other boys stay in line.

Men's fears of being judged failures as men in the eyes of other men leads often to a certain homosocial element within any heterosexual encounter: Men often will use their sexual conquests as a form of currency to gain status among other men. Such homosocial competition contributes to the strange hearing impairment that leads us to hear "no" as "yes," to escalate an encounter, to always go for it, to score. And this is occurring just as women are learning to say yes to their own desires, to hear their own voices. Instead of our socialized deafness, we need to become what Langston Hughes called "articulate listeners": we need to trust women to tell us what they want, when they want it, and what they don't want as well. And we need to listen to our own inner voices, our own real desires and needs. Not the voices that are about constantly proving something that cannot be proved, but the voices that are about connection with another and the desires and passions that can happen between two equals.

SAVING THE MALES

If men are afraid of what other men will think of them, they're also afraid of what women will do to them—just by their presence. Supporters of the male-only admissions policy at the Citadel distributed buttons that said "Save the Males!"—as if the very presence of women on campus would dilute the mystical bonding that takes place among the male cadets. Imagine a masculinity so fragile, so threatened, so besieged that the mere presence of a woman would make proving manhood impossible!

That also seems to be the fear that William (Hootie) Johnson expressed in his intransigent refusal to allow women to become members of Augusta National Golf Club. When their male-only policy was exposed by Martha Burk, the chair of the National Council of Women's Organizations, Hootie's growling resistance reminded me of those southern military schools: baffled by why women would want to join in the first place and gruffly resistant to allowing them to do so. Here was the head of the nation's premier country club, the site of its most prestigious golf tournament, acting like the Little Rascals defending their all-boy clubhouse with a hand-painted wooden sign that said, "No Gurls Allowed."

What could possibly be so scary about women's presence? I'll give you a hint: It isn't their presence. There are plenty of women at the Citadel (and at the Virginia Military Institute, another military academy that fought court orders to admit women); they cook the food and serve it, they clean the barracks and teach the classes, and they are graduate students and counselors. And there are plenty of women at Augusta National. Just who do you think serves all those cocktails at the nineteenth hole? Who serves the meals, prepares the food, makes the beds in the guest rooms? Women are all over the place—they are just not allowed to wear the fabled cadet uniform or the heralded green blazer. It's not women's presence that is threatening to men; it's their equality.

FROM THE BEDROOM TO THE BOARDROOM

Men's fear of and opposition to women's equality is found frequently in the workplace. Male doctors rarely are upset by female nurses or administrators, just by female doctors; male corporate executives don't mind female secretaries, just female colleagues. But they'd better get used to it, because women have utterly transformed the public arena, the workplace. As is true of sexuality, the real economic transformation of the late twentieth century was women's dramatic entry into the labor force in unprecedented numbers. While many working-class white women and women of color have always worked, middle-class white women have entered the workforce in such numbers that men had better get used to having them around.

That means that the cozy boys' club—a.k.a. the workplace—has been penetrated by women, and just when that arena is more suffused with doubt and anxiety than ever before. In a downwardly spiraling economy, the current generation of college students are themselves downwardly mobile. The fastest growing job category in the U.S. economy is not dot-com millionaire; of all the jobs created in the decade from 2000 to 2010, more than four-fifths will be in entry-level service and sales jobs. Most Americans are less successful than their parents were at the same age, and this will continue for their entire working lives. It takes two incomes to earn what one income earned in the early seventies (the actual income of a family of four in the United States in 2003, in constant dollars, was about eight hundred dollars less than what it was in 1973). Most middle-class Americans cannot afford to buy the house in which they grew up.

We are a nation of fewer and fewer big wheels and more and more men who feel they have to prove themselves, who feel damaged, injured, powerless. And now here come women into that arena in unprecedented numbers. It is virtually impossible for a man to go through his entire working life without a woman colleague, coworker, or supervisor. Just when our breadwinner status is most threatened, women appear on the scene as easy targets for men's anger. This may help explain men's defensiveness and resistance to women's equality in the workplace: It feels like a loss to us. This potent combination of women's increased entry into the workplace, men's declining fortunes, and men's sense of entitlement is what I often think of as the political economy of sexual harassment. I'm not referring to the less common form of quid pro quo harassment, by which sex is exchanged or demanded in return for promotions, hiring, or other job perks, but the far more pervasive hostile environment, in which women are reminded that although they may be in the workplace, they still don't belong there, it's really a man's world. The

placing of sexual harassment on the national agenda affords men a rare opportunity to do some serious soul searching. What is sexual harassment about?
And why is it in men's interests to help end it?

Sexual harassment cases are difficult and confusing precisely because one
often finds a multiplicity of truths. His truth might be that he gave an innocent indication of sexual interest or made a harmless joke with the boys in the
office (even if those "boys" happen to include women workers). Her truth is
that his remarks cause stress, anxiety about promotion and firing, and sexual
pressure.

Women and men often experience the same event differently. Men experience their behavior from the perspective of those who have power, women
from the perspective of those upon whom that power is exercised.

If an employer asks an employee for a date and she declines, he may forget about it by the time he gets to the parking lot. "No big deal," he says to
himself. "You ask someone out and she says no. You forget about it." In fact,
repairing a wounded male ego often requires that we forget about it. But the
female employee? She's now frozen, partly with fear. "What if I said yes?"
she asks herself. "Would I have gotten promoted? Would he have expected
more than a date? Will I now get fired? Will someone else get promoted over
me? What should I do?" And so she does what millions of women do in that
situation: She calls her friends, who counsel her to let the matter rest and get
on with her work. And she remembers, for a long time. Who, therefore, is
likely to have a better memory: those in power or those against whom that
power is deployed?

Using one's position to hit on women (arguably what President Clinton
did, both in the White House and when he was governor of Arkansas) is
the kernel of what is objectionable about sexual harassment. It's particularly
volatile because it fuses two levels of power: the power of employers over
employees and the power of men over women. Thus what may be said or
intended as a man to a woman is also experienced in the context of superior and subordinate. Sexual harassment in the workplace results from men
using their public position to demand or extract social relationships. It is
the confusion of public and private, bringing together two arenas of men's
power over women. Not only are men in positions of power in the workplace,
but we are socialized to be the sexual initiators and to see sexual prowess as a
confirmation of masculinity.

Sexual harassment is also a way to remind women that they are not yet equals in the workplace, that they really don't belong there. Harassment is most frequent in occupations (such as surgeon, firefighter, and investment banker) or in workplaces where women are new and in the minority. "Men see women as invading a masculine environment," says Louise Fitzgerald, a University of Illinois psychologist. "These are guys whose sexual harassment has nothing whatever to do with sex. They're trying to scare women off a male preserve."

When the power of men is augmented by the power of employer over employee, it is easy to understand how humiliating and debilitating sexual harassment can be, and how individual women would be frightened about seeking redress. The workplace is not a level playing field. Subordinates rarely have the resources to complain against managers, whatever the problem.

Although men surely do benefit from sexual harassment, I believe that we also have a stake in ending it. First, our ability to form positive and productive relationships with women colleagues in the workplace is undermined. So long as sexual harassment is a daily occurrence and women are afraid of their superiors in the workplace, innocent men's behaviors may be misinterpreted. Second, men's ability to develop social and sexual relationships that are both ethical and exciting is also compromised. If a male boss dates a subordinate, can he really trust that the reason she is with him is because she wants to be? Or will there always be a lingering doubt that she is there because she is afraid not to be, or that she seeks to please him because of his position? As men, we should work to end sexual harassment. It is more important than ever to desexualize the workplace, and to begin to listen to women—to listen with a compassion that understands that women's and men's experiences are different, and understands that men, too, can benefit from the elimination of sexual harassment.

AIDS AS A MEN'S DISEASE

Surely, men will benefit from the eradication of AIDS. Although we rarely think about HIV in this way, we need to hold this disease up to the gender lens, to see it through the prism of masculinity. AIDS is one of American men's chief health problems, among the primary causes of death for men aged thirty-five to forty-four, and AIDS is also perhaps the most gendered disease in American history. No other disease has ever attacked one gender so disproportionately except those diseases, like hemophilia, that are sex linked (to which only males or females are susceptible). AIDS could affect both men and women equally, and throughout the rest of the world (except the United States, western Europe, and Canada) the rates of infection reach gender parity; that is, of the 80 percent of HIV infections worldwide, half affect women and half men. And remember, in unprotected heterosexual intercourse, women are more at risk for HIV transmission than men. But in the United States, more than 85 percent of people with AIDS are men.

Let me be clear that in no way am I saying that one should not have compassion for women AIDS patients. Of course one must recognize that women are as likely to get AIDS from engaging in the same high-risk behaviors as men. But that's precisely my point. Women don't engage in those behaviors at rates anything like men.

One is put at risk for AIDS by engaging in specific high-risk behaviors—activities that ignore potential health risks for more immediate pleasures. For example, sharing needles is both a defiant flaunting of health risks and an expression of community among I.V. drug users. And the capacity for high-risk behavior—unprotected anal intercourse with large numbers of partners, the ability to take it, despite any potential pain—is also a confirmation of masculinity.

The victims of men's adherence to these norms of masculinity—AIDS patients, rape victims, victims of sexual harassment—did not become victims intentionally. They did not ask for it, and they certainly do not deserve blame. That some women today are also sexual predators, going to swank bars or waiting outside athletes' locker rooms or trying to score with male subordinates at work, doesn't make William Kennedy Smith, Mike Tyson, Magic Johnson, Randy Moss, or Bill Clinton any less predatory.

And the men—the date rapists, the sexual harassers, the AIDS patients—are not perverts or deviants who have strayed from the norms of masculinity. They are, if anything, overconformists to destructive norms of male sexual behavior. Until we change the meaning of manhood, sexual risk-taking and conquest will remain part of the rhetoric of masculinity. And we will scatter the victims, both women and men, along the wayside.

THE SEXUAL POLITICS OF SAFETY

What links all these struggles—against sexual harassment, date and acquaintance rape, and HIV—is that all of them require a sexual politics of safety. The politics of safety may be the missing link in the transformation of men's lives, in their capacity for change. Safety is more than the absence of danger, although that isn't such a bad thing either. Safety is proactive, the creation of a space in which all people, women and men, gay and straight, and of all colors, can experience the fullness of their beings, can work to their potential, and can express themselves fully.

Think for a moment about how the politics of safety affects the three areas I have discussed in this essay. What is the best way to prevent AIDS? To use sterile needles for intravenous drug injections and to practice safer sex. Sterile needles and safer sex share one basic characteristic: They both require that men act responsibly. This is not one of the cardinal rules of manhood. Safer sex programs encourage men to have fewer partners, to avoid certain particularly dangerous practices, and to use condoms when having any sex involving the exchange of bodily fluids. In short, safer sex programs encourage men to stop having sex like men. To men, *safer sex* is an oxymoron, one of those juxtapositions of terms that produce a nonsensical outcome. That which is sexy is not safe; that which is safe is not sexy. Sex is about danger, risk, excitement; safety is about comfort, softness, security.

Seen this way, it is not surprising to find, as some researchers have, that one-fourth of urban gay men report that they have not changed their unsafe sexual behaviors. What is, in fact, astonishing is that slightly more than three-fourths have changed and are now practicing safer sex.

What heterosexual men could learn from the gay community's response to AIDS is how to eroticize that responsibility—something women have been trying to teach men for decades. Making safer sex into sexy sex has been one of the great transformations of male sexuality accomplished by the gay community. And straight men could also learn a thing or two about caring for one another through illness, supporting one another in grief, and maintaining a resilience in the face of a devastating disease and the callous indifference of the larger society.

Safety is also the animating condition for women's expression of sexuality.

While safety may be a turnoff for men (*comfort, softness,* and *security* are the terms of postorgasmic detumescence, not sexual arousal), safety is a precondition for sexual agency for women. Only when women feel safe can they give their sexuality full expression.

This helps explain that curious finding in the sex research literature about the divergence of women's and men's sexualities as they age. Men are believed to reach their sexual peak at around eighteen and then go into steady, and later more precipitous, decline for the rest of their lives; women hit their sexual stride closer to thirty, with the years between twenty-seven and thirty-eight as their peak years. Typically, we understand these changes as having to do with differences in biology—that hormonal changes find men feeling soft and cuddly just as women are getting all steamed up. But aging does not produce such changes in every culture; that is, biology doesn't seem to work the same way everywhere.

What biological explanations leave out is the way men's and women's sexualities are related to each other, and the way both are shaped by the institution of marriage. Marriage makes one's sexuality more predictable—the partner, the timing, the experience—and it places sex always in the context of the marital relationship. Marriage makes sex safer. No wonder women find their sexuality heightening—they finally feel safe enough to allow their sexual desires to be expressed. And no wonder men's sexuality deflates—there's no danger, risk, or excitement left.

Safety is a precondition for women's sexual expression. Only when a woman is certain, beyond the shadow of a doubt, that her no means no can she ever say yes to her own sexual desires. So if we men are going to have the sexual relationships with exciting, desiring women that we say we want, then we have to make the environment safe enough for women to express their desires. We have to make it absolutely certain to a woman that her no means no—no matter how urgently we feel the burning of our own desires.

To do this we will need to transform the definition of what it means to be a real man. But we have to work fast. AIDS is spreading rapidly, and date rape and sexual harassment are epidemic in the nation's colleges and workplaces. As AIDS spreads, and as women speak up about these issues, more and more people need our compassion and support. Yet compassion is in relatively short supply among American men, since it involves the capacity to take the role of the other, to put ourselves in someone else's shoes, a capacity that contradicts the manly independence we have so carefully cultivated.

Sexual democracy, like political democracy, relies on a balance between rights and responsibilities, between the claims of the individual and the claims of the community. When one discusses sexual rights—the idea that each person, every woman and man, has an equal right to pleasure—men understand immediately what you mean. Women often look delighted and a bit surprised. Add to the Bill of Sexual Rights a notion of responsibility, in which we all treat sexual partners as if they had an integrity equal to our own, and it's the men who look puzzled. "Responsibility? What's that got to do with sex? I thought sex was about having fun."

Sure it is, but it's also political in the most intimate sense. Sexual democracy doesn't have to mean no sex. It means treating your partner as someone whose lust is equal to yours and also as someone whose life is equally valuable. It's about enacting in daily life our principles, claiming our rights to pleasure, and making sure that our partners also feel safe enough to fully claim theirs. This is what we demand for those who have come to America seeking refuge—safety—from political tyranny. Could we ask any less for those who are now asking for protection and refuge from millennia of sexual tyranny?

CODA

It's been ten years since I wrote the first draft of this essay—ten years in which dramatic progress has been matched by equally dramatic setbacks. Even though there has been a noticeable increase in the number of men who are active in these campaigns—men who organized campus groups against sexual assault, rape, harassment; men who organized programming for other men to engage them in these efforts—the majority of men continue to believe that transforming a rape culture is women's work.

And why shouldn't they believe it? After all, most of the programming we do around sexual assault and date rape on campus focuses entirely on the women. To be sure, we tell the men, "Don't do it, or else." But that's often the end of the conversation with men. The women are much better prepared. We tell them what to wear and what not to wear, what parties they can safely go to and which to avoid, what to drink and what not to drink, how late to stay out and how to get themselves home. We tell them always to go to parties with a trusted friend, never to lose eye contact, even to follow each other into the bathroom, and be sure to taste each other's drinks.

Now let me be completely clear here: Women must do all these things to reduce their risk of sexual assault. But what such programs imply about men is that unless women do all these things, unless women utterly compromise their liberties, remain eternally vigilant, and modify their activities, we men will act like out-of-control animals who will be all over them in an instant. By pitching our programs entirely to women, we assume an utterly unsavory—and unfair—view of men as no better than testosterone-crazed sexual predators.

I think we men can do better than this. Part of transforming a rape culture means transforming masculinity, encouraging and enabling men to make other choices about what we do with our bodies, insisting that men utilize their own agency to make different sorts of choices. To ignore men, to believe that women alone will transform a rape culture, freezes men in a posture of defensiveness, defiance, and immobility.

Nowhere is this better expressed than on a splash guard that a colleague devised for Rape Awareness Week at his university and that I have been bringing with me to campuses around the country. For those who don't know, a splash guard is the plastic grate placed in public urinals to prevent splatter. These simple devices are placed in urinals all over campus. This one comes with a helpful little slogan: "You hold the power to stop rape in your hand."

NOTES

. . . .

1. John Gagnon, *Human Sexualities* (Glenview, Ill.: Scott, Foresman, 1977).

2. Robert Brannon, in the introduction to *The Forty-nine Percent Majority,* edited by Robert Brannon and Deborah S. David (Reading, Mass.: Addison, Wesley, 1976).

3. Richard Kim, quoting an interview between MTV's Kurt Loder and Eminem, in *The Nation* (March 5, 2001): 4.

4. Carol Iaciofano, in a book review of *The Two-Income Trap: Why Middle-Class Mothers and Fathers Are Going Broke* by Elizabeth Warren and Amelia Warren Tyagi, *Boston Globe* (November 19, 2003).

. . . .

MICHAEL KIMMEL is professor of sociology at State University of New York–Stony Brook. Some of the more recent of his many books include *The Politics of Manhood* (Temple University Press,

1996), *Manhood: A Cultural History* (Free Press, 1996), and *The Gendered Society* (Oxford University Press, 2nd edition, 2003). He edits *Men and Masculinities,* an interdisciplinary scholarly journal, a book series on Men and Masculinity at the University of California Press, and the Sage Series on Men and Masculinities. He is the spokesperson for the National Organization for Men against Sexism (NOMAS) and lectures extensively on campuses in the United States and abroad.

HOW RAPE IS ENCOURAGED IN AMERICAN BOYS AND WHAT WE CAN DO TO STOP IT

. . . .

MYRIAM MIEDZIAN

In order to significantly decrease violence, including rape, we must begin to protect boys from violent entertainment and to teach them, from the youngest age, to view themselves as future nurturing, nonviolent, responsible fathers.

I N THE MID 1980s, when a University of Florida administrator was asked to comment on the high rates of gang rape on college campuses, he responded, "The men almost cannot say no, because if they do their masculinity will be in question."[1] In her book, *Fraternity Gang Rape*, Peggy Sanday, a University of Pennsylvania professor of anthropology, commented that "those men who object to this kind of behavior run the risk of being labeled 'wimps' or, even worse in their eyes, 'gays' or 'faggots.'"[2]

Since 1994, violent crime rates including rape have declined from the extremely high rates of the late eighties and early nineties. According to the most conservative estimates available 102,600 women were raped in 1990 and 90,178 in 2000.[3]

Surely, a minimum of 90,000 women raped in one year is not something to celebrate. If we are serious about significantly and permanently decreasing our rape rates, we must move men, and especially young boys, away from a definition of masculinity that centers on toughness, power, dominance, eagerness to fight, lack of empathy, and a callous attitude towards women. For as long as these values (which I refer to as the masculine mystique) prevail among many men, rape will continue to be viewed by them as proof that they are one of the boys, that they are "real men."

When dominance and power define masculinity, men rape as a way of putting "uppity" women in their place. Many men feel deeply threatened by the achievements of the women's movement. Some react to the greater freedom, independence, and power of women with rage and violence, including rape, battering, and killing. Masculinity must be redefined to include caring, nurturance, and empathy along with such traditionally masculine attributes as courage, strength, initiative, and adventurousness.

Since the early 1990s American society has moved in conflicting directions with respect to changing the concept of masculinity. I shall survey the positive changes first, and then the negative ones. When the first edition of my book, *Boys Will Be Boys*, was published in 1991, only one book about raising boys was on the market—a traditional child-rearing guide for parents of boys up to age eight. Since the mid-1990s, more than twenty books on raising boys and a few books on boys and violence have been published, which must be seen as a mostly positive development. Some, like Harvard psychologist William Pollack's 1998 *Real Boys*, contain recommendations that can only lead to decreases in violent behavior. With some exceptions, even those that accept much of traditional masculinity still encourage caring, nonviolent fathering, and the expression of positive emotions such as empathy and love.

As we shall see, the involvement of a loving, nonviolent father in the daily care of his children is an important factor in moving towards a more empathic, caring and less violent masculinity.

Many American fathers have become more involved in raising their children. A study of fifteen core values shared by newlywed couples, carried out by Joseph Pleck at the University of Illinois, indicated that coparenting rose from eleventh place in 1986 to second place in 1997. In his book *Fatherneed,* published in 2000, Yale psychiatrist Kyle Pruett tells us that father care has become as common as "all forms of day care combined."[4] According to surveys conducted by the Families and Work Institute of New York, in 1977 working fathers spent 55 percent of the time that working mothers did providing child care during the week. By 1997, this proportion had risen to 77 percent. As the authors of the study point out, the results might be biased "by respondents' views of what is socially desirable."[5] Nevertheless, there can be no doubt that in a large percentage of dual-parent families, fathers are considerably more involved than they were in the past. This augurs well as long as fathers are modeling caring, nonviolent behavior.

On the negative side, while fathers in dual-parent families are much more involved in the care of their children, the proportion of births to single mothers continues to grow. In 1990, it was 26.6 percent of all births. By 1998, it was 32.8 percent. Among African Americans it has gone from 66.7 percent to 69.1 percent.[6] More and more boys are growing up without fathers in the home, and often without any positive male role models in their lives.

The other factor operating against a more enlightened concept of masculinity in our unprecedented age of advanced technology is that boys and men are presented with endless violent, sadistic, rapist male role models by the media.

In order to significantly decrease violence, including rape, we must begin to protect boys from violent entertainment and to teach them, from the youngest age, to view themselves as future nurturing, nonviolent, responsible fathers. As we shall see, in doing so we would be encouraging all men, including those who never become fathers, to move away from the values of the masculine mystique.

ENTERTAINMENT

Surrounded by TV, films, videos, disks, tapes, Walkmans, video games, and computers, children today spend more time being entertained than they spend with their parents or in school. According to the American Psychological Association, the average child has watched eight thousand televised murders—most of them committed by males—before finishing elementary school. The number more than doubles by the time he or she reaches age eighteen. A major part of our children's socialization now lies in the hands of the entertainment business, where the primary goal is not to help cut down on rates of rape or other forms of violence but maximizing profit.

By the late 1980s, more than 235 studies had been done on the effects of viewing violence on the screen. Several surveys of these studies, including one by the National Institute of Mental Health, concluded that a vast majority showed that viewing violence puts children at higher risk of committing acts of violence. In the 1990s, the American Psychological Association and the American Academy of Pediatrics, among others, arrived at the same conclusion.

The catharsis hypothesis, according to which viewing violence helps viewers get violent impulses out of their system, is mistaken. Seeing women being raped or threatened with rape desensitizes male viewers and facilitates rape. For example, in their book *The Question of Pornography,* psychologists Edward Donnerstein, Daniel Linz, and Steven Penrod describe a research study in which they sought to test the desensitizing qualities of horror/slasher films. These films graphically depict people being dismembered, chopped up, burned alive, raped, or endlessly threatened with rape. Some of the victims were men, but the plot emphasis was usually the pursuit of one or more young women.

For the study, fifty-two men were chosen out of a larger group because they seemed *"least likely to become desensitized"* [my emphasis]. They were then shown one film a day for five days. Changes occurred in the men's evaluation of how violent, degrading, and offensive scenes were. Material that the men had earlier found anxiety provoking and depressing became less so. After being exposed to large doses of filmed violence against women, they judged that female victims of assault and rape were less injured than did men in a control group. They were less able to empathize with real-life rape victims. The authors point out that the frequent juxtaposition in horror/ slasher films of extremely violent scenes with relaxing music or mildly erotic scenes is similar to the techniques used in desensitization therapy to get people to engage in behavior that previously provoked severe anxiety: Anxiety-provoking stimuli are combined with stimuli that promote relaxation.

Desensitization to violence and rape starts at a very early age. While Hollywood seems to be focusing less on the horror/slasher genre than it did in the late 1980s and more on violence-filled action films, horror films still remain popular with young boys. The 1980s favorites such as *Nightmare on Elm Street* and *Friday the 13th* were replaced in the 1990s with gore-filled series like *Scream*. *Halloween,* begun in 1978, continued with its eighth installment in 2002. In addition, the old-time favorites remain available at video stores.

These films have always been rated R, but in a report released in September 2000 the Federal Trade Commission revealed that of forty-four R-rated films examined by the agency, thirty-five were consciously aimed at and marketed to teenagers under the age of seventeen. In response, the National Association of Theater Owners urged its members not to allow underage theatergoers into R-rated films. Although this has led to some increase in enforcement, it is unlikely that even this small improvement will last long since, unlike the situation in European countries, our film ratings are not buttressed by law.

If these films desensitize even men who were chosen because they seemed "least likely to become desensitized," one can imagine the effect they might have on some of the millions of boys and men in the United States who are at more than average risk for violence due to physical conditions such as mild mental retardation, a severe learning disability, or attention-deficit/ hyperactivity disorder. What about men suffering from serious emotional disorders? Not only do these films desensitize, they also serve as detailed, gruesome blueprints for violence. Even if only a small percentage of these men are affected, the results are disastrous.

In addition to the results of studies on viewing violence, we know from child-development research that children learn by imitating those they admire. So-called adventure films (they are in fact nonstop violence films), starring, among others, Arnold Schwarzenegger, Steven Seagal, and Jean-Claude Van Damme, encourage boys to associate masculinity with dominance and power and to accept violence as a normal response to conflict, anger, or frustration. These older heroes are slowly being replaced by younger men like Vin Diesel and rapper DMX.

Some heavy metal and rap lyrics encourage young boys to connect sex with dominance, violence, and rape. Different performers are popular now than in the late eighties and early nineties, but very little has changed with respect to the violent content. Around 1990, the rap group 2 Live Crew was popular. One of its songs, "Dick Almighty," included the lyrics, "He'll tear the pussy open, 'cause it's satisfaction. . . . Suck my dick, bitch, it'll make you puke."

At a 1999 concert by rage rock band Limp Bizkit, the group performed a song called "Break Stuff," which included the lyrics: "I pack a chainsaw . . . I skin your ass raw / I just might / . . . break your fucking face tonight." During the performance, a woman was allegedly raped. By the end of the concert, gang rapes, looting, and fire were reported.

In sports, fistfights, dirt throwing, and verbal insults are common among professional and even college athletes. Much of this behavior appears on TV and is viewed by young boys. A substantial number of sports heroes have been charged with rape. In a study of athletes at National Collegiate Athletic Association schools, sports researchers Jeff Benedict and Todd Crosset found that between 1991 and 1993 male athletes who represented 3 percent of the student body were responsible for almost 20 percent of sexual assaults.[7] In his 1997 book, *Public Heroes, Private Felons,* Benedict informs us that "in 1995 and 1996 alone, 199 athletes were charged with physical or sexual attacks on women."[8] For many athletes, and for millions of men who played competitive sports as children, training in violence and the denigration of women (and gay men) starts early [see Messner, p. 23].

Far too often in youth and high school sports, boys insult each other by yelling "girl," "wuss" (a cross between woman and pussy), or "faggot." Already at this level, some coaches encourage winning at any cost and an obsessive concern with dominance. Too often the result is scoring at any cost with girls and women. An extreme example of this was the Lakewood, California, Spur Posse gang. It was revealed in 1993 that these current and former high school boys, mostly athletes, were involved in a sex for points competition which allegedly included raping and molesting some young girls.

By the year 2000, some positive steps had been taken to move away from the winning at any cost mentality and to refocus youth sports as a character-building activity. At Stanford University the Positive Coaching Alliance and at Notre Dame the Mendelson Center for Sport, Character, and Culture were formed with this goal.

In the late 1980s video games were becoming popular. By 2002 they brought in $10 billion in revenue. Many are violence filled and serve to further desensitize boys and men.[9]

The development of the Internet has made violent and child pornography easily available to young boys. The National Institutes of Health has commissioned a five-year study on the effect on children of viewing raw images of sexual violence on the Web. In all probability, its effects will be found to be no different from those already confirmed with respect to TV and film violence. Chat rooms permit adults looking for illegal sexual partners to meet curious children, both girls and boys; this has opened up a whole new danger area. Among the most chilling stories, in March 2002, a twenty-five-year-old Connecticut man pleaded guilty to charges of sexual assault and manslaughter in the death of a thirteen-year-old girl he met on the Internet.[10]

Filters, which are improving in quality, can help parents protect their children. Informal interviews with librarians lead me to believe that as filters become more discriminating most libraries will no longer object to their use.

Because of their abhorrence of censorship, many well-intentioned Americans, including some feminists, continue to ignore the strong evidence that this kind of entertainment plays an important role in encouraging violence. Even Donnerstein, Linz, and Penrod, whose research was discussed earlier, are so concerned about censorship that in discussing this issue they downplay the implications of their own and others' research lest it lead to the conclusion that some regulation is desirable. All these First Amendment buffs fail to distinguish between censorship aimed at adults and regulations to protect minors.

When I researched *Boys Will Be Boys,* it became clear to me that to significantly decrease our rates of male violence we must begin to treat American children as a precious national resource rather than a commercial market. In the course of developing recommendations for the protection of children from an exploitative culture of violence, I consulted with four First Amendment law professors. They pointed out that we have a long legal tradition of regulations to protect children, including liquor, child labor, and pornography laws, and that laws to protect children from violent entertainment would be in that tradition. Unlike laws aimed at adults, they would have an excellent chance of passing Supreme Court review.

I strongly recommend that with respect to films, videos, disks, and toys, we begin to adopt regulations of the kind that already exist in many European countries, including Sweden, Belgium, and Germany. In these countries, governmental regulations and serious penalties for infractions keep movie theater owners from allowing children to see gratuitously violent films.

When it comes to television, legal experts advised me that attempts to regulate content to protect children would be very unlikely to pass Supreme Court muster because such regulations interfere with the First Amendment rights of adults. I therefore recommend a major educational campaign (similar to public health campaigns to discourage cigarette smoking) to make parents aware of the effects of viewing TV violence on their children. Parents should also be urged to acquire parental-control devices which permit them to program their TV sets so they can control what their children watch. Just like safety belts and safety seats for children in cars, they should eventually become mandatory with the sale of every TV set.

To complement parental-control devices, we need to create a Children's Public Broadcasting System with two channels, one for younger and one for older children, dedicated to top-quality TV programming that is entertaining, prosocial, nonsexist, devoid of gratuitous violence, and appealing to children of all social classes.

RAISING BOYS TO BE NURTURING FATHERS

A growing number of psychoanalytically oriented psychologists and sociologists, Dorothy Dinnerstein and Nancy Chodorow among them, analyze the difficult psychological process through which boys, who are almost all raised primarily by women, develop a masculine identity. These boys' primary identification is with their mother or female caretaker. When they begin to realize that they are not like her, that they will not be able to grow breasts, have a baby, or nurse it, their efforts to develop a male identity often include depreciating and rejecting everything feminine and embracing the qualities of the masculine mystique.

These observations are supported by sociological studies showing that while most single mothers succeed in raising decent sons, a disproportionate percentage of violent boys come from fatherless homes with no consistently present male figure they can identify with and model themselves on. Sociologists use the term *hypermasculinity* to describe the extreme concern of these boys with proving their masculinity.

Crosscultural anthropological studies indicate that violent behavior is often characteristic of males in cultures where fathers are absent or play a minor role in their sons' early rearing. In these cultures, boys are usually taken away from the women after a certain age and put through often excruciatingly painful and desensitizing initiation rites intended to turn them into "real men." Like sociologists, anthropologists have concluded that boys raised by women alone, or mainly by women, often lack a primary sense of masculine identity. In order to develop such an identity, many of them reject everything feminine and embrace *protest masculinity.*

In our society, the greater tendency toward violence on the part of fatherless boys is exacerbated by our culture of violence, which surrounds them with violent and often sadistic male role models and desensitizes them to violent, rapist behavior. Boys raised with nurturing, involved fathers develop a primary male identity. They identify with and model themselves on their fathers from the youngest age. They do not need to prove that they are "real men" by rejecting everything considered feminine, by being tough and violent. Their model of masculinity includes nurturance, caring, and empathy, which they experienced from their fathers. If there is no father, the presence of an involved, caring uncle, grandfather, male friend, or Big Brother can be a great benefit.

A twenty-six-year longitudinal study of empathy lends further support to the importance of an involved father in deterring violence.[11] Researchers found that the single factor most closely linked to the development of empathy in boys (and girls) was the level of paternal involvement in child care. Empathy is inversely related to violence.

Nurturant fathering has another beneficial side effect. A mother who raises her children together with their father is far less likely to be overwhelmed, both financially and emotionally, by the enormous demands of child rearing and is less likely to physically abuse her children. Boys who are battered by either their father or mother are more likely to become violent. If they have been abused by their mothers, wife battering, murder, and rape can be expressions of early rage and a form of revenge. In the words of one rapist, "My sisters asked me why I raped and I told 'em I wanted to hurt you females in my family, just like I'd been hurt. They knew my real mom abandoned me and that my first stepmom beat the hell out of me all the time."[12]

At the deepest psychic level, the completely helpless, dependent baby experiences the person who fulfills its needs as all powerful. It follows that as long as only women fulfill the needs of young children, men's emotional reactions to women will be overdetermined. The rapist quoted above is aware of the displacement of his early anger, but many men are unaware that their rage at and violence toward women grows out of often repressed early feelings of rage at their mothers. The desensitization and violent role models furnished by the media often facilitate the transition from anger to action.

We are the least child oriented of any advanced industrialized country, which only aggravates the problem of mother-directed rage. Lack of sufficient parental leave (some European countries offer a year or more) and flexible work hours, lack of quality day care and after-school programs, and lack of adequate medical care leave us with millions of angry, neglected young children and older latchkey children. All of this is aggravated in the case of working mothers who are single.

To significantly decrease our violence rates, including those for rape, we must do everything possible to encourage nurturing, nonviolent, responsible fathering (and mothering) and to create a society that genuinely values children and helps parents in the all-important task of child rearing.

Probably the single most effective intervention would be the introduction of mandatory child-rearing classes in our schools, starting at the very latest in fifth grade. In the course of searching for programs that would discourage violence for boys, I visited parenting classes at a private school and at several inner-city elementary, junior high, and high schools, where many, if not most, children are fatherless. Before observing these programs, I was skeptical about their impact on boys. My research had made me aware that by first grade many boys consider anything having to do with babies to be girls' stuff and won't go near it. My hunch was that most of the boys wouldn't be very interested. I was therefore all the more amazed by the level of interest and enthusiasm demonstrated by virtually every boy, regardless of race, ethnicity, or social class. I came away convinced that most boys are as capable of being interested in and involved with children and child rearing as girls. Unfortunately, our culture discourages this interest and involvement from the youngest age.

When classes in child rearing are mandatory, boys are given permission to express that interest. The elementary and junior high school child-rearing program I visited centers on a mature parent bringing a baby or toddler to class once a month. Students observe the child's behavior, interact with the child, and ask questions about what it is like to be a parent. They keep a chart of the child's progress and keep a workbook to encourage observation, psychological insight, and sensitivity. In the high school classes, teachers impart basic knowledge about child development to juniors and seniors at an appropriately sophisticated level.

These programs in child rearing deter violence in three ways: They encourage nurturing, caring, informed fathering; they make boys feel that empathy, sensitivity, and caring are acceptable—even desirable—male qualities; and they strongly discourage child battering. Sons of single teenage mothers are at particularly high risk for violence. Teachers and administrators involved in the programs report a decrease in teenage pregnancy. When girls and boys fully understand the awesome demands of responsible parenting, they decide to put off having children until they are financially and emotionally better able to deal with the responsibility.

In terms of public policy, if all women and men, including those in positions of political power, had taken child-rearing classes when they were in elementary and high school, we would be a society imbued with a much deeper sense of the importance of good parenting and far more willing to provide support for it.

It will not be easy to bring about programs that encourage caring, nurturance, and empathy in boys. Only if large numbers of Americans pressure their state legislators and school boards to appropriate funds and develop child-rearing classes is there any hope. It will be even more difficult to effect the changes necessary to protect children from a culture of violence that encourages rape, battering, and murder. Only the most intense and persistent pressure on legislators could turn protective regulations, mandatory parental control devices, and a Children's Public Broadcasting System into a reality.

The school programs, recommendations for protecting children from violence in entertainment, and research studies referred to in this essay are described in detail and discussed at length in the revised edition of my book Boys Will Be Boys: Breaking the Link Between Masculinity and Violence *(New York: Lantern 2002). Publication of the first edition of* Boys Will Be Boys *in 1991 led to the creation of The Parenting Project, a nonprofit organization whose goal is to promote the teaching of child rearing in all U.S schools. In 2002, the organization published a guide,* Preparing Tomorrow's Parents Today, *which contains detailed information concerning all aspects of teaching child rearing, including lists and descriptions of existing programs. For information go to www.parentingproject.org.*

In Canada, a child-rearing program, Roots of Empathy, was introduced in 1996 in Toronto schools. As of 2004, it was being used in 722 classrooms in eight Canadian provinces and was in the process of further expansion. For information, go to www.rootsofempathy.org.

NOTES

1. "Gang Rape: A Rising Campus Concern," *New York Times,* February 17, 1986.
2. Peggy Reeves Sanday, *Fraternity Gang Rape* (New York: New York University Press, 1990), 11.
3. These figures are from the 2001 FBI Uniform Crime Reports (Washington, D.C.: Department of Justice) and they include only rapes reported to the police. According to the 2001 National Crime Victimization Survey (Washington, D.C.: Department of Justice), which is based on interviews with women, there were 92,000 rapes, 55,000 attempted rapes, and 114,000 sexual assaults in 2000.
4. Kyle Pruett, *Fatherneed* (New York: Free Press, 2000), 1; Pleck's findings are also reported in Pruett, p. 1.
5. The 1997 National Study of the Changing Workforce, James T. Bond et al., Families and Work Institute, 1998, pp. 38–41.
6. Statistical Abstract of the United States, 2000 (Washington, D.C.: U.S. Census Bureau).
7. These articles include Jeff Benedict, Todd Crosset, and Alan Klein, "Male Student-Athletes Reported for Sexual Assault: A Survey of Campus Police Departments and Judicial Affairs Offices," *Journal of Sport and Social Issues* 19, no. 2 (May 1995).
8. Jeff Benedict, *Public Heroes, Private Felons: Athletes and Crime Against Women* (Boston: Northeastern University Press, 1997), ix.

9. "Editorial Observer: Living Under the Virtual Volcano of Video Games This Holiday Season," *New York Times,* December 16, 2002.

10. "Slain Girl Used Internet to Seek Sex Police Say," *New York Times,* May 22, 2002.

11. Richard Koestner, Carol Franz, and Joel Weinberger, *Journal of Personality and Social Psychology,* 58 (1990): 709–717.

12. Timothy Beneke, *Men on Rape* (New York: St. Martin's, 1982), 75.

· ·

MYRIAM MIEDZIAN holds both a Ph.D. in philosophy and a master's degree in clinical social work. She has served on the faculties of several universities, including Rutgers and the City University of New York. Since the publication of the first edition of *Boys Will Be Boys* (Doubleday, 1991), she has written and lectured widely on how to change the socialization of boys to decrease violence. She has testified on this subject before the U.S. House of Representatives Select Committee on Children, Youth, and Families, and has advised the Clinton Administration's Violence Prevention Interagency Task Force. In the fall of 2003, under the auspices of the peace studies program and the education department, she was the Diversity Visiting Professor at the University of Maine.

ON BECOMING ANTIRAPIST

. . . .

HAKI R. MADHUBUTI

If we men of all races, cultures, and continents would just examine the inequalities of power in our own families, businesses, and political and spiritual institutions and decide today to reassess and reconfigure them in consultation with the women in our lives, we would all be doing the most fundamental corrective act of a counterrapist.

There are mobs & strangers

in us

who scream of the women

we wanted and

will get

as if the women are ours for the

taking.

N 1991, THE CRIME OF RAPE in the United States entered our consciousness with the power of the dissolution of the Soviet Union. The trials of William Kennedy Smith (of the Camelot family) and Iron Mike Tyson, former heavyweight boxing champion of the entire world, shared front pages and provided talk-show hosts with subject matter on a topic that is usually confined to women's groups and the butt jokes of many men. Since women make up over 50 percent of the world's population and a clear majority in this country, one would think that the question of rape would not still be hidden in the minor-concerns files of men.

However, what is not hidden is that Mr. Smith and Mr. Tyson both used defenses that blamed the women in question. For Smith, that tactic was successful; for Tyson, it failed. Pages of analysis have been written in both cases, and I do not wish to add to them. But one can safely state that no woman wants to be raped, and that if men were raped as frequently as women, rape would be a federal crime rivaling murder and bank robbery. If carjacking can command federal attention, why are we still treating rape as if it's a boys-will-be-boys sport or a woman's problem, as in blame the victim? In the great majority of sex crimes against women in the United States, the women are put on trial as if they planned and executed their own rapes.

Male acculturation (a better description would be males' seasoning) is antifemale, antiwomanist, antifeminist, and antireason. This flawed socialization of men is not confined to the West but permeates most, if not all, cultures in the modern world. Most men have been taught to treat, respond, listen, and react to women from a male's point of view. Black men are not an exception here; we, too, are imprisoned within an intellectual, spiritual, and sexual understanding of women that is based on an antiquated male culture and sexist orientation—or should I say miseducation. For example, sex and sexuality are hardly ever discussed, debated, or taught to black men in a non-threatening or nonembarrassing family or community setting.

Men often see women, and specifically black women outside the immediate family, as bitches, hos, or any number of names that demean and characterize black women as less than whole and productive persons. Our missteps toward an understanding of women are compounded by the cultural environments where much of the talk of women takes place: street corners, locker rooms, male clubs, sporting events, bars, the military, business trips, playgrounds, workplaces, and basketball courts. Generally, women are not discussed on street corners or in bars as intellectually or culturally compatible partners. Rather, the discussion focuses on the best way to screw or control them.

These are, indeed, learning environments that traditionally have not been kind to women. The point of view that is affirmed all too often is the ownership of women. We are taught to see women as commodities and objects for men's sexual release and sexual fantasies; most women are considered inferior to men and thus not to be respected or trusted. Such thinking is encouraged and legitimized by our culture and transmitted via institutional structures (churches, workplaces), mass media *(Playboy and Penthouse),* misogynist music (rap and mainstream), and R-rated and horror films that use exploitative images of women. And of course there are the ever-present tall, trim, Barbie-doll women featured in advertising for everything from condoms to the latest diet cures. Few men have been taught—really taught—from birth and to the heart and gut to respect, value, or even on occasion honor women. Only very recently has it been confirmed in Western culture that rape (unwelcomed and uninvited sex) is criminal, evil, and antihuman.

> our mothers, sisters, wives and
> daughters ceased to be the
> women men want we think of them as
> loving family music & soul bright wonderments.
> they are not locker-room talk
> not the hunted lust or dirty
> cunt burnin hos.
> bright wonderments are excluded by association as
> blood & heart bone & memory

& we will destroy a rapist's knee caps,
& write early grave on his thoughts
to protect them.

Human proximity defines relationships. Exceptions should be noted, but in most cultures and most certainly within the black/African worldview family and extended family ties are honored and respected. One's sexual personhood in a healthy culture is nurtured, respected, and protected. In trying to get a personal fix here—that is, an understanding of the natural prohibitions against rape—think of your own personhood being violated. Think of your own family subjected to this act. Think of the enslavement of African people; it was common to have breeding houses on most plantations where our great-great-grandmothers were forced to open their insides for the sick satisfaction of white slave owners, overseers, and enslaved black men. This forced sexual penetration of African women led to the creation of mixed-race people here and around the world. There is a saying in South Africa that the colored race did not exist until nine months after white men arrived. This demeaning of black women and other women is amplified in today's culture, where it is not uncommon for young men to proclaim that "pussy is a penny a pound." However, we are told that the statement is not meant about the speaker's own mother, grandmother, sister, daughter, aunt, niece, close relative, or extended family. Yet the point must be made emphatically that incest (family rape) is on the rise in this country. Incest between adults and children is often not revealed until the children are adults. At that point, their lives are so confused and damaged that many continue incestuous acts.

it will do us large to recall
when the animal in us rises
that all women are someone's
mother, sister, wife, or daughter
and are not fruit to be stolen when hungry.

Part of the answer is found in the question: Is it possible or realistic to view all women as precious persons? Selective memory plays an important role here. Most men who rape are seriously ill and improperly educated. They do not view women outside of their protected zone as precious blood, do not see them as extended family, and do not see them as individuals or independent persons to be respected as most men respect other men. Mental illness or brain mismanagement blocks out reality, shattering and negating respect for self and others, especially the others of whom these men wish to take advantage. Power always lurks behind rape. Rape is an act of aggression that asserts power by defaming and defiling. Most men have been taught— either directly or indirectly—to solve problems with force. Such force may be verbal or physical. Violence is the answer that is promoted in media, from Saturday morning cartoons to everyday television to R-rated films. Popular culture has a way of trivializing reality and confusing human expectations, especially with regard to relationships between men and women. For too many black people, the popular has been internalized. In many instances, the media define us, including our relationships to each other.

Women have been in the forefront of the antirape struggle. Much of this work has been done by women working in nontraditional jobs—police officers and fire fighters, top professors and administrators in higher education, elected officials and public servants, medical workers and lawyers. However, the most pronounced presence and advancement of women has been seen in the military. We are told that the military, in terms of social development, remains at the cutting edge of changes, especially in the progress of blacks and female soldiers. However, according to an article in the *San Francisco Examiner,* the occurrence of rape against women in the military is far greater than in civilian life:

> A woman serving in the Army is 50 percent more likely to be raped than a civilian, newly released military records obtained by the *Orange County Register* show.
>
> From 1981 to 1987, 484 female soldiers were raped while on active duty, according to Department of the Army records released after a Freedom of Information Act request.
>
> The Army rate of 129 rape cases per 100,000 population in 1990 exceeds nationwide statistics for the same year compiled by the FBI of 80 confirmed rape cases per 100,000 women. The 1990 statistics are the latest comparable ones available.[1]

The brutality of everyday life continues to confirm the necessity for caring men and women to confront inhuman acts that cloud and prevent wholesome development. Much of what is defined as sexual pleasure today comes at the expense of girls and often boys. To walk Times Square or any number of big-city playgrounds after dark is to view how loudly the popular, throwaway culture has trapped, corrupted, and sexually abused too many of our children. In the United States, the sexual abuse of runaway children and children sentenced to foster care and poorly supervised orphanages is nothing less than scandalous. The proliferation of battered women's shelters and the most recent revelations about the sexual abuse of women incarcerated in the nation's prisons only underscores that a substantial number of men view women as sex objects for whatever sick acts enter their minds.

The abuse of children is not confined to the United States. Jo de Linde, chairperson of End Child Prostitution in Asian Tourism International, fights an uphill battle to highlight the physical and economic maltreatment of children. In "A New Colonialism," Murray Kempton writes about Thailand's "supermarkets for the purchases of small and disposable bodies."

> Tourism is central to Thailand's developmental efforts; and the attractions of its ancient culture compare but meagerly to the compelling pull its brothels exercise upon foreign visitors. The government does its duty to the economy by encouraging houses of prostitution and pays its debt to propriety with its insistence that no more than 10,000 children work there. Private observers concerned with larger matters than the good name of public officials estimate the real total of child prostitutes in Thailand at 200,000.
>
> The hunters and others of children find no border closed. They have ranged into South China carrying television sets to swap one per child. The peasants who cursed the day a useless girl was born know better now: they can sell her for consumers overseas and be consumers themselves. Traffickers less adventurous stay at home and contrive travel agencies that offer cheap trips to Kuala Lumpur that end up with sexual enslavement in Japan or Malaysia.[2]

That this state of affairs is not better known speaks loudly and clearly to the devaluation of female children. The war in Sarajevo, Bosnia, and Herzegovina again highlights the status of women internationally. In the rush toward ethnic cleansing and narrow and exclusive nationalism, Serbian soldiers have committed murder and other war crimes. The story of one such soldier, Borislav Herak, is instructive. According to an article in the *New York Times,* Mr. Herak and other soldiers were given the go-ahead to rape and kill Muslim women:

> The indictment lists 29 murders between June and October, including eight rape-murders of Muslim women held prisoner in an abandoned motel and cafe outside Vogosca, seven miles north of Sarajevo. There, Mr. Herak said, he and other Serbian fighters were encouraged to rape women and then take them away to kill them on hilltops and other deserted places.
>
> The indictment also covers the killings of at least 220 other Muslim civilians in which Mr. Herak has confessed to being a witness or a participant. Many of these dead were women and children.[3]

Much in the lives of women is not music or melody but a dance to the beat of the killing drums of men and male teenagers. Rape is not the fault of women; however, in a male-dominated world, the victims are often put on the defensive and forced to rationalize their gender and their personhood.

> Rape is not a reward for warriors
> it is war itself
> a deep, deep tearing, a dislocating of
> the core of the womanself.
> rape rips heartlessly
> soul from spirit,
> obliterating colors from beauty and body
> replacing melody and music with
> rat venom noise and uninterrupted intrusion and beatings.

The brutality of rape is universal. Most modern cultures—European, American, African, and Asian, religious and secular—grapple with this crime. Rarely is there discussion, and more often than not women are discouraged from being a part of the debates and edicts. Rape is crosscultural. I have not visited, heard of, or read about any rape-free societies. The war against women is international. Daily, around the world, women fight for a little dignity and their earned place in the world. And men in power respond accordingly. For example, Barbara Crossette reported in the *New York Times* about an incident in Batamaloo, Kashmir:

> In this conservative Muslim society, women have moved to the forefront of demonstrations and also into guerrilla conclaves. No single event has contributed more to this rapidly rising militancy among women than reports of a gang rape a month ago by Indian troops in Kunan, a remote village in northwestern Kashmir.
>
> According to a report filed by S. M. Yasin, district magistrate in Kupwara, the regional center, the armed forces "behaved like violent beasts." He identified them as members of the Fourth Rajputana Rifles and said they rampaged through the village from 11 p.m. on Feb. 23 until 9 the next morning.
>
> "A large number of armed personnel entered into the houses of villagers and at gunpoint they gang-raped 23 ladies, without any consideration of their age, married, unmarried, pregnancy etc.," he wrote. "There was a hue and cry in the whole village." Local people say that as many as 100 women were molested in some way.[4]

As a man of African descent, I would like to think that Africans have some special insight, enlightened hearts, or love in us that calms us in such times of madness. But my romanticism is shattered every day as I observe black communities across this land. The number of rapes reported and unreported in our communities is only the latest and most painful example of how far we have drifted from beauty. However, I have seldom hurt more than when I learned about the night of terror that occurred in Meru, Kenya, on July 13, 1991, at the St. Kizito boarding school. A high school protest initiated by the boys, in which the girls refused to join, resulted in a night of death, rapes, and beatings unparalleled in modern Kenya, in Africa, or in the world.

> The night of terror a month ago at the boarding school near Mount Kenya has torn the soul of the Kenyan people. What had the girls done to invoke the wrath of their male schoolmates?

They dared say no to the boys, who wanted them to join a
protest against the school's headmaster, according to police
and to those girls who lived through the night.

In Kenya, one-party rule has resulted in a tyranny of the
majority. Dissent, even in politics, is not welcome. "Here, the
minority must always go along with the majority's wishes,"
said a businessman who has done a lot of work with the government in the last 15 years and asked not to be named. "And
it is said that a woman cannot say no to a man."

Women's groups have said the rapes and deaths were an
extreme metaphor for what goes on in Kenyan society. The
girls of St. Kizito dared to say no to the boys, and 19 paid with
their lives while 71 others were beaten and raped. . . .

There have been many school protests in Kenya this year.
This summer alone, some 20 protests have turned into riots
resulting in the destruction of school property. There have
been rapes at other schools when girls refused to join boys in
their protests.[5]

A growing part of the answer is that we men, as difficult as it may seem,
must view all women (no matter who they are—race, culture, religion, or nationality aside) as extended family. The question is, and I know that I am
stretching, would we rape our mothers, grandmothers, sisters, or other female relatives? Would we even give such acts a thought? Can we extend this
attitude to all women? Therefore we must:

1. Teach our sons that it is their responsibility to be antirapist; that is,
   they must be counterrapist in their thoughts, conversations, raps, organizations, and actions.
2. Teach our daughters how to defend themselves and maintain an un-
   compromising stance toward men and boys.
3. Understand that being a counterrapist is honorable, manly, and necessary for a just society.
4. Understand that antirapist actions are part of the black tradition;
   being an antirapist is in keeping with the best African culture and with
   African family and extended family configurations. Even in times of

war, we were known to honor and respect the personhood of children and women.

5. Be glowing examples of men who are fighting to treat women as equals and to be fair and just in associations with women. This means at the core that we must continually reassess the family as now defined and constructed. In today's economy, most women, married and unmarried, must work. We men must encourage them in their work and must be intimately involved in rearing children and doing housework.

6. Understand that, just as men are different from one another, women also differ; therefore we must try not to stereotype women into the limiting and debilitating expectations of men. We must encourage and support them in their searching and development.

7. Be unafraid of independent, intelligent, and self-reliant women, and by extension understand that intelligent women think for themselves and may not want to have sex with a particular man. This is a woman's prerogative and is not a comment on anything other than the fact that she does not want to have sex.

8. Be bold and strong enough to stop other men (friends or strangers) from raping and to intervene in a rape in process with the fury and destruction of a hurricane against the rapist.

9. Listen to women. Listen especially to womanist/feminist/pan-Africanist philosophies of life. Study the writings of women, especially black women.

10. Act responsibly in response to our listening and studying. Be a part of and support antirape groups for boys and men. Introduce antirape discussion into men's groups and organizations.

11. Never stop growing, and understand that our growth is limited and limiting without the input of intelligent women.

12. Learn to love. Study love. Even if one is at war, love and respect, respect and love, must conquer if there is to be a sane and livable world. Rape is antilove, antirespect. Love is not easy. One does not fall in love but *grows* into love.

We can put the rape problem to rest in one generation if its eradication is as important to us as our cars, jobs, careers, sports, beer, and quest for power. However, the women who put rape on the front burner must continue to challenge us and their own cultural training, and must position themselves so that they and their message are not compromised or ignored.

> A significant few of their
> fathers, brothers, husbands, sons
> and growing strangers
> are willing to unleash harm onto the earth
> and spill blood in the eyes
> of
> maggots in running shoes
> who do not know the sounds of birth
> or respect the privacy of the human form

If we are to be just in our internal rebuilding, we must challenge tradition and cultural ways of life that relegate women to inferior status in the home, church/mosque/temple, workplace, political arena, and school. Men are not born rapists; we are taught very subtly that women are ours for the taking. Generally, these teachings begin in the family. Enlightenment demands fairness, impartiality, and vision; it demands confrontation with outdated definitions and acceptance of fair and just resolutions. One's sex, race, social class, or wealth should not determine one's entitlement or access to justice. If we are honest, men must be in the forefront of eradicating sex stereotypes in all facets of private and public life. Being honest, as difficult and as self-incriminating as it may be, is the only way we can truly liberate ourselves. If we men can liberate ourselves (with the help of women) from the negative aspects of the culture that produced us, maybe a just, fair, good, and liberated society is possible in our lifetime.

The liberation of the male psyche from preoccupation with domination, power, control, and absolute rightness requires an honest and fair assessment of patriarchal culture. This requires commitment to deep study, combined with a willingness for painful, uncomfortable, and often shocking change. We are not where we should be. That is why rape exists; why families are so easily formed and just as easily dissolved; why children are confused and abused; why our elderly are discarded, abused, and exploited; and why teenage boys create substitute families (gangs) that terrorize their own communities.

I remain an optimistic realist, primarily because I love life and most of what it has to offer. I often look at my children and tears come to my eyes because I realize how blessed I am to be their father. My wife and the other women in my life are special because they know that they are special and have taken it upon themselves, at great cost, to actualize their dreams, making what was considered for many of them unthinkable a few years ago a reality today. If we men of all races, cultures, and continents would just examine the inequalities of power in our own families, businesses, and political and spiritual institutions, and decide today to reassess and reconfigure them in consultation with the women in our lives, we would all be doing the most fundamental corrective act of a counterrapist.

It is indeed significant, and not an arbitrary aside, that males and females are created biologically different. These profound differences are part of why we are attracted to each other and are also what is beautiful about life. But too often, due to hierarchical and patriarchal definitions, one's sex also relegates one to a position in life that is not necessarily respected. Sex should not determine moral or economic worth, as it now does in too many cultures. In a just society, one's knowledge and capabilities—that is, what one is actually able to contribute to the world—are more valuable than one's sex.

As we create the definition of new men or manhood, we must put the absolute respect for and support of women at the top of our list. Remember, these women are our mothers, sisters, grandmothers, aunts, wives, daughters, close relatives, friends, and lovers. New education is required here, and it must be ongoing in all families, religious centers, male-bonding groups, educational institutions, and workplaces. I would encourage young men to start by reading *Surviving the Silence: Black Women's Stories of Rape* by Charlotte Pierce-Baker, a heart-wrenching book about black women who reveal their souls and hearts to us, and their horrible experiences of rape.

Few human acts more completely negate the human spirit than rape. The most cowardly and dastardly act against women is rape. Rape is a clear indication that a culture or civilization is out of control. Men and boys who wish to become real men do not, singly or as a group, rape women, or other men, under any circumstances. In fact, conscientious whole men are antirapist in thought, principles, and actions. An antirapist male will use all of his strength, heart, and soul to prevent rape—those that are about to begin and those in progress. Rape prevention starts early, with the proper education of boys and girls. Being an antirapist is not hard or difficult work; it is right work, it is moral and ethical work. It is work starting with the intelligent cultivation and nurturing of men who possess an undying love for life as well as respect for their mothers, grandmothers, sisters, aunts, women relatives and friends, wives, and daughters, and by extension all women regardless of race, class, religion, or ethnic identity.

Respect for the women closest to us can give us the strength and knowledge to confront the animal in us with regard to the women we consider others, because those others often *are* the women closest to us. If we honestly confront the traditions and histories that have shaped us, we may come to realize that women should be encouraged to go as far as their intellects and talents will take them, burdened only by the obstacles that all of us confront. The sexual energies of men must be checked before our misguided maleness manifests itself in the most horrible of crimes—rape.

> No!
> means no!
> even when men think
> that they are god's gift to women
> even after dropping a week's check & more
> on dinner by the ocean,
> the four tops, temptations and intruders memory tour,
> imported wine & rose that captured her smile,
> suggested to you private music & low lights
> drowning out her inarticulated doubts.
>
> Question the thousand-years teachings
> crawling through your lower depths and
> don't let your little head
> outthink your big head.
> No! means no!
> even when her signals suggest yes.

NOTES

1. Gary A. Warner, *San Francisco Examiner,* December 30, 1992.
2. Murray Kempton, "A New Colonialism," *New York Review of Books,* November 19, 1992.
3. John F. Burnes, "A Serbian Fighter's Path of Brutality," *New York Times,* November 27, 1992. Also see *Newsweek,* January 4, 1993.

4. Barbara Crossette, *New York Times,* April 7, 1991.
5. Timothy Dwyer, *Chicago Tribune,* April 18, 1991.

. . . .

As poet, publisher, editor and educator, **HAKI R. MADHUBUTI** serves as a pivotal figure in the development of a strong Black literary tradition, emerging from the era of the sixties and continuing to the present. Over the years, he has published twenty-six books (some under his former name, Don L. Lee), including *Black Men: Obsolete, Single, Dangerous?: The African American Family in Transition* (Third World Press, 1990), *Claiming Earth: Race, Rage, Rape, Redemption* (Third World Press, 1994), *GroundWork: New and Selected Poems 1966/1996* (Third World Press, 1996), *HeartLove: Wedding and Love Poems* (Third World Press, 1998), *Tough Notes: A Healing Call for Creating Exceptional Black Men* (Third World Press, 2002), and *Run Toward Fear* (Third World Press, 2004). A proponent of independent Black institutions, Madhubuti founded Third World Press in 1967 and the Institute of Positive Education/New Concept School in 1969, and he cofounded the Betty Shabazz International Charter School in 1998 in Chicago, Illinois. He is also a founder of the International Literary Hall of Fame for Writers of African Descent and is Distinguished University Professor at Chicago State University.

SEXUAL ABUSE BY RELIGIOUS LEADERS
. . . .
MARIE M. FORTUNE

Religious institutions, both formal and informal, now face the consequences of long-standing professional misconduct involving sexual abuse by their leaders. Their history of nondisclosure to authorities, and nonaction (except to protect the clergy), is now reaping a whirlwind.

THE LONG-STANDING PROBLEM of sexual abuse of congregants by clergy and religious leaders has finally made its way into public consciousness, largely due to the persistence of the media. Although religious leaders are not the only professionals to exploit those who seek their help, when they do so they betray both a helping relationship and a spiritual relationship, which can carry heavy consequences for the victims. No denomination or creed is immune from this professional pastoral problem: religious leaders, whether Protestant or Catholic, Buddhist or Jewish, Muslim or of the Native traditions, occupy positions of trust, which can easily be abused. Nor is this problem new: The historical record suggests that for many centuries some male religious leaders have used their positions to gain sexual access to women and children, and institutions of organized religion have tolerated their behavior. This particular expression of sexual violence, although long hidden, has now become public. The administrative bodies that train, oversee, ordain, and supervise religious leaders should have a primary responsibility to do all they can to ensure that faith communities and places of worship are safe for all participants.

THE PROBLEM

When a pastoral relationship becomes a sexual one, a boundary is violated, whether the context is a clergy-congregant, a counseling, a staff supervisory, or a mentor relationship. When a religious leader sexualizes the pastoral or counseling relationship, it is similar to the violation of the therapeutic relationship by a therapist. When the religious leader sexualizes the supervisory or mentor relationship with a staff member or student, it is similar to sexual harassment in the workplace, and the principles of workplace harassment apply. When a child or teenager is the object of the sexual contact, the situation is one of pedophilia or child sexual abuse, which is by definition not only unethical and abusive but criminal. Likewise, if the boundary violation is an assault, it is the crime of rape. Although most often the boundary violation is not forced or coerced but manipulated with an illusion of consent, this does not mitigate the damage it causes.

Sexual contact by religious leaders and pastoral counselors with congregants/ clients undercuts an otherwise effective pastoral relationship and violates the trust necessary for that relationship. It is not the sexual contact per se that is problematic but the fact that the sexual activity takes place within the pastoral relationship. The violation of this particular boundary changes the nature of the relationship and has enormous potential to cause harm. The behaviors that occur in sexual violation of boundaries include but are not limited to sexual comments or suggestions such as jokes, innuendoes, or invitations, touching, fondling, seduction, kissing, intercourse, molestation, and rape. There may be only one incident or a series of incidents or an ongoing intimate relationship.

Sexual behavior in pastoral relationships is an instance of professional misconduct that is often minimized or ignored. This is not just an affair, although it may involve an ongoing sexual relationship with a client or congregant. It is not merely adultery, although adultery may be a consequence if the religious leader/counselor or congregant/client is in a committed relationship. And it is not just a momentary lapse of judgment by the religious leader or counselor; often there is a recurring pattern of misuse of the pastoral role by a cleric who seems neither to comprehend nor to care about the damaging effects it may have on the congregant/client.

Research on sexual involvement between clergy and congregants is sparse, but research and media reports of charges and civil or criminal actions suggest that between 10 and 20 percent of clergy violate sexual boundaries in their professional relationships [see Flores, p. 129, and Hang and Thao, p. 201]. Although the vast majority of pastoral offenders in reported cases are heterosexual males and the vast majority of victims are heterosexual females, neither gender nor sexual orientation excludes anyone from the risk of offending (clergy) or from the possibility of being taken advantage of (congregants/clients) in the pastoral or counseling relationship.

Some of the conduct can be described as wandering. Religious leaders who wander and violate sexual boundaries are often ill trained and insensitive and use poor judgment, with complete disregard for the impact on the congregant, student, or client. If called to account and given training and supervision, wanderers may be able to return to responsible ministry. At the other end of the spectrum, however, are religious leaders whose behavior can be described as predatory. Whether they offend against children, youths, or adults, these leaders intentionally target vulnerable people, grooming them and manipulating them into crossing sexual boundaries. Some may be clinically diagnosed as sex offenders. Some may be criminally prosecuted. Most are sociopathic and thus accomplished at manipulating the system in which they operate. Once identified, they should be removed from any role of trust and responsibility for others and, if appropriate, prosecuted. They cannot be restored to responsible ministry.

CONSEQUENCES

Sexual contact with their religious leader or counselor has a profound psychological effect on congregants and clients. Initially, clients/congregants may feel flattered by the special attention and may even see themselves as consenting to the activity. Frequently, however, the congregants/clients have sought pastoral care during a time of crisis and are emotionally vulnerable.[1] Eventually they begin to realize that they are being denied a much-needed pastoral relationship and begin to feel taken advantage of. Additionally, the victims of clerical abuse may feel betrayed, victimized, confused, fearful, embarrassed, or ashamed, and may blame themselves; at this point they are not likely to discuss the situation with anyone and so remain isolated. They are at risk for depression, substance abuse, or suicide. If and when anger finally surfaces, they may be ready to break the silence and take some action on their own behalf and on behalf of others. Once having disclosed their situation, survivors depend heavily for their healing on the response of the institution or faith group. Too often survivors of clerical abuse meet a response of disbelief, blame, and ostracism. This will revictimize them, since they are abandoned by their faith community. A response of support and compassion and a willingness to hold religious leaders accountable can help survivors to heal from the abuse.

Spiritually, the consequences are also profound; the psychological pain is magnified and takes on cosmic proportions. The congregants/clients are not only betrayed by someone representing God but also feel betrayed by God and their faith community. Religious leaders/counselors are very powerful and can easily manipulate their victims not only psychologically but also spiritually and morally. Religious leaders are reported to have justified their boundary-crossing behavior in these ways:

- "He said that love can never be wrong; that God had brought us together."
- "He said we should sin boldly so that grace might abound."
- "She said that ministry was mutual and our relationship was mutual. So she shared her problems with me and the sex followed from that."
- "I was learning about God for the first time. He took me seriously. I went along with the sex so that I could continue to learn from him."

The result for congregants or students is enormous confusion and guilt; this psychological crisis becomes a crisis of faith as well, with very high stakes.

Manipulation by religious leaders or pastoral counselors compromises the moral agency and otherwise good judgment of congregants. If the person they rely on as a moral guide explains away any moral question they may have about engaging in sexual activity and requires them to keep it secret so they are not able to check this out with someone else who might help them see more clearly what is happening, it is very easy to be deceived. The result is that many survivors of clergy abuse end up feeling stupid and blaming themselves, when in fact someone they trusted stole their moral agency from them.

Entire congregations are also devastated by clergy sexual abuse. With or without disclosure, the impact of boundary violations ripples through the membership. The whole congregation feels their trust has been betrayed. Consequences can include loss of faith, financial liability, and loss of members, and the residue lasts for years unless the congregation has an opportunity to confront the truth and find healing.

Finally, the consequences are also profound for the religious leaders and their families. Not only is there the internal betrayal of their vocation, with disclosure there may well be loss of employment, status, and benefits, or imprisonment. The profession as a whole also faces consequences. Daily reports of clergy members being arrested and new civil actions against the governing bodies of religious institutions seriously compromise the credibility of all religious leaders. While not all religious leaders are engaged in boundary violations, all bear the burden of distrust created by the misconduct of a minority.

AN ETHICAL ANALYSIS

The ethical analysis of sexual abuse and boundary violation by religious leaders has been woefully inadequate in many circles. For example, in the proposed revisions to the U.S. Roman Catholic Bishops' Dallas Policy (2002) on the sexual abuse of children by priests, the bishops directly tie the definition of sexual abuse to a moral standard based on the Sixth Commandment in Hebrew scripture: "You shall not commit adultery." The average layperson would rightly ask, "I thought adultery was about adults having sex with someone they are not married to. What does sexual abuse of kids have to do with adultery?"

The fundamental ethical question is, why is it wrong for an adult to be sexual with a child or teen? The answer is not a difficult one: It is a betrayal of trust, a misuse of adult authority, taking advantage of a child's vulnerability, sexual activity in the absence of meaningful consent; it is, in other words, rape. When an ordained member of the clergy has been sexual with a child, it is also a betrayal of the role of the pastor. Our job as clergy is to nurture the flock, to protect them when they are vulnerable, and to empower them in their lives—especially children and youth. Our people assume they can trust us not to harm them, because we are clergy. Sexual abuse betrays that trust.

The bishops turned to the wrong commandment. Instead of the sixth, they should have gone to the seventh: "You shall not steal." To steal is to take something that doesn't belong to you. To sexually abuse a child is to steal the child's innocence and future, often with profound and tragic consequences. When an acknowledged pedophile priest can say that he didn't see what was wrong with his behavior with a child because he had been taught not to have sex with adult women, we can begin to see the inadequacy of this ethical analysis. The sexual abuse of a child or teen is about the misuse of power by the adult. It is about theft: taking advantage of a child's naiveté, stealing his or her future.

Clarity of ethical analysis is necessary to help shape an effective response to disclosures of abuse. It is a violation of professional ethics for any person in a pastoral role of leadership or pastoral counseling (clergy or lay) to engage in sexual contact or sexualized behavior with a congregant, client, employee, or student, whether adult, teen, or child, within the professional pastoral or supervisory relationship. It is wrong because sexual activity in this context is exploitative and abusive:

- *Role violation.* The pastoral relationship involves certain role expectations. The religious leader/counselor is expected to make available certain resources, talents, knowledge, and expertise that will serve the best interest of the congregant, client, staff member, or student. Sexual contact is not part of the pastoral professional role. Important boundaries within the pastoral or counseling relationship are crossed and as a result trust is betrayed. The sexual nature of this boundary violation is significant only in that the sexual context is one of great vulnerability for most people. However, the essential harm is that of betrayal of trust.
- *Misuse of authority and power.* The role of religious leader/counselor carries with it authority and power, and the attendant responsibility to use this power to benefit the people who call on the religious leader/counselor for service. This power can easily be misused, as is the case when a member of the clergy uses (intentionally or unintentionally) his or her authority to initiate or pursue sexual contact with a congregant or client. Even if it is the congregant who sexualizes the relationship, it is still the religious leader's responsibility to maintain the boundaries of the pastoral relationship and not pursue a sexual relationship.
- *Taking advantage of vulnerability.* The congregant, client, employee, or student is by definition vulnerable to the religious leader/counselor. She or he has fewer resources and less power, and when a member of the clergy takes advantage of this vulnerability to gain sexual access, the clergy member violates the mandate to protect the vulnerable from harm.[2]
- *Absence of meaningful consent.* In order to consent fully to sexual activity, an individual must have a choice and the relationship must be one of mutuality and equality; hence, meaningful consent requires the absence of fear or of even the subtlest coercion. There is always an imbalance of power and thus inequality between a person in the pastoral role and those whom he or she serves or supervises. Even in a relationship between two persons who see themselves as consenting adults, the difference in role precludes the possibility of meaningful consent.

AN INSTITUTIONAL CRISIS

Religious institutions, both formal and informal, face the consequences of long-standing professional misconduct involving sexual abuse by their leaders. Their history of nondisclosure to authorities, and nonaction (except to protect the clergy), is reaping a whirlwind. The enormous cost in legal fees and settlements is but a material indicator of the depth of damage done to the institutions and their members. Some dioceses are facing bankruptcy and others are cutting back funds for social programs.

The history of religious bodies' responses to complaints of sexual abuse and professional misconduct suggests that they have followed an institutional protection agenda, which, ironically, has not worked. Nonetheless, it has dominated the strategies of many governing bodies.

An institutional protection agenda uses scripture to avoid action: for example, "Judge not that you not be judged." It uses language to confuse and distort reality: "It was just an indiscretion and it only happened once." It instructs its legal counsel to protect the organization from victims and survivors. It develops policies whose sole purpose is to protect the institution from liability. It urges liturgies that immediately focus on forgiveness, which will only serve to "heal the wound lightly." It allocates funds to defend the institution in civil litigation while it shuns victims and survivors and attempts to silence them. It resists reform at all costs.

But there is another possible agenda, one more congruent with the teaching and values of religious organizations. A justice-making agenda uses scripture to name the sin and lift up victims: for example, "It would be better for you if a millstone were hung around your neck and you were thrown into the sea than for you to cause one of these little ones to stumble." It uses language to clarify: "This is sexual abuse of the most vulnerable by the powerful. It is a sin and a crime." It instructs its legal counsel to find ways to make justice for survivors and to hold perpetrators accountable. It develops and implement policies whose purpose is to protect the people from their institution and from those who would misuse their power. It encourages liturgies, when the time is right, that name the sin, confess culpability, remember the victims, and celebrate justice really made—all of which allow for healing and restoration. It allocates its funds for restitution to victims and survivors and for education and training for prevention. It does not look for a scapegoat but looks inside itself with a critical eye, focusing on power as the true issue. It seeks out those who have been harmed, thanks them for their courage in disclosing their abuse, and supports them in their healing. It has the courage to ask what reforms are needed in order to be faithful to the most important values that the religious organization espouses.

Some Roman Catholic bishops and cardinals in the United States have argued that their early management of the reports of priests' sexual abuse of children was sincerely motivated by their desire to protect the church from scandal. This translated as protecting priests from the consequences of their misconduct, keeping secrets, and limiting the financial liability of the institution. Ironically, their mismanagement now undermines the credibility of all priests, compromises the image and moral capital of the whole church, and will cost far more financially than it needed to. In other words, even the institutional protection agenda didn't protect the institution in the long run. The betrayal of any helping relationship is about the misuse of power, in this case to violate sexual boundaries. It is the importance of power in a helping relationship that led Hippocrates to formulate the Hippocratic Oath more than two thousand years ago and commit physicians "to keep [patients] from harm and injustice" with these words: "Whatever houses I may visit, I will come for the benefit of the sick, remaining free of all intentional injustice, of all mischief and in particular of sexual relations with both female and male persons, be they free or slaves." He was concerned about the helper taking advantage of the vulnerable and so offered these boundaries to remind any who would serve others of their responsibilities to protect the vulnerable.

Since the mid-1980s in the United States, the discussion of the problem of ministerial misconduct has expanded; disclosures by victims/survivors have increased; lawsuits against churches and synagogues, denominations and movements, as well as pastoral counselors, have multiplied. A crisis has come to light that now challenges the professional credibility of all religious leaders and religious institutions. A number of denominations, at the national and regional levels, have moved to develop policy and procedures as they are being faced with an increasing number of complaints. More research projects are under way. Codes of ethics have been written or revised by professional organizations. Some attention is beginning to be focused at the seminary level on preparing clergy and pastoral counselors to lessen their risk of violating the integrity of the ministerial relationship. Seminaries are key to preventing sexual abuse and boundary violations by religious leaders. Training for ministry and leadership must address professional ethics, boundaries, power, and authority. Students should be supported in exploring their own histories, especially family-of-origin issues of abuse or dysfunction, and their own healing. But religious institutions also share responsibility for effectively screening candidates, supervising and evaluating their work, and if necessary removing them if they are shown to be abusive.

People who approach a helping professional such as a religious leader should be able to trust that they will be safe and that their sexual and emotional boundaries will not be violated. This requires well-trained, sensitive, committed religious leaders whose first concern is the well-being of their congregants, students, or clients. Too often in the past, religious leaders, out of ignorance or with intention, have taken advantage of the vulnerabilities of those who came to them for help. If a religious institution or organization gives credentials to its leaders, allowing them to teach or practice ministry, then it also has the responsibility to remove those credentials when it discovers that a leader cannot be trusted and is doing harm in the community. Only this social contract can sustain the professional credibility of religious leaders, institutions, and organizations.

NOTES

1. It is not unusual for people who are exploited by a religious leader or pastoral counselor to have some history of childhood sexual abuse, or abuse within an adult intimate relationship, which may not have been addressed. Disclosing child sexual abuse or current domestic violence only increases their vulnerability to further exploitation by a religious leader.
2. For Jews and Christians, the mandate to protect the vulnerable derives from the Hebrew hospitality code.

MARIE M. FORTUNE is a minister in the United Church of Christ and founder of the FaithTrust Institute (formerly the Center for the Prevention of Sexual and Domestic Violence) in Seattle. She is the author of *Is Nothing Sacred?* (United Church Press, 1989), the story of a pastor, the women he sexually abused, and the congregation he nearly destroyed, *Love Does No Harm: Sexual Ethics for the Rest of Us* (Continuum, 1995), *Sexual Violence: The Sin Revisited* (Pilgrim Press, 2005), as well as other books that address sexual and domestic violence. She is the editor of the *Journal of Religion and Abuse,* published by Haworth Press. For more information, see http://www.faithtrustinstitute.org

HMONG WOMEN'S PEACE

· · · · · · · · · · · · · · · · · · · ·

MAYKAO YANGBLONGSUA HANG AND TRU HANG THAO

What visible and invisible barriers must be identified and overcome to bring equal value to women? As people like myself start to peel the layers and challenge the belief system, we are stamped as radicals. So be it.

MAYKAO YANGBLONGSUA HANG

I N THE MID-1990s a coalition of women's groups started Hmong Women's Peace, a grassroots effort to develop violence prevention and intervention programs in Ramsey County (St. Paul, Minnesota). More than a thousand members of the Hmong community agreed on the need for this effort.

At the time, focus groups and surveys revealed that most Hmong community members believed that Hmong males were inherently more powerful than Hmong females. This belief continues to be so strong that even before birth Hmong male fetuses are thought to have more power than females. Transforming such a culture to one in which females are also valued will require a struggle to change far more than behavior; it will have to challenge the cosmology and the belief system that govern Hmong culture.

Hmong boys and men typically have the authority to enact, learn, and enforce the traditions of Hmong culture. Girls and women participate in rituals and ceremonies but are not the main players. When my grandfather died, I was unable to formally receive funeral money from or give money to relatives in the ritual process of giving and then getting thanked. Because I am a woman, I was not able to hand money to the ushers even though this was my grandfather. Instead, my husband had to do this for me. A woman related to the person who has died must find a man in the funeral home to give the money to the ushers. When I tried to help my father receive money in this ritual process, I was told that it was inappropriate and unseemly. My male relatives in charge of the funeral ordered me to go back to the refreshment stand to organize the girls who were delivering drinks to the crowd.

Being unable to give money at a funeral may seem far removed from sexual violence; however, in the community planning process that started Hmong Women's Peace—the first and the only Hmong sexual assault program—we found that Hmong community members firmly believe that sexism is what leads to violence against women and girls, both subtle and overt. Overt sexual exploitation and abuse include polygamy and the practice of much older men marrying teenagers. These were both identified as forms of violence against women. A subtler form of sexism is women serving as the audience during clan meetings, but not as participants. More subtly still, as a Hmong woman leader I am often asked to speak last at public events. It is a victory that I am there at all, but I still get the message that I am less important than everyone else who is speaking.

What determines value in a person, generally, is one's name and reputation. Although women are starting to have public roles as executives or legislators, for example, the Hmong community still does not know how to relate to women who are powerful public figures. My position underscores this need to redefine relationships within the shifting paradigm. At work, I oversee many staff members and services in Ramsey County. Hmong staff (especially men) don't quite know what to do with me, but they acknowledge my presence because of my authority at work. At home and in the community, I hold very little power, and when I see these same staff members they are unlikely to acknowledge my presence. If they know my husband, or my father, they are likely to talk to one of them first. This is changing, and some men who work under me do acknowledge my presence both at work and in the community. However, this is still rare.

I have had many arguments with people who think I am out in left field because I talk about transforming Hmong culture to be more inclusive of women. For example, why can't I just take the money and hand it to the ushers at a funeral and be thanked? Will the world come to an end? As I sat typing dollar amounts into a laptop at the funeral, I was actually transforming culture. This simple act was radical. Was I shaming my male relatives, sending a message that even a woman could do this type of job? What visible and invisible barriers must be identified and overcome to bring equal value to women? As people like myself start to peel the layers and challenge the belief system, we are stamped as radicals. So be it.

People can howl all they want. My peers and I are tired of walking on eggshells, trying not to inadvertently cross the invisible yet tangible gender boundary. If we are ever to break away, the silence must be broken around sexism while we work on developing the capacity to intervene when violence erupts. I see no other way.

TRU HANG THAO

In 1998, I was hired to develop and coordinate Hmong Women's Peace, a sexual assault program specifically for the Hmong community. When I started the job, I wasn't sure how the community would react to me or the program, which was the first of its kind in the country, and I wanted it to be a success. My biggest fear was that there would be community resistance to the program. To my surprise, that was not the case. The first year, I spent much of my time developing and promoting the program to both the Hmong community and the mainstream community. I felt it was important to educate both communities about sexual assault in the Hmong community so there could be a mutual exchange of information about culture and systems. Since sexual assault was not openly acknowledged as a problem or an important issue in the Hmong community, I wanted to advance it as a priority. I networked with local nonprofit Hmong agencies' youth programs to raise awareness about sexual assault. I hoped that talking very publicly about sexual assault would send a message out to Hmong victims that they were not alone. The messages were that sexual assault does exist and that help is available.

Mainstream sexual assault service personnel were for the most part unaware of the barriers that Hmong women faced when they tried to get help after a rape. I strongly believed that if I was going to encourage women to step forward, then it was my job to educate mainstream agencies about the obstacles Hmong victims were facing in counseling and in the legal system. The success of the program relied heavily on this process. If a Hmong woman decides to come forward and the mainstream system is unsure of how to handle her case, then our program could be setting her up for failure. She could be revictimized, and her mistrust of the American legal system reinforced. Two groups, one a county agency (Sexual Offense Services of Ramsey County) and one a nonprofit (Minnesota Coalition against Sexual Assault), played key roles in setting up training opportunities for law enforcement personnel, advocates, and prosecutors to help improve cultural responsiveness.

Sexual assault advocacy can be stressful but rewarding. As a sexual assault advocate over the past five years, I've worked with at least forty Hmong cases. Most of the time, even when these cases are reported to law enforcement, they don't reach the American legal system. The victims' families choose to use the Hmong clan system for resolution. Many of these families feel that the traditional Hmong system is a surer route to family justice, even if the victims' personal needs are not addressed as well as they could be.

In the Hmong community, an assault brings shame upon the victim's family. The only way to make it right is to seek out the advice of clan elders, who are often leaders of the community. In the clan system, consequences for the assailant are minimal. The perpetrator's family has two ways to make amends to the victim's family. The first is for the perpetrator and his family to agree that he will take the victim as his wife. If he is already married, then she can become a second wife. The marriage has to be agreed on by both families. If marriage is not agreed on, then the only other option is for the perpetrator's family to pay a fine, anywhere between $2,000 and $5,000, to the victim's family. The fine has two purposes, first to fix the damage that was done to the victim's family reputation and second to admit that the perpetrator was wrong. The perpetrator's—or his family's—willingness to pay the fine is understood as a good faith effort to restore damage to the reputation and to admit wrongdoing.

The clan system does not work for victims of sexual assault. Instead, it revictimizes a woman by isolating her. She is not allowed to have a voice or to make her own choices. Instead of providing support, the system pressures her to go along with whatever has been decided between the two families. No personal counseling or advocacy is present.

Sexual violence is well hidden behind the walls of the Hmong community. In Hmong families, as MayKao points out, males are valued above females, and there are different expectations for each gender. As a young girl, I was constantly told that I needed to learn certain things in life in order to be a good wife. When I reached adolescence, my mother warned me always to be careful and not bring any shame to my family. It always upset me, but I knew what she was saying: "Don't come home with a full belly."

Sexuality is not discussed freely among mothers, daughters, aunts, and siblings. Premarital sex for women is looked down upon in the community. If an unmarried woman is known to be sexually involved, her family will force her to marry her partner in order to avoid scandal. Parents force marriage upon the woman because her reputation has been ruined and the likelihood of her finding a husband is very slim. If a young woman tells her parents that she has been raped, they assume she is admitting to having non-marital sex and therefore bringing shame on the family.

Having worked with many Hmong victims, I see that the majority of their families are not supportive. The family members tend to blame the victim. The victim feels an enormous amount of guilt and shame about the rape, and her own family and community ostracize her. The Hmong community is large but tightly knit, and gossip spreads quickly. The fear of further gossip pressures the victim to stay away from police and the courts, because the rape will become public. Seeking help from mainstream agencies can also be bruising for victims. Sexual assault, like domestic violence, is an intimate crime; therefore it should stay within the family. If the victim chooses to get help from outside sources, she is inviting more trouble for herself.

Most of the women who come to Hmong Women's Peace are looking for emotional support, education, explanation of a sexual assault to family members, and legal advocacy. A woman must take a number of giant steps when she chooses to come forward and ask for help. The first important step is to move away from her family and talk to a stranger about her rape. The second is to believe that it was not her fault. This can be hard, since her family and peers have told her repeatedly that the rape was her fault.

I'm going to share with you one brave Hmong woman's story. The legal system failed to respond effectively to her complaint of rape, and she endured community ostracism and lack of support from her own family. Despite these obstacles, she found the strength to move on.

Mai Xiong (her name has been changed), a Hmong woman in her late thirties, was raped by her pastor. The rapes began when she went to her pastor for counseling about and support for her troubled marriage. Her husband was a deacon at the church; therefore she did not want to go to the family elders with her marital problems because she did not want his reputation to be ruined in the community. The pastor at first was helpful, but things began to change when he asked her to meet him after church and outside of church. She found this strange, but because he was the pastor she trusted him.

The first rape occurred after church. The pastor told Mai that he had new resources that might be helpful to her. She agreed to meet with him in his chambers, where he raped her. In shock, she was not able to scream for help. After the rape, he said that if she told anyone he would deny it, and because he was the pastor no one would believe her. Scared, she left and did not attend church for several weeks. The pastor called her husband and harassed him about his wife's absence from church. Tired of arguing with her husband, Mai Xiong began attending church once more. The rapes continued. Her pastor would ask her to meet him outside of services and, if she refused, threaten to go to her husband and tell him she was having an affair.

Not wanting to further damage her already troubled marriage, she agreed to meet him.

The rapes continued for more than a year. They stopped when she finally told her rapist that she was not going to comply with his requests and that she was going to make a police report. She did gather the courage to call the police and make a complaint. However, because she did not speak English fluently, the police called for a Hmong officer to come to the scene and take the report. When the Hmong officer arrived, he asked both Mai and her husband what was going on. She told him that their pastor had raped her and that her husband did not believe her. Her husband thought she was having an affair with the pastor. Instead of believing her and reporting a rape, the officer reported it as a domestic incident between the couple.

Not knowing what the officer had written down, Mai waited for the pastor to be picked up and charged with rape. A year went by and still nothing came from the criminal justice system. She then came to see me, at Hmong Women's Peace. When we read the police report together, Mai understood why her assailant had never been charged and her case would never get to the legal system; it was never written up as a criminal sexual conduct complaint.

Prior to meeting me, she had begun a civil suit against the pastor and the church for damages from the rapes. I began working closely with her because she needed an advocate to help her through the courts. She wanted justice, and if she could not get it in the criminal court she would try the civil system. For over a year, she and I met with her attorney and went to court proceedings, and as time went by she become more comfortable with me and told me about the obstacles she faced. All the members of her church gave full support to the pastor and the church. Church members called her home, threatening her and telling her to back down. Worst of all, a well-known Hmong woman leader who was thought to be progressive on issues of violence against women was advocating on behalf of the church and the rapist by finding them a prominent law office to work on their case for free.

Even though she had no support from her husband or her family, Mai continued the civil litigation. I found it sad that every time we appeared in court her husband would be there, sitting right behind three of the defendants. In the end, the civil suit got her nowhere and she dropped the case. At our last meeting, she told me that all she wanted was for the pastor to admit the horrible things he had done to her. She wanted the community to see him for who he really was. However, she realized that no matter what happened, people would not change their opinions and attitudes. She felt that she had spent too much time trying to convince people and she needed to start her healing process. In Mai's effort to find justice for herself, she faced revictimization from her family, friends, and community and from the legal system, but those things did not stop her from telling her story. In the end, these obstacles helped her become a stronger woman.

Advocating for survivors of sexual assault can be challenging, but I am hopeful that with education and time the Hmong community's attitude toward sexual assault will change. In the two years that I coordinated Hmong Women's Peace I saw small changes in the community's attitudes. Local agencies became more open to attending training and referring victims for services. Providing the community with accurate information about the legal system demystified it and transformed some of the myths Hmong community members believed about the legal system. Success in getting justice for assault survivors also built trust.

I've met many strong survivors like Mai. I have much to thank these women for. They shared their stories and taught me many of the things I know today. Although I am no longer coordinating Hmong Women's Peace, the opportunities it has given me will always stay with me. The courage and strength of these women keeps me energized and advocating for victims of sexual assault.

. . . .

MAYKAO YANGBLONGSUA HANG was the first project coordinator for Hmoob Thaj Yeeb (Hmong Peace) and helped cofound Hmong Women's Peace, the first sexual assault program for the Hmong community. Now director of Adult Services for Ramsey Country Human Services, she is the former chair of the Hmong Women's Action Team, and still a champion for women's issues.

TRU HANG THAO was coordinator of Hmong Women's Peace and is now an advocate with Sexual Offense Services of Ramsey County and a consultant on violence against Hmong women. A trainer for the Minnesota Bureau of Criminal Apprehension, Metropolitan State University, and rape crisis centers throughout Minnesota, she is also still a member of the Hmong Women's Action Team.

RAISING GIRLS IN THE TWENTY-FIRST CENTURY
EMILIE BUCHWALD

Our daughters were able to tell us about their experience of harassment, knowing that we would do everything we could to help. At the time, though, neither they nor we knew enough to connect personal traumas to societal patterns. That connection was made when we recognized the truth of the phrase "the personal is political."

The great question that has never been answered
and which I have not yet been able to answer, despite
my thirty years of research into the feminine soul,
is, 'What does a woman want?'

—SIGMUND FREUD, TO MARIE
BONAPARTE (CA. 1935)

WHAT A GIRL WANTS, what a woman wants, is what Freud knew
is held precious by every man: self-determination, autonomy within
reason, life without undue fear, liberty without causing harm to others,
and the ability to pursue one's happiness. None of those desires can be fulfilled
for women so long as we live in a rape culture. A general recognition is dawn-
ing that our culture will need both women and men who are strong, wise, and
generous if the future is to be better than the present. The nurture and education of girls must emphasize the importance of their role in that future.

LEARNING GENDER

In my robe and hospital slippers, I spent long, delightful minutes staring
through the glass panel into the hospital nursery at the babies in their wheeled
bassinets, some crying and kicking, some asleep, a few being changed. I was
flooded with an emotion I couldn't identify. What I felt was so powerful that
I wasn't sure whether I wanted to laugh or weep. I was struck by the sight of
an entire room filled with lives just begun, one of them our daughter's. An
ID bracelet at the ankle identified the infants by name. Each wore a white
knit cap whose blue or pink pom-pom signaled male or female. The nurses
on duty sometimes had as many as twenty babies to care for. They were quick
as well as deft. I am sure they thought they were tending the babies identi-
cally, but I noticed that they hefted and handled baby boys with a heartiness
that said, "He's a male, he can take it." I know that they spent minutes of
their precious time combing our baby girl's hair into a miniature topknot,
tied with a pink ribbon. Her gender life was already under way.

A child is born with the potential ability to learn Chinese or Swahili, play
a kazoo, climb a tree, make a strudel or a birdhouse, take pleasure in finding

the coordinates of a star. Genetic inheritance determines a child's abilities and weaknesses. But those who raise a child call forth from that matrix the traits and talents they consider important.

A child is born with a sex determination but without innate knowledge of what it means to be a woman or a man. Even before its birth, the preconceptions of the parents seal a child's gender fate, and moments after birth the infant is swaddled in gender definition. Our self-image as a female or a male is a major force in creating the person we become. We exaggerate gender differences rather than celebrate what we share as human beings. Male and female are distanced from one another, made into polar opposites, as if a division into yin and yang were mandated. We sunder brother from sister and create a lifelong distrust.

Our gender lives are further burdened by thousands of years of propaganda written by men that defines the nature and role of male and female. This propaganda both demonizes and trivializes women as inferior in every particular of character and ability. I was reminded of the ancient nature of misogyny when I read the quotes in The "Natural Inferiority" of Women, a compilation by Tama Starr of men's slanders of women over the past five thousand years. Women are reviled by some of the sages she quotes for being licentious and promiscuous and by others for being frigid and asexual. Women are described matter-of-factly as the physical, intellectual, and moral inferiors of men. In the words of Saint John Chrysostom, around 380 AD, "What else is a woman but a foe to friendship, a cosmic punishment, a necessary evil, a natural temptation, a desirable calamity, a domestic peril, a delectable detriment, a deadly fascination, a painted ill!"[1]

Men of every age, including our own, have added poisonous brush strokes to the unflattering portrait of womankind. Their words of scorn, contempt, exclusion, and hatred continue to feed the male notion that women are—less. Henry Miller's comment in a 1975 interview conveys the idea: "Women have been a definite influence on my life. I adore women as a whole. I enjoy them as a breed, like a dog. They're another species that you become endeared to. I don't mean that derogatorily, but in an admiring sense, like someone would appreciate a fine breed of horse. It's like treading on eggs not to offend these people, the women's libbers. They're touchy, always on the defensive. What are they so worried about?"[2]

Freud would never have thought to ask, "What does a man want?" His vexed question speaks to his belief that women are a different, inferior kind of being, hence impossible to understand. Women are subordinate to men *by nature*. As inferiors, women must always be kept in protective custody, under the control of men. When Freud's fiancée offered to go to work to enable them to marry sooner, Freud replied, "It is really a stillborn thought to send women into the struggle for existence exactly as men. If, for instance, I imagined my sweet gentle girl as a competitor it would only end in my telling her . . . that I am fond of her and that I implore her to withdraw from the strife into the calm incompetitive activity of *my* home." [italics mine][3]

Boys take in misogyny with their breakfast cereal. Mentors and peers show them that it won't do to spend much time with girls and women. No boy wants to be told he throws like a girl or to go home to mama. When his teachers and his buddies tell him that girls are not only physically weaker but lack all the important virtues, including courage, strength, and rationality, why would he respect girls? It's easy to move from thinking that women are inferior to treating them as inferiors.

The effect of this poison on women is equally potent. Like successful advertising, the message is designed into our lives and repeated until it becomes part of stored memory, until it is thought of as a received truth, an article of faith. Sexist messages, such as "no girls in this game," have been internalized by women as well as by men.

Ideas are powerful shapers of behavior. None has had graver consequences than the idea that one group is superior to another *by nature,* but most societies have been built on the bedrock of that idea. It has been the basis for racism, sexism, nationalism, imperialism, and speciesism.

For example, many societies have considered slavery an acceptable condition for those conquered in battle or seized by force (hence, inferior) or for children born into a state of servitude. As long as people believed that it was proper for human beings to be bought and sold, slavery persisted in this country. Emancipation in the United States came after public sentiment was galvanized by abolitionists—the radicals of their day—who regarded slavery as neither natural nor legitimate. We will not see the end of a rape culture until a critical mass of people believes that violence against women is neither natural nor legitimate. And that will require rethinking and reshaping attitudes internalized from childhood. When the destructive messages that sexism broadcasts are recognized as dangerous to a worthwhile future civilization, we will have relationships that are based on mutual trust—true peer relationships built from the ground up, built on mutual respect.

THE PERSONAL IS POLITICAL

For years, I thought that acts of sexual violence were the irrational, unrelated acts of deranged strangers. Experience and study, however, have led me to conclude that a malevolent tradition and woman-hating gender training have everything to do with the universality of violence against women. The outcome of that training is evident in the imbalance of power between genders in our private and public lives but is most painfully visible when it erupts as sexual violence.

Preparing for this book has shown me how well and for how long I suppressed my own experiences of living in a rape culture when I was growing up. At that time, I didn't understand the meaning of a number of unpleasant experiences. I remember the day I first saw a man unzip his fly and expose his penis in the secluded front entry area of a subway car. I was on my way to junior high school in Manhattan. I had been staring out the front panel of the train into the void of the tunnel, hypnotized by the dazzling passage of colored lights. A blurred motion of his hand caught my attention. He was looking at my face, waiting for a reaction. I knew instinctively that his behavior was inappropriate, bizarre, and I turned and found a seat in the center of the subway car.

My best friend and I often took the long way home from school, walking across Central Park, to have more time to talk. Occasionally men followed us as we strolled across the park, but we learned that if we kept a certain distance ahead of them and didn't respond to their chitchat they would eventually leave us alone. We weren't sure why grown men would waste their time stalking high school girls.

During rush hour on the subway, a man would sometimes get close enough to rub his pelvis against my body, something I decided I would not put up with. I became expert in getting away through the crowd or, if the crush was too great, in thrusting my lumpy schoolbag between us. I pretended to ignore those men.

The summer I was fourteen, I hitched a ride back to our rented summer cottage from the little upstate town where I had been shopping. A man who had been watching me from across the street turned his car around and volunteered to drive me home. On the seven-mile drive back, he made a sexual offer that felt extremely menacing. I talked glibly about the fact that I was already late and that my parents were probably out looking for me. To my intense relief, he dropped me off at my road without another word. I've read newspaper stories about women hitchhikers found raped and murdered by the roadside. My life might have ended that way.

I wouldn't have known how to describe these incidents to my parents without using words about parts of the body they never named or spoke of and that I sensed they didn't wish to speak of. I never mentioned these incidents to anyone because they had to do with sex, and sex in the fifties was a taboo subject, an ugly, secretive activity that people were ashamed of. There was no public discussion of rape. No one said the word out loud. Each woman was alone with what had been done to her. And there were no statistics.

· · · · ·

THE FACES OF OUR DAUGHTERS look out at me from old grade-school photographs. Their expressions are hopeful. Days at school were an adventure that might or might not go well, yet each well-loved face wears the smile the photographer requested. I had learned, as most parents do, that I could not pack happiness into their lunches with the sandwich and the apple. My love and my desire to protect did not give me the power to keep them from pain and trouble. Yet I sent them off, hopeful myself that no one would deliberately make them unhappy.

Our four daughters grew up in a pleasant suburb of a Midwestern city. They were not subject to the pressures of living and going to school in a core city. They attended reputable coed schools and colleges. Their father and I told them to fight back against classroom and neighborhood bullies, but the sexual bullying and harassment they encountered as they grew up could not be dealt with so simply or directly:

In a biology lab between classes one day, a male high school classmate grabbed one of our daughters from behind. He held her and fondled her, despite her vigorous protests, until she was able to break his hold.

As an eight-year-old, one of our daughters was walking home from a friend's house a few blocks away when a man stopped his car beside her on the street, opened the passenger-side door, exposed himself to her, and told her to get into his car. Instead, she turned and ran for home. We called the police, but she was too terrified to tell the officer much of anything about the man in the car. For months, she was frightened that the stranger might come back and get her.

One of our daughters, at fifteen, was hassled and propositioned every school-day afternoon by the loungers she had to pass on her way from the bus stop to her dance class a block away.

When one of our daughters was a college freshman, a casual friend who lived down the hall in her dorm attempted to rape her in her room. A passing student heard her call out and intervened. The would-be rapist told her that no one would believe she hadn't asked for it by allowing him into her room.

At seventeen, one of our daughters found a summer job as a waitress in a busy restaurant where the tips were good. The mandatory uniform, a short skirt and form-fitting top, drew frequent sexual comments and propositions. She held her tongue and kept the job for the summer, although she was angry that she was considered fair game because she was a woman working in a service-oriented job.

As a college sophomore at a highly rated Eastern liberal arts college, one of our daughters was assigned a room in a frat house that had recently been converted into a dorm. She was terrorized for an entire semester by the ex-fraternity men next door. They threatened to beat her up and rape her because she wouldn't move out of her room, a room they thought should go to a fraternity buddy of theirs. When she complained to the dean of students, he told her that he had no power to prevent these men from threatening her. He suggested that she be cautious about walking across the campus after dark.

One of our daughters was stalked for several months by an acquaintance. Even after she assured him that she never wanted to see him again, he wouldn't leave her alone. He didn't take her no seriously. Only after he received a call from another man, her father, did he cease and desist.

During their teen years, three of our four daughters received obscene phone calls, some random, others from people who knew them from school. Several times we had to change the number of our children's line to stop the frightening calls.

These experiences are the ones that come readily to mind, although there were others, including sexual name-calling on the school bus and in high school corridors. At the time, I minimized these incidents as much as I could in order not to frighten my daughters further. As I write down these stories, I am surprised by how many there were, and by how unwilling I was then to understand what they represented. They were expressions of forces I didn't dare think about because I didn't know how to counter them.

I cite these incidents not because I believe that our daughters were singled out for harassment but because, on the contrary, what they experienced is all too customary. As our daughters grew up, they heard similar stories from their friends. We began to realize that girls leading ordinary lives in supposedly safe surroundings were in fact living in an environment latent with hostility and sexual threat.

Our daughters were able to tell us about their experiences of harassment, knowing that we would listen and do everything we could to be of help. At the time, though, neither they nor we knew enough to connect personal traumas to societal patterns. That connection was made when we recognized the truth of the phrase "the personal is political." Women sharing their experiences of sexual violence and harassment with other women in the seventies and eighties broke the silence of centuries. Their stories allowed air and light into the darkness of women's sexual ignorance and sexual abuse. This was a time when women opened rape crisis centers and educated the police and the courts to become more aware that rape was an issue that called for sensitivity and proper training. Because of feminism, because of the women's movement, because of the daring and the dedication of thousands of women who applied social and political pressure to bring violence against women into the open and to quantify the issue, we finally understand the enormity of the problem.

The fear of sexual assault that is part of the daily life of women in this country takes up a continent of psychic space. A rape culture is a culture of intimidation that keeps women afraid of being attacked and so it confines women in the range of their behavior. That fear makes a woman censor her behavior—her speech, her way of dressing, her actions. Fear undermines her confidence in her ability to be independent. The necessity to be mindful of one's behavior at all times is far more than merely annoying. Women's lives are unnecessarily constricted. As a society, this one issue hampers the best efforts of half our population, costing us heavily in lost initiative and in emotional energy stolen from other, more creative thoughts.

THE DAMAGE TO GIRLS GROWING UP NOW

Girls and boys are themselves quite aware of the differing cultural situations that confront them. In a Minneapolis newspaper survey in the nineties,[4] thousands of schoolchildren were asked whether they would prefer to be a man or a woman. Both boys and girls commented frequently that a woman is vulnerable to assault, rape, and murder. Here are three of the responses:

> The worst thing about being a woman is we get raped and
> killed. Women can get killed by their prettiness.
> —Fifth-grade girl, age ten, Mounds View, Minnesota

> The up side to being a woman is you can manipulate men
> with your body. There isn't anything a man wouldn't do for
> a gorgeous woman. . . . Even though it might be fun to be a
> woman for a little while, I wouldn't want to be one full time.
> Why? Because no matter how you slice it, men are in control
> in today's society just as they have been since man and woman
> existed. That's where I like to be.
> —Tenth-grade boy, age fifteen, Elk River, Minnesota

> The best thing about being a man is that I can do what I want,
> be as rude and disgusting as I want, and no one says anything.
> —Eleventh-grade boy, age sixteen, Grey Eagle, Minnesota

Here, in the words of those who know, is the truth about the way things continue to be in the early years of the twenty-first century. American girls grow up in an atmosphere of gender-based pressure. Although they are the objects of aggression from the time they enroll in grade school, the situation grows steadily worse in junior high and high school. The air in such an atmosphere is unfit for girls to breathe, unhealthy and depressing. It's not surprising that a number of studies have shown that the self-esteem of girls plummets when they reach adolescence.

RAISING GIRLS TO KNOW THEIR STRENGTHS

What can we do to repair the damage? What can we teach girls that will help them to grow up strong enough to resist the pressures and to change a rape culture?

• *Tell your daughters about the resources that helped you survive the traumas of growing up.* Taking Thoreau's advice, I will begin by looking into my own life to judge what may be learned from it. Since I was as unscathed by adolescent feelings of anxiety and low self-esteem as anyone in hormonal overload can be, I have tried to understand why that was so. Raised in a blue-collar neighborhood by immigrant parents, my life was bare bones in terms of what we could afford. My father worked long hours to bolster a fledgling business, and my mother was often sick and depressed. But both my parents gave me the feeling that I was important and worth their time and interest. The feeling of being valued for one's self is probably at the base of most people's self-estimate.

I learned to express myself physically, to trust and enjoy using my body. As a city kid, I had only concrete playgrounds, but I roller-skated and played long games of jump rope, stoopball, stickball, and, most glorious of all, rode my two-wheeler on long bike hikes.

My sixth-grade teacher, Mrs. Pauline Hill, cared about my future and suggested that I try to test into Hunter College junior high school, a New York City public school that offered an excellent education for girls who wanted a college preparatory course of study. My parents were doubtful about allowing a thirteen-year-old to travel by subway into the city each day, but they finally agreed that I could enroll. I consider that decision pivotal in shaping my life. Because of it, I bypassed the usual coed competition and social anxiety.

I was part of a society of girls and women from seventh grade until I graduated from high school. The atmosphere was informal. I didn't worry about what I was going to wear; a few skirts and blouses saw me through. The girls came from every ethnic group and from all the boroughs of the city. My friends were remarkably different, one from another, in temperament and background. We got to know each other through the extracurricular clubs and groups, where I spent every school afternoon from three to six o'clock.

My role models in school were women. Without thinking too much about it, I absorbed the knowledge that women were intellectual, proactive, good leaders, firm friends, and simply fun to be with.

I was encouraged academically. My teachers were women who, for the most part, cared about their students and urged them to speak in class and to go beyond what was called for in an assignment.

I was empowered by my peers. I ran for student government office, I had a small part in a school play, I joined the staff of the magazine, I was a mentor to younger girls through a Big Sister organization. My friends, too, had their activities and roles in some facet of school life: the athletic association, the French club, the school newspaper, and the honor society. No one needed to talk to us abstractly about the importance of women participating in the social or political life of our school.

Hunter is now coed, which I regret, no matter how good the school may be, because there are many coed schools and only a few that offer girls the kind of outstanding single-sex academic and social opportunity I received.

Coming out of that experience, I had great enthusiasm for going on to college and into the working world. I had learned that I could work toward a goal I cared about and have a reasonable chance of achieving it. And I never considered that my gender might be a hindrance.

Some women who have studied at single-sex schools have a different and much less enthusiastic opinion. Women have said to me, "We live in a co-educational world. Girls should learn to get along with boys in school." I agree wholeheartedly, in principle. If girls were treated as equals in the class-room, coeducation might be ideal.

I doubt that I could have convinced any of our four daughters to attend a girls' school, even had one been available. But I firmly believe that girls should have some place—a club or a team or an organization with a social goal—where they can come together to meet each other as friends and as allies.

Girls need comradeship as relief from the social-sexual competition that often makes the junior high and high school years dreadful—so much so that girls can slip into a victim mentality. These are the years when the matter of what to wear becomes, in the eyes of girls, a huge problem in the school social pressure cooker, because appearance is more important than academic achievement. No one who hasn't witnessed it can imagine the self-loathing and despair that can accompany the simple act of getting dressed for school in the morning and feeling inadequate.

• *Give girls your attention and your approval.* Teach girls to be independent entities. A girl should be raised to feel that she is a valuable person who will be taken seriously. Children's stories are sometimes serious allegories: Margery William's velveteen rabbit wishes to be a real rabbit, not a toy to be played with and abandoned at the whim of its owner. Pinocchio longs to be flesh and blood, not a marionette controlled by a master, even a kind one. It is essential that a girl think of herself as valuable in her own right, as a real person, not a toy or a marionette dancing on strings held by the men in her life.

Girls must hear repeatedly, from as many sources as possible, that their lives are as important as are those of their brothers. Girls must be told that they have the right to aspire to work they care about.

Parents complain that teenage girls won't talk to them about their problems and don't seem to value their parents' input. Early in a girl's life is the time to establish a talking relationship that will last a lifetime. She will realize that her parents think she is worth talking and listening to.

For centuries, girls have been taught to commit a kind of psychic suicide. They were required to efface any quality of self that was rebellious or enterprising or merely curious and imaginative. Girls were directed to be meek, gentle, docile, and submissive, because such qualities were considered womanly. A woman was obedient. A woman did not question, much less look directly at, a man. The idealized woman, painted as a Madonna, was portrayed with her head down, gaze lowered and averted. Girls were trained for subservience, not for personal satisfaction. Girls trained in this way do not often grow up to become independent women.

The most important gift anyone can give a girl is to instill in her a belief in her own power as an individual, her value without reference to gender, her self-respect as a person with potential. I have heard the gratitude and satisfaction in an adult woman's voice when she speaks of a father or a mother or a teacher who showed her early in her life that she mattered. Yes, a woman can overcome being shut up and toned down as a child, but recovery from that treatment takes enormous time and energy. The rambunctious girl who knows her own strengths will become a person who empowers others out of the abundance of her self-respect.

• *Encourage fathers to become active allies in remaking the culture.* Society now acknowledges what was long denied and long concealed: the fact that there are sexually abusive fathers as well as fathers who regularly batter their children. There are also fathers who permanently scar their daughters by openly preferring their sons. The misogyny of our culture is at least part of the source of these men's actions and attitudes.

We ought to recognize, though, that there are millions of supportive, nurturing fathers in this country whose efforts to promote gender equity make a large, positive difference in the lives of their daughters.

In my own life and in the lives of our daughters, it would be hard to overestimate the effect of having had a father who showed us his love and his confidence. Busy and tired as he was, my father found time to have long conversations with me, to walk with me in the evening and tell me stories, to explain his taste in music and literature. He listened without laughing to my half-baked plans for the future. In short, he treated me with respect as a person who had interesting thoughts and opinions.

Our daughters each spent considerable time with their father right from the beginning: he took on the 2 A.M. feedings, and he was the one they chose to throw up on in the middle of the night when they had stomach flu. When our daughters were young and fascinated by the process, they wanted to shave like their dad; he gave them a play razor and lathered them up, and, no, that didn't make them want to grow up to be men. No matter how cold or wet the weather, he took them trick-or-treating. He went fishing with the ones who didn't mind baiting their own hooks. He danced around the living room, as they did, to music they loved, but he didn't miss a chance to lobby on behalf of the music he cared about. He rearranged his schedule to attend their school plays, gymnastic meets, dance recitals, debates, soccer matches, and birthday parties. His pride in them is evidenced in the yard of photo albums on our bookshelf that chronicle their days in colorful detail.

The ongoing father-daughter kitchen-table debates and skirmishes about political issues and any other topic worth discussing continue to this day whenever they are together. They disagree, creatively and at length, on a variety of issues. They agree that they can disagree and still love one another. That's vital knowledge for a girl to have when she is learning to partner in her adult life.

Daughters can bring to their fathers an awareness of the prevalence of harassment in their everyday lives. For most men, sexual violence is an invisible issue, and the huge and incontrovertible fact that America is the most sexually violent country in the Western world has no impact on their consciousness. The fear of being sexually assaulted is simply not on a man's mind as it always is on a woman's. I would go further and say that sexual violence is a *nonissue* for most men, with none of the clout, say, of the state of the economy or the standing of a favorite baseball/football/basketball team.

How do we make this enormous shadow on the lives of women visible to the millions of men who are not rapists or molesters or seducers? How do we reach the men most of us know, the men who flinch at the thought of being put into the category of perpetrator but who are socialized to agree tacitly with the beliefs of a rape culture?

I believe that a father's love for his daughter, and his knowledge of what his own male socialization was like, might inspire him to look through a different lens at the familiar clubby world of male privilege; to recognize the effect that gender inequity has on his daughter's life, to be outraged by the harassment and violence that touch her in some way every day. The former navy officers who were fathers of the women officers sexually harassed at Tailhook were furious and indignant about the belief in sexual privilege that was expressed at that convention.

Fathers of daughters can actively promote the idea that sexually violent men are not real men at all but cowards and bullies. I would like to see men's groups undertake a campaign to make sexual violence not only repulsive to men but—and this could be crucial—unfashionable, uncool, unmasculine.

Fathers of daughters can turn their love and energy into practical efforts to remake this culture into one that actively promotes the growth and happiness of girls and women. Their efforts are needed and welcomed. They make a profound difference to this society.

• *Tell girls the truth; replace sexual ignorance with sexual knowledge.* Protecting girls means giving them the knowledge that will allow them to make intelligent, principled decisions about sexuality. As a society—preferably through a parent or parents—we should teach girls at an early age about the sexual functioning of their bodies. It is a mistake to wait until a girl reaches the age that's generally considered old enough.

My father and mother were themselves unsure what to say to a girl about the life of her body, so they said nothing. My mother had been trained to deny that she knew anything remotely connected with the sex act or its consequences. Once I asked her the meaning of the word *abortion*. She looked as if I had struck her and told me never again to use such a word in her presence.

Of course, I read whatever I could get my hands on about sex in an attempt to understand why there was so much mystery and secrecy. My high school didn't get around to sex education until junior year, when Miss Mildred Duffy gave her popular course, called Health Education 6, a euphemism for *sex education.*

Even though we should have been given such a course much earlier in our lives, Miss Duffy's students in the late fifties and early sixties were an immensely privileged group. We were among the tiny percentage of women in all of recorded history given accurate information—and actually taught—about human reproduction.

Miss Duffy was careful not to talk about the implications for us personally of what we were learning; she didn't teach about sexuality as a source of pleasure, nor did she speak about sexual violence against women. Nonetheless, her class was a door to what used to be called carnal knowledge, knowledge forbidden to us because we were girls and because such knowledge might tarnish our innocence.

An innocent is literally one free of guilt or sin, lacking in knowledge. The girls in my class qualified as innocents. We had little or no concept of the physiology of sexuality or reproduction. We didn't know there was an estrus cycle that regulates conception. Several years after we began wearing sanitary napkins each month, we were taught the reason women menstruate.

I wish that Miss Duffy could also have told us that boys were being socialized to become sexual marauders and to see women as sexual prey.

Our mothers, and certainly their mothers, went to their marriage beds "innocent." A woman learned about sex not from books or wall charts but from what she could glean from the hints of other women or from the experience of being sexually assailed on her marriage bed. No woman considered virtuous by her community knew anything significant about sex before she married.

Moreover, lack of information was made a virtue in a woman. To be pure was to be unaware of basic physical facts, ignorant, uninformed and hence vulnerable, pliable, obedient to the wishes of the husband who knew, more or less, what to do. A proper girl was raised to be a sexual lamb, docile and tractable. Ignorance was dressed up and paraded to women as innocence. Innocence was touted as fostering a high level of morality.

The male authority that kept girls and women ignorant of their physiology is intact in many places in the world today, and that deliberate ignorance of anything to do with her sexuality is part of the market value of a prospective bride. Even in the United States, sexual ignorance continues to make girls easy pickings for the molester and the seducer. Recently, I read a newspaper story that quoted the mother of a ten-year-old who had become pregnant. The mother lamented that she couldn't understand how such a thing could have happened when she had purposely withheld any information about sex.

Ignorance is not and never should have been considered a virtue. To keep a girl ignorant of the way her body functions sexually is detrimental. Early and thorough education for girls and boys about their sexuality is a basic need that is not met by most school curricula. Religious and political beliefs have crept into teachings about human biology. Sex education coupled with sexual harassment curricula could form the basis for school programs that talk about ethical sexual behavior.

• *Arm girls with the knowledge that they can be a part of cultural change.* Girls will find insight in the knowledge that cultures and their mores change over time—through the efforts of those who demand change. Customs that once seemed intrinsic to human nature have been abandoned or redirected. For example, human sacrifice was once practiced extensively. In the past, consigning feeble newborns, the very sick, and the old to death by exposure and starvation was routine in some cultures. The women's movement of the twentieth century secured the vote for American women after decades of protest. In other parts of the world, women are still fighting for the right to vote, to seek employment, and to make decisions about their sexuality.

Societies can adapt to new insights and change their habits and their practices, but often only through social and political pressure. Girls who grow up with a desire to work for social justice will become politically aware and active.

Girls who are taught cultural history will recognize that eradicating sexual violence is a formidable goal but no more so than cleaning up pollution on the planet, a recognized cultural objective we have embraced as worthy of time and support.

• *Enlist women mentors and role models.* We don't live in close-knit villages nor do we have readily accessible extended families where our daughters can find other listeners and guides. However, grandmothers, aunts, honorary aunts, neighbors, and family friends, no matter how far away, can become a source of knowledge and companionship. Older women are a girl's link to history, her personal knowledge of the past. Such mentors can enlarge her horizons and help her reflect upon her own future.

• *Find ways for girls to play and work together.* Athletic programs are an excellent way for girls to gain strength and competence, especially now that schools have recognized that it's not only the few girls who make a varsity team who should be trained and strengthened. All girls should be included in some athletic program and instructed in physical activities. Being able to swim or run or play volleyball can help a girl survive a socially cutthroat school.

Many studies have demonstrated the boost to self-esteem when girls become active in sports and recreational activities. A study of preteen girls in the early nineties supports the idea that girls derive a strong, positive self-image from the challenge, achievement, skill development, and risk-taking of sports involvement. The study makes a number of recommendations, including creating single-sex teams where girls can play and try new activities in a safe, uncritical environment. The Women's Sports Foundation, a national nonprofit, member-based organization dedicated to increasing opportunities for girls and women in sports and fitness through education, advocacy, recognition, and grants, was established in 1974 by tennis star Billie Jean King to create an educated public that encourages females' participation and supports gender equality in sport. Its goal is to improve the physical, mental, and emotional well-being of all females through sports and fitness participation.

According to the National Federation of State High School Associations, 2000–2001 marked the twelfth consecutive record-setting year for girls' participation in high school sports: 2,746,181 girls participated, an increase of 60,662. Girls' participation accounted for 41 percent of high school athletes, up marginally from 40.9 percent the year before.

Girls' participation in outdoor track and field also showed an increase, with 10,361 more participants than the previous year, followed by an increase of 5,763 in volleyball. These two sports rank second and third, respectively, after school spirit groups, as the most popular female sports.

Recently I watched two of our granddaughters, both five years old, playing soccer for the first time in a youth league with kind, encouraging coaches. They are enthusiastic about continuing to play.

I recommend that parents of girls investigate what's available through their daughters' schools and in their communities, and that they help to develop new programs that allow girls the experience of working cooperatively. Organizations like the Girl Scouts and the Y offer important opportunities to girls, not only as a source for camaraderie and good times, but as places where their skills and leadership abilities will be encouraged.

• *Teach girls to be both story-critical and media-critical.* Fairy tales may be all right, introducing children, as Bruno Bettelheim suggests, to the terrors of life, but frankly these stories are dreadful gender role models for girls. Most of the heroines are ladies-in-waiting: Cinderella waits humbly in the ashes for a transformation or a prince; Snow White waits primly in her bed-coffin to be kissed by a man and awakened into a real-life existence. All those princesses wait in their towers to be rescued, the pretty women of their day. Being beautiful is a storybook heroine's stock-in-trade, but waiting is her primary activity. Passivity encourages victimization. Girls want to be heroes. Find stories and books that give them women heroes worth identifying with.

Women don't always acknowledge the psychic damage caused by fear of sexualized violence. There is strong evidence that men exposed to repeated doses of violence and rape in films become increasingly desensitized to violent acts and to the effect of that violence on the victims. What is the effect of repeated doses of sexual violence on women and girls? How much anger and fear do women repress every time they watch a TV program or a film, in the company of a man, that shows women being stalked, raped, tortured, murdered? A few women say they get up and leave. Others think they need to show their tough-mindedness by watching with outward composure, although they may be uncomfortable with what is being shown. Many women don't say anything to the man they're with because, after all, sexual violence in the media is such a common plot prop that they would have to walk out on most of what's commercially available. And perhaps that's what women should be doing.

How can anyone quantify the damage done to a girl who is exposed daily to a stream of images of women being pursued, threatened, sexually assaulted, and killed? What happens to a girl's sense of adventure, her zest for living an interesting life, in the face of a world obviously hostile to women? The cumulative effect of media violence on girls is difficult to estimate, but I believe that over the years the results are visible in the lessening of self-esteem, and in the belief that women cannot effectively fight a universal predation.

We demonstrate to girls repeatedly that being beautiful and seductive are the qualities society prizes in adult women. At the same time, girls cannot help but observe that in the media beautiful and seductive women are the most likely candidates for sexual assault. A successful woman, in this unspoken double bind, is set up to be a victim of violence. As the Minnesota fifth-grader wrote, "Women can get killed by their prettiness." The media portrayal of women prepares girls to become victims, just as surely as it teaches men to be comfortable perpetrators of violence.

Watching television or a film with a girl can be a springboard for questions about what is happening on the screen and how female and male characters are presented. A parent can ask, for example, "How would you have handled that situation?" If girls learn from adults at an early age that the messages being broadcast are not necessarily in their best interests, they have the chance to reject those messages. Children can quickly become critical and reflective about what they see, hear, and read.

We ought to have alternative media, some of them created by children themselves, that present noncommercial visions. Parents' groups should discuss strategies to influence media presentations of women. Women characters who are three-dimensional human beings rather than clothes-pegs, sex objects, or villainous sexual manipulators are badly needed in the media's global village.

• *Be a part of the solution.* Whatever you find the time and energy to do that makes this society more hospitable and more equitable for women is part of creating positive change. Your actions register more deeply than you suspect with your daughters. Your behavior and your relationships with others are critical shapers of a girl's image of who she can and should become.

• *Encourage girls to be ecstatic.* At twelve, I rode my bike in the warm last light of summer evenings, swooping down the long hill just past my block, past St. Teresa's parochial school where my girlfriends learned every day that their bodies were provocations to evil, down another block, and then another and another. I have never been more completely alive than in those moments, feeling in sync with the whir of the spokes and the air I displaced. I had no word then for the ecstatic, but that was the emotion I felt. I knew what it was to be joyful and alive, on my own but not lonely, my mind and body working together.

Joy and playfulness are regarded as childish emotions instead of being recognized as lifelong resources that strengthen and invigorate. We rarely speak about those emotions, the causeless happiness that floods us and makes us grateful to be alive. The ability to feel deeply is a power and a resource that Audre Lorde evokes in her essay "Uses of the Erotic: The Erotic as Power." Whether one calls that emotion the ecstatic or the erotic, it is a source of creativity and love that nourishes a healthy sense of self and allows a human being to feel keenly with others. It is a source of happiness that can be kept and counted on, always available and infinitely renewable.

In our culture that so often and so early makes girls feel meek and powerless, whatever nourishes playfulness, joy, and the ecstatic must be cherished and cultivated every day.

NOTES

1. Tama Starr, ed., *The "Natural Inferiority" of Women* (New York: Poseidon, 1991), 19.
2. Starr, *"Natural Inferiority,"* 87–88.
3. Starr, *"Natural Inferiority,"* 181.
4. Misty Snow, "Question on Gender Brings Out Stereotypes," *Minneapolis Star Tribune,* October 6, 1992.

EMILIE BUCHWALD is publisher emeritus of Milkweed Editions and the editor of more than 190 books. She was educated at Barnard College (BA), Columbia University (MA), and the University of Minnesota (Ph.D., Doc. Humane Letters). Buchwald is the author of two award-winning children's books. She is the mother of Jane, Amy, Claire, and Dana, who provided ideas, insights, and valued suggestions for this book.

LEARNING TO LISTEN
ONE MAN'S WORK IN THE ANTIRAPE MOVEMENT
. . . .
RICHARD S. ORTON

I believe that defensiveness and discomfort are inevitable
for many men when we are challenged to acknowledge
women's vulnerability to men's violence and the impact
that it has on them.

PART I

MY TELEPHONE RANG AT MIDNIGHT. The rape hotline volunteer told me that a woman was waiting at the emergency room for a rape exam. The volunteer had been trying for an hour to locate someone to go and be with her. I was the only person available that night.

I had been on staff at the Austin Rape Crisis Center for over a year and knew that this moment might come. Even though my job focused on school and community education, I had been trained, like all staff and volunteers, to support rape survivors in crisis situations. I had done crisis counseling via the telephone, but I had never been face to face with a rape survivor shortly after the assault. My stomach tightened at the thought.

The most practical—and most difficult—part of rape crisis center training for me was the role playing, where trainees are put into unscripted scenarios similar to those they would encounter on the telephone, at the emergency room, or in other face-to-face encounters with rape survivors, their family members, or medical and law enforcement professionals. The crisis intervention skills that are taught in training get tested through role-playing. For me, it was like trying to walk through a minefield. I thought that if I failed to say the right thing, if I failed to anticipate correctly the needs of the survivor, I might set off emotional mines. No real harm was done in role-plays, but what was about to happen would not be a role-play.

I now understand that what most people need in such situations is to feel genuine concern and empathy from a helping person, to be listened to, to be allowed to express feelings (or remain silent), and to have their questions answered. But as I drove to the emergency room that night, I was only aware of how nervous I was. I went over in my mind all the do's and don'ts I had learned in training. And I had one additional concern: Having just been raped by a man, the woman I was about to meet might not want to deal with me, another man. Crisis center policy required that a female volunteer be provided in these situations, but none was available that night.

As I walked into the emergency room I saw a young woman I will call Sandy sitting on a bed dressed in a green hospital gown. A nurse stood behind her doing something to her hair. As I got closer I saw that the nurse was cleaning dried blood out of Sandy's hair and I saw a dozen or more stitches in her scalp.

I introduced myself, certain she could hear the pounding in my chest. I asked her how she was feeling. She smiled and said she was doing better now. She seemed calmer than I was.

That afternoon a young man had approached her in a mall parking lot and asked for help. His car wouldn't start, he said, and he needed a ride to a friend's house a short distance away. Accustomed to helping people out in the farming community she had recently left, Sandy agreed to give him a ride. She ended up in a ditch outside of town, raped and beaten.

In addition to stitches in her scalp, Sandy needed to undergo a rape exam and get an X-ray of her skull. As we waited for these tasks to be completed, we talked about many of the things that come up in such situations. Why would someone do something like this? What was going to happen now? What would the police want to know? What would happen if they caught him? Was she going to be all right? What would this do to her life? How could she tell her family what had happened, and how were they going to react?

I was greatly relieved that Sandy accepted my presence. Like many people in her situation, she seemed to appreciate that a stranger would come to the hospital in the middle of the night to be with her—someone whose only purpose was to support her and advocate for her.

After spending four or five hours in the emergency room Sandy needed to decide where to go now that she was about to be released. She was new to Austin and had not made many friends yet, and her family was in another state. Her employer and his wife were the only people she knew well enough to call. She asked me to call her employer's wife, explain what had happened, and ask if she could stay with them that night. I made the call and we left the hospital.

We arrived at her employer's home around 5 or 6 A.M. Sandy went to bed right away, and I stayed a moment to talk with her friends. The sun was coming up as I left. I felt strange. Fatigue, I thought. I was numb from the previous six or seven hours. But about halfway home the numbness ended and I broke down. One moment I was fine, the next I was sobbing uncontrollably. I hadn't seen this coming and I was unable to control it when it did. I was shocked and frightened at what was happening to me. I had never experienced anything like this before and now here I was, driving down the highway at daybreak, falling apart.

This was the first of several experiences I had in the late 1970s and early 1980s through my work with the Austin Rape Crisis Center that began to expose me to blank spaces in my awareness of the world. These blank spaces, which I attribute to growing up male, represented my lack of awareness of the world as women experience it, a world that in varying degrees creates in women a sense of being at risk simply because they are women. Though it took me years to fully assimilate the significance of these experiences, they ultimately had a profound impact on the way I view the world—as if I had entered a different dimension.

Being hired by the Austin Rape Crisis Center (ARCC) in 1978 was a lucky accident, though at the time I considered it only an interesting opportunity to do something different for a while. In the year or so that preceded my encounter with Sandy in the emergency room, I had learned a lot about rape from books, from the staff and volunteers at ARCC, and from several rape survivors who were volunteers. I had spoken frequently to school and community groups about rape awareness and prevention. I had helped train volunteers for ARCC.

Yet until that night, rape was only an idea to me. My connection to it was mostly intellectual. During the drive home at dawn, I felt it in my gut for the first time. Sandy's experience made it impossible for me to protect myself any longer from the emotional impact of sexual violation—something I had not allowed to touch me before. That experience put me on a different track and sent me into uncharted territory.

In August 1979, I attended the first conference of the National Coalition Against Sexual Assault (NCASA) in Lake Geneva, Wisconsin. Held at a rustic camp, the conference was attended by about two hundred people. I was one of six men. I knew that male involvement with rape crisis centers was a controversial topic for many, perhaps most, women doing the work, and that it was relatively rare at that time for centers to solicit male volunteers and practically unheard of to recruit male staff.

The Austin Rape Crisis Center had included a small number of male volunteers ever since its founding in 1974. Sylvia Callaway, who became executive director in 1977, embraced this policy wholeheartedly. She believed that the challenges male volunteers and staff might present were worth the effort. The long-term effect of meeting those challenges would be to educate a group of men about rape from a woman's perspective, and those men would then educate other men. The antirape movement's goal of ending rape could not be accomplished without male allies, and Sylvia was committed to creating male allies.

Lake Geneva was a different environment than anything I had experienced in Austin. I halfway expected to be challenged verbally, or worse. Nothing like that happened. What did happen was more subtle and indirect: I was mostly ignored. My clearest memory is of sitting in a workshop for an hour and a half, participating occasionally but not feeling part of the group. By the end of the session, I felt a combination of alienation and confusion, though I doubt I could have described my feelings so clearly then. I remember a frustrated conversation with Sylvia that evening, in which I tried unsuccessfully to understand the source of my feelings.

What was unfamiliar about that experience, as I began to understand later, was that I felt invisible. My presence was largely unacknowledged. The workshop proceeded without my influence. I might as well not have been there.

Many years after that first NCASA conference, I was at a conference for profeminist men. One of the keynote speakers, Harry Brod, was talking about his experiences with men who viewed feminism and feminists as antimale. His comments on where this attitude came from took me back to that Lake Geneva workshop. He said that what many men most misunderstand about feminism—a misunderstanding that leads them to view feminism as antimale—is that it is not about men at all. And this, he said, is what is so frightening about feminism to so many men.

What those women were doing in that workshop at Lake Geneva was not about me, and although I did not experience it as being *against* me, I did experience their way of being together without including me as something completely new, and I did not know what to make of it. It had not occurred to me before that gender might be part of what determines how a person is treated. I had not experienced the discriminatory behavior that females often do. This was largely invisible to me until the Lake Geneva conference, and it remained confusing and blurry in my consciousness for a long time afterward. To this day, I have to remind myself that women's experience in the world—women's reality—is not always the same as men's.

Another experience, this time at the second NCASA conference in Austin in 1980, exposed even more dramatically the blank spaces in my life as a man.

One of the keynote speakers suggested that we show a new film on rape made by a group of Canadian feminists, and as an organizer of the conference I ordered the film and scheduled it for viewing. It arrived at the last minute and we did not have a chance to preview it.

As I recall, the film began with a didactic section, then shifted abruptly to a rape scenario. A woman walking down a sidewalk was grabbed by a man and thrown into a van, where she was terrorized and raped. It was highly realistic. The woman's terror permeated the viewing room. As the scenario progressed, women began to leave. Finally, someone stood up and demanded that the film be stopped. Many women in the room were survivors of rape or childhood sexual abuse. Several were outraged that they had not been warned about the content of the film. Some thought that such a film should not be shown at all. Others, while agreeing that the film was extremely difficult to watch, wanted to finish it, finding value in being able to confront it. After a brief but intense discussion, the women agreed that those who wanted to finish watching the film would do so, then join the others for a processing session.

I felt both responsible for what was happening and helpless to do anything about it. Many women were clearly in pain because of the film. Again, I felt myself sliding into unknown territory.

When the fifty or so women came together after the film, I remember what happened mostly as a succession of images as I might have seen them through a gauze screen, not as words in a narrative. Even more than in the hospital emergency room with Sandy, I felt completely unprepared for what I was experiencing. I was witness to an emotional outpouring that astonished me, frightened me, and left me dumbfounded. Nothing in my thirty-plus years had prepared me for the next hour or two.

The situation felt chaotic. Some of the women were angry that other women would watch the film. Others thought that seeing it allowed them to confront their own demons. Rape survivors did not have a consistent response. Some found it a test of their recovery, while for others it was a nightmare relived. Individuals made impassioned statements. Small groups came together for support. The film had ripped off the veneer of safety for many of them, and their vulnerability and outrage were on display in such a graphic way that I could not possibly intellectualize, rationalize, or compartmentalize my response. I was confronted by the reality of women's vulnerability in a way that made me feel helpless and completely unsure of myself, as if a very large person had picked me up by the shoulders, shaken me violently for a few seconds, then put me down and walked away. Nothing looked or felt the same.

I could not fully absorb the meaning and importance of these three experiences when they happened. I did not have the emotional awareness or vocabulary to talk about them, but they burned deeply into my consciousness.

Working at the rape crisis center, I was confronted daily by the world women experience, from petty injustices to fear to actual assault. I always had the option of filtering out what I was hearing, and I often did. But the cumulative effect, year after year, of exposure to this women's world gave me information about women's experience that men rarely acquire. I had information about what the fear of male violence, as well as the actual experience of it, does to their lives. Constant exposure to this information forced me, slow as I was, to open up to my own feelings—not my thoughts—about the fear and violence that many women live with simply because they are women.

Being bombarded with information from this parallel world could be tiresome and difficult, and I didn't always want to hear it. Sometimes the information was full of anger, and the anger might be directed at me because I was a man. Women's anger was a powerful force that pushed the movement for change forward. Indeed, one could argue that women's anger was the foundation upon which the antirape movement was built. But dealing with it was never easy. I often got defensive.

Defensiveness is, still, something I have to be conscious of when challenged by women. When women express their experiences and feelings honestly, it may be difficult to hear them. Their words, coming from this parallel world, may feel assaultive and hurtful. Denial and defensiveness can be reflexive responses in such situations.

I may hear a woman's truth as an accusation, not as an expression of her own experience. I may feel threatened by the new frame of reference she is challenging me to acknowledge: hers. The tacitly accepted values of the world I live in support my need to be right because I am a man. Defensiveness and denial are tools I can use to keep from having to confront my ignorance of and insensitivity to women's experience. And they can support my complicity in maintaining a man's right to define reality in a way that excludes or diminishes important experiences that women have.

The situation may be further complicated by the dual, sometimes contradictory, effect of anger. A rape survivor's anger may be the only piece of strength she has to assert herself in the immediate aftermath of being raped, the only way for her to say "I am a human being and I demand to be treated with respect!" Hearing and acknowledging the collective anger that many women feel about their at-risk status can reveal an important perspective on the world we all inhabit, a perspective largely ignored or otherwise discounted in male-defined reality because it is so uncomfortable to deal with and challenges so much in our culture.

On the other hand, anger alone does not create change. It can become destructive if one side or the other becomes stuck there, making it an end in itself. Overcoming this anger, in my view, requires a willingness to acknowledge the validity of its source instead of denying it, and to hear it as something more than personal accusation.

As challenging as it sometimes is for me to hear what women are saying, the effort has, over the years, made a more complete and caring human being out of me. Many women have been and continue to be a part of my educational process. None has had a greater impact on me than Sylvia Callaway, the woman who hired me in 1978. Sylvia's philosophy of "loving anger" bridges the opposing forces in antirape work. It allows her to condemn the act of rape and all that supports it in our culture while acknowledging the humanity of the rapist and the necessity of understanding how such a personality comes into being. For her, rape is a "rip in the spirit" for both the victim and the perpetrator. Her philosophy of antirape work acknowledges the needs of everyone in the community, including the perpetrator and his family.

From her, I learned that doing antirape work is mostly about teaching respect to counter the disrespect taught by sexism—a disrespect that, in its most extreme form, becomes gender-based violence. Rape is an ultimate act of disrespect, yet it is a common occurrence. It is vital that we understand why it is so common and the real extent of the damage it does to our society. The path toward a rape-free society will lead men, in particular, through unmapped areas in our consciousness and into some challenging personal encounters. This journey will take us very near, if not actually into, the world as women experience it—the world of women at risk.

PART II

I left a downtown building late one night many years ago. I had just spent several hours training new volunteers for the rape crisis center. I was in a hurry to get home and my car was parked in a lot across the street. As I left the building, I saw the traffic light turn green and I started to run toward the intersection, about thirty yards away. A woman walking ahead of me toward the same intersection suddenly turned and looked at me like an animal frozen in the headlights of an oncoming car. I stopped and for a brief instant we stared at each other. In her eyes, I saw a mixture of surprise and terror. She turned and hurried across the street. I didn't move until she was out of sight.

As I stood there, I felt foolish and hypocritical, as well as responsible for her distress. By then, I had spent several years talking about rape prevention to groups of all kinds, yet apparently I had not absorbed the full meaning of my own words. While I had talked about the distancing phrases we may use when thinking about rapists—"not normal," "not one of us"—I had not yet understood that a woman might view my normal behavior as threatening. Never mind that I had no intention of harming the woman on the street that night (or any other woman who might be distressed by my behavior, intentional or not). The lesson I learned that night, at that woman's expense, was that her feelings of vulnerability to sexual violence had been largely invisible to me, even though I might claim, with some justification, to be sensitive and enlightened.

I started talking about that incident in my presentations as a way of illustrating how easy it is for men to threaten women simply because we aren't paying attention, because we don't experience the world in the same way they do. Later, I used another illustration of the different ways men and women experience the world:

Imagine walking down a sidewalk in a part of town with which you are unfamiliar—not what's considered a bad part of town, just unfamiliar. At first you appear to be alone—no one else is around. Then, a block or two ahead, you see a person coming directly toward you on the same sidewalk, someone you do not know, someone of the opposite gender. The distance between you and the other person slowly decreases until you pass within a few inches of each other.

I have used this exercise around a hundred times, mostly with college and high school classes. After presenting the scenario, I ask individuals in the group what they would be thinking or feeling as they passed the stranger on the sidewalk. I invariably get the same responses. A woman always responds first, saying she would feel anything from mild discomfort to nervousness to outright fear. The majority of women say they would be on their guard; a few say they would employ avoidance tactics such as crossing to the other side of the street.

When I ask the men to respond, there is often a long silence. After I press the issue, a man usually volunteers that he would not be thinking or feeling anything in particular, implying that he doesn't see anything remarkable about the situation, that it is not anything he has really thought about. Occasionally a man will say that if he found the woman attractive he might try to start a conversation. This usually creates a negative reaction from several women, who say they would feel even more threatened if that happened. Once in a while a man says he would feel a little nervous passing the woman because he would know she feels nervous. Some say they would consciously avoid eye contact or even cross the street to avoid making the woman uncomfortable.

I live in a relatively safe suburban environment. I would think nothing of taking a long walk in my neighborhood by myself in the middle of the night. Most of the women I know would not do that. Indeed, a woman who did and was assaulted would certainly be asked, "What were you doing walking by yourself in the middle of the night? Don't you know better?" Some people would blame her for what happened, while the actions of her nameless, faceless attacker would be taken for granted. Blame would not be placed where it belongs.

The classroom exercise I described above hardly constitutes a scientific study, but the consistency of responses it evokes shows that women as a group feel more vulnerable to harm than men as a group, even though men are victims of violence more often than women. Some men grow up in dangerous urban environments and fear walking to school or to the corner store. But the issue here is the threat of violence as women experience it and how that threat affects their lives.

For an instant on that night after volunteer training, I embodied that threat for the woman at the crosswalk. For me to argue that I did not intend to do harm would be true but irrelevant. The fact is, I did do harm.

I chose to acknowledge the experience instead of denying, ignoring, or forgetting it. It became an(other) important lesson, clarifying how invisible this women's reality can be, and challenging me again to learn to see the impact of the threat of rape on women's lives. Experiencing sexual violence is a debilitating experience, but so is living with the threat of it over a lifetime.

Becoming aware of these realities was like entering an uncharted sea without knowing that I was in a boat or on an ocean. Nothing had prepared me for the gut-level experiences, in an emergency room and at gatherings, that placed me on unfamiliar ground, in the blank spaces that came from experiences I never had or information I did not absorb because I grew up male.

Concern for my safety does not restrict my freedom now to the extent that it does for many women I know. The full impact of this threat on women is not something we talk about much—or at all—in public. Women's at-risk status is a given in our culture, something we tacitly accept as inevitable. I do not have to see or experience the world as women do. I can usually go through life with my blank spaces intact and suffer no negative consequences. If I am affected by women's vulnerability to sexual violence, it is usually because women I care about are hurt by it. A rape survivor is not the only person affected by the rape.

I learned to see the impact of the threat and experience of rape on women's lives by being willing to acknowledge and confront the blank spaces in my own. Doing this required humility and a willingness to listen to women in a way that was new to me. It required that I be willing to experience some of their vulnerability.

My blank spaces distanced me from the lives of the women I knew, allowing me, if I wanted it, the option of not thinking about their realities or doing anything about them. This distancing also allows me, if I want, to believe that the threat of sexual violence is not a serious problem, and that rape only happens to certain women and is perpetrated only by certain men—men who have nothing in common with me. It gives me deniability. I can stand on the sidelines of the issue and condemn rape without any understanding of how it looks or feels to those at greatest risk—without hearing their voices at all.

It has been hard to acknowledge that some important realities may have escaped me, or that I may have screened them out. Listening to women talk about the casual affronts and terrors they endure has challenged me.

Sometimes I don't want to hear these stories because I feel helpless, or I choose to ignore them because I can, because I have no parallel experience.

A friend told me once about being stalked and harassed on the highway by a man in another vehicle while she was driving alone. He tailgated her, then got in the lane beside her and made obscene gestures. This continued for miles. Listening to her story, I felt outraged and uncomfortable. I empathized as best I could. At a certain point in our conversation I no longer knew what to say, so we just dropped the subject. I could escape back into my own relatively safe life, but she would take those feelings of terror with her forever.

The man who harassed my friend must have engaged in similar activities on other occasions, and he must have known that he would get away with it. His chances of being held accountable were remote. He had crossed a line, but it was surely not the first line he had crossed with women. His highway terrorism may have been preceded by more subtle or customary aggression, like making women uncomfortable by the way he looked at them, by commenting about their bodies, or by being physically aggressive. Perhaps he had already raped.

If we deal with this man at all, we call him a weirdo, a psycho, or a sociopath. We may not connect his extreme behaviors with the less extreme visual and verbal intrusions into women's lives that may have preceded the highway incident. And we might not want to acknowledge the acceptability of such behaviors—the fact that men are rarely confronted or held accountable when they engage in sexually harassing behaviors. In such a world, rapists find acceptance, if not for raping, then for the harassing behaviors that lead up to their rapes. This acceptance makes what they do hard to see for what it is, which is one reason they can get away with it.

The crowning sadness of this event is that my friend not only had no access to justice for herself, but also probably told no more than a handful of close friends what happened to her. Silence overwhelmed her story, as it does so many others. Surely this silence is related to the blank spaces in men's lives.

The silencing of women also allows us to avoid a fundamental reassessment of the relative power of women and men in our society. Such a reassessment could put at risk power arrangements we take for granted in a male-defined reality, power arrangements that help hold in place our blindness to—or disregard for—women's vulnerability to harm.

As I became more aware of the parallel world women often inhabit, I could no longer avoid responding to it. Instead of spending all my time in the familiar public world largely defined and controlled by men, I was in a rape crisis center, an environment defined and controlled by women that deals with tragedies largely hidden from view in the male-defined world. Because the women who worked there treated me well, I felt at ease from day to day. But over time, the issues we dealt with put me into a mental and emotional frame of reference that I could not control, and that compelled me to deal with issues in my own life. I had to confront my own sexism. I had to acknowledge that I was not always the model citizen I wanted to believe I was. I had to absorb the meaning of the term male entitlement. It was then that I began to be aware—vaguely—of the blank spaces.

Filling in these blank spaces made me defensive. Dealing with the consequences of male violence to women on a daily basis backed me into a corner. On some level, I felt guilty. My own past behavior was cast in a new light and I was uncomfortable.

I had to take another look at my own treatment of women. I've never been physically violent with anyone, man or woman, but male entitlement casts a broad shadow. I had to acknowledge that I had been verbally and emotionally insensitive or demeaning to women, though I would not have thought of my behavior in those terms at the time, and that I had felt entitled to behave that way. My behavior was unremarkable because it was common male behavior and therefore invisible to me. But I could no longer pretend not to see connections between different kinds of demeaning behavior, ranging from visual and verbal affronts to rape. The common denominator was lack of respect.

I came to understand how male entitlement legitimizes lack of respect in subtle ways. By giving primacy to male viewpoints and male needs, it creates unequal power between men and women, making it easier for men to ignore or belittle women's voices, particularly when they are confronting our behavior. Sexual harassment provides examples of this point. Women who are sexually harassed by men in the workplace may hesitate to make their feelings known. By objecting, they may directly oppose entrenched male power and risk ridicule and further harassment. Federal legislation and judicial rulings are forcing employers to be accountable for sexual harassment, but the real human cost is paid by individuals, mostly women, whose lives have been poisoned by the once invisible range of behaviors we now call sexual harassment. The vast majority of sexual harassment victims suffer in silence because they do not think they will be taken seriously, and so they choose not to risk making a complaint.

Finally, male entitlement has maintained the blank spaces in my life. It has supported me in the mistaken belief that my experience as a male is a complete view of the world. Male entitlement and the disregard of women's experience go hand in hand. If I participate in one, I participate in the other. This is not easy for me to acknowledge on a personal level, because it requires humility and an openness to my own imperfections, and those make me feel vulnerable. But unless I am willing to take this step, I limit my own development as a human being.

I believe that defensiveness and discomfort are inevitable for many men when we are challenged to acknowledge women's vulnerability to men's violence and the impact that it has on them. Most of us aren't accustomed to viewing ourselves in this light and would insist that we are not part of the problem. I have certainly done that. But whether we commit acts of disrespect against women, large or small, or simply fail to notice that others do, we are part of the problem. Some may hear this as an accusation. I have experienced it as an opportunity to learn and grow as a human being.

Men have some good (selfish) reasons to get beyond defensiveness. In my case, defensiveness has been a block to learning some important things about my relationships and myself. My ego becomes a barrier to my emotional and intellectual growth when I am defensive. I have come to view the discomfort I feel when confronted with the blank spaces in my life as part of the process of reintegration with the female side of my psyche, correcting a separation encouraged in me—as it is in most boys—from an early age. Part of what creates our defensiveness in the first place is the loss of control we experience when we can no longer so easily define reality in our customary way. The very idea that there might be another, female-defined, reality that parallels our own can be threatening. We are forced by that knowledge into a role reversal in which women's realities challenge our own, and this is unfamiliar ground for most men.

Defensiveness seems inevitable to me when men grow up with blank spaces in our awareness of women's vulnerability to men's violence and then are confronted with the need to respond to it. Whether we are rapists, saints, or something in between, we must account for gender-based violence that normally casts men as offenders and women and children as victims.

Fortunately, this dilemma pushed me in the direction of self-examination and self-discovery. Filling in the blank spaces has helped me become more empathetic. By dealing with my defensiveness, I became more willing to open my heart and accept as a part of my reality aspects of women's lives that I had not previously acknowledged. My defensiveness and discomfort eventually led me to an honest awareness of women's vulnerability to men's violence. Once that honest awareness was in place, it required a moral or ethical response in my behavior. It became a moral imperative for me to be proactive in helping to create a different world, a world in which women's lives are not seriously eroded simply because men choose not to pay attention to the power imbalances that cause women so much suffering. Altruism aside, this journey has benefited me emotionally and spiritually beyond measure.

. . . .

RICHARD S. ORTON worked as a rape prevention educator between 1978 and 1996, including eleven years with the Austin Rape Crisis Center and four years with the state of Texas. Trained as a musician, he now earns his living as a photographer in Austin, Texas.

THE DATE RAPE PLAY
A COLLABORATIVE PROCESS
· · · · · · · · · · · · · · · · · · · ·

CAROLYN LEVY

We thought we were prepared for the response, but we were amazed at the outpouring of emotion from spectators. They greeted the play with joy and pain. For some, it reaffirmed that they were not alone in their experiences. For others, it opened a topic for discussion that had previously been closed tight. For still others, it raised questions about behaviors and attitudes.

(House lights down. Eight actors enter and face the audience. A man steps forward.)

Man: Every six minutes someone in America is raped. The vast majority of them are raped by someone they know.

(He checks his watch. A bell rings. Blackout. Throughout the play the bell will ring every six minutes.)

I N 1992, I CREATED A PLAY with a group of my students at Macalester College about the troubling issue of date rape. We titled our play *Until Someone Wakes Up.* The project grew out of our dramatic arts department's interest in community-based theater; we wanted to create an experience for our students that was outside the Broadway model of a five-week rehearsal period with a set script.

My own background had been in another form. For eight years, I was the artistic director of the Women's Theatre Project in the Twin Cities, where we had created new plays by and about women. As a collaborative enterprise, we had worked with a wide variety of writers, designers, performers, and directors as well as community groups and women's organizations. It was this experience I wanted to bring to my students, to teach them another mode of working, one that is central to some of the best theater being made in this country. We chose to do a community-based project and then cast about for appropriate subject matter.

The subject of date and acquaintance rape seemed to be everywhere around us. When I read Robin Warshaw's book, *I Never Called It Rape,* and learned that one in four college women has been or will be the victim of rape or attempted rape, I found I could not walk into any gathering of students without mentally counting off the women ("One, two, three, four"), knowing that a fourth of them had probably experienced this violence in their lives. But I read on and learned that women are not alone in being victims: Men are raped, too. I found that if I looked hard at the society and culture in which we are living, if I really examined forces at work on our students as they grow up, then the rape statistics were not a surprise. The climate is ripe for such things to happen. We are not taught well what it is to be a man or a woman. We don't have a lot of good models for healthy relationships. We receive confusing messages about who to be and how to be—both men and women. The issue had lots of gray areas—perfect for theatrical exploration.

Mom: Georgie Porgie, pudding pie,

Boy: Kissed the girls and made them cry!

Voice: One in twelve of the male students surveyed had committed acts that met the legal definition of rape or attempted rape.

Girl: Mommy, Gary threw snowballs at me today and it hurt.

Mom: Oh, honey, that means he likes you.

Voice: Only 27 percent of the women whose sexual assault met the legal definition of rape thought of themselves as rape victims.

Many groups collaborated on this project. Foremost was the support of the Dramatic Arts and Dance Department; the process owed its existence to the department's philosophy. In addition, many other groups helped in the research and development of the piece: the Sexual Assault Work Group and their sponsors in Residential Life and Health Services provided invaluable assistance, as did Campus Programs, the dean's office, and members of other academic departments who provided their expertise, notably anthropology, sociology, and women's studies. Finally, we enlisted the support of organizations in our community—rape crisis centers, treatment facilities, counselors, and the media.

The collaboration of all these groups made this a truly community-based project. In addition, however, we found that the work was intensely personal. All the participants examined their own lives and behaviors, and our collaborating groups not only helped us in our research but also made it possible for us to get support and counseling for the participants in the process and ultimately for the members of the audience who found they needed it.

> Man: It's not as if I am some rapist or something. It isn't like
> I beat her up or anything. And I was comforting her the whole
> time. I told her I didn't want her to miss out on a perfect op-
> portunity. . . . It bothers me. I thought the first time having
> sex was supposed to be something great. Something special.

I spent fall semester 1991 deep in my own research on the subject. Assisted by several students, I began to work out the details of an interim class (our intensive January term) to research and develop the play. We assembled books, videotapes, and speakers, and we put classified ads in the student newspapers of seven Twin Cities colleges for rape survivors and their loved ones who were willing to be interviewed. A counselor in a treatment center for sex offenders brought perpetrators who agreed to speak to us. As the project proceeded and word of what we were doing spread, more and more people sought us out to share their stories.

In interim term 1992, I taught a course with the cumbersome title Community-Based Theater: Script Development Workshop. Twenty-one students (ten men and eleven women) participated in what turned out to be a crash course on date rape and sex in our culture. We began with the research in books and on tapes. We heard speakers and learned about interviewing. Every member of the class conducted at least one interview with a rape survivor or perpetrator. They transcribed these and used them as the basis for monologues. We created improvisations based on this material. We examined different aspects of our culture—TV, music, commercials, magazines, toys, novels, children's literature, and so on. We discussed the lack of adequate sex-education programs. We noted the way our language expresses society's biases about sex and relationships. And we talked about ourselves and our own lives.

Writing began to pour out, some of it intensely personal. Some grew from the interviews we conducted. Some came in response to our culture watch. Some was filled with agony and some spoke to our desperate need for humor. By the end of January we had enough material for ten plays, maybe more.

Barbie: (Giggles.) Hi.

GI Joe: Well, hello.

Barbie: Where are you going?

GI Joe: On a dangerous secret mission to slay my evil enemies. And you?

Barbie: Malibu.

GI Joe: Perhaps we should go together.

Barbie: (Giggles.) You'll have to put my shoes on first.

GI Joe: No! I'll carry you! (Slings her over his shoulder.)

Barbie: Ooo! You're much more interesting than Ken!

What followed was a period of writing, rewriting, editing, and organizing. Ultimately, I worked with a small group of students to synthesize the material that had been generated in the class. From that work, we created a spine of scenes that examined how we grow up in this culture, from earliest nursery rhymes to college dating. We arranged them chronologically, as if one set of children were growing up through a series of scenes, and then we took the stories of rapes told by survivors and perpetrators in monologues, scenes, triplets, and duets, and placed them between the scenes in the spine. What emerged, with humor where we found it appropriate, chronicled the years of maturation and simultaneously told female and male tales of painful experiences.

The rewriting overlapped with the casting and rehearsals. When I cast the show in February, I knew I needed four men and four women to play a variety of roles. I looked for a diverse group of actors to tell the many stories in the play. The cast included some members of the interim class and some new people. With a production team, many of them class members, we began the next phase of the project—workshop rehearsals for public presentation. We always billed our play as a work-in-progress and allowed ourselves the freedom to change material right up until the closing performance. The whole company experienced the workshop process, and their own input in a given rehearsal might be reflected in the next night's rewrites. New scenes were born from rehearsal improvisations and old scenes were reconceived.

Waiter: Would you like some coffee?

Woman: Yes, please.

Waiter: Just say when. (*Starts to pour.*)

Woman: There. (*He keeps pouring.*) That's fine. (*He pours.*) Stop! (*She grabs the pot; there is coffee everywhere.*) What are you doing? I said *stop*.

Waiter: Yes, ma'am.

Woman: Well, why didn't you stop pouring?

Waiter: Oh, I wasn't sure you meant it.

Woman: Look, of course I meant it! I have coffee all over my lap! You nearly burned me!

Waiter: Forgive me, ma'am, but you certainly looked thirsty. I thought you wanted more.

Woman: But—

Waiter: And you must admit, you did let me *start* to pour.

Woman: Well, of course I did. I wanted some coffee.

Waiter: See, there you go. A perfectly honest mistake.

We thought we were prepared for the response, but we were amazed at the outpouring of emotion from spectators. They greeted the play with joy and pain. For some, it reaffirmed that they were not alone in their experiences. For others, it opened a topic for discussion that had previously been closed tight. For still others, it raised questions about behaviors and attitudes. The groups that had helped so much with the research were also there to help at performance time. The Sexual Assault Work Group and the Rape Crisis Center provided volunteers to hand out literature and to provide immediate help to any audience member who needed to talk. We created a program with steps to take if rape has happened to oneself or to a friend. For everyone, the play seemed to provoke discussion. We handed out response forms. Most poignant were those from several college students who said they wished they had seen the play in high school. One woman wrote, "I wish I had seen this when I was a lot younger (I'm fifty-six). I was raped when I was twenty-one and had to deal with it alone." Another woman wrote, "As a victim, it forced me to go back, get in touch, deal, and move forward to become a survivor."

In addition to informal responses from the members of the audience, we also asked two outside reviewers to critique the piece. A director and a playwright, both of whom had a great deal of experience workshopping new scripts, wrote critiques and met with us to discuss the play. From their ideas and from our own perspectives of how the play worked in front of an audience, we took a new look at the structure and the content. As we studied what we had done, several scenes seemed unnecessary; others seemed to need more focus in the writing; and still others needed additional material. Overall, our evaluation was positive: We felt that the piece accomplished what we set out to do and, with a minimum of rewriting, could be staged again.

The responses from the Macalester campus and from the other young people and educators who saw the show prompted our decision to take it on tour. We tackled the demands of rewriting and streamlined the staging to make the production more portable, and then we hit the road in September. Again, the purpose was twofold. We were anxious to bring the play to audiences who would benefit (we had already performed the play for one high school group, which discussed it for months). In addition, the theater students who enjoyed the experience of creating and workshopping a new play were able to take that play on the road and learn about touring, about doing long-term work on a role, and about meeting the variety of audiences outside the walls of our college. The whole notion of community-based theater comes full circle when you create a play out of the words and experiences of a community and then take the play back to that community for performance.

> Woman: When we're babies, we're born knowing that if we
> scream at night, someone will take care of us. And I just want
> to know where that ability goes. Because sometimes I feel like
> screaming now, just yelling, until someone wakes up.

All quotes are from the play Until Someone Wakes Up, *conceived and directed by Carolyn Levy and written by Carolyn Levy, Laura Bradley, C. Todd Griffin, Marcy Laughinghouse, David Page, Josh Schultz, Deborah Sengupta, Elizabeth J. Wood, Cara McChesney, Christopher Berg, C. Brianna Merrick, P. Jeffrey Nelsen, Philip Park, Tina Pavlou, K. Siobhan Ring, Alejandro Aguilera, Matt Lewis, Andrew Lyke, Laura E. Meerson, Jessica Mickens, Danielle O'Hare, and Jonathan Saltus.*

. . . .

CAROLYN LEVY is a theater director, teacher, and writer. She was artistic director and cofounder of the Women's Theatre Project, which from 1980 to 1988 produced new plays by women about issues of importance to women and brought these plays to the community in the Twin Cities and beyond. Most notable of these works were *The Women Here Are No Different,* about battered women; *Red Light/Green Light,* both a play and videotape about adolescent girls; and three touring shows coauthored by Levy, *Life in the Pink Collar Ghetto,* about women and work; *Make It Better,* about nurses; and *Daughters Arise,* about women in religion. These plays were performed all over the country, often in workplaces and schools and at conferences.

Levy directs for numerous professional theaters in the Twin Cities. She is the artistic associate for the Minnesota Jewish Theatre, where she has directed *The Chosen, Never the Sinner, Substance of Fire,* and *Rose.* She is also a professor of theater at Hamline University, where she teaches acting and directing and has directed plays including *The Laramie Project, for colored girls who have considered suicide when the rainbow is enuf, Waiting for Godot, Whose Life Is It Anyway?, Kindertransport,* and *The Colored Museum.* She also helps coordinate a Hamline orientation program about date rape for incoming students each fall. Often this has included a production of *Until Someone Wakes Up.*

Until Someone Wakes Up has been produced by schools and rape crisis centers all over the country. All royalties go to Sexual Offense Services, the Rape Crisis Center of Ramsey County. For information about acquiring a script or the rights to produce the play, please contact:

Carolyn Levy, Box 67
Hamline University
1536 Hewitt Avenue
St. Paul, MN 55104
(651) 523-2972
clevy@gw.hamline.edu

MAKING RAPE AN ELECTION ISSUE

. . . .

JOHN STOLTENBERG

Imagine a candidate declaring on national television, "As president, I will commit the resources of my administration to making the United States a rape-free zone." Sounds utterly farfetched, but *why?*

ELECTION AFTER ELECTION, politicians of all stripes slug it out across the country, seeing who can wave the flag the hardest, who can beat on their chest the mightiest, competing for the allegiance of voters who will decide which candidate speaks most trustworthily to their problems and fears—their longing for security and a better life. Yet no one seems to notice: The candidates never talk about rape.

Or when candidates do, they completely miss the point. In 1988, for instance, Michael Dukakis, the Democratic candidate for president, blundered in his third televised debate against George Bush Sr. when asked this question about his wife: "If Kitty Dukakis were raped and murdered, would you favor an irrevocable death penalty for the killer?" Dukakis gave a rambling and irrelevant reply—about the crime rate in Massachusetts and "the avalanche of drugs that's pouring into the country."[1] Many believe this dumbfounding display of insensitivity demolished forever his dwindling chances for the presidency. At around the same time, the Bush campaign was airing a TV spot featuring one Willie Horton, a black man convicted for rape who had been furloughed from a Massachusetts prison only to commit rape again. It was an inflammatory commercial that many believe helped boost Bush to victory.

The United States has the highest rape rate of any Western nation.[2] For any political candidate who is concerned with the safety of *all* the folks who live here, rape would seem to be a problem that desperately needs solving. But instead, political campaigns provide a national nondiscussion.

Nearly every woman lives with the terror that a rape could sometime happen to her.[3] There are significant odds that it already has. Research by sociologist Diana E. H. Russell based on face-to-face interviews with 930 women residents of San Francisco—selected at random from a scientific probability sample of households—found that 44 percent had suffered a criminal rape or an attempted rape at least once in their lifetime.[4] The 1996 National Violence against Women Survey, funded by the National Institute of Justice and the Centers for Disease Control and Prevention, found that "18 percent of women surveyed said they experienced a completed or attempted rape at some time in their life."[5] Extrapolating from both studies, there is a rape-survivor population in the United States of somewhere between 25 million and 64 million living Americans.[6]

Rape is a crisis of national security if anything is. Living in fear of forced and violent sex is much like living in a state of siege in occupied territory. Yet one candidate after another will declaim about defending this country's interests against *foreign* aggressors. Why doesn't local, homegrown, day-in-and-day-out *sexual violence against women* make it to even the bottom of their list of major social-policy questions?

Imagine candidates stumping for public office debating how best to stop rape. Imagine them inspiring us with new ideas and new programs to eliminate crimes of sexual violence completely. Imagine them promising bold and innovative leadership to set a national priority to "denormalize" rape, to refute myths about rape through all the mass media, to educate young people about personal rights and bodily integrity throughout the public school system, to create a national climate of opinion in which ending rape matters—because it gets talked about and cared about and people take it seriously. Even among groups of men, there would emerge a new kind of peer pressure, discouraging rape rather than encouraging it, labeling coercive sex as one of the most not-cool things a guy can do. Imagine a candidate declaring on national television, "As president, I will commit the resources of my administration to making the United States a rape-free zone."

Sounds utterly farfetched, but *why?* Why isn't stopping rape an election issue?

I believe there are real answers to that question—a series of interlocking explanations that, taken as a whole, signal a deep and disturbing truth about this country right now.

Answer #1: A lot of women don't like to think about rape. As a strategy for survival, most women get through each day by blocking out consciousness about sexual violence against other women. If they can't protect themselves from the violence, they can at least protect themselves from the information. Ignorance gives the illusion of strength, and their denial is like a drug. For any candidate, this is an applecart of delusion not to upset.

Even some self-professed feminist women give rape short shrift when it comes to matters of public policy. For a while, Dukakis's campaign manager was Susan Estrich, an *expert* on rape. A tenured Harvard Law School professor, Estrich had argued in her 1987 book, *Real Rape*,[7] that the law must respond not only to aggravated rape (by a stranger, for instance), but also to "simple rape" (as when a woman is victimized by a friend or acquaintance). Whatever

Estrich did or did not argue once she joined the Dukakis campaign, on the subject of rape the Duke himself kept mum.

There is evidence, however, that women in the electorate are becoming more inclined to voice their concerns about rape. For its cover story "Women Face the '90s," *Time* magazine polled 1,000 women about which issues concerned them most. Rape ranked third (88 percent of the women said the issue was important to them), just below equal pay (94 percent) and day care (90 percent)—somewhat *more* important than abortion (74 percent) and considerably more important than sexual freedom (49 percent).[8] Clearly, women's deep concerns about rape are not being spoken to.

Today, the abortion controversy has been pitched into presidential politicking, yet rape is still a campaigner's no-no—except when a so-called prolife candidate happens to mention conception through rape as a permissible qualification for abortion. The prochoice side has generally tried to keep separate the issues of reproductive freedom and sexual violence. But that sleight of hand may prove to be a serious strategic mistake. A woman's right to control her own body once she's pregnant is a rather moot abstraction for all the women whose bodies are already colonialized through forced sex. If prochoice advocates were more candid about the social reality of forced sex, they might persuade women on the antiabortion side to reexamine their forced-pregnancy position. Moreover, if prochoice advocates were more honest about the relationship between forced sex and forced pregnancy, they might successfully put pressure on *both* major parties' platforms to acknowledge women's body rights without equivocation. So long as presidential candidates think women voters can be counted on to keep silent about their human right not to be raped, the candidates can pretend to speak to women as full citizens—and really only address men.

Answer #2: A lot of men don't want to hear about rape. As things stand now, a candidate for elected office probably could not talk forthrightly about rape without alienating enormous numbers of men—and that's not just because rapists, too, vote. Violence against women is perceived by campaign managers and a huge share of the electorate as a "special interest" issue, a pejorative by definition because it affects mainly women. So the trick for the campaigner is to give the appearance of concern for women's interests—child-care, for instance—while reassuring men that all their gender-class interests will still be served. A candidate may be tough on crime, a staunch defender of law and order, but he dare not breathe a word about crimes like rape and battery—which hit too close to home.

Answer #3: To be soft on rape is to be soft on war. Rape is a significant motivating force in military strategy.[9] Uncle Sam needs to keep men's taste for rape alive—in order to forge unified combat platoons across racial and class animosities and in order to get out there and blow the heads off "the enemy."

Military-supported brothels have long been a fixture of U.S. bases around the world, while virtually every PX proffers an ample line of pornography as well. The bodies of uncounted indigenous women, garrisoned and variously impaled in the service of our far-flung armed forces, have borne silent witness to Nietzsche's dictum that "man shall be trained for war, and woman for the recreation of the warrior."

The fair-haired son of a U.S. diplomat in Southeast Asia once told me how his father used his position to secure sexual favors from Asian women in the war zone. Taken as a youth one night on a prove-your-manhood prowl of brothel life in a small town in Thailand, he watched in inner horror as his father ogled and patronized the young Thai women—some of them silicone-breasted, their eyes surgically sliced to look Caucasian and therefore more desirable to GIs. "It was simple," he told me, "the Cong were gooks to be snuffed; women were cunts to be fucked."

During the mud-and-blood Vietnam War, a training refrain from boot camp was widely reported: "This is my weapon, this is my gun [the man points to his crotch]; this one's for killing, this one's for fun." During the high-tech Persian Gulf War, this chant reverberated as news slipped past military censors that pilots on the aircraft carrier *John F. Kennedy* had watched pornographic movies before flying bombing missions.[10] The pedagogy was all too familiar: inciting men's aggression and training men to view "the other" as the enemy through sexualized hate and fear. And the current corollary is an epidemic of sexual assault at U.S. military academies.

Electoral politics do not disrupt the status quo of militarism, and they therefore do not disrupt the status quo of rape.

Answer #4: Rape sells, so rape pays. You won't find the prorape lobby in any Washington, DC, office. But you will find them marketing prorape scenarios in film and video pornography and defending their prorape propaganda in "civil liberties" circles and high-toned journals of liberal opinion. To these folks, some of whom donate generously to campaign war chests, the rapist appetite creates a lucrative market segment—for heavy-metal sadism, for hate rap, for masochistic fashion, for online bondage. It's the classic American combination of free speech and free enterprise, and no candidate for office wants to catch flak from this powerful contingent. Consider, for instance, the woes of Albert Gore in the 1988 presidential primary when his wife, Tipper, suggested a link between sexual violence and pornographic media: The music press especially treated her like a prudish cartoon. Candidate Dukakis found in his campaign manager Susan Estrich—now a Fox television commentator—someone who could perhaps keep him out of this fray. After all, in a 1985 seventh circuit court of appeals case, Estrich had signed her name to an amicus brief that, among other things, categorically denied a link between rape and pornography and in fact lauded pornography as an empowering opportunity for women to explore their rape fantasies.[11]

To really stand up forcefully to the prorape lobby, a politician would need to be unusually high-minded—and have unusually deep pockets.

Answer #5: There's a widespread belief that you can't really do anything to end rape. "Some men will inevitably rape. It's probably men's nature—who knows? Rape—like death and taxes—will always be with us. The best that can be hoped for is a few legal reforms, more humane treatment for victims, and—if you're a woman—dumb luck." This is a profoundly nihilistic view, one that is tacitly shared across most of the political spectrum, from left to right. It seems that only radical feminists still believe rape is stoppable. They are the vocal optimists—and also the "man-hating extremists" according to everyone else.

A candidate for political office won't articulate a vision of basic change if people don't believe in the possibility of basic change. And vice versa: People don't believe in the possibility of basic change in part because their leaders do not want them to.

If this deafening silence continues to surround sexual violence against women, are we as a nation left to conclude that we have both the leaders *and* the rape rate we deserve?

I fervently hope not.

Could a president or campaigning presidential candidate make specific policy proposals about ending rape—and then actually achieve them in office? I believe so. And I have several concrete ideas about where to begin.

Rally the private sector. Provide presidential leadership to enlist corporations, the advertising council, and print and broadcast media to mount a public-information campaign to refute myths about rape and to encourage rape reporting. Launch a media blitz even more massive than current ones against drug use (such as Partnership for a Drug-Free America) and HIV transmission (America Responds to AIDS). If you need to cost-justify it, tally the medical expenses and productivity losses due to sexual violence. Many good antirape media materials already exist. Find them, improve them if necessary, and—with clear-cut White House support—roll them out nationally.

Get behind sex education in public schools—seriously. Call for the development and funding of comprehensive curricula that teach not just the facts of life, not just information about safer sex, but also the meaning of informed consent and bodily integrity, together with personal self-esteem values and sexual communication skills. For a model of what can be done to promote self-respect in the young, note the child sexual-abuse prevention training program that was in place throughout the California public school system, the legacy of California state legislator Maxine Waters (until Governor Deukmejian defunded it in 1990).

Make rape a real crime—a crime someone gets convicted for. Promise to get tough with institutions receiving federal funding: Hold them accountable, vow to withhold federal monies from colleges, for instance, if they do not turn campus rape complaints over to law-enforcement agencies and if they do not implement meaningful rape-prevention education. Use your influence to urge Congress to make rape and other forms of sexual violence prosecutable as gender-bias crimes. Beef up sex-crimes prosecutorial staffs. Make sure they know what they're doing so they do it right.

Speak out against the pornography industry as a purveyor of prorape propaganda. Does pornography "cause" rape? From a purely scientific point of view, causality is no more or less than *increased probability.* And there is no doubt whatever that some rapes are committed that would not have been committed without the influence of pornography. Just because we can't be certain *which* rapes and *which* pornography does not mean there is no link. Sociologist Russell, reviewing the extensive clinical and psychological evidence, writes that pornography "intensifies the predisposition" of some men to rape (and various researchers have found that 25 to 60 percent of college-age males are already so predisposed, by their own admission). Russell also points out that pornography "undermines some men's internal inhibitions against acting out their desire to rape" (and as various researchers have found by measuring penile tumescence, 20 to 30 percent of young male subjects are sexually aroused by depictions of forced sex against a woman's will, and another 10 percent are aroused by extreme sadism as well). Citing data correlating rape with pornography distribution and consumption, Russell further points out that pornography "undermines some men's *social* inhibitions against acting out their desires." As Russell observes, in response to those who say there is no causality in all the available evidence, "If researchers had insisted on being able to ascertain why Mr. X died from lung cancer after 20 years of smoking but Mr. Y did not, before being willing to warn the public that smoking causes lung cancer, there would have been a lot more deaths from lung cancer."[12] Much pornography is actually a *documentary* of coercion and sexual abuse, and some rape-crisis centers report an increase in rapes involving videotaping by perpetrators. So forget profamily moralizing. Forget posturing about social purity. Speak to the real issue of human harm: Pornography that promotes rape is wrong. Pornography that is made from rape is wrong.

Then, once you're in office, commission a Justice Department task force to eventually replace our useless hodgepodge of obscenity laws with legislation that would allow victims of pornography to sue for violations of their civil rights. Under current laws, a movie of a rape is considered "protected speech"—and it can be sold anywhere. Commit your administration to confront pornography as a civil-rights issue—and take the profit motive out of rape.[13]

NOTES

1. *New York Times,* October 14, 1988.
2. Arthur F. Schiff, "Rape in Other Countries," *Medicine, Science and the Law* 11, no. 3 (1971): 139–43, cited in Diana E. H. Russell, *Sexual Exploitation: Rape, Child Sexual Abuse, and Workplace Harassment* (Beverly Hills, Calif.: Sage, 1984), 30.
3. See Margaret T. Gordon and Stephanie Riger, *The Female Fear* (New York: Free Press, 1989).
4. Russell, *Sexual Exploitation,* 35. Her 1978 survey used the California statutory definition of rape.
5. Patricia Tjaden and Nancy Thoennes, *Prevalence, Incidence, and Consequences of Violence against Women: Findings from the National Violence against Women Survey* (Washington, DC: U.S. Department of Justice, Office of Justice Programs, 1998), 3.
6. NVAWS extrapolation (17.6 percent) and Russell extrapolation (44 percent) based on 143,368,343, the number of females living in the United States in 2000 according to the U.S. Census Bureau.

7. Susan Estrich, *Real Rape* (Cambridge: Harvard University Press, 1987).

8. Claudia Wallis, "Onward, Women," *Time* (December 4, 1989): 82.

9. See the classic Susan Brownmiller, *Against Our Will: Men, Women and Rape,* (New York: Simon and Schuster, 1975).

10. "U.S. Censors Story on X-rated Films," *Boston Globe* January 27, 1991, 16.

11. "Brief Amici Curiae of Feminist Anti-Censorship Taskforce, et al." in *American Booksellers Association, Inc., et al.* v. *William H. Hudnut III, et al.* (7th Cir. 1985).

12. Diana E. H. Russell, "Pornography and Rape: A Causal Model," in *Making Violence Sexy* edited by Diana E. H. Russell (New York: Teachers College Press, 1993).

13. For more background on the civil rights antipornography ordinance coauthored by Andrea Dworkin and Catharine A. MacKinnon, see "Confronting Pornography as a Civil-Rights Issue" in *Refusing to Be a Man,* by John Stoltenberg (London: UCL Press, 2000); see also Andrea Dworkin and Catharine A. MacKinnon, eds., *In Harm's Way: The Pornography Civil Rights Hearings* (Cambridge: Harvard University Press, 1997).

. . . .

JOHN STOLTENBERG, a longtime radical feminist activist against sexual violence and a philosopher of gender, is the author of *Refusing to Be a Man: Essays on Sex and Justice* (revised edition, UCL Press, 2000), *The End of Manhood: Parables on Sex and Selfhood* (revised edition, UCL Press, 2000), and *What Makes Pornography "Sexy"?* (Milkweed Editions, 1994), as well as numerous articles and essays in anthologies. He is also a frequent speaker and workshop leader at colleges and conferences. He has been the managing editor of five national magazines and served as editorial and creative consultant to many other publications. For the nonprofit organization Men Can Stop Rape (www.mencanstoprape.org), he conceived and is the creative director of the "My strength is not for hurting" media campaign. He holds a master of divinity degree in theology and literature from Union Theological Seminary and a master of fine arts in theater arts from Columbia University School of the Arts. He has lived with the writer Andrea Dworkin since 1974.

ESTABLISHING RAPE AS A WAR CRIME

VESNA KESIĆ

Just as in ancient Greek history, the pattern of military
or paramilitary rapes in Bosnia and Rwanda occurred
in such a manner that a group of soldiers sexually violated women in front of their relatives or members of the
community.

THE EXPLANATIONS OF WARTIME SEXUAL VIOLENCE against women are contradictory and controversial, in theory and in everyday life. A key question appears to be, who actually rapes during wars? Is it one man, or is it men—an individual with specific psychological features or members of the male gender? Are wartime rapists members of the armed forces trained in militarized, patriarchal institutions or are they renegade soldiers, acting beyond military control? Do the rapists—as members of a particular ethnic or religious group—assert their collective identity over women's bodies as symbolic battlefields (in Susan Brownmiller's phrase) representing a different culture, or do they attempt to introduce their own genetic code to the reproductive ground of the enemy? Do the perpetrators, while raping women, act to fight and conquer men from other groups by attacking their land and property, including their women—an ethnicity definition—or do they sexually violate women as utterly other and different—a gender definition?

During the wars in the former Yugoslavia, the different meanings of sexual violence against women turned into a source of further struggle between warring sides and governments. Sexual violence in war also became a bitterly contested issue among women's groups, both within and across ethnic lines. It is easy to presume that in wartime both of these approaches, gender and ethnicity, along with their many intersections, played a major role in generating war propaganda and inciting both sexual and ethnic violence. However, theorizing gender and ethnic differences became central, not only in feminist scholarship but also in the newest development of international law concerning gender war crimes.

One of the most interesting questions is this: To what extent does gendered war violence differ from everyday peacetime violence against women, such as rape, battery, and sexual harassment? Do these different forms of violence all belong to the same continuum of violence against women? The criminal status of sexual violence, and of rape in particular, changes in national and international jurisprudence, in peace and in war. Recent changes have been introduced to international humanitarian law following the wars in the former Yugoslavia and Rwanda, thanks in part to the (recent) recognition of women's human rights and women's movements internationally.

RAPE IN WARTIME

The past century alone has seen at least six documented cases of mass sexual abuse of women during wars: the Rape of Nanjing in 1937; the "comfort women" used as sexual slaves in Japanese camps throughout Asia during World War II; the pervasive rape of German women at the end of World War II; rapes during the Bangladesh–Pakistan war in the early 1970s; and the mass rapes of women during the ethnic conflicts in Bosnia and Rwanda in the 1990s.

Numerical estimates in all these cases vary during and after wars, depending on the source and the context of the debate. The Bosnian Ministry of Internal Affairs released a statement in October 1992 saying that in Bosnia 60,000 women were raped by Serbian military and paramilitary personnel, and that many of them were intentionally impregnated, whereas the UN Commission of Experts released a report in 1994 claiming 4,500 documented cases of rape and sexual violation. At the same time, the UN Commission of Experts gave credibility to the E.C. Investigative Mission of Experts' February 1993 estimate of 20,000 women having been violated in Bosnia and Croatia. (The mission was composed mainly of European women—doctors, academics, politicians.) These distinguished international fact-finding missions agreed that all the warring sides performed rapes, and that members of Serbian military and paramilitary troops committed the greatest number of such crimes, although they disagreed as to the scale. Nevertheless, all the warring sides for a long time denied any involvement of the part of their soldiers.

From the beginning, Croatian, Bosnian, and Serbian officials in particular, but also some of the international researchers, including feminist scholars, gave very different interpretations of the purpose and meanings of wartime violence against women in the Yugoslav wars. According to some of these interpretations, the crimes committed by Serbs were planned, systematic actions for the purpose of ethnic cleansing, so-called genocidal rapes, and intentional impregnations (women were kept incarcerated for the purpose of giving birth) so as to destroy the ethnic composition of Croats and Bosnians. The term *genocide by procreation* was used in some of these claims.

The Croatian and Bosnian sides declared that rapes executed by the Serbs were unique in history and specifically inhumane. Not surprisingly, after the numbers were disputed by international fact-finding missions, various Serbian and pro-Serbian counterinformation groups and international lobbyists (again composed of "experts") began to claim there had been no mass rapes (whatever *mass* means) at all in Bosnia, and the whole story was part of international anti-Serbian propaganda and/or a conspiracy. This was not the first time women's suffering has been exploited for nationalistic purposes during armed conflicts, and thousands of brutal rapes first exaggerated, then denied, and in the end largely forgotten.

In the Bangladesh–Pakistan war, estimates ranged from 20,000 to 400,000 women raped. German historian and filmmaker Helke Sander, after meticulous research, argued that 1.9 million German women, or two-thirds of the female population in the Eastern Sector, were raped during the final operations of World War II (the battle for Berlin) and the establishment of Allied control over occupied zones between March and November 1945. The majority of the perpetrators were soldiers of the Red Army, but the French, U.S., and British militaries raped as well. Sander's conclusions were vigorously contested by the German left and right and by some U.S. academics.

In analyzing such complex phenomena as war rapes, numbers and statistics are not the best way to approach the problem. On the contrary, they easily become a new focus of conflict—something we in the Balkan region used to call the monstrous arithmetic—that is, numbers used for further warmongering and the spreading of hate. Yet in almost all cases, rapes committed during wartime are trivialized and soon after the wars pushed under the carpet and forgotten. Both winners and losers, the perpetrators and victims of wars alike, tend to repress these memories and events. The narratives sometimes re-emerge in the form of literature, movies, or memoirs but seldom in serious political or theoretical debate. Even within the growing body of feminist literature on gender and violence of the last thirty years, only one study seriously approached wartime sexual violence against women: Susan Brownmiller's classic *Against Our Will: Men, Women and Rape,* published in 1975.[1] Brownmiller argued that sexual war crimes are often traded for various peace or other political arrangements negotiated by international mediators between the winners and the losers.

Although the sexual abuse of women in war has been known throughout human history, rape has not been recognized specifically as a war crime.

Wartime rapes have not been investigated, prosecuted, or punished, because no laws covered them. Like peacetime sexual assaults against women, they remained crimes without a name.

Significant changes occurred after the wars in the former Yugoslavia and Rwanda, and not only legal changes. Even before they became a topic for international law, the atrocities gained widespread media attention, accompanied by general outrage. Hundreds of articles and television programs, conferences, round tables, expert and popular debates, and dozens of books appeared on the topic. What caused that change in reception? Was it the omnipresent, catastrophe-driven news media that shape the postmodern world? Was it because there were more women employed in leading positions in these media? Or had the world become more sensitive toward the suffering of victims? I believe it was the growing awareness of women's human rights within the global women's movement, and the recognition of women's rights as human rights, that created the space in national and international jurisdiction for recognition of violence against women as a crime, both in peace and in war.

Legally, this change became effective with the establishment of the International War Crimes Tribunal for the Former Yugoslavia (ICTY) in February 1993, and the Tribunal for Rwanda (ICTR) in 1995. The statute of the ICTY is the first international legal document that singles out rape as a crime against humanity. In order to be prosecuted under that section, rape must be proved to be part of a widespread or systematic attack "against a civilian population on national, political, ethnic, racial or religious grounds." Feminist legal scholars objected to such formulation on the grounds that, once again, the gender dimension of rape during war is subordinated to the ethnic (or national, racial, or religious) dimension, and the statute does not specify rape independent of other violence as a crime against women. Nevertheless, the statute does recognize gender-based crimes as a distinct phenomenon and provides a cornerstone for the future permanent establishment of an international criminal court that will integrate the concept of gender crimes into international justice.

The mass rapes that took place during the wars in the former Yugoslavia, particularly in Bosnia and Herzegovina, were the first in history to be brought before an international court, and these crimes, together with the mass rapes that occurred in Rwanda, contributed to groundbreaking changes in international humanitarian law. Despite these legal changes and the considerable attention these atrocities received in the news media worldwide, the origins of mass war violence against women—the mechanisms that turn relatively tolerant people and peaceful neighbors into killers and rapists—have not yet been comprehensively examined.

The exceptional levels of violence against women on all sides of the conflict remain unexplained. Attempts have been made to understand this violent "dirty war" in historical, political, and economic terms. Its ethnic dimension has been widely acknowledged and researched, although the Yugoslav wars were too often simplified and dismissed as a violent ethnic-tribal conflict. No research has yet connected the origins of the war violence to the patriarchal organization of society, to patriarchal family structure, or to gender relations. As a long-time feminist and peace activist in the former Yugoslavia, and as a scholar and social researcher, I believe that the origins of both forms of violence that occurred during these wars, ethnic and gendered, should also be researched and explained from the perspective of gender and of patriarchal social structures. In both Bosnia and Rwanda, patriarchal gender relations and the strict division of male and female roles persisted in private and in public, in the sexist culture of everyday life.

I believe that to generate ethnic wars in the former Yugoslavia—especially to incite and mobilize vast numbers of so-called ordinary people to participate in war violence—specific constructions of gender and ethnicity were used as a strategy to generate hatred and war. These two constructs intersected and reinforced each other in many ways. Whatever rationale was used for war—and it was different for different warring factions—the atrocities were aimed against those who were *other* and *different* in both ethnicity and gender. The question then is, how did those different and other people become objects of hatred to such a degree that it was possible to inflict all kinds of violence upon their bodies and communities while the perpetrators' own nation was being imagined heroically?

THE CONSTRUCTION OF GENDER

News of the massive rapes and the "sexualization of war" was a shock even to the women of the Yugoslav feminist movement. Knowledge about rape as a weapon of war throughout history did not help us to accept the unexpected. We repeated the classic feminist truisms, such as "Rape in war is horrible but still only the tip of the iceberg of patriarchal violence against women." We had difficulty admitting that sexual violence against women had become a part of the nationalist war strategy in our country. At the same time as sexualized violence was being wreaked on women's bodies, the new national leaders were using that violence to reinforce ethnic hatred. No one except a few feminist groups tried to understand or explain the roots of that violence from a gender perspective and beyond its obvious nationalistic use as a means of ethnic cleansing.

Only a few years before, in the mid-1980s, Yugoslavia seemed to be the most prosperous among the socialist countries, making considerable strides toward democracy. People of different ethnic and religious backgrounds lived together, at least in tolerance and with mutual respect for their respective cultures (if not in "brotherhood and unity," which was the official slogan of the former Yugoslavia's ruling regime [note the gender of the slogan]).

Bosnia-Herzegovina, with an almost 30 percent rate of intermarriage between Orthodox and Catholic Christians and Muslims, was a truly multicultural society without multiculturalism or diversity being particularly noted or celebrated. To my knowledge, even in such large cosmopolitan cities as New York people of different ethnic and cultural backgrounds do not live in mixed-culture families to such an extent.

Feminists knew that discrimination and violence against women existed despite the egalitarianism of the official socialist ideology and the much-proclaimed legal, economic, and political equality of women, which included women's quotas in both the republic's and the federal parliaments. Feminists were aware of the deep sexism inherent in the culture and reflected in the social structures, including the laws; however, it was fairly safe for women to walk at night in Yugoslav cities and villages, in contrast to European or American cities of the seventies or eighties.

An effective women's movement could not have developed under state-controlled civil society. In the centralized authoritarian socialist system, the women's question was officially resolved with socialist egalitarianism and class-based economic distributive justice. Autonomous women's organizing was not tolerated until the late eighties. Nevertheless, feminist initiatives emerged in Yugoslavia in the late seventies, at least a decade ahead of other socialist countries, although women activists were mostly denigrated as bourgeois imports from the West and not widely accepted by the broader population of women.

In socialist Yugoslavia, women made up 40 percent of the labor force, which meant economic independence, and legal and social advantages for women included free, legal, accessible abortion, contraception and family planning, and equal legal status for married and unmarried couples. Children born out of wedlock had the same rights and benefits as children of marriages—a great achievement for single mothers that nearly eliminated the term *illegitimate child* from popular use. In 1990, in the last Croatian socialist parliament before multiparty elections, 25 percent of deputies were women—one of the highest levels of political representation of women in the world. In other European states and the United States, women then barely exceeded 10 to 15 percent of parliamentarians. Despite these achievements and advantages, however, women were discriminated against as citizens and were not fully protected from violence. After the first democratic multiparty elections in 1990, Yugoslavia disintegrated into its constituent republics and discrimination against women in the newly emerged nation-states, founded on the principle of ethnic identity, increased due to nationalism, war, and economic crisis from what it had been in the authoritarian socialist state.

ETHNICITY

The rise of ethnic nationalisms released unexpected violence among people representing all sides in the war. As many female victims of sexual war violence have confirmed, the perpetrators were neighbors, sometimes teachers and colleagues, men they had known their whole lives. Suddenly, the people of Yugoslavia were destroying themselves and the country in a bloody civil war beyond all models of rational explanation.

Bosnia and Herzegovina has often been described as the heart of the former Yugoslavia, and not solely because of its central geographical position. The ethnic makeup of Bosnia and Herzegovina, with its historically mixed cultures, religions, and ethnicities, symbolized Yugoslavia's political and social experiment. This experiment was, among many other things, an endeavor to build a society that would find its identity in features and values other than ethnic identities and historical tensions and conflicts. Yet the cruelty of war-time sexual abuse of women exploded right in Bosnia. The three main ethnic groups in Bosnia and Herzegovina—Serbs, Croats, and Bosnians—are similar in language and social organization (family structure, education, gender relations). Their main difference is religion: Serbs are Orthodox Christians; Croats are Roman Catholics; and Bosnians are Muslims, who were in the seventies pronounced an ethnic group—a "nation"—although the term *Muslim* for a long time meant only the people of Islamic religion. (In socialist Yugoslavia religion, although a constitutional right, was completely allocated to the private sphere.)

The status of women was similar in each of the three dominant religions. The traditional cultural values of all ethnic and religious groups living in the former Yugoslavia privileged patriarchal manliness, which endorsed the inhibition of emotions and affection; put a high value on chastity and family honor; and included sexual taboos, for example on women's sexuality or on gay or lesbian expression. Sexual mockery and ridicule were common, and particularly in rural areas men and women lived in psychologically different worlds. During the wars, men from all sides engaged in all forms of violence and torture, if not to the same degree.

In traditional societies such as existed in the rural regions of the former Yugoslavia, with their rigid gender roles and division, boys and men may develop greater capacity for violence, aggression, and hatred against women in order to achieve independence from their mothers and be accepted in male society. Besides that, the nations in the region have a long history of domination by foreign colonists and occupiers, giving rise to a history and mythology of heroic resistance. Both of these were a fruitful ground for asserting masculinity as a quality needed to fight for independence, and in them may lie the origins of the overall misogynist perspective that, triggered by nationalism and war, transformed the repressed, "normal" peacetime violence into massive wartime cruelty against women.

Bosnian Muslim women have said that in traditional Bosnian culture a man's dignity depends on the purity of "his" woman. It is more damaging to family honor if their women are dishonored than if "their" men are killed. The mass rape of women functioned as *Endlösung*—a final solution—since people never return to places of such "dishonor." It is a shame that can never be forgotten. Some of my Bosnian colleagues—women scholars and intellectuals—have suggested that since the goal of the enemy was to destroy Muslim culture, Bosnian women were raped because of their role as bearers of Muslim culture and tradition. Even if I do not agree that such an insight entirely explains sexual violence, it does speak to the position of women within patriarchal culture and the construction of female and male genders. A woman is not a subject, not even a person to be exterminated; she is not an enemy who threatens the interests and lives of the other side. Rather, she occupies the position of a "symbolic battlefield," as Brownmiller states: "She is a depersonalized symbol, a bearer of man's honor, a reproducer of the culture and of other traditional values."[2]

SOCIAL AND POLITICAL ORIGINS OF GENDER VIOLENCE

Feminist scholars of violence against women have shown that until recently violence against women belonged to the private sphere into which the state and its legal instruments did not intrude. Physical violence against women entered the public sphere as a crime only with the growth of the contemporary women's movement—that is, since the 1970s. It took even longer for rape in marriage to be considered punishable violence. In the United States, for instance, marital rape became recognized in all states as a crime only during the 1990s. In the former Yugoslavia, only one of its six republics, Slovenia, incorporated marital rape into its jurisdiction, while Croatia had been about to do the same. Women still had no formal legal protection or remedy against domestic violence, even though almost everywhere in the world violence among family members or between partners is the leading cause of injury inflicted on women. Until the 1970s, courts and legislatures in the United States permitted abuses of women and children, ranging from domestic violence to date rape and childhood sexual abuse, under the cloak of privacy rights.

Rape within the public sphere by an unknown perpetrator, that is someone who is not a husband, fiancé, or lover, has been in one form or another illegal since the beginning of the modern legal system, but at least until the end of the nineteenth century redress belonged, if a woman was married, to her husband, or if she was not married, to her father or eldest male relative. Privacy rights, like other patriarchal rights, gave men the right to a woman's body.

Rape or sexual violence against women in war was condemned in the Geneva Conventions as an offense against "family honor and rights," "assault against personal dignity," and "humiliating and degrading treatment"; that is, as an assault on honor or as a crime against morality and not as an act of violence against a human being. Even the relatively recent Protocols to the Geneva Conventions from 1977, which could have been referred to as a modern-day legal platform, mention "rape, forced prostitution and any other forms of *indecent assault* [italics mine]," as "humiliating and degrading treatment," not as violent crimes against women. In legal terminology, this implies a lesser degree of criminality and, in social terms, shame and stigmatization for women.

Sexual crimes against women became subject to national and international jurisprudence only when women worked their way out of the private realm and entered the public sphere, demanding civil freedoms and women's human rights. The Vienna Declaration and Program of Action, adopted by the UN World Conference on Human Rights in 1993, is the first international document that recognizes the rights of women as human rights. The Vienna Declaration clearly states that violations of the human rights of women in armed conflicts—in particular murder, systematic rape, sexual slavery, and forced pregnancy—are violations of the fundamental principles of international human rights and humanitarian law. In the statutes of the ad hoc tribunals for the treatment of war crimes committed in the wars in the former Yugoslavia and Rwanda established in 1993 and 1995, rape was listed as a specific form of crime within the category of crimes against humanity.

War—as the highest patriarchal activity—has always reinforced the traditional roles of women, building firmly upon the concept of social motherhood, or childbearing in the interest of the nation. Women's assigned roles in war predetermine them as vulnerable civilian victims. In a similar way, Jacklyn Cock argues, "War is a gendering activity. It both uses and maintains the ideological construction of gender in the definitions of 'masculinity' and 'femininity.' Women are widely cast in the role of 'the protected' and 'the defended.' . . ."[3] Peace is seen as a feminine and war as a masculine element, or as popular literature would put it, women are from Venus, men are from Mars.

GENDER CRIMES AS WAR CRIMES: INTERNATIONAL LAW

In the past, sexual war crimes against women remained invisible, were trivialized, or were justified either as an inevitable byproduct of war or as a reward for fighting men. Thus, as well as being excluded from redress under national laws, women were also privatized in the international arena. This seems paradoxical in light of the fact that sexual and military war violence against women happens, by definition, within the public sphere, as wars between states, in legal terms, belong to the domain of international affairs and international law. As I stated earlier, even if the act of violence takes place in somebody's private premises, the function of this violence, whether it is ethnic cleansing, humiliation of the enemy, or violence against female sex, is political and the act belongs to the public sphere. Just as in ancient Greek history, the pattern of military or paramilitary rapes in Bosnia and Rwanda occurred in such a manner that a group of soldiers sexually violated women in front of their relatives or members of the community. The most intimate and personal of human relationships, as sexual intercourse is supposed to be, was turned into a public gesture and martial demonstration. To paraphrase Brownmiller, rape in war is a message that one warring male faction sends to another, using women's bodies as their battlefields.

Rape was first identified as a capital offense in the Leiber Code, which regulated the conduct of the Union Army during the American Civil War. This precedent was followed in the Hague Convention of 1907, and later in the Geneva Conventions and its Protocols of 1948 and 1949, which took force in 1950 and were to have determined the prosecution of war crimes in the Nuremberg and Tokyo tribunals. But this did not happen at Nuremberg and it was only implemented at Tokyo to a limited degree.

Rhonda Copelon, a feminist lawyer who was involved in starting a civil suit in the United States against Radovan Karadzic, the Serbian leader in Bosnia, to indict him for Bosnian military rapes, offers the following explanation for the failure of international jurisprudence to enforce the provisions given in these conventions:

> Rape was not treated as violence, and was therefore not
> named in the list of "grave breaches" subject to the universal
> obligation to prosecute. . . . [Rape had] a characterization
> that reinforced the secondary importance as well as the shame
> and stigma of the victimized women. The offence was against
> male dignity and honour, or national or ethnic honour. In this
> scenario, women were the object of a shaming attack, the
> property or objects of others, needing protection perhaps, but
> not the subjects of rights.[4]

The consequence was that, despite considerable evidence for mass rapes in occupied Europe during World War II, the International Military Tribunal at Nuremberg failed entirely to criminalize and prosecute rape and sexual violence as a war crime, a crime against humanity, or a crime of genocide. Susan Brownmiller quotes the French prosecutor asking the tribunal for forgiveness if he avoided citing the "atrocious details" from the records on sexual crimes committed against women, calling this attitude "the standard censoring mechanisms that men employ when dealing with the rape of women."

The International Military Tribunal for the Far East (IMTFE) faced a different situation in Tokyo. Throughout Asia, the Japanese military established rape camps, which they named comfort stations, and they called the women detained in these camps comfort women. In Tokyo, several high-ranking officers were held responsible for this, as was the wartime foreign minister of Japan, who was convicted of direct responsibility for violations of the laws or customs of war, including widespread rapes in Nanjing in 1937, where an estimated 20,000 women and girls were raped. During the IMTFE, though, rape was not considered a war crime or a crime against humanity, and the facts of enforced prostitution and sexual slavery were ignored under provisions for these crimes.

As in Europe, existing documentation revealed that Allied Forces knew about the Japanese rape camps and sexual slavery throughout Asia. The full scope of sexual torture against Asian as well as Dutch women in Indonesia during the Japanese invasion came to light only in the early 1990s, when

Korean and other Asian women started the first regional and then later international movement for recognition of these crimes.

Many women died in these camps—of exhaustion, malnutrition, mutilation, sexually transmitted diseases, and torture in the form of sexual violence. The rape camps in Asia, where women were forced to provide domestic as well as sexual services, could have been compared to the German forced labor camps but were not.[5]

CHANGE IN THE PARADIGM

The wars in the former Yugoslavia and Rwanda have brought about groundbreaking changes at international criminal tribunals in the treatment of sexual crimes against women in war. Both statutes of the ad hoc international criminal tribunals have listed rape as a form of crime under the category of crimes against humanity. These two tribunals have historical significance in ending impunity for sex war crimes against women, which ceased to be a crime whose name is unspeakable. Presently, at both tribunals, a number of current public indictments have laid charges of sexual violence including rape. The shift from women being seen as and protected as part of a national, ethnic, or religious community to women being recognized as having rights as women and thus legally protected is of fundamental importance in general, not only for women.

In the case of Rwanda, one of the accused, J.P. Akayesu, a former teacher and a city mayor who became a warlord during the Hutu genocide against Tutsis, was charged with rape and gender violence as a genocidal act. This charge was not included in the original indictment against Akayesu; the indictment was amended after the testimony of two Tutsi women with substantial evidence. The amendment was also requested by the amicus brief submitted to the court by a coalition of women's groups. The original indictment contained charges of crimes against humanity (article 3 of the International Criminal Tribunal for Rwanda [ICTR] with respect to rape and gender violence and with respect to outrages committed upon personal dignity under article 4 of ICTR, referring to the violations of Geneva Conventions and its additional Protocols under which rape is not explicitly listed as a form of crime.

After amending the original indictment, the chamber judgment stated that rape and gender violence can constitute genocide "in the same way as any other act as long as they were committed with the specific intent to destroy, in whole and in part, a particular group, targeted as such."[6] The key element for a case of gender violence to be considered genocidal was, in legal terms, the *mens rea,* the intention with which the crime was committed.

Akayesu was charged with command responsibility, as someone in a position of authority, for ordering, instigating, aiding, and abetting acts of gender violence. In the Akayesu case, again, it was not women as a protected group whom the Court was protecting and to whom it was making restitution, but female members of the targeted ethnic group. The case is interesting because, for the first time in the history of international law, an international court laid a charge for rape of women under the Genocide Convention (article 2 of the ICTR). In this case, wartime gender violence was treated as an integral part of the overall intention *(mens rea)* and the process of the destruction, in whole or in part, of the particular group, targeted as such, with women specifically targeted as part of that group.

The sentence and its explanation[7] did not explicitly state that sex or gender can be taken as the basis for a stable and permanent identity, as race or ethnicity can. Nevertheless, by expanding the four grounds explicitly mentioned in the notion of a stable and permanent group (religion, nationality, race, ethnicity) whose protection is secured with the UN Genocide Convention and ratified in ICTY and ICTR, some feminist lawyers argued that gender appeared as a category of rights and protection already in the Akayesu case, even though he was charged under the genocide article of the ICTR.

The definition of a stable group in the UN Genocide Convention refers to groups constituted in a permanent fashion and whose membership is determined by birth, in contrast to the more mobile groups, such as political and economic groups, which one joins through individual voluntary commitment. With the Akayesu judgment, the question of gender as a ground for war crime remained open and subject to further discussion. In fact, the ICTR's decision on Akayesu reflects the overall feminist discussion on the content of the concept of gender.

Contemporary science and life practices have shown that neither gender nor sex necessarily need be a permanent condition, and most feminist scholars have refuted an essentialist understanding of the concept. However, the same can be argued for concepts such as nation, ethnicity, and race, not to mention religion, as chosen identities. Nevertheless, most feminist theorizing has claimed the practical political, social, and legal usefulness of the concept of gender as a means for the advancement of women's status. I would like to argue that the concept of gender has also demonstrated its usefulness in legal practices of international law.

THE MEANING OF THE LEGAL CHANGES

In both the Rwandan and Yugoslavian cases, the media and local and international policymakers characterized systematic rape as a tool of ethnic cleansing or genocide. There is a common belief that this publicity against gender violence as a tool of war and ethnic cleansing influenced a major change in international humanitarian law and finally put rape and gender violence onto the list of crimes treated by international law. Many women lawyers and researchers claim that this formulation transformed rape from a private, off-duty, collateral, and inevitable excess to a public or political act in the traditional sense. Other women's groups in the former Yugoslavia and also international human rights lawyers and activists, although admitting that the ethnicization of war rape contributed to the force of condemnation and to the changing of public attitudes, launched the following critique of such a stand:

> Rape drew broad attention, at the outset, however, more
> because it was a genocidal or ethnic attack than because it was
> an attack on women. . . . Like all arguments that deflect atten-
> tion from the essential need to recognize women as subjects,
> it had a potentially regressive aspect in suggesting that this
> use of rape was qualitatively different from the traditional use
> of women as booty, . . . or as the reward for the penultimate
> expression of the norm of masculinity.[8]

But whether the rape was prosecuted as genocidal or as a crime against humanity, it seems that rape—as a specific crime against women—became visible, changed public attitudes, and was transformed from the private to the public and political sphere only when it became closely linked to already recognized and legally sanctioned crimes against ethnic/national or religious groups.

From a woman's, or at least from a feminist, point of view, we can once again argue that it was not a crime against women but a crime against women as members of an ethnic or national group that became punishable. This meant that it was not the atrocity as such (mass rape of women, harm done to the single woman), but the purpose of that atrocity, in these cases ethnic cleansing or genocide, that decided the character of the crime and decisively contributed to the change. However, there has been further development in the issue of rape as a war crime. The International Criminal Court (ICC), which has built on the experiences of the ICTY and ICTR, has embraced more radical changes in that direction.

In general, the creation of the permanent ICC[9] in July 1998, with the primary purpose of investigating and punishing "the Crime of genocide, Crimes against humanity, and War crimes" in circumstances in which the appropriate national authorities fail to do so, can be understood as important progress for humankind. With regard to war, it thoroughly shifts the existing paradigms of international law and, I hope, of relations between states. By challenging the notion of sovereignty, this change may increase the possibility that international bodies can prevent wars, because the sovereignty of the nation-state has been one of the main legal-political obstacles to preventing wars among states. The ICC has the potential to revolutionize the status of women in international law and to define, investigate, and prosecute war violence against women, as well as other forms of war crimes.

There are at least two major breakthroughs concerning gender in the statute:

1. Gender-specific crimes are now included under two of the three core crimes that are provided: crimes against humanity and war crimes.

2. The listing of these crimes covers a much broader spectrum than before (ICTY, ICTR). Rape, sexual slavery, enforced prostitution, forced pregnancy, enforced sterilization, and any other form of sexual violence of comparable gravity are defined as crimes against humanity.

Another interesting point with regard to the interpretation of war rapes as genocidal crimes or crimes against humanity is the description that the ICC Statute gives the crime of forced pregnancy. It states, "'Forced pregnancy' means the unlawful confinement of a woman forcibly made pregnant, with the intent of affecting the ethnic composition of any population or carrying out other grave violations of international law." Here we could argue that the court has made a compromise: It recognized forced pregnancy as an ethnic, and not a gender, crime, but by excluding it from the category of genocide and adding it to the crimes against humanity, and by adding "other grave violations" it also recognized its gendered dimension. Nevertheless, the ICC has ended impunity for gender crimes and has introduced sex and gender justice in international human rights and humanitarian law.

Feminist activists and lawyers claim that the Rome Statute of the ICC, after several decades of international women's activism, begins to correct many centuries of neglect by international law. From my perspective, which was to observe the process of disentangling women as a legal subject from other preexisting groups, collectivities, or categories as a ground for defining crimes, I believe that the ICC includes gender as a specifically protected social category, along with ethnicity, nation, religion, and so forth. Because of this inclusion, we can also claim that sexual violence has become recognized on a par with other egregious forms of violence, such as torture, enslavement, genocide, and other inhuman treatment. The Rome Statute of the ICC contains an impressive list of sexual and gender crimes listed as crimes against humanity or war crimes and additional provisions specific to women's issues.[10]

CONCLUSIONS

International law, both criminal and humanitarian, as well as human rights law, regulates the relations between states; by definition, this means the public sphere. The sheer fact that women traditionally belonged to the private sphere delayed the recognition of crimes against women as war crimes. War, with the exception of civil war, takes place between states, and international law itself stems from historic attempts to prevent or at least to regulate warfare.

By stating that crimes against humanity can be perpetrated against civilians, "in time of peace as well as war," "when committed as part of a widespread or systematic attack,"[11] the ICC Statute clearly refers to the crimes committed by private persons as well as state actors such as members of an army. Although it is difficult to foresee its effect in situations of defined conflict, whether international or within an existing nation-state, this is a revolutionary reversal in the potentials of international jurisprudence.

This is particularly significant for violence against women because in the existing patriarchal gender relations that characterize states and civil societies there is not always a sharp difference between violence against women in wars and other conflict situations on the one hand and everyday violence against women, such as marital rape and other domestic and private violence on the other. I know that the ICC Statute will not automatically change national or international discriminatory and sexist laws, much less the gender politics of everyday life in sexist culture. Nevertheless, by establishing basic norms of international gender justice, it provides an efficient new tool for political advocacy in the domestic and international arenas. This tool was created through the tireless efforts of the women's human rights movement to connect gender violence and sexual persecution of women in war and conflict and "in the small places close to home," as Eleanor Roosevelt said in the Universal Declaration of Human Rights.

This article is excerpted and adapted from "The Status of Rape as a War Crime in International Law: Changes Introduced after the Wars in the Former Yugoslavia and Rwanda," M.A. thesis prepared for the Committee of Liberal Studies, New School University, New York City, December 2001. The author and editors thank professors Elzbieta Matynia, Betty Reardon, and Stephanie Damoff.

NOTES

1. Susan Brownmiller, *Against Our Will: Men, Women and Rape* (New York: Simon and Schuster, 1975).

2. Brownmiller, *Against Our Will*, 31.

3. Jacklyn Cock, *Colonels and Cadres: War and Gender in South Africa* (Cape Town: Oxford University Press, 1991).

4. Rhonda Copelon, "Gender Crimes as War Crimes: Integrating War Crimes against Women into International Criminal Law," *McGill Law Journal* 46 (2000): 7, http://www.journal.law.mcgill.ca/abs/461copel.htm.

5. In Tokyo in 1993, I attended the first public hearing held in Japan on sexual crimes against Asian women committed by Japanese soldiers. The event was organized by the Asian Women's Human Rights Council.

6. ICTR Statute, International Criminal Tribunal for Rwanda Web site, http://www.ictr.org.

7. ICTY Statute, § 511, § 516, http://www.un.org/icty/basic/statut/stat2000_con.htm.

8. Copelon, "Gender Crimes," 9.

9. Rome Statute of the International Criminal Court, UN Doc. No. A/Conf.183/9, 37 I.L.M. 999, http://www.un.org/icc.

10. The following articles of the Rome Statute contain various gender provisions: 7(1:g, h), 7(2:f, g), 7(3), 8(2:b, xxii; e, vi), 21(3), 36(8:a, iii; b), 42(9), 43(6), 54(1:b), 54(2), 57(3:c), 68, 69. See http://www.un.org/law/icc/statute/romefra.htm

11. Rome Statute, Article 7(1).

· ·

VESNA KESIĆ, a graduate of the University of Zagreb, was a founder and the first director of the Center for Women War Victims, a Zagreb-based feminist organization that since 1992 has worked with women refugees and war victims. A journalist and author, she has taught and lectured widely in Europe and the United States on women's issues, specifically violence against women, and also contributed to scholarly periodicals in several languages. She lives in Zagreb.

VISIONS AND POSSIBILITIES

Here are the voices of women and men who have glimpsed the possibility of a transformed world, sharing their visions of personal as well as institutional change. Some of these visions are hard to see; many veils must be lifted. We must learn new language, new responses. As products of the rape culture, we all suffer deep interior divisions, but we can learn to speak truth, resist seduction, and come to terms. We can learn to hear the voice of the not-yet-spoken in our desire to change, to follow these promptings of our best selves.

SEDUCED BY VIOLENCE NO MORE

· ·

b e l l   h o o k s

I was surprised by the number of young black women
who repudiated the notion of male domination but who
would then go on to insist that they could not desire a
brother who could not take charge, take care of business,
be in control.

WE LIVE IN A CULTURE that condones and celebrates rape. Within a phallocentric patriarchal state the rape of women by men is a ritual that daily perpetuates and maintains sexist oppression and exploitation. We cannot hope to transform rape culture without committing ourselves fully to resisting and eradicating patriarchy. In his essay "Black America: Multicultural Democracy in the Age of Clarence Thomas and David Duke," Manning Marable writes, "Rape, spouse abuse, sexual harassment on the job, are all essential to the perpetuation of a sexist society. For the sexist, violence is the necessary and logical part of the unequal, exploitative relationship. To dominate and control, sexism requires violence. Rape and sexual harassment are therefore not accidental to the structure of gender relations within a sexist order." This is no new revelation. In all our work as thinkers and activists, committed feminist women have consistently made this same point. However, it is important to acknowledge that our movement to transform rape culture can only progress as men come to feminist thinking and actively challenge sexism and male violence against women. And it is even more significant that Manning speaks against a sexist order from his position as an African American social critic.

Black males, who are utterly disenfranchised in most every arena of life in the United States, often find that the assertion of sexist domination is their only expressive access to that patriarchal power they are told all men should possess as their gendered birthright. Hence, it should not surprise or shock that many black men support and celebrate rape culture. That celebration has found its most powerful contemporary voice in misogynist rap music. Significantly, though, powerful alternative voices exist. The mass media pays little attention to those black men who are opposing phallocentrism, misogyny, and sexism, who rap against rape, against patriarchy. The "it's-a-dick-thing" version of masculinity that black male pop icons like Spike Lee and Eddie Murphy promote is a call for real black men to be sexist and proud of it, to rape and assault black women and brag about it. Alternative progressive black male voices in rap or cinema receive little attention, but they do exist. There are even black males who do "rap against rape" (their slogan), but their voices are not celebrated in patriarchal culture.

Overall cultural celebration of black male phallocentrism takes the form of commodifying these expressions of cool in ways that glamorize and seduce. Hence, those heterosexual black males whom the culture deems most desirable as mates or erotic partners tend to be pushing a dick-thing masculinity. They can talk tough and get rough. They can brag about disciplinin' their woman, about making sure the "bitch" respects them.

Many black men have a profound investment in the perpetuation and maintenance of rape culture. So much of their sense of value and self-esteem is hooked into the patriarchal macho image; these brothers are not about to surrender their dick-thing masculinity. This was most apparent during the case against Mike Tyson. Brothers all over the place were arguing that the black female plaintiff should not have gone to Tyson's hotel room in the wee hours of the morning if she had no intention of doing the wild thing. As one young brother told me, "I mean if a sister came to my room that late, I would think she got one thing on her mind." When I suggested to him and his partners that maybe a woman could visit the room of a man she likes in the wee hours of the night because she might like to talk, they shook their head, saying, "No way." Theirs is a deeply engrained sexism, a profoundly serious commitment to rape culture.

Like many black men, they are enraged by any feminist call to rethink masculinity and oppose patriarchy. And the courageous brothers who do, who rethink masculinity, who reject patriarchy and rape culture, often find that they cannot get any play—that the very same women who may critique macho male nonsense contradict themselves by making it clear that they find the "unconscious brothers" more appealing.

On college campuses all over the United States, I talk with these black males and hear their frustrations. They are trying to oppose patriarchy and yet are rejected by black females for not being masculine enough. This makes them feel like losers, like their lives are not enhanced when they make progressive changes, when they affirm the feminist movement. Their black female peers confirm that they do indeed hold contradictory desires. They desire men not to be sexist, even as they say, "But I want him to be masculine." When pushed to define masculine, they fall back on sexist representations. I was surprised by the number of young black women who repudiated the notion of male domination but who would then go on to insist that they could not desire a brother who could not take charge, take care of business, be in control.

Their responses suggest that one major obstacle preventing us from transforming rape culture is that heterosexual women have not unlearned a heterosexist-based eroticism that constructs desire in such a way that many of us can respond erotically only to male behavior that has already been coded as masculine within the sexist framework. Let me give an example of what I mean. For most of my heterosexual erotic life, I have been involved with black males who are into a dick-thing masculinity. I was in a non-monogamous relationship of more than ten years with a black man committed to nonsexist behavior in most every aspect of daily life, the major exception being the bedroom. I accepted my partner's insistence that his sexual desires be met in any circumstance where I had made sexual overtures (kissing, caressing, etc.). Hence ours was not a relationship where I felt free to initiate sexual play without going forward and engaging in coitus. Often I felt compelled to engage in sexual intercourse when I did not want to.

In my fantasies, I dreamed of being with a male who would fully respect my body rights, my right to say no, my freedom to not proceed in any sexual activity that I did not desire even if I initially felt that I wanted to be sexual. When I left this relationship, I was determined to choose male partners who would respect my body rights. For me, this meant males who did not think that the most important expression of female love was satisfying male sexual desire. It meant males who could respect a woman's right to say no irrespective of the circumstance.

Years passed before I found a partner who respected those rights in a feminist manner, with whom I made a mutual covenant that neither of us would ever engage in any sexual act that we did not desire to participate in. I was elated. With this partner I felt free and safe. I felt that I could choose not to have sex without worrying that this choice would alienate or anger my partner. Braggin' about him to girlfriends and acquaintances, I was often told, "Girl, you betta be careful. Dude might be gay." Though most women were impressed that I had found such a partner, they doubted that this could be a chosen commitment to female freedom on any man's part and raised suspicious questions. I also began to feel doubts. Nothing about the way this dude behaved was familiar. His was not the usual dick-thing masculinity that had aroused feelings of pleasure and danger in me for most of my erotic life. While I liked his alternative behavior, I felt a loss of control—the kind that we experience when we are no longer acting within the socialized framework of both acceptable and familiar heterosexual behavior. I worried that he did not find me really desirable. Then I asked myself, would aggressive emphasis on his desire, on his need for "the pussy," have reassured me? It seemed to me then that I needed to rethink the nature of female heterosexual eroticism, particularly in relation to black culture.

Critically interrogating my responses, I confronted the reality that despite all my years of opposing patriarchy I had not fully questioned or transformed the structure of my desire. By allowing my erotic desire to still be determined to *any extent* by conventional sexist constructions, I was acting in complicity with patriarchal thinking. Resisting patriarchy ultimately meant that I had to reconstruct myself as a heterosexual desiring subject in a manner that would make it possible for me to be fully aroused by male behavior that was not phallocentric. In basic terms, I had to learn how to be sexual with a man in a context where his pleasure and his hard-on were decentered and mutual pleasure was centered. That meant learning how to enjoy being with a male partner who could be sexual without viewing coitus as the ultimate expression of desire.

Talking with women of varying ages and ethnicities about this issue, I am more than ever convinced that women who engage in sexual acts with male partners must not only interrogate the nature of the masculinity we desire, we must actively construct radically new ways to think and feel as desiring subjects. By shaping our eroticism in ways that repudiate phallocentrism, we oppose rape culture. Whether this alters sexist male behavior is not the point. A woman who wants to engage in erotic acts with a man without reinscribing sexism will be much more likely to avoid or reject situations where she might be victimized. By refusing to function within the heterosexist framework, which condones male erotic domination of women, females would be actively disempowering patriarchy.

Without a doubt, our collective conscious refusal to act in any way that would make us complicit in the perpetuation of rape culture within the sphere of sexual relations would undermine the structure. Concurrently, when heterosexual women are no longer attracted to macho men, the message sent to men would at least be consistent and clear. That would be a major intervention in the overall effort to transform rape culture.

. . . .

bell hooks is the author of more than sixteen works on feminist theory and cultural criticism, including *The Will to Change* (Atria, 2004), *Rock My Soul* (Atria, 2002), *Remembered Rapture* (Henry Holt, 1999), *All About Love* (William Morrow, 1999), *Killing Rage* (Henry Holt, 1995), and *Ain't I a Woman* (South End Press, 1981). She lives in New York City.

THE LIE OF ENTITLEMENT

. . . .

TERRENCE CROWLEY

As a man, I accrue privilege simply by remaining silent, accepting this legacy, and saying nothing about its cost in terms of women's lives.

Lying is done with words, and also with silence.
—ADRIENNE RICH, *On Lies,*
Secrets, and Silence

ECAUSE I WILL BE USING my personal experience as the vehicle for this essay, I want to start by saying a bit about who I am. I am a divorced white male in my early sixties. Reared in the south-east United States by working-class Catholic parents, I earn my living as a self-employed furniture maker. I am university educated, middle class, and straight. As such, I inherited all the privilege the rape culture provides.

The connection between my life and that culture was largely invisible to me until I began working with Men Stopping Violence, an organization dedicated to ending violence against women—specifically battering, rape, and incest. What I have learned through my associations with other men and in particular through my work with Men Stopping Violence is that, although my experience may differ from that of other men in some of its specifics, it is frighteningly similar at its core. In our childhood homes, on playgrounds, in locker rooms, in dormitories, and in fraternities of all kinds, men learned to define our masculinity in terms of our differentiation from what we felt was feminine as well as in terms of our ability to control women. The dichotomy was absolute: I was either in control or I was a pussy.

This said, what does my personal process have to do with transforming a rape culture? In particular, how do I support patriarchal values, making them seem almost natural, when I choose not to reckon with them in my own movement through the world?

For me, a hint of an explanation came while experiencing the paradigm shift that took place when I began my training with Men Stopping Violence. I was not a stereotypical villain when I came to the organization asking how I could help. I had a long history of politically correct and socially responsible behaviors. I had spent ten years in a seminary where I learned empathy for the downtrodden and how to help them while pursuing my theological studies. I was outspoken against the Vietnam War even while in the military. In the late 1960s, I participated in civil rights marches and demonstrations in my native Mississippi. I was the cofounder of a group working for environmental sanity in the panhandle of northern Florida. I studied and maintained a voluminous library of feminist writings. I was always careful to keep copies of *Z* magazine and the *Utne Reader* nearby. I worked for the passage of the Equal Rights Amendment. I made it a point to choose strong, independent women as companions. For years, I participated in men's groups where I shared feelings and supported others in doing the same. Forty years after the movement, I continued to subscribe to the hippie value that all men are brothers and conducted my business accordingly. It was difficult for me to find other men who respected and shared such a liberal belief system; as a result, most of my friends were women. I worked and read to overcome my racist, classist, and sexist beliefs. In all honesty, I felt quite good about the job I'd done. I considered myself a politically concerned, sensitive, and principled person.

It was this man, immobilized by what I now recognize as my homophobia, who resistantly followed the wise and careful shepherding of a dear friend to the Men and Masculinity Conference held in Atlanta in 1990. There I became acquainted with Men Stopping Violence through the keynote address of its executive director, Kathleen Carlin. Through her, I learned of the principle of intentions versus effects, which says that my intentions are not necessarily what gives my actions their moral value but rather their effects on others—specifically their effects on those people who are disenfranchised by my privilege, marginalized by my sense of entitlement. But Kathleen did not stop there. She went on to say that they, rather than I, were the ones to name those effects. What's more, they got to say what I needed to do to redress the damage.

Despite my liberal bent, these ideas caught me completely unaware. In that moment, my privilege was rendered visible to me in a way that was undeniable. With that epiphany came my first inkling of why my privilege remains largely invisible to me. So extreme and so complete was my privilege that to question it literally never entered my mind. My sense of entitlement insulated and isolated me from threats of any kind. I had no reason to be aware of my privilege.

The challenge to relinquish my privilege both chilled and excited me. However, the threat of that challenge made it elusive to me. Trying to examine it made it invisible. Nonetheless, with a strange mixture of apprehension, confusion, and altruism, I called Men Stopping Violence the following week. I was ready to step into a position as an instructor in their batterer intervention program after an orientation to the organization. Hold up! they said. There's a one-year training to be done. Well, after a review of my background, I was sure I would be exempted from most of the internship.

I was hurt and angry to find that before I could work with the organization, I would have to complete the entire year-long internship—a clear waste of my time and money. I thought these people were looking for help! I was incensed that my M.A. in psychology wasn't enough. I was confused that my work with prisoners while in the seminary wasn't enough. I was surprised that my former employment with vocational rehabilitation wasn't enough. I was indignant that my politics and environmental work weren't enough. I was outraged that my sagacity and righteousness weren't enough. What more did these people want?

My first class brought the answer. I began my internship as a participant in a twenty-four-week class for batterers. The initial exercise was to check in with one's worst incident of abuse to women. After several days of struggle about whether to lie or not, it dawned on me that the training was not about helping *those guys;* it was about confronting my own abusive and controlling behaviors. My world shifted 180 degrees: I was going to be held accountable in a new way, accountable to women. I felt the principle of intentions versus effects beginning to slowly recondense in my brain. I wanted out!

I wanted to be one of the good guys. I wanted to say what battering is about and who does it. I wanted to say what working on sexism looks like. I wanted to say what racism is and what to do about it. I wanted to be the one to say when homeless people, gays, people of color, and most especially women go too far in their self-expression. I wanted to define *fair and just.* I wanted to say what is appropriate and when. I wanted to say what is sensual and sexy. I wanted to say what *no* means. I wanted to say what is provocative or erotic for women. I wanted to say whether this sense of entitlement propagates and condones a rape culture. Last, if questioned, I wanted to deny this need for control.

It looked rough. I had twenty-three weeks of class and fifty-one weeks of training to go. Each week, I struggled with the principle of intentions versus effects while I identified my abusiveness and listed its effects on those I had silenced. Each week, I sat with those intense feelings of vulnerability, fear, and confusion as the reality of women was brought into the room. Through this process, my acceptance of the principle of intentions versus effects grew. Yet each week, I used my theological, psychological, social, and political training to concoct new ruses that would allow me to jump outside that system of accountability.

The challenges for me surfaced in subtle attempts to control: Why do I shield my expectations from my partner, keeping her walking on eggshells, focused on my life rather than hers? How do I store disappointment for its ambush potential at a later date? Why, to feel safe, do I present myself as an emotional enigma that she must figure out? Why does being direct with women make me feel so vulnerable and out of control? Why is being sexual with a woman so important to me? What does it mean for me to be sexual with a woman? What am I trying to do when I pout and withdraw following a refusal of sex? What does it mean when a woman agrees to be sexual with me in the face of my sulking and moping? What constitutes consent between someone of the subordinate and someone of the dominant caste? If I was unable to get control via psychological and verbal manipulation, would I take the next step—physical force? The good guy/bad guy model no longer made sense to me. I was simply another man moving across the continuum of controlling behaviors to get my way with women.

In retrospect, I needed that training with Men Stopping Violence to up- root my arrogance. To exempt myself was to lie about my involvement in a rape culture. I wanted to remain silent around my role in the perpetuation of a culture that condones violence against women.

I had not been exempted from the internship because my background and preparation had been carried out in an environment of disdain for the principle of intentions versus effects. My previous training endowed me with the authority to take control, define solutions, and co-opt the problem people into carrying out my ideas. The two types of training are not the same, and it was critical that I have a clear understanding of that. For me to have received an exemption would have been to lie about women's reality—to say that I could in fact name it.

Most of what I brought to Men Stopping Violence was of enormous help to me as I assimilated the principle of intentions versus effects, but it was and sometimes continues to be an enormous burden to me while trying to negotiate the labyrinth of my sense of entitlement; my privilege always gives me permission to frame my perceptions as the truth.

This lie of entitlement—my privilege to describe the reality of women—gives a rape culture its life. Patriarchy is predicated on this lie and on our protective silence. It is the lie I wanted so badly to tell the class. It is the lie that allows me to describe myself as one of the good guys. It is the lie not permitted in the classroom. When this lie is disallowed, the rape culture is challenged at its foundation. If I go on to name that lie, if I break ranks with the patriarchy by acknowledging that I cannot know the reality of those subordinated by the system of values that entitles me, that system is no longer seamless; its existence is endangered.

As a man, someone the rape culture has endowed with credibility, my schism has the potential to be all the more destructive. Of course my lot will be cast with women's for this betrayal. Nonetheless, just as I was moved by the honesty of other men not to lie about my worst incident of abuse to a woman, so perhaps other men will be inspired by this truth-telling to break ranks. My vision is that this personal process moves logarithmically, reaching critical mass, and ultimately destroying the institutions that support and encourage rape.

I must confess that I have difficulty holding this vision in focus, but I also know that I cannot work for something I cannot imagine. If I let my mind run wild, I can see men naming the lie of privilege in such numbers that this system of values begins to unravel. As it unravels, the rape culture begins to transform into one of respect and dignity for women.

What can keep this vision from being realized? Why is this vision so difficult for me to hold in focus? Because to stop lying means nothing less than changing what it means to be a man. Because my proclivity is to remain silent and to consolidate my power as a man—not to write this essay, not to blow the whistle on myself. Silence feels easy. I don't feel like a man when I'm not in control. I feel confused and vulnerable. It frightens me to say out loud: As long as men control women's bodies, a rape culture will continue. As long as men get to define the sexuality and eroticism of women, a rape culture will continue. As long as men link sexual excitement with control, domination, and violence, a rape culture will continue. Until the effects of men's behavior on women define the moral value of that behavior, a rape culture will thrive. Violence of all kinds can be seen as the refusal to accept the principle of intentions versus effects. Privilege is always paid for by those it subjugates.

As a man, I accrue privilege simply by remaining silent, accepting this legacy, and saying nothing about its cost in terms of women's lives. Men can stop the lie of our inherent superiority in its tracks by simply not acting as if it were true. I do not mean to imply that what is simple will be easy. It is extremely difficult for me. But the process begins with the acknowledgment of privilege; the terms of my privilege are that I do not have to acknowledge it. The process begins with me saying aloud that the standards of gender identity are contrived to accommodate my privilege. The male/female dichotomy is based on relatively minor biological differences that are eroticized, fetishized, mythologized, and exploited to declare men and women opposites. This social and political dichotomy is used to promote the idea of men as intelligent, rational, sagacious, and moral and women as our opposites: dense, emotive, obtuse, and evil. As I aggrandize myself, I demean my opposite. As I deify the masculine, I necessarily vilify women. The degradation not only makes attack permissible, it makes it a moral imperative.

When my privilege is laid out in all its ugliness, how can I remain silent? My hope is that what Gloria Steinem said of women's consciousness-raising groups in the 1970s is true for men today: "Personal truth-telling as a path to social change is the most important and enduring legacy." I am breaking my silence and trying to tell my truth, trusting that social change will follow. If men break the silence in concert with one another, we can transform this rape culture. As the perpetrators, we can bring about the transformation today if we so choose. If we maintain our silence, we doubtless will rape another 600,000 women in this country in the coming year and in each of the years to come.

My process has carried me to the point where I know that I am lying when I fail to acknowledge openly my privilege as a man and where I know that my failure to make that acknowledgment holds the rape culture in place. To transform the culture, I must transform what it means for me to be a man; I must relinquish my claim on women.

My thinking and writing is richly informed by the work of Kathleen Carlin, Andrea Dworkin, Kay Hagan, and the program staff of Men Stopping Violence.

. . . .

TERRENCE CROWLEY has been an instructor and trainer with Men Stopping Violence (MSV) since 1990, and has served as the research and evaluation team manager at MSV. He teaches classes for batterers referred by the courts, the clergy, and therapists. As part of the MSV training team, he helps conduct regional and national trainings for churches, universities, the military, and the court system. He was also the project director of the Community Intervention Evaluation Project, introducing a batterers' program into two counties and conducting a five-year research project on the effectiveness of a BIP in increasing the community's response to battering. In 2000, Crowley became manager of the publications team. He has contributed a series of essays, "Choosing Our Words: The Dilemma of Gender-Neutral Language," "Unpacking Provocation," "Chivalry and Sexism," and "Program Evaluation: A Social Change Approach," to the journal *Uptake*.

A WOMAN WITH A SWORD
SOME THOUGHTS ON WOMEN, FEMINISM, AND VIOLENCE

· · · · · · · · · · · · · · · · · · · ·

D. A. CLARKE

The man limps into the emergency room with one ear half torn off and multiple bruises. As he gasps out his story, the doctor shakes his head: "You mean you grabbed at her breasts and tried to pull her into your car? Well I mean, dummy, what did you expect?" And he gets no sympathy, not a shred, not from anyone.

JUSTICE IS A WOMAN WITH A SWORD"—as slogans go, this one is strangely evocative. The sword, after all, is the weapon of chivalry and honor. Aristocratic criminals were privileged to meet their deaths by the sword rather than the disgraceful hempen rope; gentlemen settled their differences and answered insults at swords' point. Women and peasants, of course, did not learn swordplay. The weapon, like the concepts of honor and personal courage it represented, was reserved for men, and for men of good birth only; no one else was expected or permitted to have a sense of personal pride or honor. Offenses against a woman were avenged by her chosen champion.

· · · · ·

A WOMAN WITH A SWORD, then, is a powerful emblem. She is no one's property. A crime against her will be answered by her own hand. She is armed with the traditional weapon of honor and vengeance, implying both that she has a sense of personal dignity and worth, and that affronts against that dignity will be hazardous to the offending party. This is hardly the woman of pornographic male fantasy.

In male fantasy, women are always powerless to defend themselves from hurt and humiliation. Worse, they enjoy it. Treatment that would drive the average self-respecting man to desperate violence makes these fantasy-women tremble, breathe heavily, and moan with desire: abuse and embarrassment are their secret needs. Womanliness as invented by pornographers is a deep masochism, which renders women as powerless to defend self and others as the sweetness-and-light female patience and martyrdom of Christian romanticism. It's but a short step from the ladylike and therefore ineffectual face slaps of Nice Girls to a hot and steamy surrender in the dominant male's brawny embrace.

But a woman with a sword—*that* is a different matter.

The troublesome question of nonviolence haunts the women's movement and always has. We despise the brutality to which woman are subjected by men, the arrogance and casual destructiveness of male violence as embodied in domestic battery, gang skirmishes, and officially sanctioned wars. Feminists have traditionally opposed police brutality, the draft, warfare, rape, blood sports, and other manifestations of the masculine fascination with dominance and death.

Yet, like all oppressed peoples, women are divided on the essential question of violence as a tactic. When is it appropriate to become violent? Is the use of force ever justifiable? When is it time to take up arms? to learn jujitsu? to carry a knife? Is violence just plain wrong, no matter who does it? Or can there be extenuating circumstances?

The flow of our debate is muddied by traditional ideas of womanliness with which feminists struggle. Are women really better than men? Are we inherently kinder, gentler, less aggressive? Certainly the world would be a better place if everyone manifested the virtues tradition assigns to Good Women. But will gentleness and kindness really win the hearts of nasty and violent people? Will reason, patience, and setting a good example make men see the error of their ways? Is "womanly" nonviolence "naturally" the best and only course for feminists?

Historically, the prospect for nonviolent peoples and cultures is not good. They tend to lose territory, property, freedom, and finally life itself as soon as less pleasant neighbors show up with better armaments and bigger ambitions. It's hard to survive as a pacifist when the folks next door are club-waving, rock-hurling imperialists: you end up enslaved or dead, or you learn to be like them in order to fight them. The greatest challenge to nonviolence is that to fulfill its promise it must be able to *prevent* violence. The image of the nonviolent activist righteously renouncing the use of force—while watching armed thugs drag away their struggling victims—is less than pleasing.

We have also the problem of effectiveness. Nonviolence is far more impressive when practiced by those who could easily resort to force if they chose. A really big, tough man in the prime of life who chooses to discipline himself to peace and gentleness is an impressive personality. A mob of thousands who choose to sit down peaceably and silently in the street, rather than smash windows and overrun police lines, is an unnerving sight. These kinds of nonviolence make a profound political point. But when women advocate nonviolence it may be much less effective.

Why? Because women are traditionally considered incapable of violence, particularly of violence against men. In the forties, the film beauty used to beat her little fists ineffectually on the strong man's chest before collapsing into passionate tears; in the seventies, the ditzy female sidekick inevitably left the safety catch on when it was time to shoot the bad guy. Women are commonly held to be as incompetent at physical force as they are at mechanics, mathematics, and race-car driving. The only violence traditionally permitted to women is the sneaky kind: conspiracy, manipulation, deceit, poison, a stiletto in the back.

And when women do become violent, we perceive it as shocking and awful, far worse than the male violence which we take for granted. There is a self-serving myth among men that, given power, women would be even worse than the worst men—which, of course, justifies keeping women firmly in their place and making sure no power gets into their nasty little hands. Many of us believe that myth, to some extent: I can remember my mother (a strong and resourceful woman) retailing to me the common doctrine that the female camp guards of the Third Reich were worse than the men.

Of course, only a handful of women attained power in Hitler's Germany; prison-guarding is an unfeminine occupation, also. So female camp guards, of high or low rank, were exceptional and therefore suspect. Their deeds are documented and unquestionably vile, but it's hard for me to say how they might be distinguished as measurably worse, more evil, than those of their male colleagues. What makes them worse in the eyes of Allied historians, I fear, is that in addition to their other crimes they *stepped out of women's place.*

This different perception of male and female violence, this double standard, afflicts women at the most elementary levels. Suppose a man makes unwanted social advances to a woman in, let's say, a restaurant or theater, and she eventually has to tell him loudly and angrily to get lost. *She* is the one who will be perceived as rude, hostile, aggressive, and obnoxious. His verbal aggression and invasiveness are accepted and expected; her rudeness (or mere curtness) in getting rid of him is noticed and condemned. One of our great myths is that a "real lady" can and should handle any difficulty, defuse any assault, without ever raising her voice or losing her manners. Female rudeness or violence in resistance to male aggression has often been taken to prove that the woman was not a lady in the first place, and therefore deserved no respect from the aggressor or sympathy from others.

Until recently, violent women in fiction were always evil. Competence with guns, long blades, or martial arts automatically marked a female as "mannish," possibly lesbian, destined for stereotyping as a prison matron, pervert, man-hater, sadist, and so on. On the other hand, cleverness with tiny silver-plated pistols, poison rings, or jeweled daggers identified the snakelike villainess whose cold and perfect beauty concealed a heart twisted by malice and frozen with selfishness—and so on. Heroines, predictably, fainted or screamed at moments of peril and then waited to be rescued in the penultimate chapter. By the 1920s, the Good Girls might put up a brave struggle and kick the bad guy in the shins, but they certainly did not throw furniture, break necks, cut throats, or whip out a sword-cane and chase the villain through the abandoned warehouse.

Tougher females emerged for a while in the war years, but only in the last thirty years or so have fictional females arrived who are ready with fists, karate kicks, and small arms. A new genre of Amazon Fantasy has grown up where previously there were only one or two authors who dared to put a sword in a female character's hand. Warrior women have become protagonists, with books and even epics to themselves. Admittedly, most of them are required by the author (or editor) to Learn to Love a Man Again by the end of the plot, but at least they start out by avenging their own rapes and their family's wrongs.

In commercial film (a conservative medium), fighting heroines and anti-heroines have become almost stock characters: Sigourney Weaver in the *Alien* movies, Anne Parillaud in *La Femme Nikita,* Deborra-Lee Furness in *Shame,* Geena Davis and Susan Sarandon in *Thelma & Louise,* Uma Thurman and Lucy Liu in the *Kill Bill* films, Michelle Yeoh in an endless series of martial arts/action films, and of course the immensely popular *Xena, Warrior Princess,* played by Lucy Lawless. Even in films with no pretense to social commentary or good intentions—films or TV programs clearly aimed at an adolescent male audience—fighting female sidekicks pop up fairly regularly (as in *Conan the Destroyer, The Golden Child, The Matrix, Lethal Weapon 3, Farscape*), characters who once would have been restricted to the world of Marvel Comics.

Americans are beginning to be able to handle the idea of female rage and vengeance, or at least of serious female violence, in fiction. In much the same way, the reading public of the twenties and thirties began to accept the Career Woman long before women made real inroads into the professions. Does this mean something? Is the ability to be violent a prerequisite for equality—as the maintenance of army and arsenal is for nationhood? Are these fighting females a good sign?

Maybe. In a perfect world, no. In a perfect world we wouldn't lock our doors, and no one would know how to throw a punch or how to roll with one. In this world, however, perhaps the price of full citizenship is the willingness and ability to defend oneself and one's dignity to the point of force.

We do respect people who know their limits, who cannot be pushed past a certain point—just as we mistrust and disrespect those who have no give in them at all and overreact violently to every little frustration. We respect people who can take care of themselves, who inform us of their limits clearly and look prepared to enforce them. Women are traditionally denied these qualities—the *no means yes* of male mythology—and one reason for this is that we are denied the use of force. To put it very simply, little boys who get pushed around on the playground are usually told to "stand up to him, don't let him get away with it," whereas little girls are more usually advised to run to Teacher.

The bottom line in not being pushed around is our willingness and our capacity to resist. At some point, resistance means defending ourselves with physical force. Women—kept out of contact sports, almost never trained in wrestling or boxing as boys often are, taught to flatter strong men by acting weak—are denied the skills and the emotional preparedness required to fight back.

Men commit the most outrageous harassments and insults against women simply because they can get away with it. They know they will not get hurt for saying and doing things which, between two men, would quickly lead to a fistfight or a stabbing. There are no consequences for abusing women.

There are several strategies for preventing crimes. We start with education, reason, and our efforts to bring up children to be good adults. Then comes elementary preparedness and awareness on the part of the innocent. Then there is active resistance and self-defense when a crime is attempted. And as our last resort, there is the establishment of consequences for the perpetrator.

Every time a man molests his daughter and still keeps his place in the family and community—every time a man sexually harasses a female employee and still keeps his job or his business reputation—every time a rapist or femicide gets a token sentence—there is a terrible lack of consequence for the commission of a crime.

We disagree as a society about the level of punishment or retribution or reparation we should exact. We can't agree whether murderers should themselves be killed. Most of us would agree that hanging is too severe a penalty for stealing a loaf of bread or a sheep, but is it too severe a penalty for hacking a woman to death? Some would say yes and some no. Others think we should abandon the concepts of punishment and reparation altogether, with their authoritarian implications, and concentrate on reeducating and reclaiming our errant brothers, turning them into better people.

While we argue about these things, women are steadily and consistently being insulted, molested, assaulted, and murdered. And most of the men who are doing these things are suffering no consequences at all, or very slight consequences. The slighter the consequence of their offense, the more it seems to them (and to everyone) that there is really nothing so very wrong with what they have done.

When as a society we sanctimoniously clasp our hands and reject the death penalty, letting femicides and rapists free after token jail terms and dubious therapies, we merely make a callous value judgment. We judge that a man's life—even a rapist's or a murderer's—is more valuable than the life and happiness of the next woman or child he may attack. When a killer is released and kills again, those who signed his release were signing also the death warrant for his next victim: someone they did not know and could not identify. That person's life was the price of their squeamishness and reluctance to sign for the death (or life imprisonment) of a man they could name, whose face they knew.

If the State is not going to step in and enforce severe penalties for abusing and murdering women, then is it women's responsibility to do so? When a woman's dignity, honor, and physical person are assaulted or destroyed, how shall we get justice? How shall we prevent it from happening again?

If the courtroom and the law are owned by men (if a Clarence Thomas, for example, can be appointed to the Supreme Court regardless of evidence that he routinely insulted and harassed women), at what point are women entitled to take the law into their own hands? At what point can we justify personal vendettas by angry survivors of male violence? What about violent action for political (rather than personal) agendas?

These are thorny questions, for sure. Vigilantism is so very trendy in our fragmenting culture: in films and cheap novels by the dozen, angry protagonists (almost all male) go out and shoot up the bad guys in a series of solo crusades, for revenge and the justice that a corrupt and ineffectual System cannot provide. America's love affair with flashy violence and alpha-male bravado is so traditional and distressing that one does hesitate to suggest vigilantism as a feminist tactic.

Yet—but—on the other hand—sometimes a demonstration of violent rage accomplishes what years of prayers, petitions, and protests cannot: it gets you taken seriously. (On yet another hand, it can also get you labeled crazy and put away.) Palestinian terrorists may have done more harm than good to their people's cause—or they may have been an essential part of a liberation struggle. It depends whom you ask.

When we consider violent political tactics such as terrorism and retribution, we have to remember that male implementation of these tactics is all mixed up with the traditions of male amusement and competition. Too often, the political cause of the moment is no more than an excuse for a gang of rowdy boys to play about with high explosives and automatic weapons— just another form of blood sport. Often there is more violence, and more random violence, than is called for—simply because the terrorists are having so much fun frightening and killing people. Would women succumb to this temptation?

A common belief about female violence is that it will only escalate male violence. I have heard from people of widely varying ages and politics the argument, "If women learn judo, then men will start using guns." This rather sidesteps the fact that a large number of men already own and use guns, knives, and other portable weapons; but it's an argument endemic to all liberation struggles. What if resistance to the occupier/oppressor leads only to increased brutality, repression, and suffering?

We can end up in a sadly familiar conflict: some women will hate and fear feminists and self-defense advocates because they anticipate that male anger, stirred up by these uppity females, will be vented on all women, including the "innocent." No liberation movement has ever escaped this bitter argument.

Will we make it worse by resisting? Feminists who demonstrated publicly and disruptively at the turn of the last century were accused at the time of worsening women's prospects by their violent and provocative behavior; yet today we honor them as the instigators of changes that lifted women halfway out of serfdom. Certainly forceful and loud resistance to sexual assault tends to result more often in escape or reduced injury than "womanly" tactics such as tears, pleading, or cooperation.

If the risk involved in attacking a woman were greater, there might be fewer attacks. If women defended themselves violently, the amount of damage they were willing to do to would-be assailants would be the measure of their seriousness about the limits beyond which they would not be pushed. If more women killed husbands and boyfriends who abused them or their children, perhaps there would be less abuse. A large number of women refusing to be pushed any further would erode, however slowly, the myth of the masochistic female which threatens all our lives. Violent resistance to an attack has its advantages all round.

A backlash is always possible, whether women "behave" or not. The strength and viciousness of antifeminism, and its appeal, have a lot more to do with the prevailing economic and political weather than with anything women actually do. A subject population can be as polite, conciliatory, and assimilated as possible—and still wake up one morning to discriminatory laws, confiscation of property, and all the rest.

For these reasons the argument that female violence will hurt only women, or make things worse, seems irrelevant to me. In fact, female violence that hurts only women is perfectly acceptable. Women have always been given the dirty work of disciplining their daughters into women's place, whether this meant binding little girls' feet or blaming and beating them for being raped. Today, a feminist community which claims to find violence of all kinds distasteful is still able to find lesbian sadomasochism sexy and chic. Images of women hurting other women are widely accepted, even where images of men hurting women are criticized.

Now, I am not particularly attracted to images of anyone being hurt, period. But I see potential value in fiction and film on the theme of women taking violent vengeance on rapists and femicides. One benefit is the assertion of female personal honor; another, quite frankly, is the shock value. Those who are appalled by the idea of vigilante women hunting down men should be asking themselves what they are doing about this world in which images of men hunting down, overpowering, and hurting women surround us. If violence is so terribly wrong when committed by women, then—damn it—it is just as terribly wrong when committed by men.

Let's face it, we still live in a world and a century in which a woman who walks (mistake) in the wrong part of town (oh dear) after dark (uh oh) alone (a big no-no) will be blamed by all and sundry if she is raped. People will ask what she expected, doing a fool thing like that.

It's interesting—amusing in a bitter kind of way—maybe even liberating—to envision a slightly different world. The man limps into the emergency room with one ear half torn off and multiple bruises. As he gasps out his story, the doctor shakes his head: "You mean you grabbed at her breasts and tried to pull her into your car? Well I mean, dummy, what did you expect?" And he gets no sympathy, not a shred, not from anyone.

If women become more violent, will the world be a more violent place? Perhaps, but it's not simple addition. We will have to subtract any violence that women *prevent*. So we will have to subtract a large number of rapes and daily humiliations suffered by women who today cannot or will not defend themselves. We might have to subtract six or seven murders that would have been committed by a latter-day Zodiac Killer, except that his first intended victim killed him instead. Suppose one of the women in the lecture hall in Montreal had been armed and skilled enough to take out Marc Lepine before he mowed down fourteen of her classmates.

It's not as if we were suggesting that women introduce violence into the Garden of Eden. The war is already on. Women and children are steadily losing it.

And women are already violent. Women take out the anger and frustration of women's place—and the memory of their own humiliations and defeats—on each other, on their kids, and on their own bodies. Would we rather that incest survivors mutilate themselves, commit suicide, abuse their own children—or go and do something dreadful to Daddy? We don't know for sure that doing something dreadful to Daddy will heal a wounded soul, but it does seem more appropriate than doing dreadful things to oneself or any innocent bystander.

And one last great myth: "Violence never solves anything."

In the grand philosophical sense, those words may ring true. Violence is like money: it can't make you happy, save your soul, make you a better person—but it certainly can solve things. When the winners exterminate the losers, historical conflicts are permanently solved. Many a high-ranking criminal has lived to a comfortable and respected old age only because a few pesky witnesses were no longer alive to testify. Many a dissatisfied husband has got rid of an unwanted wife. More women than we know have probably got rid of abusive husbands.

Violence definitely solves some things. A dead rapist will not commit any more rapes; he's been solved. Violence is a seductive solution because it seems easy and quick; violence is a glamorous commercial property in our time; violence is a tool, an addiction, a sin, a desperate resort, or a hobby, depending on where you look and whom you ask.

I lay before you here, not a list of easy answers, but a tangle of difficult questions. Violence may be a tool and a tactic that feminists should use; certainly we ought to be putting some serious thought into it. If we refuse it, it should not be because it offends against our romantic notion of Morally Superior Womanhood, but for some better and more thoughtful reason. If we accept it, we had better figure out how to avoid becoming corrupted by it.

This piece was commissioned originally in 1993 for the anthology Nemesis: Justice Is a Woman with a Sword, *edited by Nikki Craft.*

. . . .

D. A. CLARKE is a feminist, lesbian, and recovering technophile who has contributed irregularly to the literature of radical feminism since 1980. She has written mostly about male violence against women and its marketability—the connections between patriarchy, misogyny, and neoliberal "market values." Her essays have appeared online and in various feminist anthologies, most recently *Not for Sale*.

IN PRAISE OF INSUBORDINATION, OR, WHAT MAKES A GOOD WOMAN GO BAD?

INÉS HERNÁNDEZ-AVILA

There is an old Cheyenne saying, "A nation is not conquered until the hearts of its women are on the ground. Then it is done, no matter how strong the weapons, or how brave the warriors." How do all of us as women ensure that our hearts do not hit the ground? What strategies might we as women use to remind ourselves to hold our heads and hearts high?

AN INDIAN[1] DANCER (who is gay) tells me laughingly how a group of Indian men "trained" (gang raped) a young Indian woman dancer during a powwow weekend and then the next day bragged about it, each man taking credit for how well she was dancing.

Members of a multiethnic fraternity look on as one Chicano member drags his Chicana ex-girlfriend by her hair out of her car, throws her on the ground, and begins kicking her and beating her. None of the males moves to help her.

A distinguished senior Chicano scholar explains to me that his conflict with a younger and junior Chicana scholar is not personal, but strictly political. He tells me that he would "shoot" anyone, including his family, who got in his way politically.

I read in a San Francisco newspaper how young, mostly undocumented, women immigrants from Mexico and Central America are being offered jobs as housekeepers and domestic servants only to find once they begin working that their white male employers assume they are entitled to sexually harass and rape them.

· · · · ·

AT A UNIVERSITY AWARDS BANQUET some time ago, I found myself sitting near a white woman who informed me how much she and her husband enjoyed traveling in Mexico. Unfortunately, I was not surprised when she proceeded to tell me (knowingly) how sorry she felt for Mexican women, having to contend as they do with machismo. Instantly I heard my voice telling her, "Be careful." Startled, she answered, "What?!", to which I calmly replied, "You need to be careful about what you're saying. That particular opinion is one that has marked a battleground between white feminists and feminists of color. A male chauvinist pig is a male chauvinist pig is a male chauvinist pig, in whatever culture he is from, and in whatever language you might use to name him." As Chicana scholar Emma Pérez writes:

> Many Anglos, particularly white feminists, insist that the men
> of our culture created machismo and they conveniently forget
> that the men of their race make the rules. This leads to prob-
> lematic Chicana discourse within feminist constructs. When
> white feminists ardently insist upon discussing machismo, they

impose phallocentric discourse. By "centering" and "focusing"
upon the penis, they deflect from their racism. This evasion
is both racist and heterosexist.[2]

I need to say this because I do not want anyone to assume that if I am
critiquing my own communities, I am placing the blame squarely on our
culture. I *am* assuming my right to question and to challenge what has come
onto us *as* culture through the process of colonialism. On my dad's side,
I am Tejana (a Chicana from Texas); my Mexican ancestry is indigenous,
with a few drops of Spanish blood. On my mom's side I am Nimipu (Nez
Perce) from Washington State, of Hinmaton Yalatkit's (Chief Joseph's) band.
I identify as a native woman of this hemisphere. I do not believe indigenous
cultures before contact were perfect; however, they had not become so "civilized" that the cultures were almost completely self-destructive, as today's
"First World"[3] societies seem to be.

When Alice Walker wrote *The Color Purple,* she was criticized severely
by many people for her supposed betrayal of the African American community, because, they said, she made black men look bad. That argument is
an old line and an absurd critique. Alice Walker did not betray the African
American community. Those who condemned her betrayed her by wanting
to silence her, just as they betrayed all those who knew of what she wrote.
Walker's novel in one sense is an incisive internal critique of the dynamics
of sexual and gender relations as she sees them in her community, contextualized in a blatantly racist and classist South and grounded in a resurgent
memory and a proud consciousness of African ancestry.[4] If I criticize the men
or women of the Native American and Chicana/Chicano community who
are perpetuating oppressive regimes of being, and sustaining "oligarchies of
the spirit," that does not mean that I do not love my communities, or that
I do not want to honor them or respect them. It is because I love them and
care for them that I challenge all of us to unlearn the doctrine of subordination to which we have been subjected intentionally as colonized peoples, as
peoples who were supposed to have been conquered and so should know
their place—which is a very tiny space indeed. For many indigenous peoples,
it is not even a closet; in many parts of this hemisphere, it is often a *casa de
cartón* (cardboard house).

I want to scream it out that we should know better, those of us who have endured diaspora and genocide. I want to make us look into the mirror to see how many of us have apparently accepted terrorism against ourselves and each other as a fact of life. My critique is also internal, contextualized in the historical experience of colonialism. By acknowledging the repressive and life-draining nature of the colonial experience, I do not mean to soften my critique in a way that might excuse the men or the women who have exhibited violent behavior. I have no use for a political peace, for a false show of unity while our women and our children are being violated, battered, and abused or while our communities continue to suffer the effects of conquest. I cannot excuse the *patrón/patrona* (big boss) politics that exists in both the Chicana/Chicano and Native American communities. I will not be silent when I feel that I am being intimidated, threatened, or harassed because I want to be an example of a woman who will not be brought down to the ground. I will not be a good girl and take whatever abuse is dished out to me (nor will I keep quiet when I see it happen to others) in order to make us all look good. I have no interest in being a saint, a heroine, or a martyr. Maybe I get that from my Nimipu mother. She will not hang her head; she might look down because she does not want to watch as someone acts shamefully before her very eyes, but when she is ready she will look you straight in the eye. She is articulate both when she is silent and when she chooses to speak.

To the women of the communities I call my own, I want to ask, how can we be sure that we have divested ourselves of the imposed stereotypes of Native American women as submissive, passive squaws and drudges (or more recently, as mystical, unintellectual bringers of good feelings), and of Chicanas and Latinas as fiery, dumb, promiscuous sexpots? We must claim our power and give value to every aspect of ourselves, including our sexuality. Why can't more of us remember that we deserve to know pleasure and love? Why do so many of our women of all ages allow themselves to be co-opted and succumb to mistreatment and degradation for the sake of having a partner, for the sake of having a spouse—of either sex? How did so many of us become convinced that violence is eroticism? When did we come to feel worthless, undesirable, and crazy, as if something were dreadfully wrong with us, as if the fault were ours because we do not enjoy violent sex that is called by the name of *passion,* that is called by the name of *love*? What makes it so hard for us to say, "I was raped"?

speechless women
bartering cuerpos
succumb
> for a touch
> for that closeness
> called love
>> ("Cuernavaca-Pensavientos")[5]

Of both the heterosexual and gay men of my communities I want to ask, why do men argue that women really mean yes when they say no? Why do you try to justify your violence by insisting that the woman asked for it? Don't you see that this argument leaves you no defense when the victim of a rape or a beating is your mother, your sister, your lover, your wife, your daughter, your granddaughter, or your friend? Suddenly you will find your-self hearing someone say, "She really asked for it," or, "She meant yes"—and worse, you will find yourself believing it. I have been told by gay and lesbian sisters and brothers that these patterns of abuse apply to gay and lesbian relationships as well. How did all of us learn these patterns? Through whose eyes have we seen the dynamics of dating and courtship in, say, Hollywood movies? Through whose eyes have we seen intercultural courtship in movies and television?

I remember a *Seinfeld* show with a Latina playing the part of a cleaning lady from Panama. My reading of this so-called comedy revealed the blatant perpetuation and exploitation of racist, sexist, and classist stereotypes for the sake of supposed humor. In one scene, Seinfeld's male sidekick confides that at work he has had sex on his desk with the cleaning lady. When this buddy admits that he's always had a thing for cleaning ladies, Seinfeld responds that he's always had a thing for chambermaids. As the reader of this text, I understand white male entitlement when I see it, an entitlement that reeks of a colonialist as well as misogynist mentality. Later, the sidekick tries to pass off a defective cashmere sweater to the Latina as a thinly veiled bribe to keep her quiet about the incident. She gushes over the sweater and recalls how in her native Panama, from the moment she first saw a cashmere coat, she was enthralled, and in a heavily sexual way, she says how much she has always wanted something cashmere.

The pseudoerotic nature of this scene, in which the Panamanian woman expresses desire toward Westernization, if you will, exemplifies the justification of the right of conquest. In this white, male, capitalist (read colonialist/imperialist) fantasy, the woman of color, as well as the country she represents, *wants* to be subjugated, indeed she exists to be subjugated, and the card that entices them both is consumerism, material culture. In the end, the sidekick gets fired for sexual harassment, but the woman's boss gets to throw the sweater back at the jerk as a final message from the offended woman. The woman apparently protested only *after* she received the defective sweater, suggesting to us that the damaged goods she received upset her more than the rape. Had the goods not been defective, we are led to believe she would have been willing to continue putting out in exchange for the benefits of Western materialism (just as "Third World" countries are forced to put out because the power relations between them and First World countries are not equal). The woman's voice and her presence disappear, while the white male boss gets to deliver the blow to the errant sidekick, presumably as a way for the producers to safeguard themselves against being seen as condoning sexual harassment. In effect, we are given the message, "Now, please understand, we don't want you to get the wrong idea about us. See, we're with it, the guy gets fired. What do you want?!" I was torn while watching this show between wishing the actress had refused the part (knowing that any parts for Latinas are extremely hard to get) and realizing that her choices, and the space that she is allowed to occupy, are indeed limited. In terms of spaces for the Latina/o population in the United States (including Latina/o indigenous communities), the mainstream media tend to so excruciatingly underreport news from Mexico and Central and South America that for all intents and purposes there is an effectively enforced media blackout of information and analysis regarding a great part of the Americas.

What is the difference between the colonization process here in the area that has come to be known as the United States and in the area that has come to be known as Mexico? What does this difference mean in terms of how white America sees mestizos and indigenous peoples, for instance, from Mexico and Central and South America? Why is the guilt of much of white America (United Statesians) apparently so intense with respect to African Americans, but not so with Native Americans, Mexicans, or other Latin

Americans? Since we are the fewer in numbers, Native Americans, for the most part, have been rendered basically invisible. We purportedly have vanished and are no longer an issue. Or, as one closed-minded young white male student told me in class many years ago, "How many of them are there left anyway?" With respect to Mexicans and other Latin Americans, is this attitude prevalent because many EuroAmericans[6] clearly see the establishment of slavery as a product of British and then Southern U.S. (and therefore their own) colonialism, but do not see their complicity in the colonization of Mexico and Central and South America? Do white United Statesians see the Spanish and the Portuguese as responsible for those processes of subjugation via colonialism? Don't they see that, just as Manifest Destiny justified U.S. imperialist expansion from east to west as God's will, the Monroe Doctrine, the CIA, and the School of the Americas (along with innumerable transnational, U.S.-initiated economic, political, cultural/globalizing interventions) have perpetuated continued U.S. imperialist domination from North to South? Is it harder to recognize Native Americans (whether they are from the United States or other parts of Latin America, whether they are full bloods or mixed bloods) because this hemisphere is our land base? We have always been from here—we cannot go back where we came from.

There are stories within intertwining stories, from the local to the global level. In recent memory, the right of conquest—the privilege of the stronger to discover, invade, violate, pillage, dispossess, and appropriate—has been contested, by and on behalf of indigenous peoples, on a scale large enough to attract international attention. The quincentenary anticelebrations of 1992, Rigoberta Menchú's winning of the 1992 Nobel Peace Prize, and the ethnopolitical indigenous movements that are proliferating throughout the Americas, such as the inspired and inspiring Zapatista movement in Chiapas, Mexico, which took the international stage on January 1, 1994, are some of the contemporary narratives.

How do patriarchy, misogyny, and imperialism contribute to the forming of a rape culture such as the one that exists in the United States? Paulo Freire's *Pedagogy of the Oppressed* still serves well to explain how a person who is oppressed internalizes the oppressor; the oppressor becomes a part of the person, so much so that the oppressed person adheres to the oppressor and sees the world only through the oppressor's eyes. Indeed, once the oppressed person becomes liberated, even if only ostensibly, that person might not know how to act except to follow in the footsteps of the one who has oppressed him or her. In this state of false liberation, the dynamics of the power relations are interpreted simplistically; the oppressor has power, the oppressed does not. When the oppressed becomes free, he or she must become like the oppressor in order to manifest the power of freedom. *Freedom* in this context is defined as the freedom to do as one pleases.

When freedom is not seen in terms of personal or social responsibility, or defined with a mutuality that accords everyone the same rights, it becomes the freedom of privilege, the freedom of entitlement, authorized by right of conquest and enforced by notions of superiority. What are the manifestations of this freedom in contemporary society? Male entitlement. White skin entitlement. Class entitlement. Heterosexual entitlement. Youth entitlement. Ability entitlement. Adult entitlement. Employer entitlement. Senior worker entitlement. First World entitlement. Religious entitlement. And so on. In the United States today, Native Americans still do not enjoy freedom of religion. Those settlers who came over here for religious freedom were as rigid in their prescriptions, once they got here, as those who had oppressed them and denied them freedom. Many of the descendants of these immigrants continue to adhere to the oppressor as they persist in the need to impose their religious, cultural, and political will on those who have been forced into an unequal relationship with them. The idea of indigenous peoples as savage and primitive also serves to enforce the internalized racism that mestizos and mestizas feel toward their own Indianness, allowing them to set themselves apart from the *real* Indios and Indias, just as it continues to undermine native struggles for sovereignty. For native peoples, sovereignty is not what comes through right of conquest (that is, power over the ostensibly weaker or more vulnerable) but rather signifies empowerment through (individual and collective) autonomy, through the assumption and practice of the right as nations to (individual and collective) self-determination and self-representation.

In a most profound way, when native peoples are prevented from practicing their ways of life (such as speaking their languages) and from sustaining their ancient belief systems, what is lost or endangered are those very principles that could help give direction to the transformation of a rape

culture. Matriarchal, matrilineal cultures offer insights not only into tolerance (which to me is always begrudging) but also respect for difference, as
in sexual orientation. Even in apparently patriarchal cultures, indigenous
peoples acknowledge and honor their female principles, women's culture,
and women's teachings. As white feminist scholar Sally Roesch Wagner
has testified, Iroquois women before European contact enjoyed rights that
were unheard of for women in Europe at the time, including the right to
divorce, the right to their children, property rights, the right to give birth
or not, the right to birth control, the right to their sexuality, and the right
to their say. In the Iroquois tradition, women elders were (and are) the
clan mothers; they had, and have, the power to name the sachems or the
spokespersons for their people, and the power to depose them should they
not live up to their responsibilities. A man cannot achieve a leadership
position if he ever commits a murder or a theft or violates a woman. What
Roesch Wagner suggests is that European women brought with them from
Europe a "tradition of dissent"; what they found here in the Americas was
the "practice of feminism," which gave them their own vision.[7] It is not
hard to understand why native women had to be cast later in the most demeaning roles as women and as Indians. It was (and is) critical to Western
civilization and its sustainers to make EuroAmerican women feel that they
are in a privileged position (socially, culturally, and intellectually) with respect to all other women, and that they should be thankful that at least
they are not women of color.

How long and why have sexuality and nationality been intertwined? For a
very long time. But it has been my experience that people are uncomfortable
talking about it, at least outside of their own communities. I do know that
many men of color still hate for women of color to date white men. These
men of color see it as an affront to them personally, from a racial/ethnic viewpoint, as well as (often) a class viewpoint. They may not even know the woman
of color in question. I understand, though, because many women of color have
done this, too. In the seventies, in the Chicano/Chicana and Native American
communities, when we used to criticize Chicanos and Native American men
for wanting to date white women (in particular white women groupies who
just kind of hung around movement circles, pretty obviously waiting to be
picked up by some dark-skinned man), some of the men would respond

that they were "fucking the system," so we shouldn't worry. Interestingly enough, the men's argument postulated that white men had been doing it to women of color in this hemisphere ever since initial contact and imposition of colonial rule (witness the Spanish, the French, the British, and then the U.S. colonizing processes, including the institution of slavery), so why was it wrong for men of color to turn the tables on white men and do it to white women? As far as the men were concerned, turnabout was fair play. War was war, and the spoils of war were the spoils of war.

In Mexico, one of the most insulting things a man can say to another man is, *"Yo soy tu padre"* (I am your father). For mestizos, the conquistador and the missionary (who is called *padre)* figure into their collective memory as the fathers, which is a cause for incredible shame in what might be called the Mexican psyche. The well-known Mexican intellectual Octavio Paz (in *Labyrinth of Solitude*) and many others have pointed this out. The men feel shame about their indigenous origins because they still feel helpless against the original devastation of the infamous and horrific Conquest. The men (the native armies) were defeated overwhelmingly, even those who sought alliance with the invaders. They witnessed the end of a way of life, the rape of their women, the murder of their people, the destruction of their temples, and the burning of their sacred histories.

The women, on the other hand, witnessed the same extermination as they were being raped, as they saw their spouses go down in defeat, and as they watched their children slaughtered. They were made to go through an ethnic cleansing themselves by being forced to birth babies who were children of their own violators. As Susan Brownmiller so succinctly explains in a *Newsweek* essay, "Making Female Bodies the Battlefield":

> Rape of a doubly dehumanized object—as woman, as enemy— carries its own terrible logic. In one act of aggression, the collective spirit of women *and* of the nation is broken, leaving a reminder long after the troops depart. And if she survives the assault, what does the victim of wartime rape become to her people? Evidence of the enemy's bestiality. Symbol of her nation's defeat. A pariah. Damaged property. A pawn in the subtle wars of international propaganda.[8]

And an image engraved on the collective memory recalls the shame in a way that turns in on itself and becomes self-hatred.

Gloria Anzaldúa says in her important work *Borderlands/La Frontera: The New Mestiza:*

> The worst kind of betrayal lies in making us believe that the
> Indian woman in us is the betrayer. We, *indias y mestizas,* po-
> lice the Indian in us, brutalize and condemn her. Male culture
> has done a good job on us. *Son los costumbres que traicionan. La
> india en mí es la sombra: La Chingada, Tlazolteotl, Coatlicue.
> Son ellas que oyemos lamentando a sus hijas perdidas.*[9]

Mexican male culture, imposed through the Conquest, has betrayed Indian women and mestizas, reducing the India, Anzaldúa says, to a shadow of herself, a shadow of the historical figure Malintzin, a shadow of the powerful manifestations of the highest female principle of the Aztecas, Tlazolteotl and Coatlicue, whose voices we hear lamenting their lost daughters. Tlazolteotl is the Great Mother Confessor, who hears all, who knows the extremes of love and lust, to whom nothing is a surprise, and who helps us to release our fears, our insecurities, our guilt, and our shame, to renew ourselves; she is the GodMother of Childbirth and Grand Governess of the Cycles of Women. Coatlicue is the Great EarthMother of the Serpent Skirts, the Tremendous Regulator of the Cycles of Life and Death (these are my names for these sacred beings).[10] And Malintzin is the native woman who became the unwilling consort of the invader Cortés, the only native woman who is remembered by name in the annals of the Conquest, because she was brilliant and served as interpreter to Cortés. Malintzin—*La Malinche, La Chingada* ("the fucked-over one")—is charged in the minds of many Mexican men with the infamy of surrendering herself to the enemy (she, too, is seen as having asked for it; she, too, is seen as having wanted it). And just as many women today identify with male interpretations of female behavior, many Mexican women have bought into the story of Malintzin's betrayal.

Que me digan Malinche	Let them call me Malinche
Es un nombre que llevo con honor	It is a name I wear with honor
y doy gracias que mi lengua es mía	I am thankful my tongue is mine
y es libre	and it is free

y grita	and it shouts
y llora	and it cries
y canta	and it sings
y demanda	and it demands
y reclama	and it claims
por la justicia verdadera	a true justice
y por la justiciera paz	and a just peace

(Testimonio de Memoria)[11]

In her early work, *Woman Hating*, Andrea Dworkin says that "all women are not necessarily in a state of primary emergency as women. . . . As a Native American, I would be oppressed [she says] as a squaw, but hunted, slaughtered, as a Native American."[12] While I appreciate much of Dworkin's work, I object to her assumption about "squaws" (as well as her use of the term), and I disagree with her assessment that a Native American woman's first identity is as a Native American rather than as a woman. The two are inseparable. It is *because* of a Native American woman's sex that she is hunted down and slaughtered—in fact, singled out—because she has the potential through childbirth to assure the continuance of the people. Since the invasion that began in 1492, indigenous women have been raped and forced to give birth to their violators' offspring. In the United States many indigenous women have been sterilized and their children have been taken from them to be placed in foster homes. Some have had their own babies ripped out of their wombs (a grotesquely tactical regularity of war), as has happened in the brutal period of the early 1980s in places such as El Salvador and Guatemala, where even babies and children, if they are poor, are considered potentially subversive. At the U.S.–Mexican border between El Paso and Ciudad Juarez, young Mexican *maquiladoras* (female sweatshop workers) for years have been tracked, abducted, raped, mutilated, and murdered, their bodies dumped wherever, and the authorities have done nothing and may, many contend, be implicated in the crimes. Why? Because the women are poor and seemed to have no political leverage. However, there is a mass of international support forming to decry these atrocities and to help their families.

Five hundred years ago, in Mexico, native women were put into boarding schools to be indoctrinated into Catholicism; the Spanish missionaries knew that women were the teachers of culture, and so, for example, the collective memory of the Aztecs of a supreme being who is a Dual Duality, MaleFemale/FemaleMale, had to be erased from their minds and a male trinity put in its place. In the north, the boarding schools serve(d) much the same purpose. The spiritual traditions of native peoples in this hemisphere recognize(d) the centrality of the female principle, working in cooperation with the male principle. This reverence for the female principle, which manifests itself in a tremendous respect for women, is and has been one of the major targets of conversion. The Christian missionization campaign is still intense on Native American reservations. Institutionalized religion and capitalism both depend on patriarchal constructs for nourishment. As I said in "Open Letter to Chicanas: On the Power and Politics of Origin," "Genocide is an instrument of imperialism, and both depend on cultural imperialism and the dialectic of terror to invade, violate, traumatize, exploit, and totally control human beings throughout the world."[13] These are the intentional tools of conquest, meant to make us (as indigenous peoples) sick and keep us powerless and out of balance.

How can I speak of transformation without speaking of recovery? It has to do with how I see my own work as a scholar and professor within the evolving disciplines and the synergistic relationship (as Sau Ling-Wong and Patricia Riley might say) of ethnic studies, women's studies, gay and lesbian studies, cultural studies, and colonial discourse. What are we doing in these fields? Better yet, how do I see myself working within this vitalizing and revisionary context? The creative process for me *is* a critical process and vice versa. When I am writing and working, I am on a journey; I have a sense of where I am going and I am most comfortable when I let my intuition guide and protect me. I really believe that what we are doing in these new (relatively speaking) studies is contributing in a grand way to the healing of ourselves as a society, a global community in which humans one day will learn to coexist with each other and the rest of life, with the rest of our relations in the animal and plant worlds, the water worlds, the sky world. At least that is how I see my own work and the work of those individuals for whom I have a great respect. I am far from denying that these radical (root-digging) fields have their problems and contradictions. But I do feel that what many of us are doing is taking ourselves, and those who choose to go with us, through processes of self-realization in every sense of the word, especially when we recognize each other's work and are inclusive in our analyses of all the factors of difference that must be considered: race, ethnicity, class, gender, sexual orientation, age, religion (or spirituality), and history, to name some of the most foregrounded ones.

For peoples who have been cast as marginalized, this recovery process is a coming into consciousness that is dramatically realigning. Many Native American writers, for example, including myself, have voiced the stunning revelation, "Oh, I'm not crazy—I'm an Indian!" The field of Native American Studies has given indigenous peoples the tools and the techniques to doctor ourselves, to retrieve for ourselves, and to shape, our faces and our hearts, which in the ancient Aztec tradition was the intent of education. Gloria Anzaldúa knows this—that is why she named one of her anthologies *Haciendo Caras: Making Face/Making Soul*. From an indigenous perspective, when you doctor someone, you must know what you are doctoring in its totality. For a holistic healing to occur, you (we) must take into account the whole of the body (politic), as well as the mind, the spirit, the heart, the will. You (we) must take into account the way energy is run, the way it is blocked, and the kind of energy being perpetuated, (self)destructive or creative. Are the forces of oppression or forces of liberation being served?

We must imagine a world without rape. But I cannot imagine a world without rape, a world without misogyny, without imagining a world without racism, classism, sexism, homophobia, ageism, historical amnesia, and other forms and manifestations of violence directed against those communities that are seen to be asking for it. Even the earth is presumably asking for it, as are all the endangered species. So are children, the disabled, anyone who is different. Different from what? What scale are we using to determine who is normal, who is rational? We are pitted against each other. Why? Whose interests are being served by our mistrusting each other, fearing each other, despising each other, and even sometimes mounting holy wars against each other? And if we are to be in solidarity with each other as human beings and global citizens of our planet, how can we ask each other for support if we do not give our own?

How can my Native American brothers expect my support when they condone or participate in the hateful violation and degradation of Native American women (or any women)? How can my younger Chicano brother dare to call himself committed to the people when he brutally beats up a woman, for whatever reason? How can the ones who looked on and did nothing face themselves in the mirror? How can my older Chicano brother (who is a leader) not see that the political is indeed personal, just as the personal is political, and that the causes he espouses and the factors of analyses that he considers crucial are intimately related to the issues of gender and sexuality, and to the right of women to be included in the struggle for their own sake (even, and perhaps especially, as dissenting voices) because women's bodies are the battlefield. Why can't they see how hard it is for me to call them brother? Until they change, I can barely spit the word out. And finally, I cannot imagine a world without rape without imagining a world that is not ruled by the logic of capitalism and imperialism, which continues to justify subordination, dehumanization, and exploitation.[14]

What do I imagine, then? From my own Native American perspective, I see a world where sovereign indigenous peoples continue to plunge into our memories to come back to our *originality*, to live in dignity and carry on our resuscitated and ever-transforming cultures and traditions with liberty. I see a world where difference is respected rather than feared. Benito Juárez, the full-blood Zapotec Indian man who was the president of Mexico in the 1860s, put it succinctly: "*El respeto al derecho ajeno es la paz*" (respect for another's rights *is* peace). I see a world where Chicanos/Chicanas and other mestizos/mestizas take the radical step of getting to know the Indian side of their families in a way that is just and honorable. I see a world where native women find strength and continuance in the remembrance of who we really were and are (with all our attributes and all our faults!), a world where more and more native men find the courage to recognize and honor that they *and* the women of their families and communities are profoundly vital and creative beings. It is hard for me to hold on to this vision, this waking dream, because the invasion, after all, continues. The waves of imposed terror are felt here in the United States, as well as from Mexico to the southernmost tip of South America, particularly in communities where indigenous people predominate: in Guatemala, El Salvador, Ecuador, Peru, Colombia, Bolivia, Brazil, Hawaii, Puerto Rico, and the barrios, reservations, and *rancherías* within the United States. As citizens (especially) of the United States and of a global society, we should be as conscious of and committed to justice in this hemisphere and in this society as we are in other parts of the world. According to the Aztec oral tradition (which, yes, is very much alive), we are moving into the next sun, Coatonatiuh, the Sixth Sun of Consciousness and

Wisdom. We are presently in the tumultuous transition period between the old sun and the new. In this period of transition, women are leading the way. Women are on the front line, opening and clearing the paths. It is our turn.

There is an old Cheyenne saying, "A nation is not conquered until the hearts of its women are on the ground. Then it is done, no matter how strong the weapons, or how brave the warriors." How do all of us as women ensure that our hearts do not hit the ground? What strategies might we as women use to remind ourselves to hold our heads and hearts high? We must stay as informed as we possibly can. I am thankful for the understanding and validation of Spirit as it manifests itself in the Native American community. I am thankful for each text that opens the way for me to go through and beyond, on my own path. I am grateful for each person who wins my heart with the example of her or his integrity. I realize that any collective is only as strong as each of its members, and that the Spider Grandmother of Many Names who sustains us all doesn't need for us to be throwing rocks at the very web or net(work) that we and she are trying to create. Every connection must be delicately woven, intricately and subtly connected, and strong. There must be individual growth for any collective to evolve. I give myself time to take care of myself. I learn how to cleanse myself and heal myself. I take care of my spirit so that my spirit will help me take care of the rest of myself. I love and let myself be loved. I accept the responsibility of freedom that my *conciencia* (conscience and consciousness) offers me. I dance, I take my stands, and I choose with whom I will stand. I raise my voice in song, in prayer, in message, and, yes, in protest and challenge. These are the things that are good for me. And if, by being good to myself in this way, I am called a bad woman, a traitor, a sellout, or a bitch, I don't care. I welcome my own delicious insubordination and savor its inspiration.

I want to thank Patricia Riley, Theresa Harlan, and Juan A. Avila Hernandez for their helpful comments in the preparation of this essay.

NOTES

1. While many native people here in the United States have begun to call themselves Native American, some still refer to themselves as American Indian or Indian. All three of these labels are problematic. Everyone in the "Indian" community knows that the term is a misnomer, but it is a word we have made our own. I will use *Native American* and *Indian* interchangeably in this essay.

2. Emma Pérez, "Sexuality and Discourse: Notes from a Chicana Survivor," *Chicana Lesbians: The Girls Our Mothers Warned Us About,* edited by Carla Trujillo (Berkeley: Third Woman, 1991), 163.

3. I realize that the terms *First World* and *Third World* are shifting and inexact, and so for the purposes of this essay I have put them initially within quotation marks.

4. I am also aware of the debate within the black community surrounding the terms *African American* and *black American. Africa* and *America* were not the original names of the continents we now know by those terms. I am certain that "Africa" had as many names as there were distinct indigenous peoples to name it, which is the case for "America" as well.

5. Inés Hernandez-Avila, "Cuernavaca-Pensavientos," *Frontiers: A Journal of Women's Studies* 2, no. 2 (Summer 1980): 52.

6. Again, the terms *white, EuroAmerican, Anglo-American,* are approximations and contested terms. Whiteness is beginning to be interrogated in the same manner that the terms designating other races and ethnicities have been interrogated.

7. Sally Roesch Wagner, "The Iroquois Roots of Early Feminism" (lecture, University of California–Davis, November 30, 1989).

8. Susan Brownmiller, "Making Female Bodies the Battlefield," *Newsweek,* January 4, 1993, 37.

9. Gloria Anzaldúa, *Borderlands/La Frontera: The New Mestiza* (San Francisco: Aunt Lute, 1999).

10. I do not agree with any analysis that either rejects completely or embraces wholeheartedly the Aztec component of contemporary Chicana/Chicano identity. The fact that Aztec cultural and philosophical foundations have figured into Mexican and Chicano/Chicana (cultural) nationalism cannot be ignored. The complexity of these foundations requires, I believe, careful consideration rather than uncritical acceptance or facile dismissal. In other essays, I have urged the Chicana/Chicano community to come to terms with their actual indigenous ancestry, whatever that might be (and there are many possibilities). There are, however, useful (and by now familiar) concepts which Anzaldúa and others have employed in their discussion of the Indianness of Chicanas and Chicanos. I have participated in the Mexico City–based Conchero dance tradition since 1979 and so have had access to elders and to the dance community that carries on the Aztec dance and oral traditions. I do not pretend to be Aztec, however.

11. Inés Hernández-Avila, "Testimonio de Memoria," *New Chicana/Chicano Writing,* vol. 2, edited by Charles M. Tatum (Tucson: University of Arizona Press, 1992), 17. Translation is the author's.

12. Andrea Dworkin, *Woman Hating* (New York: Dutton, 1974), 23.

13. Inés Hernández-Avila, "Open Letter to Chicanas: On the Power and Politics of Origin," in *Without Discovery: A Native Response to Columbus,* edited by Ray Gonzalez (Seattle: Broken Moon, 1992), 155.

14. My emphasis here has been on the colonial experience as I see it affecting indigenous peoples of the Americas. By my use of the generic terms *capitalism* and *imperialism,* I do not mean to excuse or espouse other forms of state repression, such as what occurred in the former so-called socialist systems of Eastern Europe and the former Soviet Union.

. . . .

Poet **INÉS HERNÁNDEZ-AVILA** (Nez Perce/Tejana) is a professor of Native American Studies and the director of the Chicana/Latina Research Center at the University of California, Davis. She is a member of the Latina Feminist Group, who produced *Telling to Live: Latina Feminist Testimonios* (Duke University Press, 2001), which was selected by the Gustavus Myers Center for the Study of Bigotry and Human Rights as one of the ten best books of 2001. She is the coeditor, with Gail Tremblay, of a special issue on indigenous women of *Frontiers: A Journal of Women's Studies* (vol. 23, no. 2, Fall 2002), and coeditor, with Domino Renee Perez, of a special issue titled "Indigenous Intersections in Literature: American Indians and Chicanos/Chicanas," of *SAIL: Studies in American Indian Literature* (vol. 15, nos. 3 & 4, Fall 2003/Winter 2004). She also edited *Reading Native Women*, forthcoming from Altamira Press.

UP FROM BRUTALITY
FREEING BLACK COMMUNITIES
FROM SEXUAL VIOLENCE
· · · · · · · · · · · · · · · · · · · ·

W. J. MUSA MOORE-FOSTER

An assault on a woman's sexuality is the bedrock symbol of male supremacy. Those men who exult in this violation are not necessarily out of touch with their emotions. To the contrary, they may be tapping into familiar feelings of domination and gratification, however perverse, seeing in the suffering of their victims a mirror image of their own childhood experiences.

CRIMES THAT INVOLVE BLACK PEOPLE attract public commentary like few other domestic issues in contemporary America. News broadcasts and net programming are saturated with images of murder, drug dealing, violent robberies, and the self-destructive behavior of African American celebrities. These images tend to have a singularly male cast, but the reality persists that violence against Black women occurs at higher rates than in any other groups.[1] Our awareness of this situation is too often dependent on sensationalistic reporting that focuses on personalities. The underlying social relationships that have contributed to a predatory climate for women of African descent where they live, work, or worship with men is rarely explored. Cases as distant in historical context as Anita Hill vs. Clarence Thomas, Desiree Washington vs. Mike Tyson, or the Kobe Bryant and Michael Jackson trials reflect racial perspectives on culpability as much as they do the ambiguity of the public's response.

Generally, the issues of sexual and intimate violence are squeezed to the margins of public policy discussions or sabotaged by persons unwilling to face the fact of the perilous existence of Black women here in the United States. A few women and far fewer men insist on raising the question of the unconscionable maltreatment of Black women by Black men as well as the casual way it has come to be accepted as a condition of modern living. Without fail these bold souls are regularly assailed for airing dirty laundry, perpetuating negative stereotypes, or being co-opted by the man-hating feminist agenda, most often by men who assert that they really care about the sisters.

One reason for this contradiction is that African American men encounter multilayered barriers in comprehending rape and other forms of gender-directed violence. Among these are a patriarchal perspective of history; confusion over the meaning and use of power; a corroded sense of personal accountability; and a debilitating, phallocentric socialization. I fervently believe that it is mandatory for Black men to have a firm grasp of both the facts and the nuances of sexual victimization. It is the only way we will be able to do our part in the creation of a culture that does not nurture rape in any of its physical or metaphysical manifestations.

For some of us the path to a deeper understanding of rape may lie not merely in a straightforward presentation of the evidence but also in memories we have nudged aside or in stories told to us by the women we know.

Tucked beneath the floorboards of my own memory is where I rediscovered Johnson Square.

Johnson Square was a park in the Baltimore neighborhood of my child-hood and the most imposing landmark on a well-traveled stretch of Biddle Street that connected downtown to the far East Side. It was bridge and bor-der, lovers' lane and sports field. Within its arboreal walkways, the younger and elder generations of Black folks gathered to rest, talk, and escape the yardless confines of our row houses with their famous marble steps. The park proper was situated several yards back from the sidewalk in all directions. It stood atop a plateau so wonderfully steep that kids on our block found no greater delight from May through November than rolling down its grassy hills, spinning like barrels over a waterfall, screaming and laughing with the hysteria that accompanied our planned abandon. The Square belonged to the African American community during the early 1960s, in the waning years of segregation, when neighborhood boundaries were stained with the blood of racial conflict. I never imagined that there would ever be a reason preventing us from going to the park.

I can remember when that notion left me. My family was at the dinner table when the radio broadcast the news. A young woman had been as-saulted and murdered. Her body was discovered that morning behind one of the rows of hedges lining the paved paths of Johnson Square. I have always felt that from the precise moment of that brutal act, the life of the Square was utterly subverted. It not only became an unsafe place to be after dark but it also came to symbolize the accelerated decay of our community, which was reduced to several square blocks of rubble within a generation.

Since my grammar school years the Square had filled my vision like an em-erald oasis in the center of an urban desert. Now it loomed in my conscious-ness as a mecca of terror. It rose up out of fear, mocking the line between civil authority and the hood. The city government responded by flooding the neighborhood with foot patrols and German shepherds. The dogs were trained to attack and the police were trained to let them chew on whoever crossed their path. After sundown, Johnson Square took on the appearance of a perverse Sherwood Forest, a nocturnal, atavistic reminder of our pri-mordial origins. The beautiful park, which once teemed with the diversity of a coral reef, became a meeting place for antisocial bandits, a magnet for predators, a site of gun battles, and a refuge for those fleeing the police. Anti-crime lights were installed at strategic points bathing the streets in an eerie glow. The final desecration occurred when the grassy hills of the park were sealed over with concrete aggregate. In my mind, the arbor that was Johnson Square sank beneath the burden of human wrongdoing only to reemerge as a gruesome, vegetating pyramid, sheared off at its zenith and walled up at its base. It had been transformed by social neglect and civic efficiency into a stark monument to the illusion of safety.

A single experience in my adolescence is not very significant compared to four centuries of African American history, but it does support my claim that each Black man must locate the issue of rape within the context of his own life as well as within the history of our people. The timeline of African American history does not begin with servitude in colonial North America. However, the role of slavery in shaping race and gender relations is critical to understanding the sexual oppression of women.[2] Comparing the contemporary victimization of Black women by Black men to the exploitation of our slave forebears can be a fruitful exercise in this regard. It begins by debunking the idea of Black matriarchy, the most persistent myth of African American family life. The commonly held belief is that the purported psychological emasculation of Black men was a result of gender role reversal within the slave household and by extension throughout the slave community. The documented truth is that African American women were singled out to be degraded through sexual violence as well as being objectified at the hands of the slaveholders and the agents of their authority.[3]

The historical assumption regarding Black men is that they were less than men because they did not possess the resources and, therefore, did not protect the women of their community by means comparable to those of White men. As attractive as this assumption is, it is equally ironic that certain male slaves readily accepted the slaveholder's gift of access to women as a reward and as recognition of their own elevated status within the community of bonds-men.[4] Angela Davis has argued that sexual oppression is clearly conjoined to the objectification of women that is facilitated by capitalism. Others, including Claude Meillassoux, have asserted that this oppression is also derived from historical inequities rooted in and expressed through various ideologies of male supremacy not entirely dependent upon a specific economic regime.[5]

Women of African ancestry struggled against male domination in precapitalist societies before the ascendancy of the Transatlantic slave trade from 1450 to 1850. That struggle has continued in the centuries after slavery's demise, manifesting itself in Black women's fight for: equity in the workplace; equal distribution of educational resources; economic support for themselves and their dependent children; and full inclusion in the democratic political process.[6] The gender oppression of Black women by Black men is an aspect of this conflict and has been used as a tool to suppress resistance to patriarchy.

It is unsound to argue that the reluctance of many brothers to address rape through civic discourse is based on their culpability. However, the cultural representation of Black men as sexual predators has sadly produced among many African American men a defensive, knee-jerk reaction to discussing rape as if the mere mention of it were self-incriminating. Racial profiling practices of law enforcement and selective media reporting have created an indelible image of Black male criminality in the public's vision.[7] None of this came about overnight. As W. Rayford Logan has pointed out, the Black rapist stereotype was created by the slave owning class as a rationale for the impersonal brutality of the slave regime as well as a means of manipulating the fears of the White population. The reinvention of this loathsome icon was widely circulated in the print media of the post-emancipation era of 1870 to 1910, giving assistance to organized terror campaigns directed at African American communities. At this nadir of American history, lynching became as much a part of civic culture as the vaunted town meeting.[8]

D. W. Griffith's *Birth of a Nation* created the first cinematic image of White America's perpetual nightmare: Black people taking over and exacting payback. The use of corked-up White actors to depict African American political corruption and slovenliness are racist lies about Reconstruction in the South on a gross scale. But the true heart of the film is its staged scene of a depraved Black man advancing upon the flower of White womanhood. The maiden leaps to her death, escaping the greater evil, but is avenged by an army of sheet-wearing knights in an orgy of racial violence on the colored citizenry at large. Thus began an inglorious history of Hollywood hegemony in which life has imitated art in the service of white supremacy.[9]

The idea of the Black man as rapist has not only served as a barrier to dialogue on race and gender relations outside the Black community, but also on the quality of relations within it. The reception of Alice Walker's *The Color Purple* provides an example of how paranoid many brothers become when the subject of Black male sexual violence is raised. Without question, Black women have not been spared by Black rapists, but a great many African American men are innocent of any such act. Some have not only intervened in the commission of these crimes but also feel, as I do, that we must bear witness to the strength and courage of Black women.[10]

My own close encounter with an active rapist occurred in 1969 during my senior year in college. I was living in Washington D.C. and enjoyed a fictive kinship with a group of three women to whom I was intimately but not sexually attached. Our bond was based on deep affection and I was more honored to be thought of as their friend and confidant than as a lover. What we shared was rare and genuine despite the fact that many men wrongly assumed I was a wannabe polygamist.

Our apartment buildings were located a block apart but could not have been more drastically different. My residence was in a towering, greasy brown tenement whose bloom had wilted long before I showed up. My homegirls lived in the chichi Windemere, a haven for middle-class professionals and civil servants, with a sprinkling of professional artists and well-heeled students, all dutifully screened by the redoubtable resident manager, Mrs. Tilly.

One cool fall evening several squads of police arrived in the lobby of the Windemere and alerted as many occupants as they could summon to the presence of a young Black rapist, armed with a steak knife, still at large in the neighborhood. Immediately, the identity of everyone entering the building had to be verified by a resident in good standing. I was admitted as a family member by my friends and hunkered down in their shared apartment for a grim vigil. They also asked me to accompany other residents in patrolling the building and using the basement laundry room. I camped out on the floor of their apartment but seldom slept, my imagination holding my common sense at bay as I ran to the door at every noise in the hallway. I felt the ladies had asked me due to my large size although my fear nearly matched their own. I was less aggressive than other men they knew, and I had the reputation of being a bookworm, not a thug. In addition, I was reluctant to arm myself with anything for fear of being taken as a threat and injured by vigilantes or the police. The police were a greater threat given their propensity for first shooting Black men and not quite getting around to asking the questions later.

I went along with the plan to patrol the building every evening out of loyalty and love more than confidence that I could intimidate a slashing psychopath with my sheer bulk. I felt I had to do something more than merely comfort my friends with affirming words. As it turned out, I was able to intervene in a rape and contribute to the arrest of its diminutive, pathetic perp. Yet, my emotions were closer to the grief of his victims than to anything even vaguely heroic. The passage of time hasn't changed the way I feel about any aspect of it.

One afternoon when I knew they had gone shopping, I let myself into my friends' apartment with my key, hoping to surprise them with a special dinner. I worked quickly trying to time the preparation to the moment they usually ate their evening meal. I was nearly ready to get all the pots cooking when I heard terrifying screams coming from down the long hallway. They were punctuated by a series of flat thuds. I raced out of the apartment to find the prone figure of Mrs. Noble, whom I recognized as a Caribbean neighbor, straddled by a slight Black man.[11] She was winning the struggle by holding on to his collar with one hand while beating him soundly about the head with the large, square purse she wielded in the other. Seeing me, she released her wiry attacker. I saw an expression of grateful relief rather than fear on his face as he fled through the fire exit and bounded away. The clattering of his knife followed his shadow in the stairwell. The volume of the brave woman's crying diminished, but her sobs continued through the arrival of the squads and the interminable reporting process. She couldn't stop even when her adult children came home and formed a protective circle around her. I explained what I saw and praised their mother's mettle, but my attempts to comfort them were coolly received. I went back to my dinner preparations, but any heart I had left was not invested in festivity.

The Steak Knife Rapist, as the media dubbed him, was caught later that night skulking about the area, but a sound sleep eluded me. I was transformed by witnessing the kind of courage it takes for women to go about their daily lives. Mrs. Noble had fought valiantly and would live to tell others if she chose. I was paradoxically filled with awe and self-loathing. Although I had raced to her assistance, I believed that my actions were inadequate.

She was safe for that moment but her condition and that of other sisters was fundamentally unchanged. I felt as if I had helped to free a single hostage in a world of women held captive by men who looked like me.

As I reflected on the meaning of those few minutes, the romanticized notions about the moral superiority of Black people I had been carrying around were crumbling. Looking into the fearful face of a stranger, I had witnessed the bitter truth of Angela Davis's assertion that "when working-class men of color accept the invitation to rape extended by the ideology of male supremacy, they are accepting a bribe, an illusory compensation for their powerlessness."[12] My classmates and I had been enthralled by the call to arms in Eldrige Cleaver's *Soul on Ice*. Now I felt only compunction for failing to criticize his crowing manifesto about the efficacy of "practicing" sexual assaults on Black women before graduating to politically preferable White victims. I wondered if all the talk about guns was a smoke screen to hide his basic degeneracy.[13] I felt deeply betrayed but too ashamed to speak to a woman. I reached out to my best male friend and former roommate, remorsefully emptying out my heart, cursing my gullibility.

Few Black men will have the opportunity or the motivation to confront their assumptions about aggression before those assumptions emerge as codified behavior. For those of us who came to adulthood in the Sixties, aggression was politicized as a rite of passage. Our rhetoric of righteous, purifying violence, based on literal readings of Georges Sorel, Frantz Fanon, Mao Zedong, combined with equal parts of Huey Newton, Bobby Seale, and Malcom X, have a hollow ring these days. For all the hell we raised, the miles we marched, and the genuine martyrs we mourned, neither I nor many of my male peers turned our intellectual and moral scrutiny toward gender relations without the insistence of the women around us. Despite the examples of courage presented by visionary Black women in this era, ranging along the political spectrum from Fannie Lou Hamer and Ella Baker to Angela Davis and Assata Shakur, we failed to learn as much from their lives and work as we needed to know. Those lessons can't be wasted on another generation of Black males imprisoned by the pathology of patriarchy.

Male supremacy cannot be established without violence, and an assault on a woman's sexuality is its bedrock symbol. Those men who exult in this violation are not necessarily out of touch with their emotions. To the contrary, they may be tapping into familiar feelings of domination and gratification, seeing in the suffering of their victims a mirror image of their own experiences.[14] It is not uncommon in a patriarchal society supportive of rape that men can boast about their misdeeds (sometimes in the company of women) with little fear of retaliation or ostracism. Despite the heroism and sacrifices of women in the rape law reform movement, their reliance on adjudicated remedies has created another arena of power in which the oppressive values of men from the dominant culture prevail against women of color.[15]

If Black Americans are to survive as a people with a moral foundation, men's attitudes about women must be fundamentally overhauled. An urgent effort to reeducate youth about sexual violence must become a priority of the highest order. We who would be teachers and mentors must also engage young people in the rethinking of gender begun by African American womanist pioneers of the nineteenth century and continued by the inheritors of that legacy.[16] They have taught us that sexism is not only invested with explanatory power, but it is also a destructive pattern of society that defines, promotes, and rewards certain behavior. Therefore, the process of critical pedagogy is also accompanied by the need for Black men to continually reevaluate our own practice of masculinity.

There is no better starting point than in our familial relationships. We must resist the temptation to use our strength to coerce women and children or express our anger in threatening ways. For most men, it will mean going beyond the management of our animosity to the core of the hurt that produces rage. Furthermore, each of us must speak out and take action against the depiction of violence against women as well as all forms of shaming acts directed toward them. For those of us who are fathers of daughters, this action would appear to be moot, but it is not. The contradictions are evident in the ubiquitous portrayal of teenage girls as sexual commodities in every avenue of media from advertising to music videos.

Media companies are making fortunes by feeding the insatiable appetite of young Black and white males for hard-core lyrics and outlaw imagery.[17] After two decades in the margins of America's urban culture, hip-hop and rap are as much a part of the global mainstream as big band jazz was to my parents' generation. At their best, these are complex art forms, but the incorrigible misogyny of gangsta rap together with the ascendancy of *pimpnography* have incited censure from the lectern to the pulpit. The expansion of the racial parameters of this debate calls for the accountability of the corporate owners as well as their White stockholders.[18] First Amendment concerns notwithstanding, one can defend the principle of free expression while resolutely condemning the degradation of women. In some quarters, and they are not exclusively neoconservative, African Americans are speculating about warning signs that the spiritual center of our race has shifted. In the years since 1968, we have adjusted our hearing of Brother and Sister as forms of popular address to the arrival of *niggah, bitch, pimp,* and *ho* as salutations in our contemporary lexicon. There may be nearly as many who find these terms endearing and vital to *keeping it real* as there are those who sense that the value of respectful discourse in civil society has toppled. That verbal abuse attends and engenders violence is lost on an audience loyal to the histrionics of the *Jerry Springer Show* and its imitators.

Until we can commit to the overthrow of the regime of commonplace violence under which Black women and children live within our own communities, every discussion of ending violence anywhere in the world deserves a qualified and critical objection. Given the fact that nearly half of Black women report coercive contact of a sexual nature by age eighteen, the lives of African American woman are more at risk from rape than they are from the terrorist threat that grips the globe.[19]

There is cause for alarm, but there is a greater need for thoughtful action. I contend that rape is an act that begins in the soul. Black men, therefore, must set about cleansing our souls of the toxic levels of rage and alienation. Healing ourselves is an important preparation in the struggle for justice.[20]

Moral leadership is required as much as sound strategy, and men must demand a higher standard of character. The issue of morality is being lost through default to conservatives and is too often articulated as part of a reactionary political agenda. Progressive African American men must continue to work for the ascendancy of a new social order that is governed by a morality free from patriarchal ideology and firmly established in human equality.[21]

At the earliest feasible age, the social education of boys ought to embrace ideas of masculinities that are not defined by mechanistic theories of male sexuality. Character education as promulgated through athletics and pseudo-military manhood training involves barely disguised strategies for male domination. A radical pedagogy about the meanings and applications of such values as courage, self-discipline, empathy, loyalty, generosity, responsibility, integrity, fairness, respect, compassion, love, and balance is overdue.[22]

As part of that effort, African American men could benefit from a re-examination of the lexicon of intimacy. This need not be confined to the community of intellectuals attracted to semiotics. More fundamentally, I am pointing out questions about what brothers say or do not say in describing the sexual act, engaging in love play and in our casual comments to each other. The expressions I've heard are more related to acquisition than to shar-ing. Many of them are baleful synonyms for aggression, disrespect, and de-valuing that objectify the partners as well as the deed.[23] This is the language of demeaning work, violence, narcissism and alienation. It suggests that men be simultaneously immersed in intimacy but absent from it in ways that corrode affective meaning. In the interest of remedial action, a good beginning would include conversations about the uses of language to articulate our intimate needs. Young people have to be appropriately involved in these discussions and adults have to listen carefully. Some of this work has already begun on college campuses, but it needs to occur in every sector of Black communi-ties at every level. There are veritable orchards of refreshing discourse on the Internet if one has the patience and focus to continue searching for them. African American faith communities are reexamining these issues in light of the invaluable heritage of womanist activism in the civil rights epoch.[24]

On a practical level there are several ways Black men can support the struggle to end violence against women.

- Find ways of getting involved with organizations that address the issue of violence against Black women by asking what you can do to be of support, fund-raising, volunteering your labor, and informing other men of this vital work.
- Take the struggle to places where groups of men are less likely to be aware, such as fraternities, social clubs, sports teams, and the military.
- Bring a progressive perspective to organizations that mentor young males. Get this issue on the educational agenda in an open and engag-ing manner.

To Black men everywhere I direct this appeal. Now is the time to begin the long climb up and out of the hell to which we have been condemned by brutality. We must continue to change the behaviors in our lives that are unhealthy and unwise. Never be afraid to ask for and practice forgiveness. Let each day be a small victory in our struggle against complacency and may the beauty around us never be ruined.

NOTES

1. Bureau of Justice Statistics National Crime Victimization Survey: Criminal Victimization Survey (NCJ 205455), U.S. Washington: Department of Justice, September 2004.

2. Angela Davis, "Reflections on the Black Woman's Role in the Community of Slaves," *Massachusetts Review* 13 (Winter/Spring 1972): 84.

3. Darlene Clark Hine, "Rape and the Inner Lives of Southern Black Women: Thoughts on the Culture of Dissemblance," in *Southern Women; Histories and Identities,* ed. Virginia Bernhard, Betty Brandon, Elizabeth Fox-Genovese, and Theda Perdue. Columbia: University of Missouri Press, 1992, 177.

4. Angela Davis. *Women, Race, and Class.* New York: Random House, 1983.

5. Claude Meillassoux, *Maidens, Meal and Money.* Cambridge: Cambridge University Press, 1981. See also Jeanne Koopman Henn, "The Material Basis of Sexism: A Mode of Production Analysis," in Jane L. Parpart and Sharon B. Stichter, eds., *Patriarchy and Class: African Women in the Home and the Workforce.* Boulder, Colo.: Westview Press, 1988.

6. A cogent account of this struggle is presented in Paula Giddings, *When and Where I Enter: The Impact of Black Women on Race and Sex in America.* New York: Bantam, 1988. See also Manning Marable, *How Capitalism Underdeveloped Black America: Problems in Race, Political Economy, and Society.* Boston: South End Press Classics, 1983.

7. Dennis Rome, *Black Demons: Media's Depiction of the African American Male Criminal Stereotype.* Westport, Conn.: Greenwood, 2004.

8. Rayford W. Logan, *The Betrayal of the Negro: From Rutherford B. Hayes to Woodrow Wilson.* New York: DeCapo Press, 1997.

9. See Thomas Cripps, *Slow Fade to Black: The Negro in American Film, 1900–1942.* New York: Oxford University Press, 1993. The Center for History and New Media at George Mason University offers a powerful and compact online discussion, "'Art [and History] by Lightning Flash': *The Birth of a Nation* and Black Protest," at http://chnm.gmu.edu/features/episodes/birthofanation.html.

10. The better of progressive discussions is found in Joseph L. White and James H. Cones III, *Black Man Emerging.* London: Routledge, 1999.

11. "Noble" is a fictional name given to protect the victim's privacy, but the details of the account are true.

12. Davis, *Women, Race, and Class,* 194.

13. "The Color of Violence Against Women," a speech by Angela Davis, is a compelling critique of this extreme chauvinism. For the complete text, see the Color Lines journal online at http://www.arc.org/C_Lines/CLArchive/sotry3_3_02.html. See also Giddings, op. cit., 310, 322.

14. Andrew Taslitz, "Race and Two Concepts of the Emotions in Date Rape," *Wisconsin Women's*

Law Journal 15, no. 3 (Spring 2000). Cleaver's rhetoric is given a rigorous exposure to masculinity theory by Robert F. Reid-Pharr in "Tearing the Goat's Flesh: Homosexuality, Abjection and the Production of a Late Twentieth-Century Black Masculinity," *Studies in the Novel* 28, no. 3 (Fall 1996).

15. Davis, "The Color of Violence Against Women."

16. Patrica Hill Collins's *Black Feminist Thought* (London: Routledge, 2000) is a sound starting point for establishing a framework. See also Delia Jarrett-Macauley, *Reconstructing Womanhood, Reconstructing Feminism: Writings on Black Women.* London: Routledge, 1996.

17. Rome, op. cit.

18. Leola Johnson's "Rap, Misogyny and Racism," *Radical America* 26, no. 3 (1994), is among the most valuable, lucid, and critical discussions to emerge from the response to the apogee of gangsta rap. See also bell hooks's online essays at http://www.eserver.org/race/misogyny.html.

19. Michael L. Rothschild, "Terrorism and You—The Real Odds." Washington Post (November 25, 2001): D7.

20. Malidoma Patrice Somé, *The Healing Wisdom of Africa.* New York: Jeremy Tarcher/Putnam, 1999.

21. Davis, "The Color of Violence Against Women."

22. Cooper Thompson, "A New Vision of Masculinity," in Paula S. Rothenberg, ed., *Race, Class and Gender in the United States.* New York: St. Martin's Press, 1995. See also Colin Greer and Herbert Kohl, *A Call to Character.* New York: HarperCollins, 1995.

23. While neither exhaustive nor particularly current, this sample of sexual vocabulary is recognizable and includes the graphic as well as the idiomatic. Consider *waxing, boning, blending, nailing, banging, knocking boots, doing a rip job, laying pipe, rocking, taxing, digging out, flexing, delivering the wood, freaking, buck wilding, macking, getting some cut up,* and *bagging up* as illustrations of my point.

24. Rosetta E. Ross, *Witnessing and Testifying: Black Women, Religion and Civil Rights.* Minneapolis: Fortress Press, 2003.

. . . .

W. J. MUSA MOORE-FOSTER is an independent scholar-activist living in St. Paul, Minnesota, who dedicates this essay to Black womanist visionary Alice Lynch, and to the memory of her late husband, Bob, both tireless advocates for victims of domestic violence.

Musa has over thirty years experience teaching at the post-secondary level and has conducted primary research on the family life of African American males. He offers public speaking, training, research, writing, and analytical services through his consulting group, TMFG.

comin to terms

. . . .

NTOZAKE SHANGE

mandy fixed his dinner/ nothin special/ & left the door of her room open so he cd see her givin herself pleasure/ from then on/ ezra always asked if he cd come visit her/ waz she in need of some company/ did she want a lil lovin/ or wd she like to come visit him in his room/ there are no more assumptions in the house.

THEY HADNT SLEPT TOGETHER for months/ the nite she pulled the two thinnest blankets from on top of him & gathered one pillow under her arm to march to the extra room/ now 'her' room/ had been jammed with minor but telling incidents/ at dinner she had asked him to make sure the asparagus didnt burn so he kept adding water & they, of course/ water-logged/ a friend of hers stopped over & he got jealous of her having so many friends/ so he sulked cuz no one came to visit him/ then she gotta call that she made the second round of interviews for the venceremos brigade/ he said he didnt see why that waz so important/ & with that she went to bed/ moments later this very masculine leg threw itself over her thighs/ she moved over/ then a long muscled arm wrapped round her chest/ she sat up/ he waz smiling/ the smile that said 'i wanna do it now.'

mandy's shoulders dropped/ her mouth wanted to pout or frown/ her fist waz lodged between her legs as a barrier or an alternative/ a cooing brown hand settled on her backside/ 'listen, mandy, i just wanna little'/ mandy looked down on the other side of the bed/ maybe the floor cd talk to him/ the hand roamed her back & bosom/ she started to make faces & blink a lot/ ezra waznt talkin anymore/ a wet mouth waz sittin on mandy's neck/ & teeth beginnin to nibble the curly hairs near her ears/ she started to shake her head/ & covered her mouth with her hand sayin/ 'i waz dreamin bout cuba & you wanna fuck'/ 'no, mandy, i dont wanna fuck/ i wanna make love to . . . love to you'/ & the hand became quite aggressive with mandy's titties/ 'i'm dreamin abt goin to cuba/ which isnt important/ i'm hungry cuz you ruined dinner/ i'm lonely cuz you embarrassed my friend: & you wanna fuck'/ 'i dont wanna fuck/ i told you that i wanna make love'/ 'well you got it/ you hear/ you got it to yr self/ cuz i'm goin to dream abt goin to cuba'/ & with that she climbed offa the hand pummelin her ass/ & pulled the two thinnest blankets & one pillow to the extra room.

· · · · ·

the extra room waz really mandy's anyway/ that's where she read & crocheted & thot/ she cd watch the neighbors' children & hear miz nancy singin gospel/ & hear miz nancy give her sometimey lover who owned the steepin tavern/ a piece of her mind/ so the extra room/ felt full/ not as she had feared/ empty & knowin absence. in a corner under the window/ mandy settled every nite after the cuba dreams/ & watched the streetlights play thru the lace curtains to the wall/ she slept soundly the first few nites/ ezra didnt mention that she didnt sleep with him/ & they ate the breakfast she fixed & he went off to the studio/ while she went off to school he came home to find his dinner on the table & mandy in her room/ doing something that pleased her. mandy was very polite & gracious/ asked how his day waz/ did anything exciting happen/ but she never asked him to do anything for her/ like lift things or watch the stove/ or listen to her dreams/ she also never went in the room where they usedta sleep together/ tho she cleaned everywhere else as thoroughly as one of her mother's great-aunts cleaned the old house on rose tree lane in charleston/ but she never did any of this while ezra waz in the house/ if ezra waz home/ you cd be sure mandy waz out/ or in her room.

. . . . .

one nite just fore it's time to get up & the sky is lightening up for sunrise/ mandy felt a chill & these wet things on her neck/ she started slappin the air/ & without openin her eyes/ cuz she cd/ feel now what waz goin on/ ezra pushed his hard dick up on her thigh/ his breath covered her face/ he waz movin her covers off/ mandy kept slappin him & he kept bumpin up & down on her legs & her ass/ 'what are you doin ezra'/ he just kept movin. mandy screamed/ 'ezra what in hell are you doin.' & pushed him off her. he fell on the floor/ cuz mandy's little bed waz right on the floor/ & she slept usually near the edge of her mattress/ ezra stood & his dick waz aimed at mandy's face/ at her right eye/ she looked away/ & ezra/ jumped up & down/ in the air this time/ 'what are you talkin abt what am i doin/ i'm doin what we always do/ i'm gettin ready to fuck/ awright so you were mad/ but this cant go on forever/ i'm goin crazy/ i cant live in a house with you & not fu . . . / not make love. i mean.' mandy still lookin at the pulsing penis/ jumpin around as ezra jumped around/ mandy sighed 'ezra let's not let this get ugly/ please, just go to sleep/ in yr bed & we'll talk abt this tomorrow.' 'what do you mean tomorrow i'm goin crazy' . . . mandy looked into ezra's scrotum/ & spoke softly 'you'll haveta be crazy then' & turned over to go back to sleep. ezra waz still for a moment/ then he pulled the covers off mandy & jerked her around some/ talkin bout 'we live together & we're gonna fuck now'/ mandy treated him as cruelly as she wd any stranger/

kicked & bit & slugged & finally ran to the kitchen/ leavin ezra holdin her torn nitegown in his hands.

.   .   .   .   .

'how cd you want me/ if i dont want you/ i dont want you niggah/ i dont want you' & she worked herself into a sobbin frigidaire-beatin frenzy . . . ezra looked thru the doorway mumblin. 'i didnt wanna upset you, mandy. but you gotta understand. i'm a man & i just cant stay here like this with you . . . not bein able to touch you or feel you'/ mandy screamed back 'or fuck me/ go on, say it niggah/ fuck.' ezra threw her gown on the floor & stamped off to his bed. we dont know what he did in there.

.   .   .   .   .

mandy put her gown in the sink & scrubbed & scrubbed til she cd get his hands off her. she changed the sheets & took a long bath & a douche. she went back to bed & didnt go to school all day she lay in her bed. thinkin of what ezra had done. i cd tell him to leave/ she thot/ but that's half the rent/ i cd leave/ but i like it here/ i cd getta dog to guard me at nite/ but ezra wd make friends with it/ i cd let him fuck me & not move/ that wd make him mad & i like to fuck ezra/ he's good/ but that's not the point/ that's not the point/ & she came up with the idea that if they were really friends like they always said/ they shd be able to enjoy each other without fucking without having to sleep in the same room/ mandy had grown to cherish waking up a solitary figure in her world/ she liked the quiet of her own noises in the night & the sound of her own voice soothin herself/ she liked to wake up in the middle of the nite & turn the lights on & read or write letters/ she even liked the grain advisory show on tv at 5:30 in the mornin/ she hadda lotta secret nurturin she had created for herself/ that ezra & his heavy gait/ ezra & his snorin/ ezra & his goin-crazy hard-on wd/ do violence to . . . so she suggested to ezra that they continue to live together as friends/ & see other people if they wanted to have a more sexual relationship than the one she waz offering . . . ezra laughed. he thot she waz a little off/ till she shouted 'you cant imagine me without a wet pussy/ you cant imagine me without yr god-damned dick stickin up in yr pants/ well yr gonna learn/ i dont start comin to life cuz you feel like fuckin/ yr gonna learn i'm alive/ ya hear' . . .

ezra waz usually a gentle sorta man/ but he slapped mandy this time &
walked off . . . he came home two days later covered with hickeys & quite
satisfied with himself. mandy fixed his dinner/ nothin special/ & left the
door of her room open so he cd see her givin herself pleasure/ from then on/
ezra always asked if he cd come visit her/ waz she in need of some company/
did she want a lil lovin/ or wd she like to come visit him in his room/ there
are no more assumptions in the house.

. . . .

NTOZAKE SHANGE is a playwright, poet, and novelist. Her play *for colored girls who have considered suicide/when the rainbow is enuf* won an Obie Award for Best Drama and the Outer Critics
Circle Award. She is the author of numerous other plays as well as collections of poetry and novels
and has been awarded an NEA Fellowship, a Guggenheim Fellowship, and the Medal of Excellence
from Columbia University. Shange is a professor of drama and English at the University of Florida
at Gainesville.

TRANSFORMING THE RAPE CULTURE THAT LIVES IN MY SKULL

· ·

MARTHA ROTH

In the new world, women look eagerly for equal sexual
partners and participate fully in the rituals of courtship,
love, and commitment. Men lose their erections—and
their desire—if their partners aren't eager to make love.

N PREPARATION FOR EDITING THIS BOOK, I had to read a lot of rape stories. They shocked and angered but also aroused me; my body responded to the ugly facts of rape as to the most delicate insinuations of erotica, and I fought my own response and felt ashamed.

I don't like pornography and don't use it, but sometimes my fantasies speak its language. I've tried to reprogram my erotic imagination, but the old hard-core fantasies swim back, and I think of my sexuality as having been colonized by male-identified images. What Susan Griffin calls "the pornographic mind" has invaded and now occupies my most intimate space.[1] I don't know what lived in that space before, or whether the colonial invasion completely destroyed it.

. . . . .

I REMEMBER HAVING AN ORGASM at the age of two. Wearing a starched white frock, I lay across a wicker stool on my tummy, rocking back and forth. A wonderful feeling flushed me with warmth, tightening my bottom, and I kept rocking. It happened again and again, until I grew tired. My grandfather, who was supposed to be looking after me, snored in a chair.

I summoned that wonderful feeling often, sometimes picturing the little boys I lusted after, like Dukey Larson, who had dark hair and pale, pale skin. I wanted to bite into his white chest, to mark him with my teeth. As I grew older and learned to read, cruel stories aroused me: Andersen's Snow Queen, who pierced children's hearts with a sharp blade of ice, or Persephone, stolen away by the god of the underworld while she was gathering wildflowers.

During my nursery school and kindergarten years, war organized our games and fantasies. Sometimes I imagined being interrogated by Gestapo agents in shiny leather coats. Sometimes I was a captured spy sent to a camp where prisoners were tormented for the amusement of their captors. Until the 1970s, when I read *Against Our Will*[2] and heard Robin Morgan say, "Pornography is the theory, rape is the practice," it never occurred to me to wonder why I connected cruelty with sensual pleasure.

The connection seemed natural. The association of orgasmic release with fantasies of pain—either given or received—is so common that many writers believe it is hardwired into our brains, part of the same reflex. Discussions of rape often begin at this point, with the assumption that it's natural for men to experience arousal at a partner's real or fantasized pain and for women to want a little cruelty.

Yet virtually everything else about human sexuality is a learned response, including how to procreate.[3] If human arousal is labile in the sense that different stimuli can produce it (body parts, music, plastic raincoats), then why has the human species persisted over many millennia in keying to images of violence and pain? Why haven't we chosen to become aroused by tenderness?

Perhaps the answer lies in psychosexual development, in the individual histories of many millions of young humans, children who experience early genital pleasure in a context of guilt, shame, coercion, or outright abuse. Perhaps this happens to so many of us that it's almost a cultural constant.

Young children touch their genitals casually at first, then for comfort. When caregivers discourage this touching for pleasure or reassurance, children learn shame. Shame is so strongly bonded to feelings of genital pleasure that many people can't feel one without the other; hidden things become sexualized and all pleasure is guilty pleasure. Male children, as Ruth Herschberger wrote in her wonderful, ovular book, *Adam's Rib*,[4] get a double message about touching their penises. They may have their hands slapped for masturbating but they are praised for learning to aim a urine stream. Female children never get approval for touching their vulvas.

. . . . .

MY GRANDFATHER SNORED IN A CHAIR. I don't remember his speaking or touching me. I remember being careful to do my rocking quietly, while he slept. What had gone on while he was awake?

Years later, I told two friends about this memory. "My God," said one, her cheeks flaring crimson. "He diddled you." "Yup," said the second. "That's what it sounds like."

I don't remember this grandpa—bald, hawk nosed, smelling of bourbon—as a child molester, but if another woman had told me this story that's what I would think: Someone, probably grandpa, had stimulated her.

. . . . .

MANY PEOPLE ARE AROUSED BY TENDERNESS, but also by cruelty. What if our patterns of sexual arousal are set by early experiences? If our first sensual responses are drawn from us by adults we depend on, might we hold within us forever the association of pleasure with abuse? Even when the sex play is gentle and loving, even when it's intended to give pleasure to the child, the imbalance of power guarantees that the pleasure will be experienced as exploitation.

I'm guessing at things I can never know for sure. Grandpa might get a little drunk on a Sunday afternoon and amuse himself by fondling a child who couldn't tell on him. Little girls' vulvas are exquisite miniatures, with their perfect frills of flesh. But this might not be enough to cement the connection of sexual pleasure with cruelty and violence. Girls who experience sexual abuse from their mothers often report a connection to toilet training or intestinal cleansing.[5] I had a nursemaid with strict ideas about early toilet training who may have stimulated me in the course of vigorous cleaning. Add these together and you might get a girl-child who has cruel fantasies and who masturbates to ease her anxiety.

Toilet training frequently involves violence, from suppressed rage to punishments for soiling to threats of castration. I once worked with a woman who complained about her two-year-old twin boys. "They wet all the time. I tell 'em I'm going to cut it off if they can't keep it dry." "You shouldn't do that," we told her. "It's really bad for you to scare them like that." She would shrug and tell us next day about "whacking" one of her sons on his penis when he wet.

Most parents and caregivers are more sensible, I hope, but many still discourage little children from handling their genitals for pleasure or reassurance. Children are generally praised for learning to control other primitive pleasures, such as urinating, defecating, and eating, but decades must pass before genital pleasure can come out into the light, and by then it's too late. The only sexual pleasure for which most people ever reward their female children comes after a marriage ceremony, in connection with producing new children. Many young girls deafen themselves to the insistent calls of their flesh or else they sneak pleasure, barricading it with guilt and (fantasized) punishment.

· · · · ·

LITTLE BOYS have a narrower range of approved behavior than little girls. Girls can wear skirts or trousers, play with trucks or dolls, paint their faces, hammer nails, dance, run races, wear nail polish, beat drums, build blocks, cook, play ball, solve puzzles, and cuddle stuffed toys. Active play is seen as healthy and natural for little girls, while many parents worry about a boy who draws and paints, dresses up, and prefers playing house to playing ball.

Boys get the message that men like hard, heavy things. Men compete and play to win. Men armor their bodies against touch. Little boys are pressured to give up softness and imagination and to learn acceptable male behavior [see Messner, p. 23], which produces anxiety. When they become anxious, they secrete high levels of male hormones, androgens.

Teenage boys have high levels of circulating androgens, including testosterone, and testosterone correlates with aggressive behavior throughout the primate world. But when you watch very young boys, from three to six, you can see that their aggression is mainly a response to frustration or anxiety. Perhaps we train little boys to make testosterone by introducing severe anxiety into their lives—channeling them into competitive play, for example. High levels of androgen secretion in teenage boys might result from anxiety induced by pressure to perform their approved masculine roles.

Androgen secretion makes them prone to violent behavior. If they react violently, we label them as having poor impulse control. If they succeed in channeling their energies into sport, warfare, or intellectual work, we praise them. But we should not be surprised if they use violence in expressing their sexuality; sexual arousal evokes unacceptable longings for tenderness and intimacy and threatens them with vulnerability and loss of control.

We have understood for a long time that young males learn rapist behavior before they ever want sexual relations. When they do, their model for lovemaking features domination and submission. Culture encourages both men and women to associate sexuality with violence because of the haphazard, abusive ways we learn about our sexual capacities. Many children first experience genital pleasure in a context of subordination to a dominant figure, and pleasure reinforces the lesson so that every repetition forges a stronger link. Others repress the knowledge of genital pleasure, and when culture expects them to deploy it they find they cannot scale the barricade of guilt and shame.

Much of the literature of sexual violence has shown that men who rape—men who are caught—are men who have experienced physical and emotional abuse as children, including sexual abuse. Women who sexually molest children are almost invariably survivors of sexual abuse. But I'm not concerned here with criminal acts as the law defines them. I want to understand something about the rape culture that crept into my own skull and peopled my earliest erotic fantasies with torturers and murderers, because I had a safe, relatively normal and happy childhood.

· · · · ·

BEHAVIORAL BIOLOGY, as I mentioned earlier, suggests that all human sexual behavior is learned. Sexual energies may be inborn, but the range and forms of their expression are determined by multiple factors, mostly unknown. Culture does its best to turn us all into heterosexuals, but the margin of what is considered failure—gays, lesbians, bisexuals, celibates, and others who don't buy into gender-based sexuality at all—should clue us in to possibilities of resistance.

Following the clue, we might recognize that human sexual response, although sturdy, is unpredictable and that it is affected—like the human feeding response—by other pressures and currents. Anorexia and bulimia, for example, are intractable medical problems. For people with these disorders, factors beyond biology have twisted a life-sustaining response into a life-threatening one. That is something like what happens to women's sexuality when our arousal becomes keyed to cruel and violent images.

This twisting of women's sexual response is socially encouraged—as anorexia is encouraged by the presentation of skeletally thin women as beautiful—so we will be at least partially willing victims of men whose arousal has also become keyed to cruelty and violence. Sometimes this is called sexual conquest. I remember being shocked at a lover who asked plaintively, "Couldn't you just fight me a little?"

In her essay "Seduced by Violence No More" [see p. 293], bell hooks speaks of the need for a woman to "reconstruct [her]self as a heterosexual desiring subject" so that she can "be fully aroused by male behavior that is not phallocentric." For me, this means male behavior that does not center on fantasies of the phallus as a weapon and lovemaking as abuse. Too many women share the fantasies of abuse because, I'm guessing, too many of us have been abused. Defenders of consensual sadomasochism claim that bondage, spanking, and various metal and rubber toys allow men and women to explore their fantasies of domination and subordination safely—that is, with partners who won't seriously harm them. But where is the sexual variation that lets us explore fantasies of equality? How can we liberate our senses so that we are not aroused by pain?

If in raising boys we emphasize achievement more than exploration and competition more than cooperation, we will train them in competitive, goal-directed behavior, including sexual behavior, and we will give them bodies—or body images—that are dominating rather than receptive or playful. After our early freedom to be androgynous and to explore multiple roles, girls enter a cultural corral at puberty where we are stigmatized if our bodies aren't smooth and pliant and if we don't please males.

· · · · ·

HUMAN BRAINS DEVELOPED CIVILIZATION, with all its discontents. We don't know exactly what reciprocal effects these discontents have on our brains, although we now blame stress for conditions that range from baldness to stomach ulcers and heart disease. With the many miraculous interventions that doctors and scientists can perform, we're still ignorant about a wide range of interactions between physiology and behavior. We know that in young mammals the learning process physically changes the brain. Each increment of learning makes others possible. We don't know what other reciprocal influences shape our bodies and selves, and we don't know much about how developmental learning affects the endocrine system.

Human sexual arousal, in the words of philosopher Ann Snitow, is a seriously undertheorized topic.[6] Many investigators, from Kinsey and his colleagues to Robert Stoller, accept the kinship of sex and violence as a fact of human psychology.[7] For reasons I've tried to set out here, I believe this kinship is learned and not innate, and that my shamed arousal at reading about violence is an artifact of my upbringing. I believe that humans can learn to raise our children without molesting them, and that if we succeed in doing this we have the ability to end sexual violence. If young children could learn the uses of pleasure on their own terms, they might grow into adolescents and then adults whose desires are turned on by warmth and affection and turned off by violence and cruelty.

It looks like an impossible task. The history of art, literature, and a multibillion-dollar global enterprise of pornography and prostitution block our path [see Dines, p. 105]. Yet we can imagine it.

If our social priorities truly were human—if we placed the true welfare of our species above everything—we would support cooperation, not competition. We would figure out how to share the world's resources in an equitable, sustainable manner. And we would teach our children that the making of children is potentially the most important act of their lives. People would train themselves for parenthood, physically and emotionally, and they would contribute as best they could to cooperative nurseries, childcare centers, and schools. If people chose not to have children, we would support that choice as well.

But in my new world, everyone shares in the care of young children. Everyone learns that human babies come into the world as primitive as monkeys but with enormously greater capacities. Everyone knows children's genital play is healthy and good, and we give young children as much freedom as we safely can, confident that they will learn civilized behavior—including toilet training—because we would model it for them. We don't increase anxiety by encouraging children to compete. Everyone understands that children want to learn—that it's hard to keep children from learning—and that learning is a great pleasure.

We teach children reverence for their bodies and sympathy for other species, both plants and animals. As they come to express physical love for one another (and who knows when that might be?), children are taught to make love tenderly and mutually. Little girls and boys learn human anatomy and physiology all their lives; they understand that their minds and bodies are expressions of their single human selves and not separate terrains ruled by warring spirits.

Since I don't believe in the devil, or in evil except as a terrible defect in human learning, this is a world without demons. A few centuries of changed culture could root the demons out of human psyches, turning off the appetite for cruelty. In the new world, women look eagerly for equal sexual partners and participate fully in the rituals of courtship, love, and commitment. Men lose their erections—and their desire—if their partners aren't eager to make love. Because the need to dominate is no longer part of their male identity, men are able to accept tenderness as fully as women and to experience pleasure without fantasies of pain.

Sexual violence gradually becomes a memory, a story that crones and codgers tell late at night around the fire (we still make fires). Younger people can't believe the stories.

"Why would anyone want to do that?" they ask. "Where's the fun in that?"

Soon the young people don't even want to hear the old stories. Rape has become alien to human experience.

I'm sure we can do this. We can do anything.

NOTES

1. Susan Griffin, *Pornography and Silence: Culture's Revenge against Nature* (New York: Harper Colophon, 1982).

2. Susan Brownmiller, *Against Our Will: Men, Women and Rape* (New York: Simon and Schuster, 1975).

3. Harry F. Harlow, *Learning to Love* (New York: Jason Aronson, 1974); William H. Masters with Virginia Johnson, *Human Sexual Response* (Boston: Little, Brown, 1966); Shere Hite, *The Hite Report: A Nationwide Study on Female Sexuality* (New York: Macmillan, 1976).

4. Ruth Herschberger, *Adam's Rib* (New York: Harper and Row, 1970).

5. Flora Rheta Schreiber, *Sybil* (New York: Warner, 1973); Toni A. H. McNaron and Yarrow Morgan, *Voices in the Night: Women Write about Incest* (San Francisco: Cleis, 1982).

6. Ann Snitow, personal communication, 1992. Also see Martha Roth, *Arousal: Bodies and Pleasures* (Minneapolis: Milkweed Editions, 1998).

7. Alfred C. Kinsey et al., *Sexual Behavior in the Human Male* (Philadelphia: W. B. Saunders, 1948); Robert J. Stoller, *Sexual Excitement: Dynamics of Erotic Life* (Washington, DC: American Psychiatric Press, 1986).

MARTHA ROTH is a writer and editor. Raised by working parents, she absorbed a practical feminism, and coming of age in the fifties she was part of the upheavals that prepared the sixties: obscenity trials, Beat literature, and struggles for civil rights, including reproductive rights. As Martha Vanceburg, she has cowritten two books of daily meditations, *The Promise of a New Day* with Karen Casey (Hazelden, 1983) and *Family Feelings* with her late mother, Sylvia Silverman (Bantam, 1989), and written a daybook for expectant mothers, *A New Life* (Bantam, 1990). Her coedited collection *Mother Journeys: Feminists Write about Mothering* (1994) and her novel *Goodness* (1996) are both published by Spinsters Ink, and her nonfiction book *Arousal: Bodies and Pleasures* (Milkweed Editions, 1998) extends the insights of this essay. Her stories, essays, and criticism have been widely published and she has traveled and lectured in Europe and North America.

WHOSE BODY IS IT, ANYWAY?
TRANSFORMING OURSELVES
TO CHANGE A RAPE CULTURE

• •

PAMELA R. FLETCHER

Being in this intimate relationship with my young body, I grew to understand and confirm three things: My body belongs exclusively to me, my soul is not at rest when my body is detached, and we (body and soul) must take good care of each other.

RAPE

I NEVER HEARD THE WORD while growing up. Or if I did, I blocked it out because its meaning was too horrific for my young mind: a stranger, a weapon, a dark place, blood, pain, even death. But I do remember other people's responses to it, especially those of women. I specifically remember hearing about Rachel when I was in high school. The story was that she let a group of boys pull a train on her in the football field one night. I remember the snickers and the looks of disgust from both the girls and the boys around campus. It was common knowledge that nobody with eyes would want to fuck Rachel; she had a face marred by acne and glasses. But she had *some* body.

While I am writing this essay, I remember the stark sadness and confusion I felt then. This same sadness returns to me now, but I am no longer confused. At the time, I wondered how she could do so many guys and actually like it (!). Then I thought maybe she didn't like it after all, and maybe, just maybe, they made her do it. But the word *rape* never entered my mind. After all, she knew them, didn't she? There was no weapon, no blood. She survived, didn't she? And just what was she doing there all by herself, anyway? Now I know what *pulling a train* is. Now I know they committed a violent crime against her body and her soul. Now I know why she walked around campus with that wounded face, a face that none of us girls wanted to look into because we knew intuitively that we would see a reflection of our own wounded selves. So the other girls did not look into her eyes. They avoided her and talked about her like she was a bitch in heat. Why else would such a thing have happened to her?

I tried to look into Rachel's eyes because I wanted to know something—what, I didn't know. But she looked down or looked away or laughed like a lunatic, you know, in an eerie, loud, nervous manner that irritated and frightened me because it didn't ring true. Now I wonder if she thought such laughter would mask her pain. It didn't.

PAINFUL SILENCE AND DEEP-SEATED RAGE

I remember another story I heard, this one when I was in college. Larry told me that his close friend, Brenda, let Danny stay over one night in her summer apartment after they had smoked some dope, and he raped her. Larry actually said that word.

"Don't tell anyone," Brenda had begged Larry. "I never should have let him spend the night. I thought he was my friend."

Larry told me not to ever repeat it to anyone else. And, trying to be a loyal girlfriend to him and a loyal friend to Brenda, I didn't say anything. When we saw Danny later at another friend's place, we neither confronted nor ignored him. We acted as though everything was normal. I felt agitated and angry. I wondered why Larry didn't say anything to Danny, you know, man to man, something like, "That shit was not cool, man. Why you go and do somethin' like that to the sista?"

It never occurred to me to say anything to Brenda, because I wasn't supposed to know, or I was supposed to act as though I didn't know—stupid stuff like that. I sat there, disconnected from her, watching her interact with people, Danny among them, acting as though everything was normal.

DENIAL

While writing this essay, I had difficulty thinking about my own related experiences. I hadn't experienced rape. Or had I? For months, in the hard drive of my subconscious mind, I searched for files that would yield any incident, of sexual violence or sexual terrorism. When certain memories surfaced, I questioned whether those experiences were real rapes.

I have some very early recollections that challenge me: Max, my first boyfriend, my childhood sweetheart, tried to pressure me into having sex with him when we were in junior high. Two of my friends, who were the girlfriends of his two closest friends, also tried to pressure me because they were already "doing it" for their "men."

"Don't be a baby," they teased. "Everybody's doing it."

But I wouldn't cave in, and I broke up with Max because he wasn't a decent boy.

A year later, when we reached high school, I went crawling back to Max because I thought I loved him and couldn't stand his ignoring me. He stopped ignoring me long enough to pin me up against the locker to kiss me roughly and to suck on my neck long and hard, until he produced sore, purple bruises, what we called hickies. I had to hide those hideous marks from my parents by wearing turtleneck sweaters. Those hickies marked me as his property and gave his friends the impression that he had done me, even though we hadn't gotten that far yet. We still had to work out the logistics.

I hated when he gave me hickies, and I didn't like his exploring my private places as he emotionally and verbally abused me, telling me I wasn't pretty like Susan: "Why can't you look like her?" I remember saying something like, "Why don't you go be with her if that's what you want?" He answered me with a piercing don't-you-ever-talk-to-me-like-that-again look, and I never asked again. He continued, however, to ask me the same question.

In my heart, I realized that the way he treated me was wrong because I felt violated; I felt separated from my body, as if it did not belong to me. But at sixteen I didn't know how or what to feel, except that I felt confused and desperately wanted to make sense out of what it meant to be a girl trapped inside a woman's body. Yes, I felt trapped, because I understood that we girls had so much to lose now that we could get pregnant. Life sagged with seriousness. Now everybody kept an eye on us: our parents, the churches, the schools, and the boys. Confusion prevailed. Although we were encouraged to have a slight interest in boys (lest we turn out "funny") so that ultimately we could be trained to become good wives, we were instructed directly and indirectly to keep a safe distance from them.

We liked boys and we thought we wanted love, but what we really wanted was to have some fun, some clean, innocent fun until we got married and gave our virtuous selves to our husbands just as our mothers had done. We female children had inherited this lovely vision from our mothers and from fairy tales. Yet now we know that those visions were not so much what our mothers had experienced but what they wished they had experienced—and what they wanted for us.

In the early seventies, we thought going with a boy would be romance-filled fun that involved holding hands, stealing kisses, exchanging class rings, and wearing big letter sweaters. Maybe it was for some of us. But I know that many of us suffered at the hands of love.

I soon learned in high school that it was normal to be mistreated by our boyfriends. Why else would none of us admit to each other the abuse we tolerated? These boys supposedly loved us, so we believed they were entitled to treat us in any way they chose. We believed that somehow we belonged to them, body and soul. Isn't that what so many of the songs on the radio said? And we just knew somehow that if we did give in to them we deserved whatever happened, and if we didn't give in we still deserved whatever happened. Such abuse was rampant because we became and remained isolated from each other by hoisting our romances above our friendships.

We didn't define what they did to us as rape, molestation, or sexual abuse. We called it love. We called it love if it happened with our boyfriends, and we called other girls whores and sluts if it happened with someone else's boyfriend or boyfriends, as in the case of Rachel and the train.

We called it love because we had tasted that sweet taste of pain. Weren't they one and the same?

REALIZATION

One sharp slap from Max one day delivered the good sense I had somehow lost when I got to high school. After that, I refused to be his woman, his property. When I left home for college, I left with the keen awareness that I had better take good care of myself. In my involvement with Max, I had allowed a split to occur between my body and my soul, and I had to work on becoming whole again.

I knew that I was growing stronger (although in silent isolation from other young women and through intense struggle) when I was able to successfully resist being seduced (read: molested) by several college classmates and when I successfully fought off the violent advances and the verbal abuse (what I now recognize as an attempted rape) of someone with whom I had once been sexually intimate.

But how does a woman become strong and whole in a society in which women are not permitted (as if we need permission!) to possess ourselves, to own our very bodies? We females often think we are not entitled to ourselves, and many times we give ourselves away for less than a song. The sad truth of the matter is that this is how we have managed to survive in our male-dominated culture. Yet in the wise words of the late Audre Lorde, "The Master's tools will never dismantle the Master's house."[1] In other words, as long as we remain disconnected from ourselves and each other and dependent on abusive males, we will remain weak, powerless, and fragmented.

A NOT-SO-AMBIGUOUS BEGINNING

I am cute and three years old. My mother has braided my hair and decorated it with red barrettes. I sit on the edge of the couch dressed in a red checkered jumper that ties in the back. I swing my legs back and forth, back and forth. I lift and spread them in the air. I am making a discovery. I am in awe of my long legs and the way they move. My body tingles with pleasure. This is how a sparrow must feel while soaring freely in the sky.

"Don't ever do that again," my father says. "Always sit with your legs closed."

Suddenly my joy is squelched by the strange tone of his voice, and I crash.

This is a recurring and haunting memory.

Had I been my brother, I would not have been scolded for exploring my physical prowess. I would not have been commanded to stop my arousing behavior. My father was only doing his duty: to control me and to train me to be his proper, feminine little girl. But what is so wrong about a girl knowing and appreciating her body? Whose body is it, anyway? My tender, indomitable spirit would not surrender.

In discovering quite early that there is a strong and essential connection between body and soul, I could not stop loving and moving my legs. I simply moved my body out of my father's sight whenever my soul wanted to enter into the purely physical world that liberated me from my constrictive surroundings. In that other world, I ran races, climbed trees, roller-skated, hopscotched, and tussled with the neighborhood boys while wearing dresses with shorts underneath. And don't ask me why, but I never, ever thought that the boys were stronger and faster and braver than I. Many of them could not compete against me, especially in races. Fortunately, I had yet to encounter the myth that boys are inherently better athletes than girls. It never occurred to me to be worried about being a girl who was acting like a boy. I only did what was natural. I was in love with my body, so if it enjoyed doing wild things, I had to make it happy.

Being in this intimate relationship with my young body, I grew to understand and confirm three things: My body belongs exclusively to me; my soul is not at rest when my body is detached; and we (body and soul) must take good care of each other. As a black woman-child living in a predominantly white, suburban world, I had to find ways to invent an affirmative reality, and I used my body to help me cement the cracks in my soul that were split open by the daily onslaught of racism that prevailed outside my home and sexism that permeated the air inside it. In elementary and junior high school, I became an athlete, specifically a runner. I sprinted the fifty-yard dash to keep from dying inside and leaped the broad jump to forget momentarily what I had to remember: I am constantly at odds with the white and male worlds.

Ironically, my father was pleased when I took first place in the fifty- and hundred-yard dashes and by my accomplishments in the 440 relay race, in which I always held the anchor position.

"You could win gold metals just like Wilma Rudolph," he said one day. He rarely missed my practices and never missed my races.

"We're going to go to the Olympics," he announced on another day with a smile. He was serious and began to coach me on the side.

My mother, on the other hand, would have nothing to do with my athletic ability or activity. It embarrassed her. "I don't know why you want to do something that's going to make your legs look muscular and ugly like a boy's."

I longed for her approval. Since she had enrolled me in ballet and tap dance lessons when I was a child, I assumed that she would be supportive of my joining a dance troupe in high school. One day I came home with my costume, ready to demonstrate the dance I had choreographed for an upcoming performance. I put on the gold leotard and the leopard-print wraparound skirt and began to move like a sultry big cat.

"Look how skinny you are!" she laughed.

I evaporated into a wisp. Up to that moment, I had been proud of my body because it was strong and supple, so I was confused by her outburst. I didn't know what she meant by it. I just knew that somehow I felt ashamed. Later, during my dance performance, my mother's laughter and words resounded in my head and I wished she and my shame would disappear from the auditorium.

I now know that I suffered the same bewilderment I had encountered as that three-year-old child with her legs sticking straight up in the air. Just like that child, I was doing something natural and liberating, and she, just like my father, focused solely on my body and ignored my soul. Now I know that they were distracted and troubled by the freedom I granted my body and the joy I took in connecting to myself. After all, as a female I was supposed to be bashful, restrained, and disconnected. They felt uncomfortable with my love for my body and for physical pleasure; they associated the body with shame.

Both times, my soul parried their attempts to subjugate my body. I would not allow them to constrict me because I could not allow them to split me in half, taking away my selfhood, diluting my power.

I stopped running in high school and began to dance seriously, later joining a dance troupe in college. After college, I continued to dance, run, and do whatever I felt I needed to do to free myself from the trap that society had set for women like me.

THE MORE THINGS CHANGE, OR, A MODERN-DAY TALE

What I did not realize then as a woman-child and what I know now is that the body-soul connection I derived from my physical activity built a strong sense of self that I now exude. This self-contained, self-assured image is what others see, especially those men who are prone to victimize and rape women. This is not an image I can see readily, but my friends and colleagues see it. "You walk in like you own the place," they tell me, or, "You move around with that don't-you-dare-mess-with-me look." I've been told, "You don't look like a victim." This attitude that I convey is rarely staged intentionally. It must be my soul guarding my body from anyone's attempt to split me in half.

I am not naive or arrogant enough to think that, because of this image, I could never or will never be raped or molested. I know all too well that I cannot control everything—or anything, for that matter. If the conditions are just right and if someone considers you vulnerable, he will strike.

Let me illustrate. Several years ago, I was granted a six-week residency at a

Wyoming arts program to work on a novel-in-progress. During that retreat, I wrote and took the necessary time to recuperate from the recent and tragic death of my partner, with whom I had had a six-year relationship. For five of those years, we had shared a home. Wyoming's desolate but serene landscape calmed me, and each day I grew spiritually stronger as I healed.

The evening before my departure, the evening before I was to venture out into the real world again, my new friends, the other residents, and I sat together at the dining table for a special going-away meal for the three of us who were leaving the next day. During this wonderfully prepared meal, we were bothered by the thick smell of smoke, but we didn't see any sign of fire. As the sun set, we discovered a gray, ominous cloud of smoke and the glorious blaze of a brush fire. I had never witnessed such a sight in person before. I was both mesmerized and frightened by it. It seemed so close. In fact, it was rapidly approaching our ranch. Volunteer fire fighters soon lined up their pickup trucks along the dirt road next to the ranch. We were instructed to go to a neighboring town twenty miles away.

The group, seven women and one man, decided to seek refuge in a bar until further notice. I had an immediate gut reaction about going to a bar because (1) I don't drink, and (2) I don't trust drunken white males. I was the only black person and I felt unsafe. I determined, however, that I would be safer with the group than I would be staying somewhere else alone. Against my better judgment, I went to this white bar in a white town, and I held my breath.

I had been in that bar for about fifteen minutes when I encountered a large, drunken white cowboy who asked me to dance. I politely declined. Before I knew what was happening, he had put down his beer bottle and begun to fidget with the fanny bag that hung around my waist. I had everything of value that I could fit inside that small pouch: cash, traveler's checks, credit cards, airline tickets, and my medicine bag.

Alarmed, I asked him, "What are you doing?"

"I'm turning this around so we can dance."

"ButIsaidIdon'twannadance."

He ignored me and seized me by my waist, lifting me up from my stool. Then he began to carry me to the dance floor with his arms wrapped tightly around my torso. The right side of my face was smashed against his chest.

My feet dangled. Realizing that my legs could not touch the ground, I suddenly became unglued. I felt shocked and afraid. How could I get away if my legs were immobilized? I repeated as calmly and slowly as possible, "I told you I don't want to dance with you. Leave me alone." I also felt stupid and wondered how I could have allowed myself to be in this white bar surrounded by virtual strangers.

When I told him that there was no music playing, he said, "Who needs music?" He continued to carry me toward the bandstand. Nearby was a pool table. Scenes from *The Accused,* a movie based on a true story in which a woman gets raped on a pool table in a bar in Bedford, Massachusetts, played in my head in accelerated motion. I thought, "I'm going to be raped. This is how it happens. I'm going to be raped." I could not believe this situation was happening to me; I felt utterly alone and terrified. Would anyone help me? Would anyone care?

Although I did and said all I could to resist, this man, who held me so tightly that I felt as if he were crushing my bones, would not hear my voice. Finally John, the lone man in my group, jumped up.

"Leave her alone; she's with me," he said, rushing up to him.

John had to say it several times before the drunk acknowledged his male voice and released me.

"All right, buddy, she's all yours," the cowboy said, jovially slapping John on his back. Actually, I was bracing myself for a barroom brawl.

What struck me at that point was that it was not safe for me to be there without a man to claim me; it took a man to save me from another man. Crudely speaking, it was a transfer of property. My body did not belong to me. It belonged to one of them. And I could not help but wonder how much of a part my color played in this madness. After all, when the cowboy entered the bar with two of his friends, they immediately walked up to me, and one of them announced, "We saw you walking around today." One frightening thing about this announcement was that when they had seen me that afternoon I was twenty miles away from that bar, strolling along the dirt road near the ranch, and I had not noticed them driving by.

The other frightening thing is that they paid little or no attention to the white women in my group. As John so astutely observed, "You were prey, Pamela. I've never seen anything like it. It was like watching *Thelma and*

Louise." John also said that he could vividly imagine what fantasies went through their minds earlier when they spied me, an attractive African American woman wandering around the countryside (an odd sight, indeed), and when they saw me later as they walked through the door of that bar. I, too, can imagine what they saw: a hot, wild, and wanton dark body for their pleasure.

Lord knows I was fortunate to escape that place physically unscathed. But days later, I could still feel his rough grasp around my waist. My body felt so sore, I wondered if I was only imagining that the hurt was there when it was really in my soul; I felt like such a fool. That night, as it had at no other time, my soul suffered a deep wound that has yet to heal. I'm certain that other such incidents pierced my soul, but this time was different somehow. This time it happened in the presence of other people, other women, who felt no affinity with me, who could not or would not identify with my precarious condition. As a result, it is difficult not to blame myself or not to feel ashamed, especially when the women in my group told me, "It wasn't personal, Pamela. They were only trying to be friendly, but they didn't know how to be," and "It's because you look so exotic, you know." And the final blow, delivered with sharp laughter: "Do you always get hit on like this?" Their insensitivity stabbed me. I wonder just how impassive they would have been had the situation been reversed, had one of them found herself molested by a large, drunken black man in a black bar in a black town. I found it ironic and painful that John realized and admitted what they dared not acknowledge. He was the courageous and compassionate one. Those women epitomized the mark of female oppression: They entered into a conspiracy with the white patriarchy in exchange for a false sense of security. Did they forsake their femaleness to reap the benefits of their white skin privilege? If I had been white, would they have had a similar response? Whatever influenced them consciously or unconsciously, they merely reaffirmed and reinforced a sexist and racist white-male-dominated culture. I fear that I could have been raped and those women would have done nothing to help me.

Despite how alone and frightened I felt, I knew that I was not going to yield to that man under any circumstances. My body is mine, and I had a right to refuse to give it to him, even in a dance. Somehow I remained calm, even when another man, who walked into the bar immediately after the incident, approached only me for a dance. I wanted to scream, "Do I have a goddamn Open Season sign on my forehead, you crazy jerks?" I felt so angry and violated, I wanted to blast all of them, both the men and women. My friends tell me that I managed to get out of there safely because I didn't break under the man's pressure. I am uncertain and full of rage.

A CALL FOR SELF-EXAMINATION AND TRUE CHANGE

I am certain, however, that while today we females cannot control the violent world in which we live, we must take control over our bodies. To me, it is at least one step we can take to challenge this rape culture in which we live. In protecting ourselves, we must realize that we cannot afford to continue dissociating our bodies from our souls. We must claim ourselves as whole human beings. When we are empowered physically, we are both spiritually and physically strong. Being in tune with our bodies helps us to trust our instincts. We are aware of what is going on around us and are able to guard ourselves against danger. When and if we are in danger, we are able to rely on our physical selves as much as possible to free ourselves from harm because we know and trust our strength. When our souls are connected to our bodies, we do not allow our bodies to be taken for granted or to be taken away from us—at least not without a struggle.

I envision a world in which all girls are free to experience and move our bodies as we grow into ourselves. I hope for a time when females are no longer afraid to move and push our bodies because we no longer believe the myths that competition is not feminine, that we are less competitive and aggressive than males, that we cannot attain peak athletic performance during menstruation, that weight lifting builds large muscles in females, that contact sports harm our reproductive organs and breasts, and that we cannot regain physical prowess after childbirth. I envision a world in which it is just as common and natural for females as it is for males to be physically active in any sport or activity we choose.

This new world is only possible when we women take control over our body imagery. As long as we believe that we are weak and dependent on men for our self-definition, body definition, and safety, we will continue to be paralyzed by our fears and controlled by our sense of inferiority.

Moreover, we must realize how much we, ourselves, perpetuate our rape culture when we abandon, reject, and alienate ourselves and each other. Yes, it is difficult to admit, but we must be honest with ourselves and each other if we are ever to heal. Just imagine how different our lives would be today if we were not injured by internalized misogyny and sexism. Imagine how different our lives would be if we would only open our mouths wide and collectively and loudly confront males and *really* hold them accountable for the violent crimes they perpetrate against females. Imagine how our lives would be if all mothers told their daughters the truth about romantic love and taught them to love themselves as females, to value and claim their bodies, and to protect themselves against violent and disrespectful males.

What if we girls in junior high and high school had believed that we deserved respect rather than verbal and sexual abuse from our male classmates? What if we girls in my high school had confronted the gang of boys who raped Rachel that night on the football field twenty years ago instead of perpetuating that cycle of abuse and shame she suffered? What if Larry and I had confronted Danny for raping Brenda that summer night in her apartment? What if Brenda had felt safe enough to tell Larry, me, and the police? What if the women in Wyoming had confronted that man while he terrorized me instead of defending him? What if they had protected, comforted, and supported me? What if we females believed ourselves and each other to be as important and deserving of our selfhood as we believe males to be? Just imagine.

Envision a time when we women are connected to ourselves and each other, when we no longer feel the need and desire to conspire with men against each other in order to survive in a misogynist, violent culture. We must alter our destructive thinking about being female so that we can begin to accept, love, and cherish our femaleness. It is the essence of our lives.

Readjusting our lens so we can begin to see ourselves and each other as full, capable, and mighty human beings will take as much work as reconstructing our violent society. Neither job is easy, but the conditions and the tasks go hand in hand. Two ways to begin our own transformation are to become physically active in whatever manner we choose so we can take pleasure in fully connecting to ourselves and in growing physically stronger, and to respect, protect, support, and comfort each other. Once we stop denying that our very lives are endangered, we will soon discover that these steps are not only necessary but viable ways to empower ourselves and claim our right to exist as whole human beings in a peaceful, humane world.

NOTES

1. Audre Lorde, *Sister Outsider* (New York: Crossing Press, 1984), 112.

PAMELA R. FLETCHER is a writer and an editor who teaches creative writing, expository writing, and literature courses. She is on the faculty of the department of English at the College of St. Catherine in St. Paul, Minnesota.

MORE GENDER, LESS PRESUMPTION
CYBERSEX AS AN ALTERNATIVE TO
A CULTURE OF VIOLENT SEXUALITY
· ·

KIM SURKAN

In online genderqueer communities, there appears to be a degree of sensitivity to issues of sexual violence even as there is a strong commitment to maintaining freedom of speech and the right of all members to freely articulate their erotic fantasies in sex-positive spaces.

THE STUDENTS in my Introduction to Women's Studies class at a suburban community college are discussing an essay on adolescent female sexuality. Oddly enough, they don't have much to say. On sexual harassment and discrimination in the workplace, they have plenty of thoughts; about fraternities and date rape, the conversation can barely be contained. But when the topic is sexuality, the room goes strangely quiet. They struggle for words; the culture, it seems, is saturated with images of sex, but it is surprisingly difficult to find a language for desire.

The experience gets me thinking. Most of the students in my classes were born in the 1980s; theirs is a generation steeped in the relentless stream of images and information emanating from an increasingly media- and consumer-focused society. The messages are conflicting and contradictory, from Nancy Reagan's Just Say No mideighties antidrug campaign mantra to Dan Wieden's Just Do It ad slogan for Nike in 1988. There is no need to explain the virgin/whore conundrum to this audience; they've been peppered with it all their lives.

Underlying the just say no/just do it dichotomy is heterosexual presumption based on a static notion of gender identity. In this configuration, women are nothing more than the passive objects of male desire—their choices are to resist or respond to a man's advances. What's missing in this picture is what women themselves want, a sense of female desire independent of the well-worn scripts of conventional heterosexuality, which at best limit possibilities and at worst lead to sexual violence [see Kimmel, p. 139, and Miedzian, p. 159]. In order to truly transform the culture in which we live, we need radically new ways to think about and articulate desire. This isn't about male sensitivity or female assertiveness; it's a question of tearing apart the most basic assumptions about sex, gender, and sexuality.

We live in a society in which men are male, women are female, and everyone is presumed to be heterosexual based on those definitions—yet none of these "truths" are self-evident, and they drastically limit the possibilities for conceptualizing and articulating desire. Times, however, are changing. Over the last decade, a profound challenge to these assumptions has been made, giving a new face to sexual politics at the end of the twentieth century. Whereas lesbian feminists in the 1970s politicized sex by drawing a connection between compulsory heterosexuality and the patriarchal oppression of women, today people calling themselves genderqueer are taking things a step further by refusing to be categorized as men and women in the first place. In so doing, they slam the door on the conventional understanding of sexuality, rendering the notions of hetero-, homo-, and bisexuality meaningless. Sexual power is being reconfigured in radically new terms, and much of it is happening online.

The challenge to binary thinking about sex, gender, and sexuality has coincided with the rise of the Internet as a popular means of communication. If discussions about sexual desire are not happening in the classroom, they *are* happening online—in chat rooms, on listserves, and in weblogs. In virtual spaces, Web users are finding the freedom to explore new sexual identities, desires, and practices in an uncensored way without inviting physical danger. In this sense, Internet technology has created a safe space in which gender roles can be critiqued and new dialogues about sexuality can (and do) take place. This essay considers several examples of genderqueer Web sites where these dialogues are taking place, evaluating the ways in which they are changing basic assumptions about sex and power that often foster sexual violence.

CYBERSPACE AND THE FALSE PROMISE OF GENDER NEUTRALITY

During the 1990s, as the number of Internet users began to rise exponentially, cyberspace began to be touted as a utopian form of democracy, an environment in which users could be free of discrimination based on gender, race, age, or other visible markers of social identity. In interactive forums, the logic went, if people chose gender-neutral aliases or pseudonyms, there would be no way to tell what their sex was in real life. The promise was that cyberspace would revolutionize our social interactions by eradicating gender entirely. Online, gender would simply not matter. As it turned out, the result was quite the opposite: As more and more people began to log on and hang out in virtual spaces, it became apparent that users consciously gendered their online personas in chat rooms, MUDs (multiuser dimensions), listserves and bulletin boards. Whether or not each online persona matched up with the real-life gender identity of the person behind the keyboard, Internet researchers have observed that most people are no more comfortable with gender neutrality in online conversations than they are with the ambiguously gendered in the real world.

As Lori Kendall observes in her essay on gender in MUD environments, characters who designate their gender as neutral are commonly understood as having neglected to describe themselves fully rather than having made a purposeful decision not to be categorized.[1] This reaction is encouraged by the convention of designating guest characters gender neutral by default when they log in. The expectation that everyone must be either male or female is carried over into online interactions, as Kendall points out: "No one encountering someone using the pronoun *e* is likely to believe that this expresses their 'true' gender, and is thus likely to treat the character's gender designation as a mere mask."[2] MUD users presenting gender-neutral characters are consequently often asked whether they are male or female in real life.

MUD environments in particular are highly social virtual locations in which people develop close relationships, both platonic and sexual, over time. Kendall's discovery, therefore, that great emphasis is placed on gender identity in these contexts is not as surprising as it is informative about how entrenched gender identity is in all social interaction, whether in real life or online:

> Although individuals can choose their gender representation, that does not seem to be creating a context in which gender is more fluid. Rather, gender identities themselves become even more rigidly understood. . . .
> . . . The online environment is not itself a solution. Understandings of gender and the hierarchical arrangements based on these understandings do not simply disappear in forums where we can't see each other. We carry these understandings with us and re-create them online.[3]

The revelation that gender neutrality in cyberspace was a false promise, then, is anchored in two observations: first, that users tend to recreate gender stereotypes as a shorthand way of making their characters socially intelligible (and in some cases sexually attractive) to others; and second, that even when consciously attempting to abandon gender, the online experience is always mediated through the knowledge of one's "real" (offline) gender identity.[4] Although technology's promise of a posthuman, nongendered virtual existence is seductive in its offer of freedom from the limits of the body, Lisa Nakamura cautions that we must not abandon the specificity of lived bodies in imagining new cyberidentities:

> This is the paradox: In order to think rigorously, humanely, and imaginatively about virtuality and the "posthuman," it is absolutely necessary to ground critique in the lived realities of the human, in all their particularity and specificity. The nuanced realities of virtuality—racial, gendered, othered—live in the body, and though science is producing and encouraging different readings and revisions of the body, it is premature to throw it away just yet, particularly since so much postcolonial, political, and feminist critique stems from it.[5]

Rather than pinning our hopes on a false promise of gender neutrality associated with a theoretical posthuman virtuality, we should use the disembodied aspects of cyberspace to challenge ourselves to invent new and more specific language about gender, sexuality, and desire as they refer back to our lived experiences.

If totally eliminating gender is not an option, and if successfully performing male or female online means conforming to recognizable (and limiting) stereotypes of masculinity and femininity, how can we begin to think about new articulations of desire—either on or offline—that break away from the misogyny and sexism that so often lead to sexual violence? The answer coming from transgender activists and queer theorists is that we need to consciously identify and articulate more specific gender identities and sexual practices if we hope to have more freedom and autonomy in creating new mappings of desire.

"MORE GENDER, MORE OF THE TIME"

Even within the field of queer studies, the understanding of desire has been limited by an insistent focus on categories of identity rather than sexual practice. As queer theorist Judith Halberstam puts it:

> Surprisingly, we talk about sex—sexual practices and erotic variation—much less than we might imagine, and this is at

least partly because we talk a great deal about categories such
as "lesbian" and "gay." We almost seem to assume that particular practices attend particular sexual identities even as we
object to the naturalization of the homosexual–heterosexual
binary.[6]

The academic discussion of sexuality in terms of categories rather than
practices limits the scope of sexual imagination and contributes to a political
hierarchy of sexual behaviors from the sanctioned to the taboo. The inability
to articulate desire outside of prescriptive definitions of lesbian, gay, and
straight sex acts for fear of being deemed perverse or politically incorrect is
disempowering and results in exactly the sort of silence that I encountered at
the community college.

In contrast to the nonconversations happening in the classroom and in
academic circles about desire and sexual practice, animated engagement with
these topics is going on in certain segments of the queer community. By calling into question notions of appropriate sexual acts corresponding to conventional gender roles, such discussions enable new articulations of desire.
As Halberstam notes:

> The development of a new sexual vocabulary and a radical
> sexual discourse is happening already in transgender com-
> munities, in sexual subcultures, in clubs, in zines, in queer
> spaces everywhere. Female masculinity within queer sexual
> discourse allows for the disruption of even flows between
> gender and anatomy, sexuality and identity, sexual practice
> and performativity.[7]

Allowing for the possibility that gender expression does not necessarily
have to map onto the biological sex of each person frees us from thinking of
sex as merely gay or straight; instead, we can conceive of a range of practices
that might be negotiated between people in a consensual relationship.

Transgender activist Dean Spade calls for "more gender, more of the time"
in an essay that appeared in both the print zine *Cocksure* and on his Web site
makezine.org in June 2002. Spade writes:

> I don't see myself as falling into either of the imaginary two
> categories "man/woman," and I don't approach the people I

want to fuck with those categories in mind. I am committed
to an idea of gender that is about an ever-changing layering
of gendered characteristics and perceptions, not at all about
two poles, a continuum, or any boxes. Please don't understand
me to be promoting "non-labeling." What I love is specific,
detailed, stimulating, inventive uses of language to constantly
re-inscribe and re-identify body and sex experiences, rather
than simplistic terms that shut down conversations about how
hot we all really are.[8]

Refusing to be shoehorned into a paradigm of four possible sexual identities (bi/straight/fag/dyke) based on two genders (man/woman), Spade also
rejects the mythic promise of gender neutrality in his call for specificity. "If
I'm chasing a scrawny, new-wave, eyeliner wearing faggotbutchswitch lesbian, and a jocky-but-sensitive preppy trannyfag, and a tough-but-gentle punk
activist translady top, how can that be made to fit me into one of four categories?" he asks. "Why would we want to do that?"[9]

Spade's position is fundamentally different from the gender-bending
MUD player in that his gender fluidity is rooted in his own real-life transgender experience, rather than something he is performing solely in the context of a virtual environment in opposition to a "real" offline identity. The
authenticity of Spade's transgender identity situates his comments within a
genderqueer framework that enables a particular critical approach to questions of sexuality. The fact that Spade and other transgendered people are
able to develop "a new sexual vocabulary and a radical sexual discourse"
(in Halberstam's words) is greatly facilitated by the Internet, communication
technology that enables conversation between people living at great distances
from each other.

SEX, PORN, AND CENSORSHIP

To date, feminists have been deeply divided on the implications of new digital
communications technology, some arguing it is hindering rather than helping
forge a more egalitarian sexual future for women by enabling the rapid distribution of pornographic images and promoting sex tourism, prostitution, and

trafficking in women and children. In fact, recent feminist debates over new media and Internet technology could be characterized as a revival of the sex wars of the 1970s and 1980s, in which antipornography activists like Andrea Dworkin and Catharine MacKinnon butted heads with sex radicals such as Susie Bright and Pat Califia. If anything, widespread use of the Internet has intensified arguments over freedom of speech and the censorship of sexually explicit materials, largely because of its contribution to the expansion of the porn industry [see Dines, p. 105].[10]

Attempts to regulate or censor sexually explicit material on the Internet have met with resistance from free speech activists, who argue that to do so is not only practically unfeasible but would also result in a colossal shutdown of valuable nonpornographic content as well.[11] The Hyde amendment to the telecommunications bill of 1995 (which was ultimately defeated) was one such example, a provision that Jonathan Wallace and Mark Mangan describe in *Sex, Laws, and Cyberspace* as "the worst nightmare of those committed to free speech on the Net." They argue that the amendment's treatment of cyberspace as a broadcast medium rather than a "constellation of printing presses and bookstores" would have disastrous consequences. "[The Hyde amendment] implemented a broadcast-style indecency standard, with no exceptions for material with scientific, literary, artistic, or political value. Therefore, it would ban serious discussion of rape, safe sex, or breast cancer on the Net."[12]

Although Wallace and Mangan do not dispute that there is some "very disturbing speech on the Internet," the solution they advocate is to "fight speech with speech" rather than censorship and implement client-side filters and controls rather than banning content from servers. The choice to access violent or sexually explicit text or images thus ultimately remains with the user; each individual can make his or her own decision about whether or not to see or read such content.

What we find in examining genderqueer and sex-positive Web sites is precisely this suggestion in action. Online communities of people interested in talking about nonnormative sexuality and desire are actively engaged in negotiating questions of censorship and freedom of speech issues in relationship to the content on the Web sites they visit. In an examination of conversations taking place on messageboards at Strap-on.org and in the LiveJournal community ftm_undressed, we can see how such communities make space for rape survivors, S/M sex radicals, and sex workers to respectfully and even playfully explore new articulations of desire.

STRAP-ON.ORG

Strap-on.org is "a progressive, queer-centered, sex-positive, girl-friendly on-line community that started in November 2000," according to the site's mission statement. The central feature of the site is a massive messageboard, divided into sections called community, identity, body/mind/support, and diy (do it yourself) and media. Most of the site's content is provided by community members, people who visit regularly and log in with a username of their choosing. An ezboard.com-hosted site, Strap-on.org has more than 3,800 registered members.[13] From the launch of the site in November 2000 through May 2003, more than 80,000 messages were posted. The site is expressly feminist, and it is managed by six administrators. On the About Us page, they describe the intent of the community and address the significance of its queer, sex-positive name:

> Mostly, it's a place for us to talk about personal, political, and
> other issues related to queer and feminist identities and ideas.
> and queer/punk music. or something. strap-on.org is a fun
> name and the domain was available. it doesn't mean we all
> necessarily like or use strap-ons. we come here to share and
> discuss and learn from each other. if you're only here to solicit
> sex, look somewhere else.[14]

The primary purpose of the site is to foster discussion rather than to serve solely as a dating service or a source of online personal ads. The community section of the messageboard does include a forum called depictions and debauchery, however, which is denoted as the "official cruising section" and invites members to post pictures and declare and respond to crushes on each other. As is true on many bulletin boards and multiuser journal sites, users may incorporate icons or thumbnail images of themselves in their signatures when posting. However, Strap-on.org has a policy against posting or linking to nude images, which prevents the site from resembling the graphic online porn sites so prevalent on the Web. Other Strap-on.org policies establish ground rules for discussion that address issues of sexual harassment and other hate speech. The messageboard administrators reserve the right to ban users from the community if they do not comply with these policies, which are designed to make Strap-on.org a safe place in which to have discussions about sex, gender, and sexuality. They write:

> strap-on.org is a girl-friendly and queer-positive (that means all queers) place for us to have fun, discuss stuff we care about, and support each other. disagreements, political debate, etc. are encouraged—but play fair. that means no sexism, racism, homophobia, biphobia, transphobia, classism, sizeism, ableism, etc.. it's important to educate each other, but if you persistently post bigotry, you will be banned. if you post bigoted shit with the intent of humiliating or harassing other users, you will be banned. accounts that are created to make posts which look like they are from other users (imposters) will be banned. accounts that are created simply to harass other users will also be banned. these are very simple guidelines to follow and we hope you'll understand that they are here for the safety, security, and general well-being of this space, not to stifle discussion.[15]

With this policy of discussion etiquette in place, the site has established an environment that enables frank and playful conversation among a wide range of people, many of whom would likely never encounter each other in real life.

Strap-on.org enables the sort of client-side selectivity that Wallace and Mangan advocate in lieu of censorship through clearly delineated, thematic message forums based on both identity and content. Visitors can choose which forums they want to read and respond to, and each forum includes specific guidelines for posting in that section. Some forums restrict posting to those belonging to specific groups, with the intent of offering members safe, exclusive spaces in which to discuss issues with others of similar backgrounds and identities. For example, separate forums exist for people of color, transgendered/transsexual/genderqueer people, fat people, working class/poor people, gay/lesbian-identified people, femmes, people with mental illness, survivors of abuse, significant others, and sex workers. Although posting to identity-based forums is restricted to those who self-identify as members of those communities, the forums are not locked and may be read by anyone. Consequently, they serve not only as supportive spaces for people of particular identifications, but also as educational resources for others interested in those groups.

The surprising coexistence of explicit discussions of S/M sex practices in the let's talk about sex forum and threads on sexual abuse in the survivors forum suggests that Strap-on.org has succeeded in creating an inclusive space for radical sexual discourse. Undoubtedly, this is largely due to good moderation and the existence of the ground rules and guidelines established by the site administrators. The convention of adding the words "possibly triggering" to the subject line of a thread that might cause associations with prior sexual abuse is one example of accommodations that have been made on the site to enable users to avoid posts that might cause them distress. In several cases, requests for more careful labeling of potentially triggering posts initiated thoughtful dialogue about violence, erotica, and age-of-consent issues.

In the context of a site dedicated to the frank discussion of sexual practices that presumes nothing about its users' gender identities, participants often refer to each other solely by username and use gender-specific pronouns only when it is clear what gender expression is preferred by the individual in question. The prevalence of non-gender-specific usernames by many Strap-on.org members has the effect of separating sexual acts from the anatomical sex of the bodies performing them. The result is a practical example of the kind of reinscription of bodies and sexual practices Spade calls for in "More Gender, More of the Time."

The mediated discussion on the Strap-on.org messageboard is a good example of how open communication about sex on an online forum can be transformative, breaking down boundaries between people of different sexual orientations, gender identities, and race and class backgrounds. The frank and specific conversations occurring on the site document the positive potential of Internet technology to push the limits of our assumptions about sexual practice and gender identity that have until now left young women in particular caught in a polar virgin/whore sexual paradox. Such communities are increasingly offering us new ways to think and talk about sexuality, which can only help in the quest to eradicate sexual violence.

LIVEJOURNAL AND WEBLOGS

Another popular form of online dialogue can be found in online journals, sometimes also referred to as weblogs, or blogs. Like their bulletin board predecessors, they often are designed interactively to allow multiple users to respond to individual entries. Some of the most popular online journal communities geared toward sexuality and genderqueer populations today can be found on LiveJournal.com. LiveJournal was the accidental success story of University of Washington student Brad Fitzpatrick, who created the server software in March 1999 so that he and his friends could more efficiently post and respond to each other's online journal entries.

As word spread, more and more people opened online journals at LiveJournal.com. As of June 2003, more than one million accounts had been created and more than 400,000 users had updated their journals in the past thirty days. Of those reporting their gender, 62 percent say they are female, and most of them fall between the ages of fifteen and twenty-two.[16] LiveJournal hosts community discussion boards as well as individual journals, and the content on many of these boards resembles the frank discussion about sex and gender found on Strap-on.org.

The high numbers of teens and women actively posting on LiveJournal sites recalls Dale Spender's comparison of Internet technology with the telephone in her 1995 book *Nattering on the Net*. "The telephone is an integral part of the information infrastructure," she writes, "yet women's easy and ready use of this form of technology usually goes unnoted."[17] Distressed by the technological gender gap that she found was limiting women's access to and use of computers, Spender argues that the history of the telephone as a key piece of communication technology is a good model for how women should view the Internet:

> The telephone . . . has helped forge new networks and
> communities.
> And this is how I would urge women to start seeing the

computer: as a means of communicating, of plugging into the
biggest network to be devised, of making and maintaining
friendships and contacts.

Computers are for nattering on the net.[18]

The friendships established online through LiveJournal sites do in fact
carry over to real life; the sites are so popular in the queer and transgender
communities that national activist conferences frequently designate social
spaces for online friends to meet each other in person. Such real-life encounters establish a connection between the alternative virtual sexual and gender
identities people construct online and the bodies that often perform them in
the real world. The intersection of these cyber-identities with the actual em-
bodiment of lived experience lends authenticity to the online conversations
occurring on LiveJournal and other genderqueer Web sites.

Thousands of LiveJournal communities are devoted to a vast number of
topics, ranging from music and other hobbies to sexual identities and support
groups. Like Strap-on.org, LiveJournal community journal sites are moder-
ated, and posting is often restricted to members who have joined specific
communities based on a shared interest. Some individual journals are designated as closed forums and are restricted to viewers designated as the author's
friends. The friends feature links individual users together, creating a massive
web of journals on the LiveJournal site. Consequently, one is always just a
click or two away from a radically different topic of conversation.

The decentralized aspect of Internet networks is illustrated in microcosm
within the LiveJournal entries, as each individual may edit his or her own
posts but not the posts of others. In May 2003, on a LiveJournal billed as
ftm_undressed, a site dedicated to "tranny porn ftm style," a controversy arose
in response to one female-to-male transman's post of a piece of erotic fiction
that several other users objected to on the grounds that it was a rape fantasy.
They demanded that it be removed from the site. Although the author himself considered the story an example of "Domination by two Androgynous
tops, on a femme female" rather than a rape narrative, he was flamed by a
flurry of angry responses and the story was removed from the site. After more
discussion, in which several community members defended his right to post
the story on a journal site dedicated to transgender porn, the author restored
the original fiction with a trigger warning at the beginning.[19]

What is most interesting about this incident is that it resulted in a change of policy on ftm_undressed regarding the format of all journal entries on the community board. Following the uproar, the moderators decided that all subsequent entries must include what is called an lj-cut. Each lj-cut creates a buffer between the reader and potentially offensive or traumatizing content by establishing a hypertext skip in the text from the initial introduction of an entry to its full posting on a second screen. In addition, a brief description of the content of the posting must accompany each lj-cut so "people can pick and choose what they would like to read and what they would not like to read." Like the trigger warnings implemented to enable survivors and others sensitive to sexual violence to avoid posts with S/M content on Strap-on.org, the lj-cut functions as an intervention between the reader and potentially triggering erotic stories. By mandating these hypertext skips for all posts on ftm_undressed, the moderators chose to enable client-side selectivity, as Wallace and Mangan suggest, rather than pursuing a strategy of outright censorship.

In online genderqueer communities, there appears to be a degree of sensitivity to issues of sexual violence even as there is a strong commitment to maintaining freedom of speech and the right of all members to freely articulate their erotic fantasies in sex-positive spaces. The peaceful coexistence of support groups, journals on gender identity, and discussions of sexuality and sexual practices within the LiveJournal domain points is a strong argument for moderation and negotiation of contentious entries through public discussion rather than censorship. Although some users will undoubtedly be alienated by what they see as political correctness on the part of their peers in determining what is and what is not appropriate, once again the decentered nature of LiveJournal (and the Internet at large) always offers such people the option of moving to another interest community or starting their own on a topic of their choice.

CONCLUSION

In thinking about the transformative implications of new technologies in relationship to sex, gender, and sexuality, it is important to make a distinction between the utopian promise of gender fluidity operating on a theoretical level and the reality of how cyberspace is being used and by whom. Rather than focusing on an idealized notion of gender neutrality in cyberspace as the answer to discrimination and disempowerment, we should turn our attention to the specific diversity of alternatively gendered lives and their cyber-representations. As Web demographics continue to evolve, and a more and more diverse group of people begin to use the Internet on a regular basis, new conversations about gender and sexuality can be observed online. In many ways, this is less due to anything inherent in the technology itself than it is a byproduct of its function as a tool of communication.

Cyber-communities like Strap-on.org and LiveJournal's ftm_undressed are two examples of how genderqueer people online are profoundly stretching the limited discourse about sexuality and desire that has been available until now. Bringing like-minded people together electronically—people who might be geographically separated from each other but who are actually embodying and enacting alternative gender identities and sexual practices—the Internet accelerates dialogue and the development of new language, promoting new ways of thinking and writing about desire. By embracing Spender's notion of nattering on the net, Internet users of all genders and sexualities can capitalize on the opportunity this new technology presents to connect with and respond to others about potentially uncomfortable topics from a safe distance. In the end, I believe that it is precisely this sort of participation that we will find transformative in the ongoing quest to break the awkward silence around sexuality and establish a more creative, playful, and egalitarian language of desire.

NOTES

1. Lori Kendall, "MUDder? I Hardly Know 'Er! Adventures of a Feminist MUDder," in *Wired_ Women: Gender and New Realities in Cyberspace,* edited by Lynn Cherny and Elizabeth Reba Weise (Seattle: Seal, 1996).

2. Kendall, "MUDder?", 217

3. Kendall, "MUDder?", 221–222.

4. In a related argument, Lisa Nakamura has coined the term *cybertype* in order to discuss race in cyberspace. In her book *Cybertypes: Race, Ethnicity, and Identity on the Internet* (Routledge, 2002), she explains that the word describes "the distinctive ways that the Internet propagates, disseminates, and commodifies images of race and racism" (3). Cybertypes both reflect and produce identity stereotypes as they are collaboratively replicated again and again throughout the Internet.

5. Nakamura, *Cybertypes,* 7.

6. Judith Halberstam, *Female Masculinity* (Durham: Duke University Press, 1998), 113–114.

7. Halberstam, *Female Masculinity,* 139.

8. Dean Spade, Makezine.org, "More Gender, More of the Time," accessed June 1, 2002, http://makezine.org/bibi.html.

9. Spade, Makezine.org.

10. Paul Keegan, "Prime-Time Porn," *Business 2.0,* June 2003, 97–103. In this story on Vivid Entertainment's CEO Steve Hirsch, a leader in the hard-core porn film and video industry, Keegan reported that "obscenity cases have proved increasingly difficult to prosecute . . . as digital technology and the pervasiveness of sexual imagery have weakened the Supreme Court's famous 1973 decision holding that 'community standards' are the crucial factor" (103). According to Keegan, Hirsch is hoping that widespread digital distribution of his porn videos will become a reality once broadband Internet TV is viable.

11. One famous example of such an argument was made by anticensorship feminist activists in the 1994 attempt by Carnegie Mellon University to ban many sex-related usenet groups from being accessed on campus. Donna M. Riley writes about the incident in greater detail in "Sex, Fear, and Condescension on Campus: Cybercensorship at Carnegie Mellon," in *Wired_Women,* 158–168.

12. Jonathan Wallace and Mark Mangan, *Sex, Laws, and Cyberspace* (New York: Holt, 1996), 190.

13. Registration is free; visitors may establish either a local or global ezboard account, which they can then use to log in and post messages. Although anyone hitting the site can read messages, registered members are only counted as belonging to the Strap-on.org community when they first post to the messageboard, so the number of members represents the total of those who have actually contributed to the conversation. One can surmise that a larger number of visitors read the board but do not log in or post responses.

14. Strap-on.org, "Frequently Asked Questions," accessed June 5, 2003, http://www.strap-on.org/faq.html.

15. Strap-on.org, "Messageboard Policy."

16. LiveJournal.com, "LiveJournal Statistics," accessed June 6, 2003, http://www.livejournal.com/stats.bml.

17. Dale Spender, *Nattering on the Net: Women, Power, and Cyberspace* (North Melbourne: Spinifex, 1995), 191.

18. Spender, *Nattering,* 192.

19. LiveJournal.com, "ftm_undressed," accessed June 6, 2003, http://www.livejournal.com/community/ftm_undressed/.

· ·

KIM SURKAN has completed a dissertation on gender passing and transgender subjectivity at the University of Minnesota. After teaching women's studies in the Twin Cities and at Minnesota State University in Mankato, Surkan relocated to western Massachusetts to begin a study of female masculinity at women's colleges as a research associate at the Five College Women's Studies Research Center at Mount Holyoke.

ORGANIZATIONS TO CONTACT

There are hundreds of organizations in the United States working on issues related to *Transforming a Rape Culture*. The following list includes just a few of the national organizations and resources, many of which have state or local chapters as well.

AN ABUSE, RAPE AND DOMESTIC VIOLENCE AID AND RESOURCE COLLECTION (AARDVARC)
606 Calibre Crest Parkway #103
Altamonte Springs, FL 32714
www.aardvarc.org

COALITION AGAINST TRAFFICKING IN WOMEN (CATW)
Dr. Janice Raymond
University of Massachusetts
P.O. Box 9338
North Amherst, MA 01059
(413) 367-9262
www.catwinternational.org

COMMITTEE FOR CHILDREN
568 First Avenue S., Suite 600
Seattle, WA 98104-2804
(800) 634-4449
www.cfchildren.org

FAITHTRUST INSTITUTE
2400 N. 45th St., Suite 10
Seattle, WA 98103
(206) 634-1903
www.faithtrustinstitute.org

FAMILY VIOLENCE AND SEXUAL ASSAULT INSTITUTE

6160 Cornerstone Court East
San Diego, CA 92121
(858) 623-2777 ext. 416
www.fvsai.org

MALESURVIVOR

PMB 103
5505 Connecticut Ave. N.W.
Washington, DC 20015-2601
(800) 738-4181
www.malesurvivor.org

MEN CAN STOP RAPE

P.O. Box 57144
Washington, DC 20037
(202) 032-6530
www.mencanstoprape.org

MEN OVERCOMING VIOLENCE (MOVE)

1385 Mission St., Suite 300
San Francisco, CA 94103
(415) 626-6683
www.menovercomingviolence.org

NATIONAL CENTER FOR ASSAULT PREVENTION

606 Delsea Dr.
Sewell, NJ 08080
(856) 582-7000
www.ncap.org

NATIONAL CENTER FOR VICTIMS OF CRIME

2000 M St. N.W., Suite 480
Washington, D.C. 20036
(202) 467-8700
www.ncvc.org

NATIONAL CLEARINGHOUSE ON CHILD ABUSE AND NEGLECT INFORMATION

330 C St., S.W.

Washington, D.C. 20447

(800) 394-3366 or (703) 385-7565

http://nccanch.acf.hhs.gov/

NATIONAL CLEARINGHOUSE ON MARITAL AND DATE RAPE

2325 Oak Street

Berkeley, CA 94708

www.members.aol.com/ncmdr

NATIONAL COALITION AGAINST DOMESTIC VIOLENCE

1532 16th Street N.W.

Washington, D.C. 20036

(202) 745-1211

www.ncadv.org

NATIONAL DOMESTIC VIOLENCE HOTLINE

P.O. Box 161810

Austin, TX 78716

(800) 799-SAFE

www.ndvh.org

NATIONAL ORGANIZATION FOR MEN AGAINST SEXISM (NOMAS)

P.O. Box 455

Louisville, CO 80027-0455

(303) 666-7043

www.nomas.org

NATIONAL ORGANIZATION FOR WOMEN

733 15th St. N.W., 2nd Floor

Washington, D.C. 20005

(202) 628-8669

www.now.org

NATIONAL ORGANIZATION OF MEN'S OUTREACH FOR RAPE EDUCATION (NOMORE)

John D. Foubert

William and Mary School of Education

P.O. Box 8795

Williamsburg, VA 23187-8795

(757) 221-2322

www.nomorerape.org

NATIONAL SEXUAL VIOLENCE RESOURCE CENTER

123 North Enola Dr.

Enola, PA 17025

(877) 739-3895

www.nsvrc.org

OFFICE ON VIOLENCE AGAINST WOMEN

810 7th St. N.W.

Washington, DC 20531

(202) 307-6026

www.ojp.usdoj.gov/vawo

RAPE, ABUSE, AND INCEST NATIONAL NETWORK (RAINN)

635-B Pennsylvania Ave. S.E.

Washington, DC 20003

(800) 656-HOPE

www.rainn.org

SPEAKING OUT AGAINST RAPE (SOAR)

69 E. Pine St.

Orlando, FL 32801

(407) 836-9692

www.soar99.org

ADDITIONAL READING

Allen, Beverly. *Rape Warfare*. Minneapolis: University of Minnesota, 1996.

Alsdurf, J. *Battered into Submission: The Tragedy of Wife Abuse in the Christian Home*. Downers Grove, Ill.: Inter Varsity, 1989.

Annis, Ann W., Michelle Loyd-Paige, and Roger R. Rice. *What the Church Needs to Know from Survivors of Abuse*. Lanham, Md.: University Press of America, 2001.

Ashworth, Georgina. *Of Violence and Violation: Women and Human Rights*. London: Change, 1986.

Assiter, Alison. *Pornography, Feminism and the Individual*. Concord, Mass.: Pluto Press, 1989.

Bart, Pauline B., and Eileen G. Moran, eds. *Violence Against Women: The Bloody Footprints*. Thousand Oaks, Calif.: Sage, 1993.

Bart, Pauline B., and Patricia H. O'Brien. *Stopping Rape: Successful Survival Strategies*. New York: Pergamon Press, 1985.

Benedict, Helen. *Virgin or Vamp: How the Press Covers Sex Crimes*. New York: Oxford University Press, 1993.

Bergen, Raquel Kennedy. *Wife Rape: Understanding the Response of Survivors and Service Providers*. Thousand Oaks, Calif.: Sage, 1996.

Bevacqua, Maria. *Rape on the Public Agenda: Feminism and the Politics of Sexual Assault*. Boston: Northeastern University Press, 2000.

Bode, Janet. *Voices of Rape*. New York: Franklin Watts, 1990.

Boonprasat-Lewis, Nantawan, and Marie Fortune, eds. *Remembering Conquest: Feminist/Womanist Perspectives on Religion, Colonization, and Sexual Violence*. New York: Haworth, 1999.

Brandenburg, Judith B. *Confronting Sexual Harassment: What Schools and Colleges Can Do*. New York: Teachers College Press, 1997.

Brandwein, Ruth A., ed. *Battered Women, Children, and Welfare Reform: The Ties That Bind*. Thousand Oaks, Calif.: Sage Publications, 1999.

Brittan, Arthur. *Masculinity and Power*. New York: Basil Blackwell, 1989.

Brownmiller, Susan. *Against Our Will: Men, Women and Rape.* New York: Simon and Schuster, 1975.

Burns, M. C., ed. *The Speaking Profits Us: Violence in the Lives of Women of Color.* Seattle: Center for the Prevention of Sexual and Domestic Violence, 1986.

Bussert, Joy M. K. *Battered Women: From a Theology of Suffering to an Ethic of Empowerment.* New York: Division for Mission in North America, Lutheran Church in America, 1986.

Conte, Jon R. *Critical Issues in Child Sexual Abuse: Historical, Legal, and Psychological Perspectives.* Thousand Oaks, Calif.: Sage Publications, 2001.

Cook, Rebecca. *Women's Health and Human Rights: The Promotion and Protection of Women's Health through International Human Rights Law.* Geneva: World Health Organization, 1994.

Counts, Dorothy Ayers, Judith K. Brown, and Jacquelyn C. Campbell, eds. *To Have and To Hit: Cultural Perspectives on Wife Beating.* Urbana: University of Illinois Press, 1999.

Criminal Victimization in the United States (A National Crime Victimization Survey Report). Bureau of Justice Statistics, U.S. Department of Justice. 1992. NCJ-139563.

Cuklanz, Lisa M. *Rape on Trial: How the Mass Media Construct Legal Reform and Social Change.* Philadelphia: University of Pennsylvania Press, 1995.

Davies, Miranda. *Women and Violence.* London: Zed Books, 1994.

Dobash, R. Emerson, and Russell P. Dobash. *Rethinking Violence Against Women.* Thousand Oaks, Calif.: Sage Publications, 1998.

Dworkin, Andrea. *Pornography: Men Possessing Women.* New York: GP Putnam's Sons, 1979.

———. *Intercourse.* New York: Free Press, 1987.

Eisenstein, Zillah. *Hatreds: Racialized and Sexualized Conflicts in the 21st Century.* London: Routledge, 1996.

Eisler, Riane. *The Chalice and the Blade: Our History, Our Future.* New York: HarperCollins, 1987.

Faust, Beatrice. *Women, Sex and Pornography: A Controversial Study.* New York: Macmillan, 1980.

Female Victims of Violent Crime. Prepared by Carolyn Wolf Harlow. Bureau of Justice Statistics. U.S. Department of Justice. 1991. NCJ-126826.

Fontes, Lisa A., ed. *Sexual Abuse in Nine North American Cultures: Treatment and Prevention.* Thousand Oaks, Calif.: Sage Publications, 1995.

Forell, Caroline A. *A Law of Her Own: The Reasonable Woman as a Measure of Man.* New York: New York University Press, 2000.

Francis, Leslie, ed. *Date Rape: Feminism, Philosophy, and the Law.* University Park: Pennsylvania State University Press, 1996.

French, Stanley E., Wanda Teacys, and Laura M. Purdy. *Violence Against Women: Philosophical Perspectives.* Ithaca, N.Y.: Cornell University Press, 1998.

Gender Violence and Women's Rights in Africa: A Symposium. New Brunswick, N.J.: Center for Women's Global Leadership, 1994.

Gilligan, Carol, Nona P. Lyons, and Trudy J. Hanmer, eds. *Making Connections: The Relational Worlds of Adolescent Girls at Emma Willard School.* Cambridge: Harvard University Press, 1989.

Gilman, Charlotte Perkins. *Herland and Other Stories.* Ed. Barbara H. Solomon. New York: Signet Classic, 1992.

Gilmartin, Pat. *Rape, Incest, and Child Sexual Abuse: Consequences and Recovery.* New York: Garland Publishing, 1994.

Girshick, Lori B. *Woman-to-Woman Sexual Violence: Does She Call It Rape?* Boston: Northeastern University Press, 2002.

Gonsiorek, John C., ed. *Breach of Trust: Sexual Exploitation by Health Care Professionals and Clergy.* Thousand Oaks, Calif.: Sage Publications, 1994.

Gordon, Margaret T., and Stephanie Riger. *The Female Fear: The Social Cost of Rape.* Urbana: University of Illinois Press, 1991.

Gorman, Carol. *Pornography.* New York: Franklin Watts, 1980.

Griffin, Susan. *Pornography and Silence.* New York: Harper and Row, 1981.

Gubar, Susan, and Joan Hoff. *For Adult Users Only: The Dilemma of Violent Pornography.* Bloomington: Indiana University Press, 1989.

Guberman, Connie, and Margie Wolfe, eds. *No Safe Place: Violence Against Women and Children.* Toronto: Women's Press, 1985.

Guernsey, JoAnn Bren. *The Facts about Rape.* New York: Crestwood House, 1990.

Hagan, Kay Leigh, ed. *Women Respond to the Men's Movement.* San Francisco: HarperSanFrancisco, 1992.

Hazen, Helen. *Endless Rapture: Rape, Romance and the Female Imagination.* New York: Charles Scribner's Sons, 1983.

Heilbrun, Carolyn G. *Reinventing Womanhood.* New York: W. W. Norton, 1979.

Jackson, Donna. *How to Make the World a Better Place for Women in Five Minutes a Day.* Los Angeles: Hyperion, 1992.

James, Joy. *Resisting State Violence: Radicalism, Gender and Race in U.S. Culture.* Minneapolis: University of Minnesota Press, 1996.

Kappeler, Susanne. *The Pornography of Representation.* Minneapolis: University of Minnesota Press, 1986.

Keshgegian, Flora. *Redeeming Memories: A Theology of Healing and Transformation.* Nashville: Abingdon Press, 2000.

Kimmel, Michael S., ed. *Men Confront Pornography.* New York: Crown Publishers, 1990.

Kivel, Paul. *Men's Work: How to Stop the Violence That Tears Our Lives Apart.* Center City, Minn.: Hazelden, 1992.

Lamb, Sandra. *Rape in America: A Reference Handbook.* Santa Barbara, Calif.: ABC-CLIO, 1995.

Le Guin, Ursula K. *Always Coming Home.* New York: Bantam Books, 1985.

Leghorn, Lisa, and Katherine Parker. *Woman's Worth: Sexual Economics and the World of Women.* Boston: Routledge, 1981.

Leone, Bruno, ed. *Rape on Campus.* San Diego, Calif.: Greenhaven Press, 1995.

Levy, Barrie, ed. *Dating Violence: Young Women in Danger.* Seattle: Seal Press, 1990; revised edition, 1998.

MacKinnon, Catharine A. *Feminism Unmodified: Discourses in Life and Law.* Cambridge: Harvard University Press, 1987.

Madigan, Lee, and Nancy Gamble. *The Second Rape: Society's Continual Betrayal of the Victim.* New York: Lexington Books, 1991.

Mamonova, Tatyana. *Women and Russia: Feminist Writings from the Soviet Union.* Boston: Beacon Press, 1984.

Medea, Andrea, and Kathleen Thompson. *Against Rape: A Survival Manual for Women.* New York: Farrar, Straus and Giroux, 1974.

Miedzian, Myriam. *Boys Will Be Boys: Breaking the Link between Masculinity and Violence.* New York: Doubleday, 1988.

Miles, Rosalind. *Love, Sex, Death, and the Making of the Male.* New York: Summit Books, 1991.

Naples, Nancy, ed. *Community Activism and Feminist Politics: Organizing across Race, Class and Gender.* New York, Routledge, 1997.

Nordquist, Joan. *Violence Against Women: A Bibliography.* Santa Cruz, Calif.: Reference and Research Services, 1992.

Omvedt, Gail. *Violence Against Women: New Movements and New Theories in India.* Delhi: Kali for Women, 1990.

Parrot, Andrea. *Coping with Date Rape and Acquaintance Rape.* New York: Rosen Group, 1999.

Parrot, Andrea and Laurie Bechhofer, eds. *Acquaintance Rape: The Hidden Crime.* New York: Wiley, 1991.

Pierce-Baker, Charlotte. *Surviving the Silence: Black Women's Stories of Rape.* New York: W. W. Norton, 1998.

Plaskow, Judith, and Carol P. Christ, eds. *Weaving the Visions: New Patterns in Feminist Spirituality.* San Francisco: HarperSanFrancisco, 1989.

Provenzo, Eugene F., Jr. *Video Kids: Making Sense of Nintendo.* Cambridge: Harvard University Press, 1990.

Ranke-Heinemann, Uta. *Eunuchs for the Kingdom of Heaven: Women, Sexuality, and the Catholic Church.* New York: Penguin Books, 1988.

Rape in America: A Report to the Nation. Washington, D.C.: National Victim Center and Crime Victims Research and Treatment Center, 1992.

Reflections of Risk: Growing Up Female in Minnesota. Minneapolis: Minnesota Women's Fund, 1990.

Reiss, Albert J., Jr., and Jeffrey A. Roth, eds. *Understanding and Preventing Violence: National Research Council Panel on the Understanding and Control of Violent Behavior.* Washington, D.C.: National Academy Press, 1993.

Renzetti, Claire, and Charles Harvey Miley, eds. *Violence in Gay and Lesbian Domestic Partnerships.* New York: Harrington/Haworth, 1996.

"The Response to Rape: Detours on the Road to Equal Justice." Senate Judiciary Committee, Majority Staff Report, 1993.

Richters, Johanna Maria. *Women, Culture and Violence: A Development, Health and Human Rights Issue.* Leiden: Netherlands Women and Autonomy Centre (VENA), 1994.

Rosenblum, Rachel, ed. *Unspoken Rules: Sexual Orientation and Women's Rights.* New York: Cassell, 1996.

Ruether, Rosemary Radford, ed. *Religion and Sexism.* New York: Simon and Schuster, 1974.

Russell, Diana E. H. *The Politics of Rape: The Victim's Perspective.* New York: Stein and Day, 1975.

———. *Rape in Marriage.* Bloomington: Indiana University Press, 1990.

———. *Sexual Exploitation: Rape, Child Sexual Abuse and Workplace Harassment.* Beverly Hills: Sage Publications, 1984.

Russell, Diana E. H., and Rebecca Morris Bolen. *The Epidemic of Rape and Child Sexual Abuse in the United States.* Thousand Oaks, Calif.: Sage Publications, 2000.

Russo, Ann. *Taking Back Our Lives: A Call to Action for the Feminist Movement.* New York: Routledge, 2001.

Sanday, Peggy Reeves. *A Woman Scorned: Acquaintance Rape on Trial.* Berkeley: University of California Press, 1997.

———. *Fraternity Gang Rape: Sex, Brotherhood, and Privilege on Campus.* New York: New York University Press, 1990.

Sanday, Peggy Reeves, and Ruth Gallagher Goodenough. *Beyond the Second Sex: New Directions in the Anthropology of Gender.* Philadelphia: University of Pennsylvania Press, 1990.

Schuler, Margaret, ed. *Freedom from Violence: A Study of Convicted Rapists.* Cambridge, Mass: Unwin Hyman, 1990.

Searles, Patricia, and Ronald J. Berger, eds. *Rape and Society: Readings on the Problem of Sexual Assault.* Boulder, Colo.: Westview Press, 1995.

Shuker-Haines, Frances. *Everything You Need to Know about Date Rape.* New York: Rosen Publishing Group, 1990.

Smith, Joan. *Misogynies: Reflections on Myths and Malice.* New York: Fawcett Columbine, 1989.

Snodgrass, Jon, ed. *For Men Against Sexism.* Albion, Calif.: Times Change Press, 1977.

Sobsey, D. *Violence and Abuse in the Lives of People with Disabilities: The End of Silent Acceptance.* Baltimore: Paul H. Brookes, 1994.

Spohn, Casia. *Rape Law Reform: A Grassroots Revolution and Its Impact.* New York: Plenum, 1992.

Stiglmayer, Alexandra. *Mass Rape: The War Against Women in Bosnia-Herzegovina.* Lincoln: University of Nebraska, 1993.

Stoltenberg, John. *Refusing to Be a Man: Essays on Sex and Justice.* New York: Meridian, 1990.

Tavris, Carol. *The Mismeasure of Woman.* New York: Simon and Schuster, 1992.

Thorne, Barrie. *Gender Play: Girls and Boys in School.* Piscataway, N.J.: Rutgers University Press, 1993.

Tomaselli, Sylvana, and Roy Porter, ed. *Rape: An Historical and Social Enquiry.* New York: Basil Blackwell, 1986.

Tong, Rosemarie. *Women, Sex, and the Law.* New Jersey: Roman and Allanheld, 1984.

Vanderbilt, Heidi. "Incest: A Chilling Report." *Lear's* (February 1992).

Vickers, Jeanne. *Women and War.* London: Zed Books, 1993.

WAC Stats: The Facts about Women. New York: New Press, 1993.

Warshaw, Robin. *I Never Called It Rape.* New York: Harper and Row, 1988.

Wiehe, Vernon R., and Ann L. Richards. *Intimate Betrayal: Understanding and Responding to the Trauma of Acquaintance Rape.* Thousand Oaks, Calif.: Sage, 1995.

Wisechild, Louise M., ed. *She Who Was Lost Is Remembered: Healing from Incest through Creativity.* Seattle: Seal Press, 1991.

Wolf, Naomi. *The Beauty Myth: How Images of Beauty Are Used Against Women.* New York: Anchor Books, 1991.

Woll, Pamela, and Terrence T. Gorski. *Worth Protecting: Women, Men, and Freedom from Sexual Aggression.* Independence, Miss.: Herald House Press, 1995.

SUBJECT INDEX

Founded in 1979, **MILKWEED EDITIONS** is the largest independent, nonprofit literary publisher in the United States. Milkweed publishes with the intention of making a humane impact on society, in the belief that good writing can transform the human heart and spirit. Within this mission, Milkweed publishes in five areas: fiction, nonfiction, poetry, children's literature for middle-grade readers, and the World As Home—books about our relationship with the natural world.

JOIN US

Milkweed depends on the generosity of foundations and individuals like you, in addition to the sales of its books. In an increasingly consolidated and bottom-line-driven publishing world, your support allows us to select and publish books on the basis of their literary quality and the depth of their message. Please visit our Web site (www.milkweed.org) or contact us at (800) 520-6455 to learn more about our donor program.

Interior design by Christian Fünfhausen.
Typeset in Adobe Garamond
by Stanton Publication Services.
Printed by Edwards Brothers.